MEDIUM ÆVUM MONOGRAPHS
NEW SERIES XIV

THE POET'S ART

Literary Theory in Castile *c.* 1400–60

JULIAN WEISS

The Society for the Study of
Mediæval Languages and Literature
Oxford
1990

This volume is printed and published with the assistance of
the Modern Humanities Research Association

British Library Cataloguing in Publication Data
Weiss, Julian
    The poet's art: literary theory in Castile c. 1400–60
(Medium Ævum monographs. New series; v.14).
1. Literature. Theories, history
I. Title   II. Series
801

ISBN 0-907570-07-0

Typeset by Oxbow Books
at Oxford University Computing Service
Printed in Great Britain
by Short Run Press, Exeter

For Joan Weiss, and in Memory of Ivor

FOREWORD

This book has its origins in a doctoral thesis completed in 1984 at the University of Oxford. I owe a substantial debt of gratitude to those who supervised successive stages in my postgraduate research: Professors Peter Russell, Ian Michael and Alan Deyermond (who first awakened my interest in this subject and who meticulously read through the final draft of the book). Their encouragement and guidance were invaluable as I shaped and clarified my ideas, not just on this particular topic, but on the Middle Ages as a whole. Their judicious comments saved me from many blunders, though needless to say none of them can be held responsible for the shortcomings of the finished product. And the same goes for Professor Nicholas Round, Dr David Pattison, Dr Jeremy Lawrance, Dr Clare Lees and Dr Angel Gómez Moreno, who gave generous and forthright advice on all kinds of matters relating to the content and form of the present book. I should also like to thank Mr John Wainwright of the Taylor Institute for supplying a constant stream of bibliographical information during my time at Oxford.

Much of my early research in Spanish libraries was made possible thanks to the financial support of a 'De Osma' studentship from El Instituto de Valencia de Don Juan, Madrid (1981), and a Laming Travelling Fellowship from The Queen's College, Oxford (1982–83). In this connection, it is a pleasure to record here my gratitude to the García-Badell family for the warmth of their hospitality during my frequent stays in Madrid. Finally, I should like to thank the University of Liverpool for a Research Fellowship (1984–86) which enabled me to make headway with many of my research projects—and to write some of them up.

To all intents and purposes, the revision of this thesis for publication was completed in late 1987. This is not the place for second thoughts on matters of detail, nor to discuss more fundamental changes in theoretical approach that have occurred to me since then. I ought to draw attention, however, to three books which appeared since this study first went to press and which have a special bearing upon its subject: A. J. Minnis and A. B. Scott,

Medieval Literary Theory and Criticism c. 1100–1375: The Commentary Tradition (Oxford: OUP, 1988); J. N. H. Lawrance, *Un episodio del proto- humanismo español: tres opúsculos de Nuño de Guzmán y Giannozzo Manetti*; and Pedro M. Cátedra, *Traducción y glosas de la 'Eneida'*, published, like the previous volume, in the new Biblioteca Española del siglo XV (Salamanca: Diputación, 1989).

TABLE OF CONTENTS

ABBREVIATIONS

N.B. Works cited more than once in the text and notes are referred to by short title. For full publication details, see bibliography.

ACCP	*Arquivos do Centro Cultural Português*
AEM	*Anuario de Estudios Medievales*
AFE	*El Crotalón: Anuario de Filología Española*
BHS	*Bulletin of Hispanic Studies*
BOOST	*Bibliography of Old Spanish Texts*, 3rd ed.
BRABLB	*Boletín de la Real Academia de Buenas Letras de Barcelona*
BRAE	*Boletín de la Real Academia Española*
C	*La Corónica*
Can.cas.	*Cancionero castellano del siglo XV*, ed. Foulché-Delbosc
CCMe	*Cahiers de Civilisation Médiévale*
DCECH	Corominas and Pascual, *Diccionario crítico etimológico castellano e hispánico*
GRLM	*Grundriss der romanischen Literaturen des Mittelalters*
HR	*Hispanic Review*
HSMS	Hispanic Seminary of Medieval Studies
IR	*Iberoromania*
JHI	*Journal of the History of Ideas*
JHP	*Journal of Hispanic Philology*
JMRS	*Journal of Medieval and Renaissance Studies*
KRQ	*Kentucky Romance Quarterly*
MA	*Le Moyen Age*
MAe	*Medium Aevum*
MLR	*Modern Language Review*
MP	*Modern Philology*
MS	*Mediaeval Studies*
N	*Neophilologus*
NCSRLL	North Carolina Studies in Romance Languages and Literatures
NBAE	Nueva Biblioteca de Autores Españoles

NRFH	*Nueva Revista de Filología Hispánica*
PL	Patrologia Latina
PFG	*Portugiesische Forschungen der Görresgesellschaft*
PQ	*Philological Quarterly*
R	*Romania*
RCEH	*Revista Canadiense de Estudios Hispánicos*
RF	*Romanische Forschungen*
RFDUCM	*Revista de la Facultad de Derecho de la Universidad Complutense de Madrid*
RFE	*Revista de Filología Española*
RH	*Revue Hispanique*
RLit	*Revista de Literatura*
RPh	*Romance Philology*
Sp	*Speculum*
SP	*Studies in Philology*
T	*Traditio*
UCPMP	University of California Publications in Modern Philology
VR	*Vox Romanica*
ZRPh	*Zeitschrift für Romanische Philologie*

A NOTE ON TRANSCRIPTION

For the sake of consistency, all medieval Castilian quotations, whether from manuscript or printed sources, have been transcribed respecting the orthography of the original, except in these cases: accents, word separation, capitals follow modern practice; 'ç' retained only before 'a', 'o' and 'u'; 'u' and 'v', 'i' and 'j' transcribed according to phonetic value; initial 'rr' and 'R' transcribed as 'r'; I have expanded abbreviations and added my own punctuation (emending that of modern editions where necessary); τ transcribed as 'e'.

INTRODUCTION

1 Aims and scope

The fifteenth century in Castile saw an astonishing outburst of poetic creativity which, at least in terms of quantity, was unmatched by any other European country.[1] The early decades of the period also witnessed important changes both of a literary and a linguistic nature. Galician finally gave way to Castilian as the dominant lyric medium; the latinizing school of the *modernos* began, led by Villena and Juan de Mena, whose experiments in the sublime style earned the reprobation of generations of scholars from Alonso de Cartagena to Menéndez y Pelayo and beyond.[2] From both France and Italy, new poetic themes were being introduced, together with new genres, such as the allegorical narrative *dezir* and the sonnet form.[3]

Equally striking is the self-consciousness that pervades the fifteenth-century court poetry. On one level, this is reflected by its very preservation in nearly two hundred manuscript, and over two hundred printed anthologies. Some of the former, like the *Cancionero de Estúñiga*, were copied out with remarkable care and beauty, and were luxury items in aristocratic libraries. The existence in such large numbers of these *cancioneros* is a mark not just of the literary, but also of the social status that was attached to the composition of this kind of verse: a point thrown into sharp relief by the quite distinct situation in England, where the courtly lyric is

---

[1] The full scope of this increase may be judged by the *Catálogo-índice de la poesía cancioneril del siglo XV*, ed. Brian Dutton *et al.* (Madison: HSMS, 1982).

[2] See Rafael Lapesa, 'La lengua de la poesía lírica desde Macías hasta Villasandino', *RPh*, 7 (1953–54), 51–59; on the latinizing movement see Lapesa's *Historia de la lengua española*, 9th ed. (Madrid: Gredos, 1983), pp. 265–71; María Rosa Lida de Malkiel, *Juan de Mena: poeta del prerrenacimiento español*, 2nd ed. (Mexico City: El Colegio de México, 1984), pp. 125–322.

[3] For a comprehensive (though somewhat biased) account, see Pierre Le Gentil, *La Poésie lyrique espagnole et portugaise à la fin du Moyen Age*, 2 vols (Rennes: Plihon, 1949–53); further bibliography from Alan D. Deyermond, *Historia de la literatura española*, I: *La Edad Media*, Letras e Ideas: Instrumenta, I (Barcelona: Ariel, 1973); Deyermond and Francisco Rico, *Historia y crítica de la literatura española*, I: *Edad Media* (Barcelona: Editorial Crítica, 1980).

often preserved merely on fly-leaves of non-literary manuscripts.[4] On a different level, a sense of artistic self-consciousness emerges too from explicit statements about literary craft. This mood is very pronounced in the first and second generation of poets who, as they write, often seem to step back from their poetry and comment on it, so to speak, from outside. Their frequent references to matters of technique and style, their comments on the social value of letters and on the work of fellow poets, and their appeals to the literary discrimination of the audience, all give to much of the poetry of this period the character of a public declaration of artistic principles.

This fondness for striking literary poses and the new developments that were taking place in the form, language and written presentation of poetry is a compelling combination, one that demands a detailed and broad-based survey. What were the theoretical assumptions that supported the literary vitality of the reign of Juan II? What importance was attached to the composition of verse, and what benefits were to be derived from the study of it? What kinds of literary theories attracted men like Baena, Mena and Santillana, and where did they get their ideas from? These are the main questions this book attempts to answer.

To do this I have compiled evidence from a wide range of sources: raw material can obviously be had from the well-known (though little understood) prologues of Baena and Santillana. There is also a fragment of a preceptive poetic: Villena's *Arte de trovar*. But in addition to these, the stray though calculated remarks made in the poems themselves and in the prose prologues and introductory stanzas yield a rich harvest of ideas about the nature and function of poetry. Also of great value are the commentaries and glosses that survive in such a surprisingly large number in contemporary manuscripts. Two of these literary commentaries are particularly rewarding sources: the vast allegorical exposition of Virgil's *Aeneid* (Bks I–III) by Enrique de Villena, and Juan de Mena's *Coronación*, a fascinating exercise in self-exegesis and literary propaganda.

The period covered in this study is relatively brief: it embraces the literary polemics that took place between Villasandino, Fray Diego de Valencia, Manuel de Lando and others, who wrote at the start of the fifteenth century, and the ideas of Mena and Santillana, who died in 1456 and 1458 respectively. The decision to limit the

---

[4] Julia Boffey, *Manuscripts of English Courtly Love Lyrics in the Later Middle Ages*, Manuscript Studies, 1 (Cambridge: D. S. Brewer, 1985).

chronological scope in this way was dictated, in the first place, by the wealth of material that emerged in the course of research. Many of the theories, it is true, are not unique to this period: ideas about poetic inspiration, the therapeutic value of literature and so on, could have been illustrated by drawing examples from writers living at the end of the century, like Juan del Encina. But despite important continuities, some issues—which I mention below—clearly had a powerful hold over the minds of the earlier poets and give a certain homogeneity to the period I have chosen. Moreover, in view of the present state of scholarship it makes better methodological sense to concentrate on a clearly defined period, and to try to characterize the main trends in its poetic theory in as precise a manner as possible. In this way, we shall be able to build up to a broader understanding of the scope of literary theory and criticism in medieval Spain by gradually accumulating a series of detailed case studies, which analyse the ideas of individual authors or trace the historical development of a particular theoretical issue.

There is a discernible social bias in the literary thought of the four main figures whose work is examined here, and for this reason thematic, as well as chronological, limits have been imposed. Baena, Villena, Mena and Santillana were at the centre of the social changes that were taking place in the early decades of the century—the arms versus letters debate, the spread of lay literacy, in short, the polemical question of vernacular humanism. These issues influenced what they had to say about the nature and value of poetry. The theories they selected to explain their craft and justify their involvement with it give us a new perspective on some of the more problematic aspects of contemporary culture; also, and this is equally important, the way they manipulated these often conventional ideas tells us something about the literary personae they tried to create for themselves in their work. My main (though not exclusive) focus, therefore, is on the social and personal implications of literary theorizing. Because of this, a number of important theoretical issues will not be examined here. There is ample material, for example, to reconstruct a theory of the creative process: writers like Villena, Fernán Pérez de Guzmán and Gómez Manrique often used their prose prologues and prefatory stanzas to explain the methods and circumstances in which they wrote, and to discuss the relative importance of reason and raw emotion in the act of composition. An examination of this subject would make a fascinating study in comparative literature, and would enable us to trace a line of continuity in medieval literary thought, linking these men with other writers who shared similar preoccupations, such as Dante, Juan Manuel and Guillaume de Machaut.[5] The fifteenth-century concept of genre is another subject not touched on here: this, however, is one of the few topics that has attracted critical attention; although I could have added more evidence to the discussion of terms such as comedy, satire and tragedy which under the influence of ancient and modern classics became so popular at this time, my findings would not have altered the conclusions of recent scholars to any significant extent.[6]

This study, therefore, operates on two axes. Its principal contribution is to the history of literary theory: it identifies some of the major theoretical issues of the later Middle Ages and places them within their historical traditions. Secondly—as an inevitable consequence—some light will be shed on the broader intellectual aspirations of the Castilian aristocracy at the court of Juan II. My approach has been to concentrate upon what the writers themselves say and to describe how they go about their task of literary criticism. I have not gone 'à la recherche d'une poétique médiévale' (to employ Vinaver's phrase). This is to say that I have not attempted by means of a deductive method to reconstruct from the basis of literary practice the techniques and attitudes underlying the work of the late medieval Castilian poets. The possibilities of this approach have been explored in depth during the past forty years, by scholars of English, French, and, more recently, Spanish literature.[7] Nevertheless, where appropriate and as far as space

[5] See Dante's *Vita nuova*, packed with references to the need to assimilate emotion thoroughly in order to 'disfogar la mente'; in *Opere*, various eds, *Enciclopedia Dantesca* (Rome: Istituto della Enciclopedia Italiana, 1978), VI, 619–1002, at pp. 623–43; see also Ian Macpherson, 'Don Juan Manuel: The Literary Process', *SP*, 70 (1973), 1–18; Shirley Lukitsch, 'The Poetics of the *Prologue*: Machaut's Conception of the Purpose of his Art', *MAe*, 52 (1983), 258–71.

[6] See Francisco López Estrada, *Introducción a la literatura medieval española*, 5th ed. (Madrid: Gredos, 1983), pp. 193–207 and notes for bibliography.

[7] See, for England: H. J. Chaytor, *From Script to Print: An Introduction to Medieval Vernacular Literature* (1945; London: Sidgwick and Jackson, 1966); A. C. Spearing, *Criticism and Medieval Poetry*, 2nd ed. (London: Edward Arnold 1972); for France: Robert Guiette, 'D'une poésie formelle en France au Moyen Âge', *Revue des Sciences Humaines*, 54 (1949), 61–68; Eugène Vinaver, 'A la recherche d'une poétique médiévale', *CCMe*, 2 (1959), 1–16; Paul Zumthor, 'Recherches sur les topiques dans la poésie lyrique des XIIᵉ et XIIIᵉ siècles', *CCMe*, 2 (1959), 409–27; *Essai de poétique médiévale* (Paris: Seuil, 1972); on this, perhaps Zumthor's

allows, attention will be drawn to the fluctuating relationship
between statements of theory and actual literary practice.

2 Medieval literary criticism: general principles

In a useful preliminary survey of literary theory in Spain and
Portugal during the fifteenth and sixteenth centuries, Karl Kohut
observed that 'según un prejuicio ampliamente difundido, en
España no hay teoría y crítica literaria más que a partir de fines del
siglo XVI'.[8] The roots of this prejudice, according to Kohut, are
deep: in 1596 López Pinciano introduced his *Philosophía antigua
poética* with the comment that Spain, 'florecida en todas las demás
disciplinas' was, in matters of poetic theory, 'tan falta y necessitada'
(*Las teorías literarias*, p. 3). This view proved remarkably persistent,
and in the twentieth century received the added impetus of such
influential authorities as Menéndez y Pelayo, Spingarn and
Saintsbury. Kohut's monograph goes some way toward explaining
why there is no broad survey of literary criticism in Spain during
the late Middle Ages and Renaissance. Put simply, critics had been
looking in the wrong places: the history of literary theory is not the
same as the history of formal poetics. The development of formal
poetic treatises can usefully be traced, as Walter Patterson has
shown in his study of French texts (see below), but such surveys
cannot pretend to offer a comprehensive account of the literary
thought of an age. This point is of fundamental importance, and I
shall return to it shortly.

It is worth dwelling for a moment on the fact that, at least as far
as the earlier literary historians were concerned, the prejudice to

most influential book, see Francisco López Estrada, 'La teoría poética medieval de
Paul Zumthor', *AEM*, 9 (1974–79), 733–86; López Estrada has pioneered the
study of the literary esthetics of Medieval Castile: in addition to his *Introducción*, see
'Poética medieval: los problemas de la agrupación de las obras literarias', in
Manuel Alvar *et al., El comentario de textos*, 4: *La poesía medieval* (Madrid: Castalia,
1983), pp. 7–31. The most recent general work in this field for Castile is Colbert I.
Nepaulsingh, *Towards A History of Literary Composition in Medieval Spain* (Toronto:
Univ. of Toronto Press, 1986). Finally, an important collection of essays which
cuts across national boundaries (though it excludes the Iberian Peninsula):
Vernacular Poetics in the Middle Ages, ed. Lois Ebin, Studies in Medieval Culture, 16
(Western Michigan Univ., Kalamazoo: Medieval Institute Publications, 1984).

[8] *Las teorías literarias en España y Portugal durante los siglos XV y XVI: estado de la
investigación y problemática*, Anejos de R*Lit*, 36 (Madrid: CSIC, 1973), p. 3.

which Kohut alludes was not directed simply at Spain, but at the very concept of medieval poetic theory. There were three main reasons, it seems to me, why Saintsbury, Spingarn and Menéndez y Pelayo found little to say about literary criticism in the Middle Ages. The first was a question of historical approach. 'Whatsoever the Middle Ages were or were not', wrote Saintsbury, 'they were certainly not Ages of Criticism'.[9] For Spingarn, the intellectual dominance of the Church meant that there was a 'theoretical and fundamental objection to all works of the imagination'.[10] In these circumstances, philosophical analysis of poetry and fiction was said to be impossible. Secondly, there was the conviction that all artistic endeavour was based on eternal esthetic values: 'Los canones que han presidido al arte literario de cada época ... se apoyan', in the words of Menéndez y Pelayo, 'en fundamentos matemáticos e inquebrantables, a lo menos para mí, que tengo todavía la debilidad de creer en la Metafísica'.[11] And the Spanish scholar never concealed his disappointment when he discovered that medieval poets and theorists were interested merely in rhetorical and grammatical precepts. Finally, even though guided by similar 'metaphysical' principles, Saintsbury was not primarily interested in esthetic theory. He sought to trace a particular critical approach to literature: broadly speaking, his history is of what we should call descriptive criticism.[12] Thus, apart from Dante's *De vulgari eloquentia*, he found no 'real criticism or matured judgment on existing work in the vernacular' (pp. 7–8).

It is true that there is no substantial evaluative criticism of the

[9] George Saintsbury, *A History of Criticism and Literary Taste in Europe from the Earliest Texts to the Present Day* (1900; Edinburgh: William Blackwood, 1949), I, 373.

[10] Joel E. Spingarn, *A History of Literary Criticism in the Renaissance*, 2nd ed. (1899; New York: Columbia Univ. Press, 1954), p. 4.

[11] Marcelino Menéndez y Pelayo, *Historia de las ideas estéticas en España*, Edición Nacional, 4 vols (1883–89; Madrid: CSIC, 1962), I, 5. Spingarn is more specific: 'the function of Renaissance criticism was to reestablish the aesthetic foundations of literature, to reaffirm the eternal lesson of Hellenic culture, and to restore once and for all the element of beauty to its rightful place in human life and in the world of art'; *A History*, p. 4.

[12] He defines criticism as 'that function of the judgement which busies itself with the goodness or badness, the success or ill-success, of literature from the purely literary point of view'; his study is confined 'wholly to the particular and the actual'. Nevertheless, he aims 'to extract from all literature, ancient, medieval and modern, lessons of its universal qualities which may enable [the reader] to see each period *sub specie aeternitatis*'; *A History*, pp. 3–4 and 8.

modern kind in the Middle Ages: this is a comparatively recent development.[13] It is also true that medieval poetic treatises were concerned first and foremost with teaching poets how to write. But this is not all they attempted to do. It is worth remembering that many vernacular poetics were also directed at the discerning reader: they provided rules not just for the composition, but also for the critical assessment of poetry. The author of the first vernacular poetic, Raimon Vidal de Besalú, for example, compiled his treatise 'per far conoisser et saber qals dels trobadors an mielx trobat et mielx ensenhat'.[14] The fact that he passes no value-judgement on the poems to which he refers is significant: evaluative criticism was a matter for private discussion amongst circles of poets and friends—it does not mean that Vidal and the public for whom he was writing were uncritical, or lacked literary discrimination, or had no interest in the nature and function of their art. It is simply that these were not expressed in the formal medium of a poetic treatise. As George Watson has observed, criticism that survives in print 'is the very tiny tip of an impossibly vast iceberg. Verbal (not to say unspoken) comment on poetry must be as old as poetry itself, and in any age the proportion of comment that sees print must fortunately be very small'.[15]

It is interesting that the need to look beyond formal poetics had, in fact, been intimated by Menéndez y Pelayo himself, but with regard to the Renaissance:

> No conoce del todo las doctrinas literarias del siglo XVI quien no ha leído más que sus *poéticas*. En otros libros de aspecto menos didáctico se tropieza a cada momento con principios de crítica luminosísimos, con observaciones de un gusto intachable. (*Ideas estéticas*, II, 252)

Leaving aside the matter of 'un gusto intachable', this applies with even greater force to the Middle Ages, and it is unfortunate that the great scholar did not bring this approach to bear in his work on that period. As I mentioned at the outset, valuable insights may be had from a wide range of sources: not just the poetics, but philosophical treatises, secular and theological commentaries, and of course, the literary text itself. The manuscript too can frequently

---

[13] Its history in Spain has yet to be written; in England it starts with Dryden: see George Watson, *The Literary Critics: A Study of English Descriptive Criticism* (Harmondsworth: Penguin, 1962).

[14] *The 'Razos de trobar' of Raimon Vidal and Associated Texts*, ed. J. H. Marshall (London: Oxford Univ. Press, 1972), p. lxxix.

[15] *The Literary Critics*, pp. 14–15.

help us to understand how contemporaries read a particular work: its literary status can be judged by the number of extant manuscripts, by the other texts with which it was originally copied, by its *mise-en-page*, and, as some excellent recent studies on Chaucer and Gower have shown, by scribal inaccuracies and interpolations—evidence that is usually scorned by modern scholars and editors.[16] In short, only by adopting a flexible approach is it possible to gauge the vitality of literary thought during the various periods of the Middle Ages.

In some quarters, the negative influence of Spingarn, Menéndez y Pelayo and Saintsbury has continued to inspire the view that between classical Antiquity and the sixteenth century there is little to interest the historian of literary theory.[17] However, since the 1930s there has been a steady growth in interest in medieval literary theory and criticism. Crucial landmarks in this development were the studies of Faral, Curtius and de Bruyne on scholastic esthetics and Latin grammatical and rhetorical treatises.[18] But the field of inquiry has broadened considerably during the past fifty years, and the full potential of the subject is now appreciated by those working with vernacular, as well as Latin, sources. A full bibliographical account is beyond the scope of the present work; but most of the research has focussed on the theories of an individual writer (such as Dante, Machaut, or Chaucer), or on the development of a single concept (literature as recreation, ethical poetics, theories of authorship and imagination). Even so, occasional attempts have been made on a broader scale to write the

[16] Elspeth Kennedy, 'The Scribe as Editor', in *Mélanges de langue et de littérature du Moyen Age et de la Renaissance offerts à Jean Frappier* (Geneva: Droz, 1970), I, 523–31; Barry A. Windeatt,'The Scribes as Chaucer's Early Critics', *Studies in the Age of Chaucer*, 1 (1979), 119–41; valuable essays also in Derek Pearsall (ed.), *Manuscripts and Readers in Fifteenth-Century England: The Literary Implications of Manuscript Study* (Essays from the 1981 Conference at the University of York) (Cambridge: D.S. Brewer, 1983).

[17] See the sections dedicated to the Middle Ages in the manuals by William K. Wimsatt and Cleanth Brooks, *Literary Criticism: A Short History* (New York: Alfred Knopf, 1957); and Sanford Shepard, *El Pinciano y las teorías literarias del Siglo de Oro* (Madrid: Gredos, 1962).

[18] Edmond Faral, *Les Arts poétiques du XII et du XIII siècle: recherches et documents sur la technique littéraire du Moyen Age* (1924; Paris: Champion, 1962); Ernst Robert Curtius, 'Zur Literarästhetik des Mittelalters', *ZRPh*, 58 (1938), 1–50, 129–232, 433–79; *European Literature and the Latin Middle Ages*, trans. Willard R. Trask (London: Routledge and Kegan Paul, 1953); Edgar de Bruyne, *Études d'esthétique médiévale*, 3 vols (Bruges: De Tempel, 1946).

history of literary theorizing carried out in a particular language or country. There is, for example, Patterson's early survey of French poetic treatises, a volume on English medieval criticism by Atkins, and Greenfield's account of Italian literary polemics. With regard to Spain, although no broad-based monograph has been written as yet, the bibliographical outlines for such a study are gradually emerging, thanks in large measure to the work of Kohut, Faulhaber, Gómez Moreno and Alvar. Such progress has been made on a variety of fronts that the history of European literary theory during the Middle Ages is now, for the first time, a feasible proposition.[19]

It would not, I think, follow the guidelines offered by O. B. Hardison in an article written in 1976.[20] He makes some valuable observations: he stresses, for example, the importance of avoiding a nationalistic approach to the earlier Middle Ages, and of separating the history of poetics from that of rhetoric.[21] Wholly unacceptable, however, are the criteria by which Hardison defines the scope of medieval literary criticism: the field, in his view, should be confined to works composed in Latin from the fourth to the fourteenth centuries (p. 12). The inappropriateness of the chronological limit is obvious: although, as I hope to show, the criticism of fifteenth-century Castile (like that of any other) has its own characteristics, the real change did not come until the renewed interest in Aristotle and Horace in the sixteenth century. It is also hard to understand why we should ignore the views of vernacular poets: to concentrate exclusively on the treatises written by, say, John of Garland or

---

[19] The monographs on particular theoretical concepts, by such scholars as Glending Olsen, Judson Boyce Allen, Douglas Kelly and Alistair Minnis, are cited in the following chapters where bibliographic references will be found. For national histories, see W. F. Patterson, *Three Centuries of French Poetic Theory* (Ann Arbor: Univ. of Michigan, 1935), 2 vols; J. W. H. Atkins, *English Literary Criticism: The Medieval Phase* (Cambridge: CUP, 1943); for Italy, see Concetta C. Greenfield, *Humanist and Scholastic Poetics, 1250–1500* (Toronto: Associated Univ. Presses, 1981); for Spain, see Kohut's *Las teorías literarias*, Faulhaber's research on rhetorical theory (to which I return in the conclusion), and the useful bibliographical sketch by Carlos Alvar and Angel Gómez Moreno, *La poesía lírica medieval*, Historia Crítica de la Literatura Hispánica, 1 (Madrid: Taurus, 1987), pp. 125–40.

[20] 'Toward a History of Medieval Literary Criticism', *Medievalia et Humanistica*, n.s., 7 (1976), 1–12; the issue is devoted to medieval poetics.

[21] See p. 6; the most likely target for his criticism are histories such as that by Charles Baldwin for whom rhetoric and poetic are merely different words for the same thing; see ch. II, below, for further details.

Geoffrey of Vinsauf would restrict our perspective to that of a thirteenth-century *grammaticus* addressing himself to an audience made up in the main of university students. The attitudes of the Provençal troubadours, for example, were shaped by a wider range of practical considerations (e.g. ethical and political) than were dealt with in Latin poetics. As Linda Paterson, among others, has pointed out, the precepts of formal treatises were merely a point of departure for vernacular creative writers.[22]

A far richer view is offered by the forthcoming volume on the Middle Ages to be included in *The Cambridge History of Literary Criticism*. The contributors to this book not only cover the academic traditions of school and cloister (embodied principally by the exposition of biblical and classical literature), they also trace critical developments in the vernacular, examining, where appropriate, their academic origins, and placing them in their broader cultural contexts.[23] In short, the volume attempts to demonstrate the diversity of channels through which ideas about literature passed, and tries to do justice to questions that were not dealt with in formal poetics. The section devoted to Castilian vernacular literary theory and criticism ranges from the thirteenth to the fifteenth century, and for the later period draws on much of the material discussed in the present study. For the earlier period, it examines, to cite obvious examples, the debates over the poet's status as troubadour and lover that are such a prominent feature of the early lyric and satiric verse; the scholastic concept of multiple interpretation which provides a thematic framework for the *Libro de buen amor*; Juan Manuel's theories of brevity and obscurity, expounded in *El conde Lucanor* and other treatises.[24]

---

[22] Linda M. Paterson, *Troubadours and Eloquence* (Oxford: Clarendon, 1975), pp. 5–6. The distortion inherent in Hardison's approach is even plainer in his discussion of the relation between poetry and music. Having discounted the *artes rhythmicae* and Dante's *De vulgari eloquentia* on the grounds that they are technical rather than theoretical (a distinction he fails to apply to the *artes poeticae*), he asserts that 'the first critical treatise to pay serious attention' to the subject is the first book of Salutati's *De laboribus Herculis*, written in 1416. Thus Machaut (see the prologue to his *Chansonnier*, pre 1377) and Deschamps (*Art de dictier*, 1392) would play no part in his history of this particular theory.

[23] *The Cambridge History of Literary Criticism*, II: *The Middle Ages*, ed. A. J. Minnis.

[24] In writing this section, I have benefited from a number of important studies: e.g., on the debate between Alfonso X and Pero da Ponte over whether to 'trobar come proençal' see Saverio Panunzio (ed.), Pero da Ponte, *Poesie*, Biblioteca de

Most of these comments about the nature and function of literature are made in the literary text itself. This point is important and deserves special emphasis, since the implications of what might be called incidental theorizing have not, I think, been fully recognized. Our aim should not be simply to reconstruct a poetic on the basis of remarks extracted from poems and prologues, and to imagine, in other words, what poets would have said if it had occurred to them to write a formal poetic. This would be to neglect one of the most fascinating aspects of the subject, since the context of a theoretical statement very often determines what is said (a point usually lost to earlier historians, who, when summarizing the contents of a theoretical text, generally ignored its structure and function). As a result, we need constantly to ask whether a writer would have formulated a theory in the same way in different circumstances. In the course of the following study we shall frequently see how theories are chosen for their rhetorical effect. Because of this, the arguments selected do not necessarily represent the whole range of theories with which a writer may have been familiar, and often give the impression of simply being those that support the stance he has adopted at that particular moment.

3 Literature and society: some new developments

The reign of Juan II saw a new class of landed aristocracy consolidate its political power, and, like the Mendoza clan, attempt to buttress and justify its strength by its literary pursuits.[25] This

---

Filologia Romanza, 10 (Bari: Adriatica, 1967), pp. 43–59; on the Galician-Portuguese poetic, see Jean-Marie d'Heur, 'L'Art de trouver du chansonnier Colocci-Brancuti', ACCP, 9 (1975), 321–98; on the Libro de buen amor, see Anthony N. Zahareas, The Art of Juan Ruiz, Archpriest of Hita (Madrid: Estudios de Literatura Española, 1965); Alan Deyermond, 'Juan Ruiz's Attitude to Literature', in Medieval, Renaissance and Folklore Studies in Honor of John Esten Keller, ed. Joseph R. Jones (Newark, Delaware: Juan de la Cuesta, 1980), pp. 113–25; Dayle Seidenspinner-Núñez, The Allegory of Good Love: Parodic Perspectivism in the 'Libro de buen amor', UCPMP, 112 (Berkeley: University of California Press, 1981); on Juan Manuel, see Macpherson, 'Don Juan Manuel'. Further bibliography on these last two authors is given in chs III and V; previous scholarship on XVc Castilian literary theory is also listed below, in the relevant chapters.

25 Helen Nader, The Mendoza Family in the Spanish Renaissance, 1350–1550 (New Brunswick: Rutgers Univ. Press, 1979), pp. 77–100. See also Roger Boase, The Troubadour Revival: A Study of Social Change and Traditionalism in Late Medieval Spain (London: Routledge and Kegan Paul, 1978). In spite of their many valid points, I

development coincided with social changes that were also taking place beyond the boundaries of Castile: the spread of literacy amongst the non-professional classes, and the accompanying emancipation of the lay voice, which is one of the defining peculiarities of fifteenth-century Europe.[26] The combination of these factors gave rise to a mode of humanistic culture that is characteristic of what is often called Spain's Pre-Renaissance. It should not be confused (as it sometimes has been) with the humanism made famous by professional Florentine scholars, whose interests extended into areas of classical philology unknown in Spain before Nebrija. A blend of influences from France, Burgundy and Italy, the humanism of early fifteenth-century Castile was essentially vernacular, and, with its dominant concern for the education of the statesman, civic. Salient features include a nascent antiquarianism and a revival of nationalism, both stemming from a patriotic interest in such 'Spanish' writers as Quintilian, Lucan and, above all, Seneca. But its most striking qualities are to be seen in the enthusiastic patronage of translations from antiquity, especially of those authors who, like Livy and Vegetius, catered for the taste for the exemplary history of the Roman *militia*. One of the ideals that these translations were designed to foster was the union of arms and letters, which derives from the classical topos of *sapientia et fortitudo*. As is well known, it was thought that in practical terms the finest embodiment of this ideal was the Marqués de Santillana, whose famous library is the most important evidence for the fondness for book-collecting amongst the aristocracy.[27]

do not share the overall interpretations of the period offered by either of these writers.

[26] Margaret Aston, *The Fifteenth Century: The Prospect of Europe* (London: Thames and Hudson, 1968), pp. 117–47; Juan Marichal, *La voluntad de estilo: teoría e historia del ensayismo hispánico* (Barcelona: Seix Barral, 1957), chs 1 and 2 (on Díez de Games, cut from the revised ed. of 1984); José Antonio Maravall, 'El Pre-Renacimiento del siglo XV', in *Nebrija y la introducción del Renacimiento en España: Actas de la III Academia Literaria Renacentista*, ed. Víctor García de la Concha (Salamanca: ALR, Univ. de Salamanca, 1983), pp. 17–36.

[27] The status of the humanistic endeavour in XVc Castile is controversial. Nicholas G. Round argues that apart from an isolated minority there was a general antipathy towards letters amongst the nobility: 'Renaissance Culture and its Opponents in Fifteenth-Century Castile', *MLR*, 57 (1962), 204–15; 'Five Magicians, or the Uses of Literacy', *MLR*, 64 (1969), 793–805; 'The Shadow of a Philosopher: Medieval Castilian Images of Plato', *JHP*, 3 (1978–79), 1–36. Peter E. Russell adopts a similar view, but finds an incipient lay humanism similar to that which was taking root in Northern Europe: 'Fifteenth-Century Lay

As I have already mentioned, one of the most powerful factors that promoted the humanistic culture of the time was the spread of literacy amongst the laity. In recent years, numerous scholars have tried to describe the increase in the reading habit amongst the non-clerical classes and to explain the enormous effects this had upon the kinds and quantity of vernacular literature produced in the late Middle Ages.[28] As far as Castile is concerned, the study of lay literacy is still in its infancy, but there has been a recent and concerted effort to draw a more detailed picture of the contents of medieval libraries and to trace the scope of book-collecting amongst the aristocracy. Notable advances in this field are the bibliography of medieval Spanish library inventories compiled by Charles Faulhaber and the 1985 article by Jeremy Lawrance. The latter points to the re-establishment in the fifteenth century of what Erich Auerbach had called the ancient literary public: 'Reading', he explains, 'became not merely a means to an end for a professional minority, but an end in itself for a whole privileged section of society'.[29] In essence, the privileged layman sought three things

---

Humanism', in *Spain: A Companion to Spanish Studies*, ed. P. E. Russell (London: Methuen, 1973), pp. 237–42; 'Las armas contra las letras: para una definición del humanismo español del siglo XV', in *Temas de 'La Celestina' y otros estudios: del 'Cid' al 'Quijote'* (Barcelona: Ariel, 1978), pp. 207–39; *Traducciones y traductores en la Península Ibérica (1400–1550)* (Bellaterra: Universidad Autónoma de Barcelona, 1985). Jeremy Lawrance argues that the climate of the times was far less negative: 'Nuño de Guzmán and Early Spanish Humanism: Some Reconsiderations', *MAe*, 51 (1982), 55–85; 'Nuño de Guzmán: Life and Works', unpublished D. Phil. thesis (Univ. of Oxford, 1983), esp. pp. 12–24 and chs 2 and 3; 'Nueva luz sobre la biblioteca del conde de Haro: inventario de 1455', *AFE*, 1 (1984), 1073–111; 'The Spread of Lay Literacy in Late Medieval Castile', *BHS*, 62 (1985), 79–94; 'On Fifteenth-Century Spanish Vernacular Humanism', in *Medieval and Renaissance Studies in Honour of Robert Brian Tate*, ed. Ian Michael and Richard A. Cardwell (Oxford: Dolphin, 1986), pp. 63–79. Less convincing (mainly because of his interpretation of Cartagena's role) is Ottavio Di Camillo, *El humanismo castellano del siglo XV* (Valencia: Fernando Torres, 1976).

[28] Chaytor, *From Script to Print*, ch. II; Erich Auerbach, *Literary Language and its Public in Late Latin Antiquity and in the Middle Ages*, trans. Ralph Manheim, Bollingen Series, 74 (New York: Bollingen Foundation, 1965), pp. 235–338; Malcolm B. Parkes, 'The Literacy of the Laity', in *Literature and Western Civilization*, II: *The Medieval World*, ed. David Daiches and Anthony Thorlby (London: Aldus Books, 1973), pp. 555–77; Paul Saenger, 'Silent Reading: Its Impact on Late Medieval Script and Society', *Viator*, 13 (1972), 367–414.

[29] 'The Spread of Lay Literacy', p. 80; see also Deyermond, *La Edad Media*, pp. 238–41; for the fullest account of primary and secondary material see Charles F. Faulhaber, *Libros y bibliotecas en la España medieval: una bibliografía de fuentes impresas*,

from reading: enjoyment, ethics and the emulation of a social ideal. And the ways in which these three objectives, coupled with other aspects of Castilian vernacular humanism, influenced literary thought during the reign of Juan II will be examined in the course of the following chapters.

The fashion for Dantesque allegories, introduced to Castile by Francisco Imperial, and the fondness for briefer verse-forms of a marked intellectual character (most notably the *preguntas y respuestas* of Baena's anthology) are an indication of the great changes in poetic taste that were taking place at the start of the fifteenth century. To some, these innovations are symbolized by the contrast between the esthetics of Villasandino and Imperial: the former is often labelled as the defeated champion of the obsolete Galician-Portuguese school, the latter as the leader of the new Italianate movement. The contrast is only incidentally one of esthetics, however: there is no substantial evidence to suggest that Villa-sandino was truly opposed to Dante and the style of writing which he was thought to represent.[30] What he did resent were the changing attitudes towards the nature and function of the poet. With the examples of Dante and Jean de Meun before them, vernacular writers throughout Europe began to emulate the concept of the philosophical poet, embodied by the term *poeta*. For some, this may have meant no more than applying a thin veneer of erudition to one's verse; but for others, such as Guillaume de Machaut, it entailed a radical change in poetic voice, and implied a different relationship between the writer and his public.[31] If Villasandino gives the impression of being a literary outcast it is because he saw that his status as a professional pundit was being undermined. His traditional role consisted not only in entertaining but also in being a commentator on contemporary affairs, and a guardian of moral and political truth. And this latter function,

---

Research Bibliographies and Checklists, 47 (London: Grant and Cutler, 1987). See also the announcement of a projected union catalogue of medieval Castilian libraries, to be compiled by John Dagenais and William D. McHugh, in *C*, 16, no. 2 (1988), 118.

[30] See Nelson W. Eddy, 'Dante and Ferrán Manuel de Lando', *HR*, 4 (1936), 124–35; similar points are made about the Provençal debate by Panunzio, ed. *Pero da Ponte*, pp. 52–59; for a contrasting view, see Giovanni Caravaggi, 'Villasandino et les derniers troubadours de Castille', in *Mélanges offerts à Rita Lejeune* (Gembloux: Duculot, 1969), I, 395–421.

[31] Kevin Brownlee, *Poetic Identity in Guillaume de Machaut* (Madison: Univ. of Wisconsin Press, 1984).

which stretches back to the ethical verse of the Provençal school, was being challenged by aristocratic poets, who did not depend on poetry for their livelihood, but relied on it as an essential ingredient in their 'True Nobility'.

This is one of the most significant points to emerge from an analysis of the *Cancionero de Baena*, assembled shortly before the compiler died in the early 1430s.[32] The social aspirations of the poets whose work it contains are expressed nowhere better than in the debate over the relative force of free will and predestination initiated by Ferrán Sánchez Calavera. This is a sequence of seven poems, written in the first decade of the new century, in which the main participants are Pero López de Ayala, Imperial, the Franciscan Fray Diego de Valencia and Ferrán Manuel de Lando. Attention was first drawn to it by Joaquín Gimeno Casalduero, who compared Ayala's reluctance to take part with the enthusiastic theologizing of the younger poets.[33] The contrasting attitudes towards what constitutes a legitimate poetic theme, coupled with Ayala's quotation of some lines of outmoded *cuaderna vía* verse, epitomized for Gimeno the new departures in poetry that were taking place in the early years of the fifteenth century. But it is worth looking more closely at Sánchez Calavera's motives for putting the learned question to Ayala: 'que mi entinción es querer disputar,/ mas non poner dubda nin fazer errar'.[34] And at the end of the sequence he congratulates his fellow poets with the words:

---

[32] New documentary evidence for the life of Baena and the date of his *Cancionero* is supplied by Manuel Nieto Cumplido, 'Aportación histórica al *Cancionero de Baena*', *Historia, Instituciones, Documentos*, 6 (1979), 197–218; 'Juan Alfonso de Baena y su Cancionero: nueva aportación histórica', *Boletín de la Real Academia de Ciencias, Bellas Letras y Nobles Artes de Córdoba*, 52 (1982), 35–57. The extant manuscript is not the original version, but a copy made *c*. 1470: see Barclay Tittman, 'A Contribution to the Study of the *Cancionero de Baena* Manuscript', *Aquila*, 1 (1968), 190–203; Alberto Blecua, '"Perdióse un quaderno": sobre los *Cancioneros de Baena*', *AEM*, 9 (1974–79), 229–66.

[33] 'Pero López de Ayala y el cambio poético a comienzos del XV', *HR*, 33 (1965), 1–14; see also Jacques Joset, 'Pero López de Ayala dans le *Cancionero de Baena*', *MA*, 4th series, 40 (1975), 475–97; Michel García, *Obra y personalidad del Canciller Ayala* (Madrid: Alhambra, 1983), pp. 270–77.

[34] *Cancionero de Juan Alfonso de Baena*, ed. José María Azáceta, Clásicos Hispánicos, 3 vols (Madrid: CSIC), III, 1022 (no. 517, ll. 114–15). I have corrected Azáceta's misreadings against *'Cancionero de Baena' Reproduced in Facsimile from the Unique Manuscript in the Bibliothèque Nationale*, ed. Henry R. Lang (New York: Hispanic Society of America, 1926). This ed. is to be preferred to the 1971 reprint from which the foliation has been trimmed away.

'todos nobleza e mesura fizieron' (no. 525, l. 157; III, 1062).
Elegant discussion, rather than philosophical inquiry undertaken
for its own sake, is the aim of these doctrinal debates. They are a
medium for a display of *ingenio*, which, allied to noble manners and
practical wisdom, constitutes the basis of courtliness.

There was never any theoretical objection to the nobleman
taking an interest in a certain class of *letras*: on the contrary,
authorities such as Alfonso el Sabio, Juan Manuel and Juan García
de Castrojeriz encouraged the literary pursuits that led to a greater
'nobleza de costumbres'.[35] According to Maravall, this concept of
courtliness was similar to the Arabic *adab*, and gradually evolved
into a notion summed up in the term *humanitas*: it was 'una manera
de conducta, basada en una sabiduría práctica y social, una
disposición del ánimo, apoyada en una disciplina intelectual' (p.
258). Thus, the learned *preguntas y respuestas* of the early decades of
the century were a new variation on the old theme of *cortesía*. Noble
poets such as Sánchez Calavera and Manuel de Lando strove to add
an extra dimension to their courtly wisdom by discussing issues not
traditionally considered to be pertinent to their social position.

As is well known, the anthology compiled by Baena is an
important source of literary theory, and much has been written
about the *Prologus Baenensis* and about the poems allegedly written
under the influence of a *gracia infusa*. My own approach, as I have
described it above, is to examine the theoretical issues in the context
of the personal concerns and aspirations of individual writers. This
means, for example, interpreting the theory of divine inspiration not
just as an extension of the age-old notion of the *poeta theologus*, but,
equally importantly, as a weapon in a struggle for literary status. As
we shall see in the first chapter, the literary polemics of this
anthology are examples of a kind of public poetry that has many
parallels in late-fourteenth-century France and England. They are
public in the sense that they are vehicles for an ostentatious display
of courtly learning—wit in its broadest sense—believed to be

---

[35] García de Castojeriz's phrase, quoted from José Antonio Maravall, 'La
"cortesía" como saber en la Edad Media', in *Estudios de historia del pensamiento
español: serie primera—Edad Media*, 3rd ed. (Madrid: Ediciones Cultura Hispánica,
1983), pp. 257–67, at p. 263. See also Jole Scudieri Ruggieri, *Cavalleria e cortesia
nella vita e nella cultura di Spagna* (Modena: Mucchi, 1980), who quotes Juan
Manuel's precept that hunting should alternate with study in the life of the knight,
and that after the hunt he should 'oír su lección et fazer conjugación, et declinar et
derivar o fazer proverbios o letras', pp. 31–32.

indispensable to the well-mannered aristocrat.

As in France and England, noble ideals were often fostered by members of the rising class of *letrados*, so it is appropriate that of the four central figures of this book, two, Baena and Mena, are *letrados*, and two, Villena and Santillana, are aristocrats. The support offered by these professional men of letters could be illustrated in many ways. It could range from the overt literary *apologiae* of Pero Díaz de Toledo to the more complex stance of Juan de Mena. His *Laberinto de Fortuna* is a political poem, certainly, but it is also a piece of cultural propaganda; its learned style encourages the confident belief that the reader's gentility was based on more than just noble blood. In Baena's case, the portrait he paints in his prologue of the ideal nobleman has a much less philosophic hue to it in comparison with the meditative *generoso entendimiento* present in the works of Villena, Mena and Santillana. Nevertheless, the influence on his prologue and rubrics of the academic *accessus* offers a classic example of the fact that when the *letrado* class put themselves at the service of the royalty and nobility, they brought with them methods of textual presentation traditionally employed in the schools. In the process, they strove to elevate the status of the vernacular literary text.

The same motive provides the central theme for chapter II, which examines the implications of the belief that poetry was a branch of knowledge, *una ciencia* or *arte*. This belief offered Baena and his contemporaries convenient labels with which to describe their craft, but, like Baena, writers were not necessarily sure about the branch to which it belonged. This, of course, was an issue that had preoccupied countless poets and philosophers before them, and would continue to be a matter of dispute for literary theorists throughout the sixteenth century. For the most part, therefore, Castilians used the terms *ciencia* and *arte* interchangeably, without regard to their philosophical connotations. But this was not always the case, and Enrique de Villena was the outstanding exception. Not only did he draw attention to poetry's status as a form of knowledge, he also attempted to define its position within a general scheme of wisdom. On a theoretical level, his discussion of this subject is occasionally enigmatic; nonetheless, in practice his aim is clear: implicitly denying the argument of theologians such as Alonso de Cartagena that poetry came low down on a scheme of values, he sought to advertise its claims as a worthy means of educating a noble elite.

We shall see that Cartagena drew partial support for his negative classification of poetry from the writings of Thomas Aquinas. And one of the main props in Aquinas's reasoning was that secular poetry possessed no allegorical significance. This view, which achieved wide currency in scholastic thought, was disseminated in Castile by the preaching of Vicente Ferrer. Chapter III examines the arguments to the contrary, as expressed by Enrique de Villena in his commentary on the first three Books of the *Aeneid*. Here, the author postulates a theory of allegory designed to explain to the Castilian aristocracy why Virgil should be held in such great esteem as a poet-philosopher. But not only Virgil; Villena's theoretical statements on the function of allegory are to a great extent coloured by his personal aspirations as a man of letters. Much has been made—too much, I think—of the notion that his political failure was largely the result of his literary pursuits: that he was marginalized by his contemporaries because they believed that, in the phrase handed down by Fernán Pérez de Guzmán, 'sabía mucho en el cielo e pocco en la tierra'.[36] History certainly does not suggest that he was at all adept at handling his political career, but in one respect at least he did not miscalculate the mood of the times. In Juan of Navarre's commission of a new, complete, translation of the *Aeneid* he saw the opportunity to cater for the fashionable belief that certain literary classics had a part to play in the well-run *respublica*. His commentary, therefore, brings out the exemplary civic qualities of the poem and at the same time stresses the political utility of its creator at the court of Augustus. But on every possible occasion, Villena tries to cast himself in the same role as Virgil, suggesting also that the classical poet wrote with him in mind; poet-philosophers resorted to allegory, he explains, so that future exegetes might interpret their words to the unlearned. In this way, a theoretical statement is incorporated into the larger strategy of the text, which is to proclaim Villena's intellectual talents and potential usefulness as a political propagandist.

The *Aeneid* commentary exemplifies how the spread of private reading brought into being a new, more intimate, relationship between author and public and allowed for the creation of structurally more complex works. To facilitate their study, writers would borrow devices first elaborated in academic, legal and theological circles, such as rubrics, chapter headings and summaries,

---

[36] *Generaciones y semblanzas*, ed. R. B. Tate (London: Tamesis, 1965), p. 33.

and often set their work within a framework of prologues, commentaries and glosses.[37] But it needs to be emphasized that although vernacular writers borrowed methods of textual presentation—such as the *accessus*—from the academic world, they did not imitate them slavishly, but adapted them according to their own needs.

This point, which is the subject of chapter IV, may be illustrated in an interesting way by an anonymous translation (possibly by Pero López de Ayala) of Boethius's *De consolatione Philosophiae*. This was commissioned at the turn of the century by Ruy López Dávalos, who asked for a new translation of the work because he found the existing ones too difficult to read; interpolated in the text were the lengthy and erudite glosses by Nicholas Trevet: 'pienso fazerme algún estorvo estar mesclado el texto con glosas, lo qual me trae una grand escuridat'.[38] (This was not an unusual complaint: it echoes Canals' reasons for retranslating Valerius Maximus into Valencian; the style of the original Catalan was 'casi confuso, entremesclado glosas con el testo'.)[39] In compliance with his patron's request, the translator took out the interpolations. But he obviously thought it inappropriate to do away with Trevet altogether and let Boethius stand alone before someone who described himself as 'venido novicio al estudio'. So, basing himself in part on the Dominican's exegesis, he wrote his own series of

---

[37] See Malcolm B. Parkes, 'The Influence of the Concepts of *Ordinatio* and *Compilatio* on the Development of the Book', in *Medieval Learning and Literature: Essays Presented to Richard William Hunt*, ed. J. J. G. Alexander and M. T. Gibson (Oxford: Clarendon, 1976), pp. 115–41; Saenger, 'Silent Reading', pp. 373–77, 392–93, 408–10.

[38] BN Madrid MS 10.220; quoted from Mario Schiff, *La Bibliothèque du Marquis de Santillane: Étude historique et bibliographique de la collection de livres manuscrits de don Iñigo López de Mendoza, 1398–1458, marqués de Santillana, conde del Real de Manzanares, humaniste et auteur espagnol célèbre* (1905; Amsterdam: Van Heusden, 1970), p. 177. On the authorship of this translation, see García, *Obra y personalidad del Canciller Ayala*, pp. 208–10; 'Las traducciones del Canciller Ayala', in *Studies in Honour of R. B. Tate*, pp. 13–25, at pp. 16–19.

[39] I quote from the Castilian text commissioned by Juan I; BN Madrid MS 10.807, f. 2^r. Alonso de Cartagena wrote a compendium of Aristotle's *Ethics* expounded by Thomas Waleys so that Prince Duarte of Portugal could read it 'sin rebolver de los libros . . .; las quales [obras] con muchas divisiones e sodivisiones de los glosadores se suelen leer, lo qual si por toda la moral filosophía se fiziere segund que trabajoso, así por ventura sin provecho serié' (*Memorial de virtudes*, anon. trans. dedicated to the mother of Queen Isabel, Escorial, MS h-III-11, f. 41^v).

'glosas y declaraciones', placing the briefer glosses in the margins, and reserving the more substantial commentary until the end of the translation.[40] The function of this new *declaración* is twofold:

> Donde se tocare fictión o ystoria que no sea muy usada, reduzirse ha brevemente .... E fallando alguna razón que paresca dubdosa en sentencia será le puesta adición de la que el nonbrado maestro en su letura ha declarado sólo tocante a la letra. (Schiff, *La Bibliothèque*, p. 179)

Textual paraphrase and the clarification of classical myth and history are the two sorts of guidance offered by the majority of fifteenth-century vernacular commentaries. Indeed, in some notable cases, the delight in retelling vignettes from Roman history and myth seems to have overridden the purely functional concerns of the commentators, and inspired them to write glosses of a marked literary character.

But this was just one of the ways in which commentaries and glosses could transcend their purpose as vehicles for factual information about the author and the literal level of the text. Self-exegesis, for example, enabled men like Santillana and Mena to exert greater authorial control over their work, and thus helped foster the new concept of *poeta* that began to take root in the early decades of the century. To return to the Boethius commentator, his attempt to solve the problems faced by Ruy López is part of a broader pedagogic trend underlying the composition of many of the vernacular commentaries. The *nuevo leedor* may have known what to read, but did he know how to extract the full benefit from his new skill? Such doubts seem to have inspired Villena and Mena to set about improving the literary competence of their public, by embedding in their commentaries advice on how to read the sophisticated texts they had before them. On the basis of this

[40] For the author's explanation of this procedure, see BN Madrid MS 174, ff. 6[r-v]. To my knowledge the commentary is found only in this MS (ff. 142[r]–160[r]). It was cut in the copy owned by Santillana (BN Madrid MS 10.220), which contains only the marginal glosses. I am not convinced by García's hypothesis that MS 174 was the version López Dávalos found difficult and that MS 10.220 represents the translator's revision ('Las traducciones', p. 19). Even though MS 174 lacks the introductory letters and contains more exegetical material, both its meticulous layout and its text (virtually identical with that of MS 10.220) indicate that it too is a copy of the version commissioned by Ruy López. More plausible is that the Condestable was offended by one of the other vernacular versions containing Trevet's interpolations: e.g. the Castilian BN Madrid 10.193, a most obscure text, based on the Catalan version of Saplana. On these MSS, see Jaume Riera i Sans, 'Sobre la difusió hispànica de la *Consolació* de Boeci', *AFE*, 1 (1984), 297–327.

advice, it is possible to reconstruct a theory of reading, similar to the scholastic concept of *lectio*: the nobility was encouraged to read not simply for pleasure or example, but also as a means of conjoining the active and contemplative lives, and thus of emulating the ideal of the prudent warrior-statesman.

The final chapter of the book is by far the longest section dedicated to a single author, but its length is justified both by the nature of its subject and by the present state of scholarship. On a purely theoretical level, Santillana's *Proemio* does not add much to contemporary thinking about the nature and function of poetry. The section devoted to tracing the history of vernacular verse—generally considered to be Santillana's most original contribution—is an adaptation and extension of a device used in laudatory orations of the arts. But seen in its proper context, the work breathes life into old topics, and becomes a vital record of a nobleman's experience of writing verse and collecting books. In this sense, *El proemio* is, to borrow a phrase, 'not epoch-making, but it is epoch-marking'.[41] For as well as being a personal gift, Santillana's *Proemio e carta al condestable de Portugal* is a diplomatic one; cementing an alliance formed after the victory at Olmedo, it advertises to the Portuguese nobility the literary aspirations and achievements of their Castilian neighbours.[42]

The research so far carried out on the text has led to a strikingly disparate set of conclusions. As regards its general cultural background, *El proemio* has been seen as the product of an aspiring (or even fully-fledged) humanist in the Italian mould, and also as that of a writer entrenched in medieval attitudes. In the narrower field of literary theory, it has been paraded both as a radical manifesto and as a reactionary tract. And no less disconcerting has been the conflict of opinion concerning its sources and influence upon later generations. The principal cause of this diversity in critical opinion has been the tendency to force the work to supply evidence that supports preconceived ideas about the nature of Castilian culture during the reign of Juan II. Put simply, this has

[41] Geoffrey Shepherd's comment on a later aristocratic text that has many similarities in function, tone and structure with Santillana's defence: Sir Philip Sidney, *An Apology for Poetry or the Defence of Poesy* (Manchester: University Press, 1973), p. 16.

[42] I am grateful to Professor Nicholas Round for pointing out this aspect of the text to me. For the date, see Maximiliaan P. A. M. Kerkhof, 'Acerca da data do *Proemio e carta* do Marqués de Santilhana', *PFG*, 12 (1972–73), 1–6.

meant that most interpretations have depended upon whether the critic regards this period as part of the Middle Ages, the Renaissance or Pre-renaissance (three terms which are often used in discussions of Santillana's work but seldom defined). This approach has deflected attention from the analysis of El proemio's content and structure, without which there can be no solid basis for any inquiry into its broader cultural implications.

But for a number of reasons, the task of interpreting El proemio is a delicate one. For one thing, as a direct result of the highly Latinate vocabulary and syntax, certain key passages are open to a variety of possible interpretations. The occasional ambiguity in the text is compounded by the difficulty of ascribing precise sources to a given statement (this has been a particularly controversial topic in recent years). But before Santillana's theorizing is accused of vagueness and superficiality, we should not forget that his work is, by and large, a eulogy not a polemic: the arguments of the detractors of poetry are occasionally mentioned in passing, but never examined at length, as they are in the fourteenth-century Italian debates between, say, Mussato and Domenici. Because of this, it is sometimes hard to identify the motives behind a particular statement, or to define the exact scope of an idea. Moreover, as a eulogy, El proemio demands not only a lofty style, but also that the argument should maintain a certain momentum: Santillana cannot afford to pause and analyse.

The fact that the most important poetic treatise of the century belongs to the tradition of a laudatory oration of the arts, and lacks an obviously polemical tone, is significant. Notes of protest were periodically sounded, mainly by theologians, against the literary pursuits of the nobility. But it would be a severe oversimplification to describe the history of literary criticism during the reign of Juan II according to the pattern encountered in Italy during the previous century, when there was a continuous series of bitter polemics between scholastic theologians and humanist defenders of poetry. The Castilian nobility did not engage in outright confrontation, but preferred to rebut opposing arguments implicitly. After all, they looked to theologians like Cartagena and Alfonso de Madrigal to supply many of their literary interests, by commissioning translations from the classics and original works in the vernacular. It seems that they realized that, for the most part, the theologians' objections were directed not at poetry per se, but at the depth of aristocratic involvement with it, and at particular poetic genres.

A good example of this is the debate over predestination and free will initiated by Sánchez Calavera in the first decade of the century. The reaction of Fray Diego de Valencia shows how clerics did not disapprove of learned debates on certain scholastic themes. They were thought, perhaps, to offer a valuable source of edification for the layman and a useful outlet for the aristocrat's desire 'con letrados atanto arguyr' (no. 525, l. 150). Moreover, the *preguntas y respuestas* had great comic potential; amusing parodies of the scholastic method could be written by dressing up trivial or obscene themes in the philosophical jargon of the schools (e.g. no. 377 by Diego de Valencia). However, the toleration of the theologians clearly had its limits. Fray Diego rebuked Sánchez Calavera for posing a question about the Holy Trinity, warning him to avoid theology 'ca es muy más fonda que la poetría/ e caos es su nombre e lago profundo' (no. 528, ll. 11–12; III, 1066). A certain amount of intellectual posturing was acceptable, but the Franciscan sensed perhaps that the nobleman's amateur theologizing was getting out of hand—fears that were evidently shared by the anonymous author of the prose treatise on predestination and free will, which was intended as the last word in the debate dedicated to Ayala, and was written 'por responder a muchos hombres sin ciencia y a otros que luego topan en hacer cuestión sobre esta materia'.[43] Similar developments were taking place in France at this time. The formidable theologian Jean Gerson was provoked into taking part in the debate over the *Roman de la Rose* because the extravagant interpretations of the poem by the early humanists Montreuil and the Col brothers typified for him the sin of intellectual *curiositas* which had been so strongly condemned by St Augustine. Like Diego de Valencia, he was horrified at the layman's ambitions to speculate on profound spiritual matters. His distrust of contemporary aristocratic taste spurred him to publish his views on the kind of reading matter best suited to the literate French noble. The main ingredients in this programme of studies were edifying chronicles and works of lay piety.[44]

---

[43] Ed. Isaac Vázquez Janeiro, *Tratados castellanos sobre la predestinación y sobre la Trinidad y la encarnación, del Maestro Fray Diego de Valencia OFM (siglo XV): identificación de su autoría y edición crítica* (Madrid: CSIC, 1984), p. 103; his attribution of these texts to Fray Diego is a mistake. On this theologian, see Wolf-Dieter Lange, *El fraile trobador: Zeit, Leben und Werk des Diego de Valencia de León (1350?–1412?)*, Analecta Romanica, 28 (Frankfurt: Klostermann, 1971).

[44] See Christine de Pisan, Jean Gerson, Jean de Montreuil, Gontier et Pierre Col, *Le Débat sur le 'Roman de la Rose'*, ed. Eric Hicks (Paris: Champion, 1977);

These men were writing at the turn of the century, yet their
reservations continued to be voiced in later decades. Jean Gerson's
ideas obviously anticipate the views of one of the most influential
of all Castilian theologians, Alonso de Cartagena. Though early in
his career he seemed to adopt a flexible attitude toward the literary
ambitions of the aristocracy (illustrated for example by his
translations of Boccaccio and Cicero), by the mid 1440s he became
much more severe. He was deeply suspicious of the fashion for
book-collecting among certain sections of the nobility, and his
preoccupation led him to attempt to control their reading habits. In
his Latin Epistle to the Count of Haro, he lists the kinds of book
most appropriate for the educated aristocratic layman. As for
Gerson, exemplary histories and devotional texts come high on this
list; at the bottom are the figments of the poets, both classical and
modern, Virgil's *Aeneid* and the tales of Amadís and Lancelot:
these, he declared, contribute nothing whatsoever of value to the
life of the aristocrat.[45] As we shall see, the case for the defence was
most eloquently put by Santillana. His literary achievements,
enhanced by his social position, made him the most effective
spokesman for the increasingly powerful, and increasingly literate,
nobility. Those members of his caste who, like him, aspired to the
unity of arms and letters would have found encouragement in his
arguments in favour of poetry, and in his desire to create an
autonomous national literature with its own canon of contemporary
auctores.

Pierre-Yves Badel, Le '*Roman de la Rose*' *au XIV siècle: étude de la réception de l'oeuvre*
(Geneva: Droz, 1980), pp. 454–61. The two Latin texts are ed. by Antoine
Thomas, *Jean de Gerson et l'éducation des dauphins de France* (Paris: Droz, 1930), see
esp. pp. 48–51. Some of Gerson's works of lay piety achieved wide diffusion in
XVc Castile see *BOOST* (author index).

[45] *Un tratado de Alonso de Cartagena sobre la educación y los estudios literarios*, ed.
Jeremy N. H. Lawrance, Publicaciones del Seminario de Literatura Medieval y
Humanística (Bellaterra: Universidad Autónoma de Barcelona, 1979), especially
pp. 49–55. Cartagena's ideas were similar to those of the Catalan theologian
Eiximenis, who was attempting to dictate the literary tastes of the clergy. The
ideas of both men go back, in part, to Gratian: on this, and other relevant issues,
see Karl Kohut, 'Zur Vorgeschichte der Diskussion um das Verhältnis von
Christentum und antiker Kultur im spanischen Humanismus: die Rolle des
Decretum Gratiani in der Übermittlung patristischen Gedankengutes', *Archiv für
Kulturgeschichte*, 55 (1973), 80–106; 'Der Beitrag der Theologie zum Literaturbegriff
in der Zeit Juans II von Kastilien: Alonso de Cartagena (1384–1456) und Alonso
de Madrigal, genannt el Tostado (1400?–55)', *RF*, 89 (1977), 183–226.

CHAPTER I

Polemic and Theory in *El cancionero de Baena*

In large, bold script at the top of the first folio of the extant manuscript are two lines of doggerel: 'Unicuique gratia est data/ Secundum Paulum relata'.[1] This reference to Ephesians, 4.7 ('Unicuique autem nostrum data est gratia secundum mensuram donationis Christi') is a wholly appropriate motto for this first anthology of Castilian lyric poetry. It expresses the self-confidence of a new generation of court poets, who believed themselves to be in possession of a special gift, 'por gracia infusa del señor Dios', as Baena put it (I, 14). The concept of poetic grace is one of the most important themes of the *Cancionero*; it occupies a key position in the structure of Baena's prologue, and is the subject of debate for all the major poets (with one interesting exception, as we shall see). It has also proved to be a controversial topic for modern scholars, who have had difficulty in agreeing about its precise meaning and sources. The problem, in part, has been one of context. The idea of poetic grace involves more than a dispute over the nature of the creative process. To understand its full significance, we need to adopt a different perspective, and examine a wider range of issues.

1 *Gracia* and the poet's status

Charles F. Fraker was the first critic to devote serious attention to the repeated references to *gracia* in Baena's anthology.[2] He surveys a series of *preguntas y respuestas* in which the secular poets Baena, Villasandino and Ferrán Manuel de Lando argue amongst themselves, or with theologians and scholastic writers, about the presence of the divine in their work and their ability to discourse

---

[1] Ed. Azáceta, I, 3.
[2] *Studies on the 'Cancionero de Baena'*, NCSRLL, 61 (Chapel Hill: Univ. of North Carolina Press, 1966), pp. 63–90.

on learned topics. In brief, he argues that *gracia* is both 'a rather specialized doctrine of poetic inspiration and an apology for ignorance', applying both to the content and to the form of poetry (p. 63). Invoked mainly by Villasandino and Manuel de Lando, it was supposed to justify the temerity of the unschooled lay poet who dared to compete with learned men in discussing spiritual or erudite subjects. Finally (and this is his most intriguing conclusion), it was 'an original application of the Franciscan, vaguely Joachimite notion that God enlightens His simple followers directly in such a way as to confound the wise of the world' (p. 64).

Fraker's insistence that to invoke *gracia* was to hold bookish learning in contempt, and his belief in the influence of radical Franciscan spiritualism, were not well received. Critics soon challenged him—with some, though not total, justification—both on the grounds that his interpretation of the evidence was inaccurate, and, equally seriously, that he was blind to the theoretical tradition of poetry as an *ars divina*.[3]

For Wolf-Dieter Lange, this last point is crucial. He makes much of the argument that the references to poetry as a divine grace can be understood only in relation to the concepts of theological and biblical poetics. According to the former, which was based ultimately on a distortion of Aristotle's *Metaphysics* and St Augustine's *City of God*, pagan poets of antiquity could be called primitive theologians because, though they were not illumined by true knowledge of God, they spoke with an intuitive awareness of divine matters. According to biblical poetics, which had its origins in the Church Fathers' attempts to reconcile Christian and classical culture, metre was employed by Moses, David and other Old Testament prophets, and parables (another form of poetic language) by Christ.[4] With examples drawn mainly from Curtius, therefore, Lange proceeds to enumerate a long list of classical, patristic and medieval writers who, in one way or another, voice the idea that poetry began as a form of theology, a science sent down to man by God. To lend more weight to his rejection of

---

[3] See the review by Alberto Vàrvaro, *RPh*, 22 (1968–69), 108–11; Lange, *El fraile trobador*, pp. 94–103; Karl Kohut, 'La teoría de la poesía cortesana en el *Prólogo* de Juan Alfonso de Baena', in *Actas del coloquio hispano-alemán Ramón Menéndez Pidal*, ed. Wido Hempel and Dietrich Briesemeister (Tübingen: Max Niemeyer, 1982), pp. 120–37.

[4] His main source is Curtius, 'Zur Literarästhetik, III', 459–79; *European Literature*, pp. 214–21. See also below, pp. 205–08.

Fraker's thesis that the notion has anything to do with Franciscan spirituality, he points to other fifteenth-century Castilian poets who talk of poetry as a divine gift in terms identical to those employed by Baena and his fellow versifiers.[5]

The tradition of theological and biblical poetics, however, provides only a partial frame of reference for the concept of *gracia* as it occurs in this *cancionero*. It also embraced the age-old debate about whether a poet was born or made: as Horace said, 'Natura fieret laudabile carmen an arte/ Quaesitum est'. The relative importance of *ingenium* and *ars* in the creative act was a commonplace issue in literary and rhetorical theory from Antiquity to the Renaissance and beyond.[6] Attitudes varied, but the consensus was that poetry was a gift from God, implanted in the poet at birth. Talent alone, however, was never enough; it was necessary to refine one's skills through constant practice and imitation of great writers. This issue underlies many of the references to *gracia*, particularly those of Villasandino. But given the polemical nature of the poems in which it occurs, it is never expressed as a lucid theoretical statement. For this, we must turn to an anonymous mid-century Castilian glossary which, under the heading 'trobar', explains that:

> No se puede esta arte aprender ni mostrar, mas es avida por gracia. Verdad es que quien por gracia la ha, después, o leyendo historias o oyendo obras que algunos grandes trobadores fizieron, puédese mucho ayudar en ello, pero el fundamento por gracia se ha de aver.[7]

This passage introduces yet another theoretical problem. When the Baena poets talk of *gracia*, they do not mean that their poems were composed in a state of numinous inspiration. For them, poetry was not the product of a divine frenzy, but of a natural inclination of the mind; it was a divine grace only in the sense that all human talents originated in God. To be sure, the notion of *furor*

---

[5] See pp. 100–01, where he refers to Santillana's *Proemio*, Pero Guillén's *Gaya ciencia* and Mena's famous invocation to the 'cristiana Musa' in st. 1 of *Las coplas de los siete pecados mortales*.

[6] See Heinrich Lausberg, *Manual de retórica literaria: fundamentos de una ciencia de la literatura*, trans. José Pérez Riesco, 3 vols (Madrid: Gredos, 1966–69), §§ 1–6, 37–41, 1152; William Ringler, '"Poeta Nascitur non Fit": Some Notes on the History of an Aphorism', *JHI*, 2 (1941), 497–504.

[7] Biblioteca de la Real Academia de la Historia, Col. Salazar, MS N-73, f. 16ᵛ. Extracts are published by Fernando Huarte Morton, 'Un vocabulario castellano del siglo XV', *RFE*, 35 (1951), 310–40, and by Jeanne Battesti-Pelegrin, *Lope de Stúñiga: Recherches sur la poésie espagnole au XVᵉ siècle*, 4 vols (Aix-en-Provence: Université de Provence, 1982), pp. 370–71.

poeticus was not unknown to fifteenth-century poets: Baena himself refers to it on one occasion, and so, possibly, does Santillana.[8] Nonetheless, with certain debatable exceptions in the work of Manuel de Lando the references to divine grace imply a wholly rationalistic approach to the subject of poetic creativity.

One final introductory point. While it is important to place the theory of *gracia* in its broad historical context, this approach (especially as applied by Lange) is not on its own sufficient. To show that the concept of poetry as an *ars divina* was a commonplace of literary thought leaves a great deal unsaid. For if it was something of a topos it could, like all topoi, be used for a variety of rhetorical effects; individual writers will borrow the theory to serve their own ends, giving it different shades of meaning according to their particular needs. Santillana, as we shall see in the final chapter, employs it mainly as a defensive measure, to bolster the historical authority of verse; for Mena, in his *Coplas contra los pecados mortales*, it is a means of re-affirming orthodox religious values, and distancing himself from the secular, classicizing verse of his youth. Such variations as these illustrate how, as I pointed out in the introduction, poetic theories were often used as rhetorical devices, tailored to suit the demands of the specific moment. As far as possible, therefore, they must be examined in the context both of the argument of a particular poem, and of the general literary persona a poet strove to project. With a concept as flexible as poetic grace this approach is of fundamental importance.

Why, then, did some of the early Castilian poets claim to be in possession of a divine gift? It is worth starting with Alfonso Alvarez de Villasandino, 'el qual', as Baena declares in the general rubric to this poet's work:

> por gracia infusa que Dios en él puso, fue esmalte e luz e espejo e corona e monarca de todos los poetas e trobadores que fasta oy fueron en toda España. (I, 16)

As this fulsome eulogy indicates, he was acknowledged after his death in the early 1420s as having been the finest troubadour of his day. His own verse, however, does not convey the impression of a man overly confident in his status as 'el señor de la floresta', as Baena once dubbed him (no. 261, l. 32; II, 537). Indeed, an acute

---

[8] See Baena's *pregunta* no. 429: '... ssy es por ciencia/ o es por engenio o es por ffemencia/ o es por abdacia o es por cordura' (ll. 10–12). For Santillana, see ch. V, section 2.

sense of rivalry pervades much of his work, particularly his later poems, and is the most interesting feature of his literary personality.

His insecurity is vividly expressed in three 'requestas contra los trobadores', written in the style of the literary *gap*, or boast, of earlier Provençal and Peninsular troubadours (nos 80, 96 and 200). In these, he adopts the voice of an outsider, contrasting the originality and excellence of his own verse with the plagiarism and distorted literary values of his contemporaries. The best example of his defensiveness is poem no. 80, which, though it has attracted the interest of recent scholars, has yet to be interpreted correctly. This is especially true of the first stanza:

> A mí bien me plaze porque se estienda
> la gaya ciencia en bocas de tales
> que sean donossos fydalgos [leales],
> e troben limado syn pavor de emienda;
> mas pues que los torpes ya sueltan la ryenda,
> quemen sus libros doquiera que son
> Virgilio e Dante, Oracio e Platón,
> e otros poetas que diz la leyenda.
>   (st. 1; I, 170)

This is not a rejection of the growing taste for the allegorical, pseudo-erudite verse that was introduced by Imperial, as Fraker and Scudieri have maintained.[9] It is a cry of irritation directed at the poetically incompetent, and has little to do with schools. Villasandino's distrust of the spread of the fashionable pastime of writing verse is rooted in the fear of being overwhelmed by a rising tide of mediocrity: 'Aquellos que non/ resciben por gracia divina este don/ de la poetría', he declares, should be brought to heel and silenced. Then, in the stanzas that follow, metaphors of craftsmanship, war and hunting belligerently affirm the virtuosity of his technique and the originality of his invention.[10] Those who plagiarize his verses and vulgarize his art 'por plazas e ostales' should not be allowed the same honor as is due to him: 'non deven bevir en onras yguales/ el muy lindo sastre con el que remienda' (ll. 19–20; I, 170). The poem ends with a veiled threat:

> Pues quien poco sabe conviene que se ryenda,
> como se rynde la garça al falcón,

---

[9] Fraker, *Studies*, pp. 68–69; Scudieri Ruggieri, *Cavalleria e cortesia*, pp. 244–45. I have adopted Scudieri's emendation of l. 3.

[10] See also nos 167, 200, 223, 225, 255.

> ca en sus Proverbios el sabio Catón
> diz qu'el bien suba, el mal que descenda.
> (ll. 33–36; I, 171)

There are several issues at stake here, and the concept of *gracia* is central to each.

Firstly, the pun on 'remendar/ remedar' ('to mend' and 'to copy', in l. 20) is bitter reference to the *remedadores*, that despised category of travelling entertainer who imitated and reworked other poets' material.[11] This is a dying echo of an age-old complaint. As a creator of original verse, who might also be a skilled musician, the troubadour was constantly on his guard against the literary and social pretensions of the multitude of minstrels, mimes, jugglers and acrobats who frequented the royal and noble courts. Satires on the attempts of this lowly and disparate group of performers to encroach on the domain of the troubadour abound in both Provençal and Galician-Portuguese lyric traditions—it was almost a genre in itself.[12] The *locus classicus* of this conflict comes in the late thirteenth century, when Guiraut Riquier entreated Alfonso el Sabio to make a formal distinction between the various kinds of *juglars*.[13] This he did (though only in fiction: the reply came from the pen of Guiraut himself), and several separate categories were established, ranging from the humble entertainers, such as the *remedadors* mentioned above, to the exalted *trobadors*.

The basic qualification of the *trobador*, according to the *declaratio*, was that he should be a skilled composer of original verse and music (ll. 250–55). More interesting than this, for our purposes, is what Guiraut has to say about his function. The status of the troubadour rests on his moral integrity; he has a mission not only to write fine verse, but to instruct. He must provide:

---

[11] Ramón Menéndez Pidal, *Poesía juglaresca y orígenes de las literaturas románicas: problemas de historia literaria y cultural*, revised ed. [of *Poesía juglaresca y juglares*, 1924] (Madrid: Instituto de Estudios Políticos, 1957), pp. 11–12, 22–23.

[12] See, for example, the *tensones* between the *juglar* Lourenço and Galician noblemen such as Joan de Guilhade in the late XIIIc (Menéndez Pidal, *Poesía juglaresca*, pp. 13, 175–80). Fifteenth-century examples are Gómez Manrique's vitriolic attacks on Juan Poeta, and the invectives between Montoro and the Comendador Román.

[13] See Valeria Bertolucci Pizzorusso, 'La supplica di Guiraut Riquier e la risposta di Alfonso X di Castiglia', *Studi Mediolatini e Volgari*, 14 (1966), 9–135; Menéndez Pidal, *Poesía juglaresca*, pp. 10–24; Edmond Faral, *Les Jongleurs en France au Moyen Age* (Paris: Champion, 1920), pp. 73–79.

de bels ensenhamens,
mostran temporalmens
o espiritual,
per c'om pot ben de mal,
sol se vol, elegir.
(ll. 267–71; p. 105)

He must guide men's actions and point out the road to honour,
employing his art as a means of clarifying obscurity ('per bel saber/
gen l'escur declaran', ll. 280–81; p. 106). The troubadour who is
capable of teaching and bringing truth to light in this way is
worthy of the title 'doctor de trobar' (because 'doctrinar/ sabon
ben', ll. 305–07; p. 106). Needless to say, this coincides with the
picture Guiraut drew of himself in the exordium to his supplication:

Mas Dieus m'a dat saber
que, segon mon semblan,
trac lo ver ad enan
declaran so que dic.
(ll. 10–13; p. 50)

These ideas were by no means unique to Guiraut; poets from the
classical period of Provençal verse until its end in the thirteenth
century frequently advertised themselves as guardians of political
and moral truth (though Guiraut seems to have insisted on the
divine authority of his position with greater emphasis than most).[14]
The tradition continues with Villasandino, who, as a Castilian,
would have been able to find extra support in the ethical theories of
Alfonso el Sabio: God gave man the power of speech 'para fazer
departimiento entre la mentira que non es sana e complida, de la
verdad e lealtad'.[15] Like Guiraut, Villasandino had an acute, and in
practical terms very flexible, sense of his political utility: his
God-given art enabled him to bring truth out into the open—the
truth, that is, of whoever hired him. The *finida* of poem no. 80
contains a menace typical of those poets who put their rhetorical

[14] See, for example, the mid-XIIc poet Marcabru who condemned his
contemporaries' tendency to distort truth ('so que veritatz autreia') through false
eloquence (Paterson, *Troubadours and Eloquence*, p. 10); also Cerverí de Girona,
poems 21, 100, 115 in *Obras completas*, ed. Martín de Riquer (Barcelona: Instituto
Español de Estudios Mediterráneos, 1947); and Joseph Anglade, *Le Troubadour
Guiraut Riquier: étude sur la décadence de l'ancienne poésie provençale* (Bordeaux: Féret et
Fils; Paris: Fontemoing, 1905), pp. 263–82.

[15] Partida II, 13, 5; quoted from Hans-J. Niederehe, *Alfonso el Sabio y la
lingüística de su tiempo*, Historiografía de la Lingüística Española (Madrid: Sociedad
General Española de Librería, 1987), p. 70.

prowess at the service of others. To compare himself to a falcon is not merely to exalt the quality of his verse over that of the poetically inept; it is also an advertisement for his ability to write effective political and personal propaganda. To Alvaro de Luna, for example, he promises that he sells 'palabras de buen mercado', and that 'quanto puedo maldigo/ a qualquier vuestro enemigo' (nos 177, l. 22 and 178, ll. 23–24; II, 326–27).[16]

But Villasandino was caught in a cross-current of literary tradition. The real challenge came not from the *juglares* but from the dilettante court poets and *letrados* for whom the composition of verse was not a means of livelihood. The end of his career coincided with the growing taste for a more philosophically oriented verse, and with the birth in Castile of the *poeta*. As a result, the old view of the troubadour as one who perceived and propagated truth took on a new dimension, and Villasandino, the political prophet of Juan II, began to be put to the test in ways that he could not have foreseen.

It is well known that the popular *pregunta y respuesta* genre stretched back through Galician-Portuguese to the Provençal *tenso* and *joc-partit*. As far as I can tell, however, there was little or no precedent in poetry for the avid interest in astrological or theological matters which make up a large part of the debates in *El cancionero de Baena*.[17] Villasandino was frequently interrogated on these subjects, his most critical adversaries being poets from a professional background: the Dominican Fray Pedro de Colunga, the Franciscan Fray Diego de Valencia and an anonymous 'Bachiller en artes' from Salamanca. These debates were conducted partly as entertainment, partly as expressions of *cortesía*. Nevertheless, they occasionally afford an insight into more fundamental differences of literary outlook.

---

[16] Villasandino also wrote propaganda for Ruy López Dávalos and Archbishop Pedro de Luna, and against Cardenal Pedro de Frías; in nos 152 and 192, he describes himself as a prophet of contemporary political upheaval; see Ingrid Bahler, *Alfonso Alvarez de Villasandino: poesía de petición* (Madrid: Ediciones Maisal, 1975), ch. 4.

[17] John G. Cummins, 'The Survival in the Spanish *Cancioneros* of the Form and Themes of Provençal and Old French Poetic Debates', *BHS*, 42 (1965), 9–17; le Gentil, *La Poésie lyrique*, I, 459–80; Alfred Jeanroy, *La Poésie lyrique des troubadours* (Paris: Henri Didier; Toulouse: Édouard Privat, 1934), II, 247–81. N'At de Mons, Riquier's contemporary, shows a fondness for scholastic and theological subjects comparable to the *Baena* poets (e.g. a long epistle to Alfonso X on astrology); he too occasionally claims divine inspiration, see Anglade, *Le Troubadour Guiraut Riquier*, p. 280.

One such occasion is poem no. 88, one of six questions the Bachiller de Salamanca addresses to Villasandino. As in so many others, a problem of astrology is posed; the solution, says the Bachiller, should be given 'por los almanaques de fylosoffýa/ o por vuestra bondat, o por cortesýa' (ll. 14–15; I, 186). Replying that the answer is one of God's secrets, Villasandino makes a remark that typifies the attitude he adopts in his exchanges with professional scholars:

> que yo no entiendo qu'es astrología
> nin sus almanaques, mas por poetría
> faré mi razón limada, compuesta.
> (no. 89, ll. 14–16; I, 187)

He makes no attempt to hide behind a façade of erudition; on the contrary, here, as elsewhere, he insists that he is unschooled—his only learning is poetic, and this, in his view, qualifies him to speak as a 'clarificador de toda escureza'.[18] This merely provokes sarcasm from the Bachiller. In the following *pregunta* (which, judging by the changed rhyme scheme, belongs to a separate sequence), he ridicules the troubadour's belief that technical virtuosity is enough for this kind of poetry (ll. 14–16). The Bachiller's irony cannot be explained entirely by the fact that these poems are written in the style of the *tenso*, in which poets deliberately set out to insult each other: the conflict originates in contrasting views about the quantity of formal erudition one need to become a true poet.

The group of four poems nos 473–76 presents a similar pattern of responses. Fray Diego de Valencia eulogizes Villasandino's versifying skills then quizzes him on the relationship between 'fortuna', 'ventura' and 'natura'. Though the latter's reply employs scholastic jargon, it remains nonetheless that of a 'rudo, synple feligrés' (no. 474, l. 5; III, 953). It is rustic only with regard to erudition, however. Villasandino wraps his answer up in a clever display of wit, in which mock modesty and self-pity are blended with praise for God and Diego de Valencia, all leading up to a petition for a new cloak. This humour is lost on the Franciscan (as it seems to have been lost on modern scholars; the sly, facetious and often ambiguous character of this poet's verse has never received the recognition it deserves). All Diego de Valencia can do is to resort to a dry and arrogant exhibition of learning, for which,

---

[18] The label was given to him (perhaps ironically) by Fray Pedro de Colunga (no. 136, l. 2; I, 259).

significantly, he feels justified in adding an extra stanza to the prescribed scheme (no. 475). This allows Villasandino to make up for being patronized in matters of philosophy; he pounces on the unwarranted addition of the stanza with a proud boast of technical superiority: 'los consonantes a vos fallescientes/ a mí non fallescen sy en el mundo son' (no. 476, ll. 17–18; III, 956). A brave try, comments Baena in the rubric, but not enough to overcome the Franciscan's superior intellectual power.

It is, then, a conflict of innate wit (understood both as humour and natural insight into obscure affairs), allied to poetical virtuosity, against scholastic learning. In most cases, Villasandino's combination of talents served him well; faced with philosophical enigmas he undermines his opponents with comic touches and protestations of ignorance. Never does he refuse to answer. But what is surprising about his exchanges with professional scholars is that he never claims the authority of divine grace to support either his arguments or his status as a poet. He is not reluctant to do this when addressing aristocrats, like Juan Furtado de Mendoza:

> ... non se engañe
> alguno diziendo que só letrado,
> pues cada qual tiene su don otorgado
> d'aquel glorioso que es más que profeta,
> e sy yo abriere mi arte secreta
> daré que fazer a algunt graduado.
> (no. 103, ll. 27–32; I, 209)

He might have thought it tactically unwise to compromise the divine source of his genius in learned debates which, in the eyes of many, he was bound to lose.

No such qualms were felt, it seems, by Ferrán Manuel de Lando in his confrontations with theologians and scholastics. He resorts without the slightest hesitation to the *gracia* topos in the poems he exchanges with the Franciscan Fray Lope del Monte, to prove that he too was capable of discussing deeply learned subjects; but, in doing so, he gives the device an original, and in view of his adversary, an ingenious twist. He begins his *pregunta* (no. 272) in the usual manner: praising Fray Lope's wisdom, excusing his own ignorance and setting him an astrological conundrum. But Manuel de Lando adds a new ingredient. He asks the Franciscan not to be surprised, or indeed envious, if he speaks 'en discreta forma', since:

> ... Dios sus secretos quiso revelar
> a párvulos symples, pessados e rudos;

e a los prudentes dexólos desnudos,
escondiendo d'ellos el su resplandor,·
segunt verifica nuestro Salvador
en su Evangelio de testos agudos.
(ll. 27–32; II, 551) ´

But Fray Lope remains unimpressed by the nobleman's claim to speak with the wisdom of the simple. If my interpretation is correct, he accepts that, when appropriate, it is perfectly legitimate for the unlearned to 'fablar de escripturas'; but he adds the important rider: 'Pero sy me fabla Remón Lulista/ sofryr non me cunple sus dichos ceviles' (no. 273, ll. 20–22; II, 552). Moreover, he has no reason to be envious of Ferrán Manuel: 'nunca vy ssecretos de Dios en ditar,/ nin al tal saber non somos tenudos' (ll. 27–28; II, 553).

These passages provided the main support for Fraker's theory that Manuel de Lando invoked the support of radical Franciscan spirituality, which in certain respects looked for authority in the works of Ramon Llull. The conclusions he draws about this issue and about the religious ideas of Manuel de Lando are in many ways questionable. It is not my purpose here to rehearse all the evidence for and against Fraker's arguments, but he was, I think, correct to situate the notion of *gracia infusa*, as it occurs in Baena's anthology, within the context of contemporary religious trends. The accusation that Lando was a 'Remón Lulista' testifies to the spread of popular Llullism, one of whose principal tenets was that Llull wrote his main theological tract, the *Ars maior*, not by a rational process, but illuminated by divine inspiration. In view of this, it is not surprising that Lando's use of the wisdom of the simple topos should have aroused suspicions that he was, in fact, a *Lulista*. It is also possible that Lando was drawn to this Evangelical concept by the example of Vicente Ferrer who, though he was treated with hostility by members of the religious establishment, acquired an enormous popular following at the time. In spite of the extraordinary eloquence of this friar, he was not thought to have derived his skills from scholastic bookishness, since 'no traía otro libro ninguno consigo sino la Biblia e el Salterio en que reçava'.[19]

---

[19] In addition to works cited in note 3, see Fraker's review of Lange, *El fraile trobador*, *HR*, 42 (1974), 341–43; on popular Llullism in Spain, see Tomás and Joaquín Carreras y Artau, *Historia de la filosofía española: filosofía cristiana de los siglos XIII al XV* (Madrid: Asociación Española para el Progreso de las Ciencias, 1943), II, 14–30, 30–44, 517–22. Poets living in and around Córdoba showed particular

Although there is not much in Lando's poetry to confirm that he aligned himself with any specific theological standpoint, both the spread of popular Llullism and the preaching of Vicente Ferrer help to explain why he was able so easily to invoke the concept of *gracia infusa* in support of his poetic debates with theologians and professional poets. The religious context also helps us to differentiate the early Castilian treatment of poetic grace from the theoretical debates of contemporary France. On the surface, they are identical: lay poets argue with University scholars over a range of learned matters, and claim authority for their position by the fact that poetry is 'une science infuse'. But these debates were motivated by a distinct set of national rivalries (Burgundian poets versus Paris University clerics), and, more importantly, they belong to quite different intellectual traditions. In France, the explicit frame of reference for theories of inspiration was Plato: not the Neo-Platonism of the Florentine Humanists, but that of a national tradition that went back to twelfth-century Chartres.[20]

To return to Castile, we must not lose sight of the fact that the real issues are not theological (Fraker's conflict between Illuminists and Conventual Franciscans), but literary. Manuel de Lando's dispute with Fray Lope is conducted on the same terms as those between Villasandino and the two scholastic poets mentioned above. As poem no. 274 clearly demonstrates, Manuel de Lando uses the concept of *gracia* to counter the accusation that lay poets cannot capture 'ssecretos de Dios'. Recalling his earlier threat that he might reply 'en discreta forma', he boasts of his ability to compose 'metáforas fondas, sutiles', and to invent 'secretos en forma' which are impossible to decipher (ll. 22–27; II, 554). In other words, it is an exaltation of the troubadour's special verbal powers, which enable him to mystify the untalented, and convey concepts that are deceptively profound. These are exclusively poetic gifts, denied to the 'letrados e frayles faludos' who lack 'gracia qu'es virtud mayor/ e fablan syn orden como tartamudos' (ll.

---

interest in Llull; see Baena's rubric to no. 342, on Pedro González de Uceda. Baena himself was commissioned to copy this philosopher's texts: see Nieto Cumplido, 'Aportación histórica al *Cancionero de Baena*', p. 199. On Vicente Ferrer, see Pedro M. Cátedra, 'La predicación castellana de San Vicente Ferrer', *BRABLB*, 39 (1983–84), 235–309, at p. 242.

[20] See C. Henry Bodenham, 'Doctrines de l'inspiration dans la poésie française du quinzième siècle', *Studi Francesi*, in press. On the poverty of platonism in XVc Castile, see Round, 'The Shadow of a Philosopher'.

29–32). However, the way in which he formulates the concept of grace suggests that he thought of his gift not so much as a constant talent, but as something that functions only when God wishes. While never going so far as to describe it as a divine frenzy, he seems, on some occasions, to give more emphasis to the impulsive and unpredictable nature of his gift.[21]

The notion of poetic grace plays a different role in the polemics between Manuel de Lando and Villasandino. In these, the central issue does not concern scholastic erudition and native wit, but is a conflict over such literary matters as originality and plagiarism, natural talent and craftsmanship. The *preguntas y respuestas* nos 253–59 represent the fragments of a continuous rivalry between the two poets (nos 253–54 and 257–58 are pairs; the other three, by Villasandino, are isolated replies to poems that are no longer extant).

The principal theme of the first pair is Manuel de Lando's refusal to accept his fellow poet's claims of absolute superiority (as illustrated, for example, by the *requesta* no. 80). He wheels out the old topos of *gracia* simply to prove that poetic skill is not confined to one man. 'Ca Dios reparte sus dones/ a todos', he declares, with a reference to 'el Apóstol' and the wisdom of the unlearned, adding that:

> Como fyzo a vos dyleto,
> profundo de grant saber,
> bien assý pudo fazer
> otro mucho más discreto.
> (no. 253, ll. 17–36; II, 519–20)

This argument, as Villasandino points out in the following three poems, is totally inadequate in terms of both theory and practice: some poets (such as 'Dante, Vergylio e Catón') are naturally finer than others, and we should not question the way God deals out his gifts, since it is obvious that he, Villasandino, is superior (no. 254; II, 521–22); his pre-eminence is founded not just on innate talent, but on long experience and training in poetic technique (no. 255, sts 2–3), which are lacking in Manuel de Lando, a mere *parvenu*: 'en tan breve tienpo tan alto sobistes', he sneers (no. 255, l. 10; II, 523; a theme taken up in no. 258, with the contrast between

---

[21] See especially nos 260, 263 (where he refers to the *metáforas* and *figuras* 'que Dios le muestra de depara', l. 50), and 275 ('. . . en quanto Dios quiso/ fize algunas symples obras', ll. 5–6).

Villasandino as 'viejo e antygo/ syempre onrado e sabidor', and
Manuel de Lando as 'un nuevo trofador', 'novel cavallero', ll. 5–7,
82); equally serious, the younger poet is simply a plagiarist:

> Quando bien mi rostro afilo
> pensando en vuestra carrera,
> fallo qu'es tener dentera
> de quantas cosas copylo.
> (no. 258, ll. 73–76; II, 532)

What is remarkable about Villasandino's arguments, especially in
this last poem, is his refusal to discuss the issue of divine inspiration
on his opponent's terms. Manuel de Lando had asserted (nos 257
and 263) that his powers of invention were based on '[la] gracia del
señor', not on scholastic learning—exactly the same Evangelical
attitude as he had adopted in his debates with the Franciscan Fray
Lope del Monte. For Villasandino, however, the implications of his
opponent's biblical arguments for a theory of poetic inspiration
seem to be of little interest. He accepts that the nobleman has a gift
('Ya mostrades que en la cuna,/ antes de vuestro bautissmo,/
rescebistes por vos mismo/ muchas gracias, que non una'; no. 258,
ll. 49–53; II, 531), but focusses his attention on the concrete
products of talent: in other words, on *ars*, rather than *ingenium*. In
the absence of evidence to the contrary, Manuel de Lando's
repeated claims to possess the wisdom of the simple are just so
much hollow rhetoric.

The purely rhetorical possibilities of the concept of *gracia* are
precisely what seem to have attracted Baena. In a *pregunta* to
Manuel de Lando, he invokes it simply to provoke his opponent
('por que se publique/ la vuestra ciencia.../ conviene forçado que
alguno vos pique', no. 359, ll. 1–4; III, 813): the assertion that
'unicuique/ data es gracia' (ll. 9–10) is the catalyst for the series of
mutual insults that stretch over the following four poems. Apart
from this, Baena does not pretend to possess divine grace in the
same way as the other two secular poets I have been discussing.
Nevertheless, he emerges as a poet of supreme self-confidence, with
a more complex literary persona than one might at first suspect.
The roles he adopts are numerous: apart from compiler, editor and
critic, he challenges Villasandino as a writer of personal propaganda; he vaunts his rhetorical prowess and ability to solve riddles;
he is also, sometimes deliberately, sometimes not, the court
buffoon. But above all, he portrays himself as a man of books;

unlike Villasandino and Manuel de Lando, he does not seem to have felt the need to call on *gracia* as a means of acquiring *auctoritas*. His self-justification was rooted in his adherence to the new ideals of lay culture, based on a show of wide reading.[22] In this respect, his status was bolstered by his occupation as a scribe: literacy and penmanship were his means of rivalling established poets and gaining honour at court. To Villasandino, insolently appropriating this troubadour's own imagery, he brags that he is the new bird of prey:

> por quanto vuestro omilano
> bola poco e con presura,
> e non sube en el altura
> donde sube don Fulano,
> el muy sotil escrivano.
>   El muy sotil escrivano
> que trabaja noche e día
> con su linda escrivanía
> en papel lisso, toscano,
> por pitarvos el tolano
> en la su ryca escritura
> de letra tajante e pura,
> bien escripta con su mano
> non por cierto de villano.
>   (no. 180, ll. 5–18; II, 330)

It is interesting to note that in the right-hand margin, against the following stanza, is the word 'unicuyque': Baena's boast had the desired effect on one reader at least (ed. Lang, f. 55ᵛ).

For the same reasons, it is perhaps also relevant that Francisco Imperial never asserts the divine origin of his talent. Like Baena, it could be that he did not feel it necessary. In his case, his *auctoritas* as a writer stemmed from the fact that he portrayed himself not as a 'trobador', but as a 'poeta'; that is to say that he thought of himself as a polymath or philosopher, like Dante. This tradition, which I shall examine later in more detail, made it unnecessary for him to fall back on the topos of grace, since wisdom already lay at the core of his literary persona.

To sum up, the concept of *gracia*, as it occurs in *El cancionero de Baena*, is best situated in two literary contexts. It enabled Villasandino

---

[22] See Francisco Márquez Villanueva, 'Jewish "Fools" of the Spanish Fifteenth Century', *HR*, 50 (1972), 385–409; Jeremy N. H. Lawrance, 'Juan Alfonso de Baena's Versified Reading List: A Note on the Aspirations and the Reality of Fifteenth-Century Castilian Culture', *JHP*, 5 (1980–81), 101–22.

and Manuel de Lando to strengthen their position as men endowed with special verbal and perceptual powers. Villasandino conforms to an older troubadour tradition; the parallels with Guiraut Riquier are notable: both were poets who, with their livelihood threatened, advertised their God-given talent to perceive truth in its various forms. Manuel de Lando, on the other hand, exploited the concept of the wisdom of the simple to compensate, perhaps, for his alleged inexperience in the complex verse forms, and the new, doctrinally-biased content of poetry. Secondly, the references to divine inspiration are part of the old debate over the relative importance of innate talent and acquired skill. Villasandino represents the view that poetry was the product both of *ars* and *ingenium*, whereas Manuel de Lando, with his constant references to biblical authority, seems to place greater emphasis on the influence of an arbitrary divine inspiration.

2   Baena as compiler and critic

We can only guess at the practical difficulties that faced Baena as he set about compiling his *Cancionero* (assembled, as the rubric tells us, 'con grand pena'). How reliable were his sources for the brief biographical and circumstantial details which precede the poems? Did he work entirely alone? Did he attempt to edit the poems or select the most reliable texts? How much was gathered aurally? Unfortunately, there is inadequate evidence to attempt firm answers to these questions, especially since the original anthology is no longer extant. It is possible, however, to say something about his methods of presentation and their relationship to those employed in earlier European anthologies of vernacular lyrics. Baena's approach to his task sheds further light on his historical position and on the changes that were occurring in the literary culture of early fifteenth-century Castile.

As is well known, very few manuscripts have survived containing examples of the lyric tradition that immediately preceded Baena. Apart from the single sheet of seven songs by Martin Codax, the entire corpus of Galician-Portuguese secular lyric is preserved in just three major collections: the fragmentary *Cancioneiro da Ajuda* (*c.* 1300: possibly the work of the Alfonsine scriptorium), and the two *cancioneiros* compiled for the Italian humanist Angelo Colocci (*c.* 1500: the *Colocci-Brancuti* and *Vaticana*).[23] Though it is slender, the combined evidence of these manuscripts makes it possible to reconstruct the organizational procedures adopted by the Galician-Portuguese compilers. The basic arrangement of the three large *cancioneiros* is by genre, and within that by author; but internal evidence also proves that in smaller anthologies the opposite practice (by author, then genre) was also followed, and this was the system selected by Baena.[24] These *cancioneiros* supply the additional precedent for Baena's anthology in the occasional use of rudimentary rubrics. These come down to us mainly via the section devoted to satiric verse in the two Italian collections (unfortunately, the scribes never filled in the spaces left for rubrics in the *Cancioneiro da Ajuda*). For the most part their function is simply to summarize the circumstances and aims of isolated *cantigas d'escarnho e de maldizer*, and they do not represent a sustained attempt—as do those of the *Cancionero de Baena*—to pass critical comment on the poets and their work. There is an interesting exception, however, in a rubric attached to a *tençon* between Pay and Martin Soares where the compiler gives rare details about Martin's origins and his excellence as a poet.[25] This may have reflected a wider practice, current in smaller anthologies now lost to us, whose purpose was to preserve and confer authority upon the work of an individual or local community of poets.

It is clear, therefore, that Baena could have drawn partial inspiration from the Galician-Portuguese school for his use of rubrics and for the particular format he adopted in his anthology. However, we should not forget that these methods of presentation were by no means unique to this lyric tradition, but were common elsewhere in Europe, in the compilations of the Old French and Provençal schools.[26] Could Baena have been attempting to copy the *vidas* and *razos*, which were such a distinctive feature of the

[23] Giuseppe Tavani, *Poesia del duecento nella penisola iberica: problemi della lirica galego-portoghese* (Rome: Ateneo, 1969), pp. 77–179.

[24] Tavani, *Poesia del duecento*, pp. 153–75.

[25] 'Esta cantiga fez Martin Soárez como en maneira de tençon con Paai Soárez, e é d'escarnho. Este Martin Soárez foi de Riba de Límia, en Portugal, e troubou melhor ca tôdolos que trobaron, e ali foi julgado antr'os trobadores', in *Cantigas d'escarnho e de mal dizer dos cancioneiros medievais galego-portugueses*, ed. M. Rodrigues Lapa (Coimbra: Galaxia, 1965), p. 445.

[26] For a pioneering survey of the compilatory techniques of Old French *chansonniers*, see Sylvia Huot, *From Song to Book: The Poetics of Writing in Old French Lyric and Lyrical Narrative Poetry* (Ithaca: Cornell Univ. Press, 1987).

Provençal anthologies from the thirteenth century onwards? The *vidas* are, in their basic conception, similar to the general rubrics preceding the work of the major poets in Baena's anthology. But they are far more elaborate than anything written by the Castilian: only the rubric to Garci Fernández de Gerena has the anecdotal quality that characterizes the *vidas*—and this, if Alberto Blecua is right, is a later interpolation. Baena's rubrics focus more on the wisdom and work of the poet, and supply little extra-literary information. The *razos*, which describe the circumstances of composition, correspond in their basic function to the rubrics of the individual poems; yet as far as style and substance are concerned, they share nothing in common. In view of this, it seems to me unlikely that the Provençal criticism exerted a direct formative influence on Baena, and unwise to consider his methods as a conscious continuation of it.[27] The similarities in function between the Castilian rubrics and the *vidas* and *razos* stem from something much more simple: they both originate in the desire of compilers to sell their wares and at the same time to extol the literary and social merits of their patrons. Indeed, as Elizabeth R. Wilson has suggested, the social information contained in the Provençal rubrics was a form of implicit literary propaganda.[28]

But the most overt example known to me of a scribe acting as a literary apologist for a poet is the Englishman John Shirley. A contemporary of Baena, he devoted much of his long working life to copying the works of Lydgate. The exhortatory style and tone of his many rubrics and glosses have caused some modern scholars to consider him a combination of publisher and literary agent.[29] His activities illustrate the growing importance of the scribe as

---

[27] For a contrasting view, see Alan Deyermond, 'Baena, Santillana, Resende and the Silent Century of Portuguese Court Poetry', *BHS*, 59 (1982), 198–210, at pp. 204–05. The texts of the *vidas* and *razos* should be consulted in *Biographies des troubadours: textes provençaux des XIIIe et XIVe siècles*, ed. Jean Boutière, A. H. Schutz, Irénée-Marcel Cluzel, 2nd ed. (Paris: Nizet, 1973).

[28] 'Old Provençal *Vidas* as Literary Commentary', *RPh*, 33 (1979–80), 510–18.

[29] See A. I. Doyle, 'More Light on John Shirley', *MAe*, 30 (1961), 93–101; A. S. G. Edwards, 'Lydgate Manuscripts: Some Directions for Future Research', in *Manuscripts and Readers*, ed. Pearsall, pp. 15–26, at pp. 19–21; Richard F. Green, *Poets and Princepleasers: Literature and the English Court in the Late Middle Ages* (Toronto: University of Toronto Press, 1980), pp. 131–33; examples of Shirley's work are in *The Minor Poems of John Lydgate*, ed. Henry MacCracken, EETS Extra Series, 107 and Original Series, 192 (London: for the Early English Texts Society by Oxford Univ. Press, 1911–34).

intermediary between the poet and his audience and offer an interesting parallel for the life and work of Baena. Though working in different circumstances, both men had an eye for a market at a time when poetic accomplishment was an increasingly important sign of good breeding.

In short, Baena structured his *Cancionero* in a way that was common in the European lyric tradition. His structuring principle draws attention to poets before genres, and thus reflects a desire to publicize the literary-social qualities of a particular community of men, a goal which is also reflected in the rubrics. These are best appreciated when they are situated, not in the Galician or Provençal tradition, but in that of another kind of criticism, that of the schools.

The relevance of scholastic criticism becomes especially apparent when the rubrics are considered in conjunction with the novel *exordium* and *Prologus Baenensis*. Prose prologues such as these appear to be a new feature in European lyric anthologies. In fact, I know of only one example of a prose introduction to a general anthology of Provençal verse: the fourteenth-century *Chansonnier de Bernart Amoros*.[30] Although, like Baena, Bernart Amoros was a clerk who prided himself on his knowledge of poetry, his brief prologue does not compare to the *Prologus Baenensis*. His main concern, apart from advertising his own literary discrimination, is to stress the textual authenticity of his collection: a preoccupation which is notably absent from Baena's prologue, but which re-emerges in the preface to the *Cancionero general*. Like other vernacular scribes and authors of the late Middle Ages, Baena was drawn to the format and terminology of the academic *accessus*. The history, function and influence of this form of critical preface will be examined in chapter IV, where we shall see how it supplied a wide range of vernacular authors with a new means of introducing their works to a reading public. That Baena also borrowed from this source is evident from a survey of his rubrics. With slight variations, these follow the same general pattern. The form of the poem is listed, followed by the name of the author; occasionally there are remarks on its purpose and quality. These headings correspond to some of the topics of the *accessus*, such as *auctor, forma tractatus, intentio*, and *materia*. In some cases, Baena's vocabulary is

---

[30] 'Le Chansonnier de Bernart Amoros', ed. E. Stengel, *RLR*, 41 (1898), 349–80 (prologue and first section only).

clearly based on academic terminology: he refers to the poem's 'intención' (e.g. nos 36, 336, 531), or to 'la materia que tracta' (nos 293, 510).[31]

His prologue, at least as far as its basic concept is concerned, originates in a branch of the *accessus* known as the *ars extrinsecus*. As Richard Hunt has explained:

> The *ars extrinsecus* belongs to the theoretical and gives us knowledge, but does not teach us how to practise the art; the *ars intrinsecus* belongs to the practical and both teaches us how to practise the art and gives us knowledge.

The consequence of this division, which goes back to Victorinus's fourth-century commentary on Cicero's *De inventione*, was that scholars 'arrived at a schema by means of which a general introduction to an art, e.g. grammar, could be combined with, yet kept separate from, the introduction to the book to be expounded, e.g. Priscian'.[32] Baena's prologue illustrates how this academic technique could be applied in a vernacular context. It gives the aspiring poet an insight into the theory of his art and some of its philosophical implications; the techniques and rules of the art are to be learnt by imitating the poems which have been arranged and methodically labelled in the main body of the collection. The same academic influence is at work in Santillana's *Proemio*, Encina's *Arte*, and, in a different context, in what remains of the introduction to Villena's *Arte de trovar*; it may also be seen in some French poetics of the fifteenth century.[33]

---

[31] According to Margarita Egan, the Provençal *vidas* also owed a debt to the *accessus*: 'Commentary, *vita poetae*, and *vida*: Latin and Old Provençal "Lives of Poets"', *RPh*, 37 (1983–84), 36–48. However, I am not convinced that the vernacular biographies were adaptations of the Latin ones, and find her application of the *accessus* paradigm to the Provençal criticism rather forced. She promises a study of the relation between the Provençal anthologies and the *Cancionero de Baena* (p. 37, n. 4).

[32] Richard William Hunt, 'The Introductions to the *Artes* in the Twelfth Century', in *Studia medievalia in honorem admodum reverendi patris Raymundi Josephi Martin* (Bruges: De Tempel, 1949), pp. 85–112, at p. 109. See also A. J. Minnis, *Medieval Theory of Authorship: Scholastic Literary Attitudes in the Later Middle Ages*, 2nd ed. (Aldershot: Wildwood House, 1988), pp. 30–33.

[33] For Santillana, Villena and an anonymous XVc *Art de seconde rhétorique*, see below, pp. 219–20; Encina's *Arte de poesía castellana* precedes the *cancionero* dedicated to the Infante don Juan, and subsequent editions of his work; for a late French example, see *Le jardin de plaisance et fleur de réthorique (reproduction en fac-simile de l'édition publiée par Antoine Verard vers 1501)*, ed. E. Droz and A. Piaget, 2 vols (Paris: Didot and Champion, 1910–25).

Baena's rubrics encapsulate some of the principal esthetic ideals of the day. They also contain attempts at evaluative criticism; this, without exception, is insubstantial: its value lies in the way it reflects the compiler's ambition to be the arbiter of literary taste at the court of Juan II. Considered separately from the poems they accompany, the rubrics are not a rewarding subject for systematic analysis. Moreover, little can be added by me to the work already done on them.[34] The *exordium* and the *prologus Baenensis*, however, are another matter.

In the former, three claims are made for the 'muy famoso e notable libro'. Firstly, it is a compendium of almost encyclopedic proportions containing:

> todas las cantigas ... todas las preguntas ... todos los otros muy gentiles dezires ... e todos los otros muy agradables e fundados processos e requestas que en todos los tiempos passados fasta aquí fizieron ... el muy esmerado e famoso poeta ... Alfonso Alvarez de Villasandino e todos los otros poetas, frayles e religiosos, maestros en theología, e cavalleros e escuderos, e otras muchas e diverssas personas sotiles que fueron e son muy grandes dezidores e ommes muy discretos e bien entendidos en la dicha graciosa arte. (I, 3–4)

I have quoted this passage at length because no paraphrase could convey the full extent of Baena's boast. It would be idle to speculate too deeply on its accuracy, since it represents—like the rubrics of John Shirley—an early example of publisher's 'hard sell'. It does seem, however, that this *cancionero* is much more parochial and selective than its compiler would have us believe; and perhaps deliberately so. A significant number of the poems are connected, in one way or another, to Seville and Córdoba. Also, as Brian Dutton has observed, though it was compiled roughly at the same time as *El cancionero de Palacio*, it reflects, with its emphasis on the work of Villasandino and learned *preguntas y respuestas*, a substantially different, and very personal, literary taste.[35] It could be,

---

[34] See Colbert I. Nepaulsingh's introduction to his ed. of Micer Francisco Imperial, '*El dezir a las syete virtudes' y otros poemas*, Clásicos Castellanos, 221 (Madrid: Espasa-Calpe, 1977), pp. xxxvi–lxvii; Claudine Potvin, 'Les Rubriques du *Cancionero de Baena*: étude pour une gaie science', *Fifteenth Century Studies*, 2 (1979), 173–85.

[35] 'Spanish Fifteenth-Century *Cancioneros*: A General Survey to 1465', *KRQ*, 26 (1979), 445–60, at p. 448, where he also makes the less convincing suggestion that *El cancionero de San Román* was a second *cancionero* by Baena, compiled to appeal to the more lyrical tastes of Juan II's court. For the connections of *El cancionero de*

therefore, that the verse of the young Santillana, to take an obvious example, was deliberately excluded: this hypothesis is feasible on chronological grounds, and seems to be supported by a derogatory remark made by Baena in a snide poem about the literary competence of Diego de Estúñiga: 'En Buytrago o en Villena/ aprendiste el deytar' (no. 425, ll. 46–47; III, 894). Not too much should be read into a stray comment such as this; even so, as with Villasandino's reference to Manuel de Lando's imitation of Imperial, it raises inevitable suspicions about the literary conflicts of the time, and about the personal enmities that underlie them. Dutton, in fact, has suggested that Diego de Estúñiga was excluded from *El cancionero de Palacio* because of his antagonism with Alvaro de Luna, who seems to have been one of its patrons. The same hypothesis could also apply to the present anthology.[36]

We return to safer ground with the second of Baena's claims, which concerns the effects of the *Cancionero*. Two theories are introduced: the ludic and the therapeutic. 'Ca sin dubda alguna', Baena promises the King:

> si la su merced en este dicho libro leyere en sus tienpos devidos, con él se agradará e deleytará e folgará e tomará muchos comportes e plazeres e gasajados ... averá reposo e descansso en los trabajos ... e tirará de sý todas tristezas e pesares e pensamientos e afliciones del spíritu que muchas de vezes ... acarrean a los príncipes los sus muchos e arduos negocios reales.
> (I, 4–5)

The belief that poetry gave pleasure, refreshed the spirit and offered relief from daily care was amongst the most common tenets of medieval literary thought. There were serious, and often highly complex, ethical and medical justifications for these ideas, as Glending Olson has shown. His book, which relates the attitudes of vernacular authors (principally Chaucer, Boccaccio and the writers of *fabliaux*) to their philosophical background (e.g., Aristotle's *Ethics*, Aquinas, Hugh of St Victor and medical treatises), makes it unnecessary for me to go into detail here.[37] Baena's treatment of the

---

Baena with Andalusia, see the two studies by Nieto Cumplido (cited above, Introd., note 32).

[36] For Dutton, see previous note; also Battesti-Pelegrin, *Lope de Stúñiga*, I, 377–84.

[37] *Literature as Recreation in the Later Middle Ages* (Ithaca: Cornell Univ. Press, 1982); also Curtius, *European Literature*, pp. 478–79; Otis H. Green, *Spain and the Western Tradition: The Castilian Mind in Literature from 'El Cid' to Calderón* (Madison: Univ. of Wisconsin Press, 1963), I, ch. 2.

subject, either in the *exordium* or later in the prologue (I, 14), does not differ in its basic concept from the countless references to literature as *ocio* that one finds in Castilian texts of the fourteenth and fifteenth centuries. One fact, of course, does set him apart from the earlier period. The contents of this *cancionero* were meant both to be read and recited (and to a lesser extent sung); but the unambiguous reference to private reading, in the first line of the passage quoted above, shows that Baena too was influenced by the gradual spread of lay literacy, the details and implications of which I examine in later chapters.[38]

The third claim made in the *exordium* also relates to the effects of poetry. Its ludic and therapeutic value, we are told, holds good over a wide audience, spanning not only the royal household, but also the many ranks of the noble and clerical estates (I, 5). To stress the universal appeal of poetry was by no means unusual: the theme occurs in the earliest vernacular *ars*, the *Razos de trobar* by the Catalan Raimon Vidal, and re-emerges over two centuries later in Santillana's *Proemio* and in the anonymous Castilian glossary to which I refer above.[39] Unlike these other writers, however, Baena fails to acknowledge the literary interests of the third estate. Though Santillana does not consider very highly the verse of 'las gentes de baxa e servil condición', it figures as a vital part of his literary defence. Baena ignores it entirely; the significance of this will be discussed below.

The *exordium* closes with a reference to the importance of literary discrimination. Baena dedicates the anthology to those who 'entender bien quisieren', adding that the prologue was written 'por que la obra tan famosa d'este dicho libro sea más agradable e mejor entendida ... por fundamento e raýz de toda su obra' (I, 5–6). The explanation that follows, therefore, was given in the belief that theoretical knowledge constituted an integral part of the pleasure to be derived from poetry; in this respect, the prologue is a guarantee of the anthology's therapeutic value. Baena's readers may have been surprised, however, to find that only about ten per cent is devoted

---

[38] Compare with Juan Manuel: 'fago que *me lean* algunos libros o algunas estorias por sacar aquel cuidado del coraçón' (*Libro del cavallero et del escudero*, 9, 5; my italics); see Macpherson, 'Don Juan Manuel', p. 7.

[39] *The 'Razos'*, ed. Marshall, p. lxxxi; similar claims in the *Vocabulario*: 'fue esta arte aplacible y agradable universal y generalmente a toda gente y nación', including the angels, emperors, Church Fathers, nobles, 'aun ... el pueblo común y grosero', Biblioteca RAH, MS N-73, f. 17ᵛ; for Santillana, see below, pp. 213–14.

specifically to poetry, and an even smaller proportion to theoretical details.

The bulk of the prologue is taken up by a eulogy of books (I, 7–11). The themes which provide the main substance of this section are all commonplace: the power of writing to preserve wisdom (the topos of 'scripturae tenacitas'); the ethical and educational function of chronicles; the obligation of rulers to know about the past and encourage the composition of all kinds of useful and pleasurable books (the topos of 'imperator litteratus'); man's natural urge for wisdom (the well-worn dictum of Aristotle). It has only recently been recognized, however, that a substantial part of this opening argument is, in fact, based word for word on the prologues to Alfonso el Sabio's *General estoria* and *Estoria de España*.[40]

A transition is marked by the assertion that just as diversity in books is a source of delight, so it is with clothes and food (I, 11–12). At this point, Baena veers off into a lengthy consideration of the benefits that are to be had from court pastimes: jousting, bull-fighting, fencing, cards, chess, dice and hunting. Of all these activities, the last is the most noble and profitable, being a means of improving the temperament and physique, and of training the nobleman for war (I, 12–13). Yet none of this, Baena concludes, can compare to the intellectual, emotional and spiritual benefits that accrue from a close study of the 'grandes fechos passados' (I, 14).

Baena now feels that he has prepared the ground sufficiently for the reader to grasp the finer points of his explanation of *la gaya ciencia*. But his long-awaited transition from a discussion of letters and court entertainments comes—for me at any rate—as something of an anti-climax. After his effusive praise of 'los libros notables e loadas escripturas', he declares that the art of poetry 'es una escryptura e conpusyción muy sotil e byen graciosa' (I, 14). It is disappointing to find Baena saying that poetry is merely '*una* escryptura', when the tone and general build-up of the argument lead one to expect the superlative, such as, 'es la más sotil e graciosa'. He could, after all, have drawn on the theory that verse was an earlier and more authoritative form of discourse than prose (a theory which was well known to writers at this time: Santillana was to put it to effective use a few years later in his *Proemio*).

---

[40] The relevant passages are printed by Francisco López Estrada (ed.), *Las poéticas castellanas de la Edad Media* (Madrid: Taurus, 1984 [1985]), pp. 29–33; see also Kohut, 'La teoría de la poesía cortesana', p. 133.

The line of Baena's argument has a rather evasive air about it. It may be reduced to these simplified terms: letters are highly important and beneficial and poetry is very subtle and enjoyable. The former contain 'muchas virtudes e muy sabyos e provechosos enxenplos', and the latter is 'muy sotil e byen graciosa e es dulce e muy agradable' (I, 14): not exactly a *non sequitur*, but there is a distinct shift in emphasis. One may object, of course, that Baena intends the reader to infer from the previous discussion that poetry should be classed under the double heading of letters and court pastimes, and hence that it shares their functions and effects. This is true, though only, I would emphasize, by implication. It is interesting that Baena feels impelled to follow this circuitous route in order to arrive at his principal subject. When he gets there, he changes tack from a eulogy of the therapeutic and ethical value of letters to a description of the qualities necessary to write verse. His method of argumentation is reminiscent of the technique advocated by rhetoricians of judicial oratory, who recommended that when one is unsure of one's case the most seductive way to influence the public is to employ the subtle approach of *insinuatio*. The orator should work round gradually to his main point 'con una simulación e con obscuro rodeo' (as Cartagena translated Cicero's *De inventione*, I, xv, 20).[41]

That Baena chooses to explain poetry by means of insinuation rather than by direct statement has a number of implications. For one thing, it reflects the difficulty of situating poetry within a broader scheme of knowledge. The emphasis on the topos of 'scripturae tenacitas', and the repeated references to letters as a means of preserving 'los grandes fechos passados' (a phrase that occurs three times in the sentence), suggests perhaps that poetry was to be classified as a form of history. His *Cancionero* records events and anecdotes from the reigns of three Castilian monarchs;

[41] *La rethórica de M. Tullio Cicerón*, ed Rosalba Mascagna, Romanica Neapolitana, 2 (Naples: Liguori, 1969), p. 54; see also Lausberg, *Manual*, § 281. This section of the prologue is reminiscent of a document of the Aragonese court, written in 1398 on behalf of Martí I, relating to the constitution of the Barcelona poetic consistory: the first half, which is a eulogy of knowledge on Alfonsine lines, ends by extolling the effects of oratory; it then describes those eloquent men who are honoured by the poetic consistories of Paris and Toulouse. The passage from the purpose of knowledge to the practice of poetry is smooth and uncomplicated, but it obscures the precise nature of their relationship: as in Baena's prologue, outright statement gives way to implication; see Boase, *The Troubadour Revival*, pp. 133–38.

as a collection of witty poems, it is also a kind of intellectual chronicle: a *speculum* of Castilian *ingenio*.

Though the weak transition from the general context to the characteristics peculiar to poetry may indicate uncertainty on Baena's part, there is also the possibility that he was being deliberately non-committal. One of the most contentious issues in the anthology was whether poetry was merely another court pastime, designed to keep the mind in agile working order, or something of an altogether higher intellectual and moral value, important in its own right. Severe doubts were expressed about its validity as a medium for philosophical or theological matters: 'nunca vy ssecretos de Dios en ditar/ nin al tal saber non somos tenudos', argued Fray Lope del Monte. Baena's silence in the prologue with regard to this dispute may have been motivated by a desire not to offend the 'perlados', 'maestres', 'pryores', and 'dottores' who, he hopes, will form a substantial part of his audience (I, 5). Nonetheless, his reluctance to specify the relationship of poetry to other branches of knowledge does not obscure the belief that the composition and study of verse constituted a more valuable exercise than other court pastimes. Though this would not necessarily have elicited universal agreement among contemporary aristocrats, it is an explicit acknowledgement of an important trend in noble attitudes. In short, Baena's presentation of the status of poetry seems to be governed by a spirit of compromise, by a deference toward noble aspiration and theological reservation.

The same may also be true of the next theoretical point, which concerns the nature of poetic grace. The art of poetry, writes Baena:

> es avida e recebida e alcançada por gracia infusa del Señor Dios que la da e la enbýa e influye en aquel o aquellos que byen e sabya e sotyl e derechamente la saben fazer e ordenar e conponer e limar e escandir e medir por sus pies e pausas, e por sus consonantes e sýlabas e acentos, e por artes sotiles e de muy diversas e syngulares nonbranças. (I, 14)

This formulation seems to me to fudge the issue that lay at the heart of the concept of *gracia*: poetry was a natural gift which, in the course of time, was brought to perfection by studying the complex rules of the art. For Baena, on the other hand, the art precedes—indeed is a precondition of—the gift: poetry is infused into those who have mastered its technique. Either this is just an unfortunately clumsy articulation of the *ars/ ingenium* dichotomy, or Baena has deliberately glossed over the controversial implications of divine inspiration. *Gracia* amounts to little more than a divine sanction, allowing the poet to practice what he has already learnt after serious and dedicated study. As expressed here, the poet is bound by something akin to a legal contract.[42]

Considerable importance is attached to understanding the complex poetic techniques which are at the disposal of the aspiring author. But, as we learn in the final lines of the prologue, many other factors contribute to the creation of the ideal poet: 'Es arte de tan elevado entendimiento e de tan sotil engeño', explains Baena, that it can be learnt only by those who satisfy certain preconditions. These may be loosely grouped under six heads:

i) intellectual qualities: the poet must be 'de muy altas e sotiles invenciones, e de muy elevada e pura discreción, e de muy sano e derecho juyzio' (I, 14–15);

ii) literary and linguistic knowledge: 'que aya visto e oýdo e leýdo muchos e diverssos libros e escripturas e sepa de todos lenguajes' (I, 15);

iii) courtly and practical wisdom: 'que aya cursado cortes de reyes e con grandes señores, e que aya visto e platicado muchos fechos del mundo';

iv) rank and gentility: he must be a 'noble fydalgo e cortés e mesurado e gentil e gracioso e polido e donoso';

v) eloquence and verbal wit: the noble poet should have 'miel e açucar e sal e ... donayre en su razonar';

vi) love: 'que sea amador e que siempre se precie e se finja de ser enamorado, porque es opynión de muchos sabyos que todo omne que sea enamorado ... de todas buenas dotrinas es doctado'.

Overall, Baena presents an image of courtliness that corresponds to a model that began to emerge in French and German courts as early as the tenth century, but which, in the view of Stephen Jaeger, 'came to expression in the courtly literature of the twelfth and thirteenth centuries'.[43] Nevertheless, without exaggerating the point it is worth observing that there is a certain gap between this traditional portrait and the practical realities of the *Cancionero* itself. On the one hand, there can be no doubt about the significance of

---

[42] I owe this last point to Bodenham, 'Doctrines de l'inspiration'.

[43] C. Stephen Jaeger, *The Origins of Courtliness: Civilizing Trends and the Formation of Courtly Ideals 939–1210* (Philadephia: University of Pennsylvania Press, 1985), p. 173. I am grateful to Mark D. Johnston for bringing this important study to my attention.

the intellectual and rhetorical qualities listed under i and v. Numerous poems endorse the importance of wisdom expressed in a lucid, free-flowing verse as well as of the need to subject one's *donayre* to a strict ethical control or *mesura* (e.g. no. 260, by Manuel de Lando). This blend of qualities echoes the Latin term *facetia*, understood both as witty speech and courtly refinement of manners (Jaeger, *The Origins*, pp. 162–68). On the other hand, conventional though they may have been, the relevance to this anthology of some of the remaining attributes is harder to assess.

To begin with the last qualification, Baena's assertion that the courtly lover is endowed with 'todas buenas dotrinas' seems to constitute a backward glance at the ideas of an earlier poetic generation. The belief that love had all kinds of ennobling powers and was the origin of *la gaya ciencia* had been emphatically stated by an Aragonese document of 1393, in which Joan I agreed to the establishment in Barcelona of a poetic consistory. This decree constitutes an important link with the earlier tradition of poetic inspiration through love which had provided the basis of Provençal and *stilnovisti* verse.[44]

Yet in spite of the undoubted influence of the tenets of courtly love in fifteenth-century Castile, one should not exaggerate their significance for contemporary poetic theory. *Pace* Lange and Kohut, *cancionero* verse offers no parallels for the concept of love as a powerful and spontaneous force of poetic inspiration, as expressed by Bernart de Ventadorn, Arnaut Daniel or Dante. A distinction should be drawn between a poet who is merely in love (common enough in Castile), and one whom love compels to write, and for whom there is a definite causal connection between the quality of his verse and the intensity of his emotion. The latter is peculiar to the earlier period: 'I' mi son un, che quando/ Amor mi spira, noto, e a quel modo/ che' e' ditta dentro vo significando'.[45] In fact, for some poets, the violent impulse of love, or indeed raw emotion of any kind, was a positive hindrance to the creation of polished verse. Excusing his work's lack of finesse, Alvarez Gato once remarked that 'los que liman sus razones/ son los libres coraçones/ quando fingen la pasión': an echo of Baena's statement

---

[44] This letter may have had some diffusion in Castile: there is a copy of it in the Biblioteca Colombina; Boase, *The Troubadour Revival*, pp. 127–32.

[45] Dante, *Purgatorio*, xxiv, 52–54; for this, and quotations from Provençal poets, see Lange, *El fraile trobador*, pp. 101–02; Kohut 'La teoría de la poesía', p. 131 and note 27.

that the courtly poet is one who 'siempre se precie e *se finja* de ser enamorado'. As José María Aguirre has suggested, the love poetry of fifteenth-century Castile has more to do with the expression of the intellectual delight taken in the code of courtliness than with the direct display of vividly-felt emotion.[46] And it is worth bearing in mind not only that the idea of love inspiration is conspicuous by its absence from Baena's *Cancionero*, but also that love poetry is by no means its dominant mode: Baena himself writes not a single line of love lyric.

Though highly apt for the contemporary *caballero andante*, from a strictly literary viewpoint, the inclusion of linguistic skill seems, like the reference to love, to be determined by the requirements of an earlier age, when Castilians used Galician-Portuguese as their lyric medium, and Catalans used Provençal. There are isolated examples of foreign languages in Castilian verse in the first half of the fifteenth century, but nothing that approaches the kind of macaronic *tour de force* attempted by earlier itinerant troubadours.[47] For Baena's contemporaries, the practical value of this recommendation lay elsewhere: to enable them to read the fashionable masterpieces of the day, notably the *Roman de la Rose* and the *Divina commedia*, and to appreciate musical lyrics (see Villasandino's reference to the *juglar* Martín, 'cuando canta ... asý en castellano commo en lymosýn'; no. 97, ll. 33–36; I, 200).[48]

---

[46] Juan Alvarez Gato, *Obras completas*, ed. Jenaro Artiles Rodríguez, Los Clásicos Olvidados, 4 (Madrid: Compañía Ibero-Americana de Publicaciones, 1928), p. 54; José María Aguirre, 'Reflexiones para la construcción de un modelo de la poesía castellana del amor cortés', *RF*, 93 (1981), 55–81, at pp. 60–61, 66.

[47] Villasandino, for example, writes a couple of lines in Catalan (nos. 178, l. 27; 182, ll. 51–53); see also Imperial (no. 226, ll. 12, 14, 16 in English, Latin and Arabic; no. 248, st. 6, in French); Santillana, *La comedieta de Ponza*, sts 19–20 (Italian). In contrast, see *Los trovadores: historia literaria y textos*, ed. Martín de Riquer, 3 vols (Barcelona: Planeta, 1975): Raimbaut de Vaqueiras, no. 164 (II, 840), Bonifaci Calvo, no. 296 (III, 1422), Cerverí de Girona, no. 330 (III, 1571), whose multilingual poems are made up of Galician-Portuguese, Provençal, French, Gascon, Italian and Castilian.

[48] As well as following the fashion for French clothes and armour, Alvaro de Luna had a taste for French minstrelsy: see the *Crónica de don Alvaro de Luna, Condestable de Castilla, Maestre de Santiago*, ed. Juan de Mata Carriazo, Colección de Crónicas Españolas, 2 (Madrid: Espasa-Calpe, 1940), p. 370. The later *cancioneros musicales* (such as those in the Colombina Library and the Cathedral Library of Segovia) indicate that the court of Ferdinand and Isabella was highly receptive to songs sung in a variety of languages (e.g. Latin, Flemish, Castilian and Italian).

A certain disparity between theory and practice is to be expected, but one cannot help wondering how Baena's readers would have judged the contents of his anthology when measured against the standards represented by his ideal poet. What, for example, would they have made of the contradiction between his demand for a widely-read poet and his eulogy of Villasandino, who consistently denies the necessity of bookish erudition? And what of the claim that the poet should be a 'noble fidalgo', when none of the three most prolific poets in the collection—Villasandino, Baena himself, and Fray Diego de Valencia—possessed noble blood, however much they might aspire to the other ideals of courtly conduct? But one should not labour the absence of rigorous empirical principles in the final section of the prologue. This is not descriptive, but prescriptive criticism. Hence, it is more profitable to draw conclusions about Baena's choice of comments than about the practical application of what he has to say.

As Kohut has rightly observed, the relatively small space devoted to formal aspects of poetry indicates that Baena's main motive for writing the prologue was to 'sacar la poesía cortesana del ámbito de los juegos y elevarla al nivel de la filosofía, que, a su vez, está definida como atributo necesario del cortesano perfecto' ('La teoría de la poesía', pp. 134–35). But we can go further than this. The portrait he sets before his readers in the final stages of the prologue is not that of a poet but of a model courtier. This distinction, though a fine one, is important. That, in the final stages of the prologue, he discusses poetry less in terms of poetics than in those of social theory is ample proof of his awareness of the changes that were taking place in his lifetime. He defines the qualities not of a professional troubadour like Villasandino, for this was a dying breed, but of the nobility, whose aspirations were to determine the future course of Castilian poetry.

Most interesting of all, however, is the air of inconclusiveness that prevails at the end of the prologue. Doubts remain over a number of issues: the precise status of poetry as a branch of letters; the effect of *gracia* as an inspirational force; the relative importance of the various courtly attributes. These topics were all to some degree controversial; whether Baena's ill-defined position is the result of uncertainty, evasiveness or just poor articulation is impossible to tell.

CHAPTER II

Enrique de Villena's 'Gaya ciencia'

The commonest way to describe poetry, especially during the early decades of the fifteenth century, was to label it *una ciencia* or *arte*. Though in scholastic philosophy these terms denoted two distinct kinds of knowledge (learning acquired intellectually or as a craft), the writers of the Castilian courts employed them in a loose sense to emphasize that poetry possessed a set of rules and hence constituted a valid branch of knowledge. Like Baena, they were not concerned with poetry's precise relationship with other forms of human wisdom. They were motivated less by an interest in philosophical speculation than with the desire to elevate the status of poetry by association with academic discourse. The treatment of the subject by Enrique de Villena, however, deserves a closer analysis. For though he too often proceeds by implication rather than by explicit argument he tackles the issue at greater depth than any of his contemporaries.

Though considerable attention has been devoted to Villena as the prime example of an intellectual outsider in fifteenth-century Castile, no-one has yet examined his views on the social importance of letters and on the writer's position in the state.[1] This is an important subject, however, because one of the recurring themes of his work is his attempt to project the image of a contemporary

---

[1] Until recently, most biographies merely elaborated upon the romantic image established by Emilio Cotarelo y Mori in *Don Enrique de Villena: su vida y obras* (Madrid: Sucesores de Rivadeneyra, 1896). Fresh and challenging insights, however, are offered by Pedro M. Cátedra in *Exégesis—Ciencia—Literatura: la 'Exposición del salmo "Quoniam videbo"' de Enrique de Villena*, Anejos del *AFE*, 1 (Madrid: El Crotalón, 1985); 'Algunas obras perdidas de Enrique de Villena con consideraciones sobre su obra y su biblioteca', *AFE*, 2 (1985), 53–75; see also Derek C. Carr and Pedro M. Cátedra, 'Datos para la biografía de Enrique de Villena', *C*, 11 (1982–83), 293–99. The evidence for and against Villena's possible poetic output has been surveyed by John K. Walsh and Alan Deyermond, 'Enrique de Villena como poeta y dramaturgo: bosquejo de una polémica frustrada', *NRFH*, 28 (1979), 57–85.

sage, an intermediary between a world of official learning (represented by the classics of literature and academic philosophy) and the vernacular lay culture of his aristocratic friends and patrons. His self-portrait, which we can piece together from remarks scattered throughout his work, is based upon a coherent theory of knowledge, covering such things as the origin of wisdom, its means of preservation and transmission, and its ethical function.[2] Here, I must pass over the details and wider implications of this subject in order to focus more clearly on the literary aspects of his concept of wisdom.

1 The science of poetry

La definición de sciencia según Galter Burley en la *Summa de las artes*: sciencia es complida orden de cosas immutables e verdaderas.[3]

Concerning this key passage, Menéndez y Pelayo has written that Villena's *Arte* '[no] responde de ningún modo al alto concepto que él da de la ciencia'.[4] This conclusion needs to be revised, since this concept of philosophy does in fact exert a powerful influence over the portrayal of poetry in the treatise.

The work opens with the kind of flourish that one would expect from a preceptive *ars poetica*: 'Por la mengua de la sciencia todos se atreven a hazer ditados'. The motivation to write is rooted in the desire to dispel ignorance. Other vernacular *artes* contain similar expressions of the theorist's concern for the literary incompetence of contemporary poets. In the earliest of them, the *Razos de trobar* (*c.* 1200), Raimon Vidal de Besalú roundly criticizes his fellow Catalans for not having understood what he considers to be 'la

---

[2] For general background, see José Antonio Maravall, 'La concepción del saber en una sociedad tradicional', in his *Estudios de historia*, pp. 203–54.

[3] 'El *Arte de trovar* de don Enrique de Villena', ed. F. J. Sánchez Cantón, *RFE*, 6 (1919), 158–80, at p. 169 (corrected against the original MS: Escorial K-III-31). Apart from supplying incorrect folio numbers, Sánchez Cantón's attempts to distinguish the original text from Alvar Gómez de Castro's interpolations (enclosed in brackets) are often misleading. He underestimates the difficulty of determining how far the XVIc humanist altered the original in the course of taking extracts from it. Critics were at one time puzzled by the date of the text (1417, 1423 or 1433?): see Elvira de Aguirre, *Die 'Arte de trovar' von Enrique de Villena* (Cologne, 1968), pp. 31–33, who shows that it can be dated 1427–33.

[4] *Historia de las ideas estéticas*, I, 467; see also Di Camillo, *El humanismo*, p. 101.

dreicha manera de trobar' (*The 'Razos'*, ed. Marshall, p. 2). His much later compatriot, Luis de Averçó, explains that he too was moved to write his *Torcimany* (*c.* 1400) by the realization that 'la gaya sciencia de trobar entre los homens no sabens ne enteses en gramatiqua es posada sotz compreniment escur o no be intelhigible'.[5] Implicit in this conventional exordial censure is the boast that the rules offered by the treatise in question will provide the cure for the decadence of contemporary verse. Villena, however, adds an interesting qualification to this idea. As a consequence of imperfect knowledge, he argues, 'no es fecha diferencia entre los claros ingenios e los obscuros' (p. 163). In other words, his treatise is based not on the assumption that all aspiring poets will be raised to the same standards of excellence (as in the *Torcimany*, for example), but on the belief that knowledge and observance of the rules of the art will establish an intellectual hierarchy.

This belief is restated on two further occasions. The first is at the start of the summary of the vernacular poetics, when he refers to the *Razos de trobar* by Raimon Vidal: 'Esmerándose con aquellas reglas los entendidos de los grosseros' (p. 164); and the second follows the famous description of the prize-giving ceremonies at the Consistory of Barcelona. As a result of the competition, explains Villena: 'mostrávase aquel aventaje que Dios e natura fizieron entre los claros ingenios e los oscuros ... e no se atrevían los ediothas' (p. 169). This expression of contempt returns us to the words that introduced *El arte*: the order of the past is contrasted with 'la mengua de la sciencia', the literary and intellectual chaos of the present.

If we bear in mind the major theme of Villena's *Los doze trabajos de Hércules*, the implications of this preoccupation become clear. Through the character of Hercules, this work depicts the actions of the 'valientes en sciencias': men whose wisdom was put at the service of the state, propagating knowledge and correcting morals.[6]

---

[5] '*Torcimany*' de Luis de Averçó: tratado retórico gramatical y diccionario de rimas, siglos XIV–XV, ed. José María Casas Homs (Barcelona: CSIC, 1956), I, 15. The aspiring poet is encouraged with the assertion that if the rules are studied assiduously, 'siatz cert que no-us será dificil cosa de saber-la perfetament ... Volenti nitxil [sic] est dificile' (I, 19).

[6] Los doze trabajos de Hércules, ed. Margherita Morreale, Biblioteca Selecta de Clásicos Castellanos, n. s., 20 (Madrid: Real Academia Española, 1958), p. 133; especially relevant are chs III, IV, IX and XII; see Maravall, 'La concepción del saber', p. 218.

In *El arte*, he indicates how the practice of poetry is a means by which the wise display their God-given talents and make themselves known to the community. More important still, perhaps, the ability to cope with the rules of poetry reveals in turn the presence of divine will, by laying bare the hierarchy imposed upon mankind by God. In this way, when practised according to its immutable rules, poetry helps to maintain a world order in which the ignorant and wise belong to quite separate ranks. The existence of intellectual elitism of this kind was justified on the grounds that equality would obscure knowledge of God. As the fifteenth-century commentator on Santob's *Proverbios morales* put it, if God had given his wisdom to every man at birth, 'non se le entendría, nin sería sabido que le bynýa de Dios, nin por acarreamiento del Espíritu Santo: asý que non sería Dios tan conosçido'.[7]

By implication, another important consequence of the 'mengua de la sciencia' which Villena attributes to his contemporaries is that the art of poetry itself is in danger of dying out. Adherence to the rules of knowledge provides the means whereby it is regenerated: Atlas 'dio ciertas reglas' to the science of astrology, 'por sostenimiento e durada de aquel saber' (*Los doze trabajos*, p. 129). Hence, in Villena's account of the Barcelona Consistory, the *libros del arte* acquire a distinctly symbolic significance. Particularly revealing is the remark that part of the money made available by Martí I was spent 'en la reparación de los libros del arte' (p. 166: presumably copies of the vernacular treatises listed earlier in the description). Carried at the head of the procession which opened the poetic competition, they were placed in the centre of the room, upon 'un bastimento quadrado tan alto como un altar, cubiertos de panios de oro' (p. 167): they represent the permanence of knowledge embodied by the written word, the 'complida orden de cosas immutables e verdaderas' (p. 169).

This 'complida orden' constitutes the necessary framework for each science; it provides the 'ciertos principios e proprios que dan entrada e son puerta de saber' (*Los doze trabajos*, p. 41). And Villena directs his sharpest criticism in *El arte* at those who possess only partial knowledge of such principles and who make the error that 'la igualdad de las sýllabas y concordancia de los bordones' are the sole ingredients of 'la rímica dotrina' (p. 163). In the rest of the

---

[7] Santob de Carrión, *Proverbios morales*, ed. Theodore A. Perry (Madison: HSMS, 1986), p. 6.

treatise, divided into ten sections on phonology, grammar and orthography, he rectifies this situation by giving a full account of all the rules which would enable his contemporaries to understand the poetic art.[8] These precepts, however, not only make up the structure of poetry, but also provide the criteria by which it is judged.

Each poet attending the Consistory would present a poem on a preordained theme, and these works would then be taken away by the members to be assessed in private, impartially and 'según las reglas del arte'. Villena's account continues:

> cada uno dellos apuntava los vicios en ella contenidos, e señalávanse en las márgenes de fuera. E todas así requeridas, a la que era fallada sin vicios, o a la que tenía menos, era judga[da] la joya por los votos del consistorio. (p. 168)

Although there are no extant manuscripts of the poems submitted to the Consistory which could illustrate how this procedure was carried out in practice, there is an interesting example of this form of literary criticism in the unique manuscript of the *Doctrinal de trobar*, by Raimon de Cornet (1324). This verse poetic was later corrected, on the grounds both of content and style, by Joan de Castellnou, who inserted his *Glosari* in the margins of the earlier work. His emendations are made strictly on the basis of the rules laid down by *Las Leys d'amors*.[9]

This seemingly mechanical approach to poetry has been severely castigated by many modern critics, who were repelled by the reduction of literary creativity to what Menéndez y Pelayo called 'pueril gimnasia de rimas ... ostentación de una falsa ciencia'.[10] But enough has been written so far about Villena's attitude toward knowledge to explain his concern, at least on a theoretical level, for all the precepts which formed the common subject matter of the vernacular poetics of that period. Grammar, orthography, punctuation, etc. were thought crucial to the art of writing poetry. It

---

[8] See Aguirre, pp. 51–54, 63–127; Ramón Santiago Lacuesta, 'Sobre "el primer ensayo de una prosodia y una ortografía castellanas": el *Arte de trovar* de Enrique de Villena', *Miscellanea Barcinonensia*, 42 (1975), 35–52.

[9] See J.-B. Noulet, Camille Chabaneau (eds), *Deux manuscrits provençaux du XIVᵉ siècle* (Montpellier: PSELR; Paris, Maisonneuve et Charles Leclerc, 1888), pp. 119–239, at p. 216.

[10] *Antología de poetas líricos castellanos*, 14 vols [in 11] (Madrid: Viuda de Hernández, 1890–1916), V, xxvi; *Historia de las ideas estéticas*, I, 410 and 419; Di Camillo, *El humanismo*, pp. 94–97.

should not be deduced from this, however, that Villena took only formal aspects into consideration in the belief that fine poetry could be produced simply by carrying out a set of rules. At the very start of *El arte*, he tells Santillana that although his *trobas* have become extremely popular:

> por mengua de la gaya dotrina no podéis transfundir en los oydores de vuestras obras las escelentes invenciones que natura ministra a la serenidat de vuestro ingenio, con aquella propiedat [con] que fueron concebidas. (p. 164)

This criticism raises two theoretical issues: one rhetorical (which I examine later), the other moral.

Villena's criticism has serious ethical connotations. If Santillana is incapable of giving concrete shape to the concepts transmitted to him by 'natura', he fails the most important test of the wise man: the ability to communicate. *Comunicar* was a key verb in Villena's philosophical vocabulary; Hercules, for example, represented 'el hombre virtuoso que ha doctrina por sí, e puede della a los otros comunicar'.[11] Santillana's ignorance of the rules of his art obscures 'aquel aventaje que Dios e natura fizieron entre los claros ingenios e los oscuros'; and in this sense, he frustrates the two-way process by which God endows man with talent or wisdom in order that it should then serve as a revelation of His presence.

El arte was influenced by yet another important characteristic of wisdom: namely that what develops is not the fundamental nature of a given science (the static 'reglas del arte'), but the extent of man's understanding within its preordained limits.[12] Villena's summary of his predecessors opens with a reference to the *Razos de trobar*, by Raimon Vidal de Besalú: 'por ser començador', we are told, 'no fabló tan complidamente' (p. 164).[13] This remark recalls

[11] *Los doze trabajos*, p. 88; see also chs IV and XII; the topos is given special emphasis in *Tratado de aojamiento* ed. Ana Maria Gallina, Biblioteca di Filologia Romanza, 31 (Bari: Adriatica, 1978), pp. 95–96. For the duty of the sage to disseminate wisdom, see Maravall, 'La concepción del saber', pp. 215–18; Curtius, *European Literature*, pp. 88–89.

[12] Maravall, 'La concepción del saber', pp. 210–12. See *Los doze trabajos*, ch. XII, and the prologue to his *Arte cisoria*, ed. Enrique Díaz Retge, Selecciones Bibliófilas, 1 (Barcelona, 1948), p. 80.

[13] Before this, Villena writes: 'El consistorio de la gaya sciencia se formó en Francia en la cibdad de Tolosa por Ramón Vidal de Besaldú. Esmerándose con aquellas reglas los entendidos de los grosseros' (p. 164). Scholars have pounced on what they consider to be an error in making Vidal the founder of the Toulouse Consistory. But Gómez de Castro's notes are clearly inadequate, since a few lines

what is said in *El arte cisoria* about Cam's attempt to classify the diverse branches of knowledge: he was the first to undertake this task, 'maguer tan complidamente como hoy se fallan non las tractasse' (p. 80). These statements are based on notions of historical change that are commonly found in medieval discussions of grammar. Commentators on one of the seminal grammatical treatises, Priscian's *Institutiones*, often said that the first grammarians wrote obscurely because they came at the start of the tradition. According to one writer, the *primus inventor* spent his whole life studying four letters; the subject then grew to perfection through the additions and emendations of successive scholars. Parallels for this view may be found in the fourteenth-century *Leys d'amors*: 'a penas obra noela se pot far al comensamen ayssi del tot complida que no sia deffectiva d'alcuna cauza e no haja mestiers d'alcuna reparacio'.[14] And, in a different context, the idea is present in Santillana's hypothesis about the work of the earliest writers of sonnets and *terza rima*. Though he has not seen the poems of Arnaut Daniel and Guido Guinizelli, he assumes that they could not have been entirely successful, since 'commo dize el philósofo, de los primeros, primera es la especulación'.[15]

Villena's summary continues with the statement that Jofre de Foixà 'dilató la materia, llamando a la obra que hizo *Continuación del trobar*' (p. 165; i.e. *Las Regles de trobar*). Given the commonplace notion that learning in its early stages is imperfect, the relationship between these two works could hardly be described in any other terms.[16] There was indeed a connection between the two treatises, though in reality it was not quite as clear-cut and uncomplicated as Villena suggests. In spite of its author's ambitious opening claims,

---

further on, Villena again refers to its foundation, but this time in the correct context of *Las Leys d'amors*. Aguirre suggests the following emendation: 'el consistorio [...] se formó [...] en la cibdad de Tolosa. [Las primeras reglas de arte de trovar fueron escritas] por Ramón Vidal de Besaldú' (p. 55).

[14] Guilhem Molinier, *Las Leys d'amors: manuscrit de l'Académie des Jeux Floraux*, ed. Joseph Anglade, 4 vols (Toulouse: Édouard Privat; Paris: Auguste Picard, 1919–20), at I, 15. See also Mortimer J. Donovan, 'Priscian and the Obscurity of the Ancients', *Sp*, 36 (1961), 75–80.

[15] *El proemio e carta*, in *Obras completas*, ed. Angel Gómez Moreno and Maximilian P. A. M. Kerkhof (Barcelona: Planeta, 1988), p. 444.

[16] Neither of the two extant MSS with textual authority gives the titles of the *Regles* as *La continuación*; on these MSS and later copies, see Marshall, *The 'Razos'*, pp. xi–xiii; Jaume Massó Torrents, *Repertori de l'antiga literatura catalana: la poesia* (Barcelona: Editorial Alpha, 1932), pp. 327–28.

Las Razos is not an exhaustive treatise on grammar and versification; it is a highly personal statement about the errors of contemporary verse, directed at a Catalan aristocracy closely acquainted with the late Provençal language and literature under discussion. Foixà's *Regles*, on the other hand, offers much more information (particularly on versification), but it is not so much an expansion of Vidal's work as an elementary explanation in non-technical terms of theories derived partly from Vidal and partly from his own reading of poetry. In the very first lines, Foixà actually pays tribute to his predecessor, whom he describes as 'en art de trobar savis e entendens', adding that his own aim is, by contrast, to write for those who 'no.s entenen en gramatica'. In short, Foixà's treatise is a simplified yet fairly detailed clarification of Provençal poetics for the benefit of a completely different public: that of a late thirteenth-century Sicilian court which hoped to preserve the literary style of the Provençal classics.[17]

As the text of *El arte* stands, Villena does not establish a direct link between these two works and those that are thought to follow them chronologically: Berenguer de Noya's *Mirall de trobar* and *La summa vitulina* by Guilielmo Vedel de Mallorca. The former is not easy to date, but Palumbo, its recent editor, assuming that Villena's chronology is exact, places it between Foixà's *Regles* (*c.* 1290) and the three versions of *Las Leys d'amors* (1328–56).[18] As far as its contents are concerned, the work has very few parallels with other poetics, including those mentioned by Villena (and there is certainly no evidence to support Sánchez Cantón's assertion that the Spaniard's *Arte* owes a special debt to it; *ed. cit.*, p. 162). The author shows scant interest in grammar, and the briefest of the four sections is devoted to the alphabet. However, the technique and tone of the treatise bring it closest to *Las Razos*, in that Berenguer includes a wealth of carefully selected illustrations culled from Provençal poets. It is, therefore, totally unlike the massive and impersonal tracts of *Las Leys d'amors*, which offer scarcely any verse quotations (*Mirall*, ed. Palumbo, pp. xiv–xxii).

The work entitled *Summa vitulina* is, on the other hand, an utter mystery: nothing of this name has yet been discovered, and its author is similarly unidentified. Furthermore, the syntax and

---

[17] Marshall, *The 'Razos'*, pp. xcvi–xcviii; Martí de Riquer, *Història de la literatura catalana* (Barcelona: Ariel, 1964), I, 170–80.

[18] *Mirall de trobar*, ed. Pietro Palumbo (Palermo: Manfredi Editore, 1955).

punctuation of Gómez de Castro's notes shroud the circumstances of the text's composition in ambiguity: 'De[s]pués escrivió. Guilielmo Vedel de Mallorca. la *Summa Vitulina*. con este tratado, por que durase la gaya sciencia se fundó el collegio de Tholosa de trobadores:' (f. 70ᵛ; ed. Sánchez Cantón, p. 165). The phrase 'con este tratado' suggests that Villena thought the work to be connected in some way to the Toulouse Consistory.

Las Leys d'amors is the next treatise to be mentioned. This exists in three versions, of which only the first two appear to have been known to Villena (Gómez de Castro's notes do not refer to the final reworking, and Guilhem Molinier's account of the foundation of the Consistory, which is included in its introduction, does not tally with Villena's description in *El arte*; see below). However, the Barcelona Consistory probably possessed the manuscript of the first version which is now in the Archivo de la Corona de Aragón: it would have been one of the 'libros del arte' paraded around the 'altar' during the prize-giving ceremony.[19] The existence of this manuscript helps to explain why Villena considered *Las Leys d'amors* to be an extensive emendation and synthesis of all previous vernacular poetics. The seven *mantenedores*, he writes, 'hizieron el tratado intitulado *Leyes de amor*, donde se cumplieron todos los defetos de los tratados passados' (p. 165). This is an echo of the introductory paragraphs of the first version. Two of the reasons for its commission are, we are told:

> per so que ayssi hom puesca trobar plenieiramen compilat e ajustat tot so que denan era escampat e dispers ... Per so quel sabers de trobar lo qual havian tengut rescost li antic trobador et aquo meteysh quen havian pauzat escuramen, puesca hom ayssi trobar claramen.[20]

[19] Massó Torrents, *Repertori*, p. 75; Sánchez Cantón, p. 165, n. 4; extracts from this lavish MS, whose text has been heavily influenced by Catalan, have been published by Anglade, *Las Leys*, IV, 136–41. Some scholars (e.g. Massó Torrents, *Repertori*, p. 331, Palumbo, *Mirall*, p. vii) have suggested that another extant MS from Barcelona was also owned by the Consistory. It contains nine vernacular treatises, including Vidal's *Razos*, Foixà's *Regles*, Noya's *Mirall*, Cornet's *Doctrinal* with Castellnou's commentary, and *Las Flors*, all of which were cited by Villena. Whether he knew this MS is open to question, since it contains four treatises not mentioned in *El arte*. While speculating on the MSS available to Villena, it is worth adding that his great protector Martí I possessed two vernacular poetics: the *Compendi* by Joan de Castellnou (not on his list), and one of the versions of *Las Leys*: see Jaume Massó Torrents, 'Inventari dels bens mobles del rey Martí d'Aragó', *RHi*, 12 (1905), 413–590, at pp. 416 (no. 14), and 451 (no. 270).

[20] *Las Flors del gay saber estier dichas las Leys d'amors*, ed. A. Gatien-Arnoult, 4 vols (Toulouse: J.-B. Paya: 1841–48), at I, 2. See also Alfred Jeanroy, 'Les *Leys*

Leaving aside the accuracy and validity of these claims, Villena was clearly influenced by the belief that *Las Leys d'amors* fulfilled the fundamental requirements of all works of learning, in that it gathered together threads of diversity and, as he wrote in connection with Cam's reorganization of knowledge, 'las puso en buena horden' (*Arte cisoria*, p. 80).

Villena continues his survey by relating how the tradition was taken a stage further by the verse abridgement of the cumbersome five-book *Leys*: 'Este era largo', he comments in a moment of rare understatement, 'por donde Guillén Moliner le abrevió, y hizo el *Tratado de las flores*, tomando lo sustancial del *Libro de las leyes de amor*' (p. 165). *Las Flors del gay saber* was written between 1337 and 1343, that is to say anything up to fifteen years after the composition of the first prose version (1328–37).

A certain inaccuracy now creeps into Villena's chronology:

> después vino fray Ramón de Cornet e fizo un tratado en esta sciencia, que se llama *Dotrinal*. Este no se tuvo por tan buena obra, por ser de persona no mucho entendida; reprehendiósela Johan de Castilnou asumando los vicios esquivadores.[21]

The unique extant manuscript of the *Doctrinal* clearly states in the *explicit* that Cornet wrote it in 1324, that is to say well before the first redaction of *Las Leys d'amors*. Villena's error may be explained by the possibility that his sources (if indeed he knew the work at first hand) lacked the *explicit* of the *Doctrinal*, but preserved that of Castellnou's *Glosari*: not unnaturally, Villena assumed Castellnou to have corrected a newly-finished treatise, rather than one which had

---

d'amors', in *Histoire littéraire de la France*, 38 (Paris: Imprimerie Nationale, 1949), pp. 139–233. Molinier's sources were academic grammars (Priscian, Donatus, Albertano de Brescia) and Latin *artes rhetoricae* (e.g. *Ad Herennium*) rather than vernacular poetics; there is also little textual evidence that Molinier was at all well acquainted with the poems of the 'anticz trobadors'; see 'Les *Leys*', pp. 162, 165–66, 221–22; J. H. Marshall, 'Observations on the Sources of the Treatment of Rhetoric in the *Leys d'amors*', *MLR*, 64 (1969), 39–52, especially pp. 50–51.

[21] Sánchez Cantón appears to be unaware of the existence of Castellnou's *Glosari* and states that the text referred to here is the fourth part of Noya's *Mirall* (entitled 'dels vicis qui son squividors', ed. Palumbo, p. 3). He adds that Villena may have had in mind the former writer's *Compendi de la conaxensa del vicis que poden sdevenir en los dictats del gay saber*. However, it seems to me an error to make the phrase 'los vicios esquivadores' the title of the treatise mentioned by Villena at this point. Preceded by the verb *asumar*—which Sánchez Cantón incorrectly believes to be Gómez de Castro's interpolation—the phrase means, 'And Joan de Castellnou corrected it, adding up the errors to be avoided'.

been in existence for fifteen years, as was in fact the case.

At this point the survey ends, and in what is either a paraphrase of the original or a personal note from the pen of Gómez de Castro himself, we are told that, 'Después déstos, no escrivió otro, hasta don Enrique de Villena'.[22]

Whatever the true chronology of the texts and the real relationship between them, Villena appears to present the history of poetics as a coherent development in which the same body of learning is passed from treatise to treatise and subjected to correction, expansion, synthesis and abbreviation. Scanty though the evidence is, an order is implicitly imposed on them: an order determined by traditional theories concerning the evolution of wisdom. It was duty of the learned writer to synthesize past knowledge, using his 'entendimiento colectivo', so as to consolidate it, taking it a stage further with the addition of his own work.[23] Learning progresses by continuous accumulation and refinement. And these ideas no doubt had a powerful effect on a man like Villena, who was always keen to cultivate the image of the ideal sage. His historical survey demonstrates that he too possesses this synoptic vision of the past, and has full understanding of the intellectual tradition of which his own work is a logical extension. Moreover, the statement that he reformed the Barcelona Consistory after the death of Martí I and the subsequent political turmoil (p. 167) is further evidence that he wished to portray himself as fulfilling the obligations of the wise: like Hercules in the final chapter of *Los doze trabajos*, he took over an interrupted and threatened intellectual enterprise, regenerated it, and, in short, preserved an institution which bestowed 'tanto . . . provecho . . . a la vida civil' (p. 166).[24]

---

[22] The intervening treatises were Jacme March's rhyme dictionary, *Libre de concordances* (1371), and Luis de Averçó's '*Torcimany*' (*c.* 1400), which exists in a unique MS, probably autograph, now in the Escorial.

[23] See *Arte cisoria*, pp. 69–70; *Los doze trabajos*, ch. XII; *Tratado de aojamiento*, p. 129; *Tratado de la consolación*, ed. Derek C. Carr, Clásicos Castellanos, 208 (Madrid: Espasa-Calpe, 1976 [1978]), p. 16.

[24] Martín de Riquer believes that Villena's reformation of the Consistory took place not after 1413, when Fernando de Antequera came to the throne, but during Martí I's lifetime. Although he proves that Villena was in Barcelona during the Martí's reign, he has been misled by Sánchez Cantón's guess that the reference to this King's death is an interpolation by Gómez de Castro. There is no evidence to suggest that this is so: 'Don Enrique de Villena en la corte de Martín I', in *Miscelánea en homenaje a Monseñor Higinio Anglés* (Barcelona: CSIC, 1961), II, 716–21.

But the chain of knowledge, represented by the succession of poetics, does not end with *El arte*. Just as the wisdom contained in *Los doze trabajos*, for example, passes from the author to the patron and then to society at large, so Santillana inherits the accumulated doctrine of the poetics and himself becomes a source of literary learning. In this way, *El arte* transcends its dedicatee, and illuminates the community of practising poets: 'e vós', declares Villena, 'informado por el dicho tratado seas originidat donde tomen lumbre e dotrina todos los otros del regno que se dizen trobadores, para que lo sean verdaderamente' (p. 164).

This section of *El arte* presents a distinctly idealized picture of the nature and development of vernacular poetics; but idealization of history is at work in other passages too. Scholars have already remarked on the fact that Villena is wholly inaccurate with regard to the foundation of the Toulouse Consistory. He asserts that it was set up with the permission of the King of France, who endowed it with 'libertades e privillegios, e asinó ciertas rentas para las despensas del consistorio de la gaya dotrina. Ordenó que uviese siete mantenedores que hiziesen leyes' (p. 165). The King, however, played no part in its organization and funding: the Consistory was a purely municipal affair (this would have been clear to Villena had he been able to read the prologue to the third version of *Las Leys d'amors*). Villena's account is obviously influenced in the first instance by what he doubtless knew of the important royal support given to the Catalan Consistories. Joan I (in 1393 and 1396), Martí I (in 1398 and 1399) and Fernando de Antequera (in 1414), all issued decrees to establish and give financial aid to the academies.[25] But in addition to this, historical verisimilitude would have given considerable authority to his portrayal of events. He may have had in mind the concept of *imperator litteratus* (which helped to shape his own account of Augustus's lavish patronage of Virgil in the prologue to the *Aeneid* translation), or the precepts laid down in the influential *Siete partidas*, according to which, popes, emperors and kings were responsible for the establishment of the *estudio general* (II, xxxi, 1).

Villena writes that the Toulouse Consistory was founded 'por que durase la gaya sciencia' (p. 165). Like any other branch of

---

[25] Latin decrees (1393, 1398 and 1414) in '*Torcimany*', ed. Casas Homs, II, 441–49; Catalan text (by Metge) of 1396 decree in Riquer, *Història*, I, 567; translations of all four in Boase, pp. 127–42.

knowledge, poetry is preserved by means of the constant verification of its 'reglas invariables e términos seguros' (*Los doze trabajos*, p. 42): the competitions are a ritualistic purification of the art.[26] The Consistory ensures the lasting vitality of poetry in another way too. In a hierarchical vision of society, where there was a direct relation between qualitative and quantitative value, it was thought that knowledge flourished best wherever large numbers of scholars gathered together: 'Mejor aprenden los muchos escolares que los pocos', observed Alfonso el Sabio, 'e mejor en las escuelas grandes e en gran estudio que en pequenno'.[27]

Some historians have discussed the accuracy of the assertion that Joan I sent an embassy to the King of France 'pidiéndole mandase al collegio de los trobadores que viniesen a plantar en su reyno el estudio de la gaya sciencia' (p. 166). It matters little that there are no records of this mission; that Villena was writing nearly forty years after the alleged event; that the first poetic competitions in Catalonia took place long before Joan I was even born: this passage is based not on fact but on historical verisimilitude. It is determined by a vision of how poetry ought to have been transferred from one nation to another: in short, by the concept of *translatio studii*. Joan I's embassy corresponds to what Maravall has described as 'la imagen del filósofo que viaja para averiguar dónde se halla el saber ... con objeto de recogerlo y llevarlo a su pueblo'.[28]

El arte clearly demonstrates the extent to which Villena's attitudes towards learning guided his attempts to describe the fundamental nature of the 'poetic science'. It is subject to all the general principles that governed intellectual theory in the Middle Ages: it is endowed with its own framework of immutable rules which enable it to be preserved and transmitted; the books which contain these rules (and symbolize their permanence) develop according to a gradual process of synthesis and cumulative growth; its practitioners are urged to observe the demands imposed on them

---

[26] Maravall, 'La concepción del saber', p. 221.

[27] Francisco Rico, *Alfonso el Sabio y la 'General estoria': tres lecciones*, 2nd ed. (Barcelona: Ariel, 1984), p. 134.

[28] 'La concepción del saber', p. 214. In the absence of independent sources, Aguirre believes the episode to be improbable (p. 59; and n. 2 for those who share her views); for Riquer, the sending of the delegation is feasible, given Joan I's, admiration for French culture (*Història*, I, 570); Boase, misled by the historian Zurita (whose only source is Villena himself), accepts it as fact (pp. 123–26, 195, n. 1).

by the need to communicate their wisdom to their fellows.

The concepts which have been examined here are wholly characteristic of the medieval attitudes towards wisdom described in such detail by Maravall. For this very reason, it is interesting to note that Italian humanists also described poetry in terms of a universal and static science. In fact, they exploited this approach to the full: it was one of their most powerful arguments in defence of poetry. Petrarch, in his first invective, for example, argues that although the words of poetry change, its underlying principles remain constant: 'Mutantur verba, manent res, in quibus scientie fundate sunt'.[29] Boccaccio is even more categoric, asserting that:

> Poetry ... constitutes a stable and fixed science founded upon things eternal, and confirmed by original principles; in all times and places this knowledge is the same, unshaken by any possible change.[30]

We should not be misled by this similarity. It is not evidence for the influence of humanistic thought on the early fifteenth-century Castilian writers, but just one example of the continuity of literary thought that existed in Europe until the arrival of new approaches and ideas in the sixteenth century.

2   Poetry and the classification of the sciences

a) *El arte de trovar*

With few exceptions, poetics was not considered an independent branch of knowledge during the Middle Ages. It was studied as part of the grammar curriculum, taught in connection with rhetoric, or classified as moral philosophy, even as part of logic.[31] If

[29] Quoted from Giorgio Ronconi, *Le origini delle dispute umanistiche sulla poesia (Mussato e Petrarca)*, Strumenti di Ricerca, 11 (Rome: Bulzoni, 1976), pp. 99 and 135, n. 51.

[30] *Boccaccio on Poetry: Being the Preface and the Fourteenth and Fifteenth Books of Boccaccio's 'Genealogia Deorum Gentilium'*, trans. Charles G. Osgood (1930; New York: Bobbs-Merrill, 1956), p. 25 (Bk XIV, 4). For a different perspective, see Averroës's commentary on Aristotle's *Poetics*, which concerns 'the universal rules of poetry common to all nations *or most*' (my italics): a qualification that indicates Averroës's awareness of the differing conventions of Greek and Arabic poetry; see *The Middle Commentary of Averroës of Cordova on the 'Poetics' of Aristotle*, in *Classical and Medieval Literary Criticism: Translations and Interpretations*, ed. Alex Preminger *et al.* (New York: Ungar, 1974), pp. 349–82, at p. 349.

[31] See Charles Sears Baldwin, *Medieval Rhetoric and Poetic (to 1400), Interpreted from Representative Works* (1928; Gloucester, Mass: Peter Smith, 1959); Richard

we were to concentrate only on the technical details contained in the main body of *El arte de trovar*, we might reasonably assume that, for Villena, poetry was simply a part of grammar, defined according to one branch of the tradition as the 'ars recte loquendi' (the definition given, for example, by Isidore). But this would be misleading. Even considering that poetry was often defined purely in grammatical terms (i.e. according to its prosodic structure as metrical discourse), it seems to me that Villena establishes a much more significant relationship with the art and ideals of rhetoric.[32]

To understand this, we must return to the opening lines of *El arte*, which criticize Santillana's youthful verse for that lack of clarity which stems from inadequate knowledge of literary technique:

> E por mengua de la gaya dotrina no podéis transfundir en los oydores de vuestras obras las escelentes invenciones que natura ministra a la serenidat de vuestro ingenio con aquella propiedat [con] que fueron concebidas. (p. 164)

Villena focusses here on the three divisions of classical oratory which dominated medieval rhetorical thought: *inventio, dispositio* and *elocutio* (the ability to discover material, to arrange it correctly, and to clothe it in appropriate form). And his principal stylistic ideal, suggested by the term 'propiedat', seems to be that of *convenientia*, the harmonious blend of form and content whose most coherent theoretical articulation is found in Dante's *De vulgari eloquentia*. As a whole, the passage corresponds to the basic rhetorical principle of effective communication of thought: 'eloqui enim hoc est: omnia

---

McKeon, 'Poetry and Philosophy in the Twelfth Century: The Renaissance of Rhetoric', in *Critics and Criticism Ancient and Modern*, ed. R. S. Crane (Chicago: Univ. Press, 1952), pp. 297–318; Curtius, *European Literature, s.v.* 'poetry'; Osborne Bennett Hardison, *The Enduring Monument: A Study of the Idea of Praise in Renaissance Theory and Practice* (Chapel Hill: Univ. of North Carolina Press, 1962), pp. 3–23; Hardison's introduction to the medieval section of *Classical and Medieval Literary Criticism*; 'Toward a History', pp. 6–12; Karl Kohut, 'La posición de la literatura en los sistemas científicos del siglo XV', *IR*, n.s., 7 (1978), 67–87. The classification of poetry was by no means an exclusively medieval concern: see Bernard Weinberg, *A History of Literary Criticism in the Italian Renaissance* (Chicago: Univ. Press, 1961), I, 1–37.

[32] For the metrical definition, see Curtius, *European Literature*, pp. 45 and 147; Baldwin, *Medieval Rhetoric*, pp. 90, 110–11, 184; Hardison, *Classical and Medieval Literary Criticism*, p. 268. For XVc Castile, see Pero Díaz de Toledo's commentary on the *Exclamación e querella* by Gómez Manrique, in *Can. cas.*, II, 131; also Kohut 'La posición', pp. 79–80.

quae mente conceperis promere atque ad audientes perferre'.[33]

Close parallels with this section of *El arte* may be found in the preceding tradition of late Provençal and Catalan poetics. The royal decrees written by Bernat Metge concerning the establishment of the poetic Consistories in Barcelona are obvious examples. The first of these, written on behalf of Joan I in 1396, was ill-fated. In it, Metge explained that poetry was 'fundada en rectorica', and that it not only encouraged courtiers to shun idleness, but also taught them to express themselves in a learned and elegant manner— 'saviament e ornada dictar' (which obviously did not convince the city councillors: refusing to fund the prizes because of allegedly grave financial difficulties, they refer to 'lo poch millorament que aconsequeix de la dita gaya sciencia').[34] Perhaps to overcome this reluctance, the second document, written two years later at the request of Martí I, makes more extravagant claims for rhetoric, though in the process it is less explicit about its relationship with poetry: it is taken for granted that they are both an art 'qua principum atque regum iam gratia capitur, lingua prerudis acuitur et possessor eiusdem de infimis ad honoris fastigia sublevatur' (Boase, p. 134). These ideas were not restricted to the official documents of the Consistory, but also appear in Metge's philosophical treatise, *Lo somni*. In this work, however, he brings an extra element into play: the finest 'danses e cançons', he remarks, are a combination not only of rhetoric and poetry, but also of music. The value of such compositions, he continues, is that they enable men to 'fugir ociositat e per poder dir bé lo concebiment de llur pensa'.[35]

For any writer involved with the Barcelona Consistory, the most authoritative source for views on the relation of poetry to rhetoric was Guilhem Molinier. In the final version of his *Leys d'amors*, he makes what by that time had become a common distinction between two categories of eloquence: prose and verse.[36] And among the many qualities attributed to verse rhetoric (he comments on its esthetic, emotional and moral effects), he mentions its power

---

[33] Quintilian, *Institutio*, VIII, pref., 15; see Lausberg, *Manual*, § 455.

[34] Boase, *The Troubadour Revival*, pp. 132–33; Antoni Rubio i Lluch, *Documents per l'història de la cultura catalana mig-eval*, 2 vols (Barcelona: Institut d'Estudis Catalans, 1908–21), I, 384–85.

[35] *Lo somni*, ed. Marta Jordà (Barcelona: Edicions 62, 1980), p. 139.

[36] Molinier's source is probably Brunetto Latini's *Li Livres dou trésor*, III, x, 1; see Jeanroy, 'Les *Leys*', pp. 220–21.

to enhance the individual's capacity for self-expression. 'Esta sciensa', we are told, 'trobada fo ... per miels dir sa voluntat' (ed. Anglade, II, 31).

Apart from *El arte*, only one other early fifteenth-century Castilian text gives such prominence to the rhetorical theory of poetry being examined here: the allegorical exegesis of Petrarch's sonnet 116, recently published by Derek Carr.[37] According to the commentator, this sonnet conveys the poet's almost unquenchable desire 'de obtener el plazer e fartura de la plática poetal' (p. 135; in fact it describes Petrarch's love for Laura). This 'plática poetal' is, we learn, the act of direct and positive communication. As such, it is fully realized only when one is in possession of 'la eloqüencia ... para recitar e representar propriamente las concebidas cosas, en cuyo decurso nasce la poesía' (p. 135). The similarity between the way this notion is formulated here and in *El arte* may well be more than mere coincidence. A number of factors, including other verbal and thematic parallels with certain of Villena's works, suggest that this erudite allegorical exegesis was in fact carried out by him.[38] Both these works draw our attention to the fact that poetry is a form of eloquence: the poet's task is to communicate directly with his public, to convey his thoughts 'con aquella propiedat [con] que fueron concebidas', or, as the Petrarchan commentator put it, 'para recitar o representar propriamente las concebidas cosas'. The association with rhetoric is a forceful reminder that the poem will depend for its effect upon the technical abilities of the poet. This is an obvious point; but it acquires greater significance, indeed a certain irony, when one considers the vogue for allegory in early fifteenth-century Castile. As we shall see in the next chapter, in works such as the *Aeneid* there is much less emphasis on the author as the positive communicator of his own message than on the reader as the discoverer or creator of numerous personal meanings within the text.

El arte, therefore, preserves the close association between poetry and rhetoric which had been established by the Provençal and Catalan schools. Stated in these bald terms, this is hardly a remarkable conclusion; it needs, however, to be placed in its proper

[37] Derek C. Carr, 'A Fifteenth-Century Translation and Commentary of a Petrarchan Sonnet: Biblioteca Nacional MS 10.186 folios 196ʳ–199ʳ', *RCEH*, 5 (1980–81), 123–43.

[38] I examine this issue in 'La affección poetal virtuosa: Petrarch's Sonnet 116 as Poetic Manifesto for Fifteenth-Century Castile', *MLR*, in press.

perspective. For many medieval writers, both rhetoric and poetics implied little more than the technique of verbal adornment.[39] However, the emphasis placed by Molinier, Metge and Villena on lucid and forceful self-expression shows that they entertained much less simplistic notions of rhetorical poetics. That they had in mind a kind of poetic eloquence that went beyond the mere manipulation of tropes is confirmed by their remarks on the function and content of poetry.

With regard to function, Villena writes: 'tanto es el provecho que viene desta dotrina a la vida civil, quitando ocio, e ocupando los generosos ingenios en tan honesta investigación' (p. 166). The notion that the social value of poetry was to enable men to avoid idleness was wholly commonplace in texts relating to the Provençal and Catalan Consistories (see, for example, Metge's comments quoted above, p. 70). But the 'provecho ... a la vida civil' surely consists in something far more significant. The phrases 'generosos entendimientos' and 'honesta investigación' hint at the concepts of intellectual nobility and meditative study which played such an important part in the literary theorizing of the *Aeneid* commentary (see ch. IV). Moreover, Di Camillo has suggested that this passage, with its emphasis on the smooth running of the 'vida civil', betrays the influence of Italian civic humanism. This is a plausible hypothesis, especially in view of Cátedra's discovery of Villena's reading of Coluccio Salutati's *De seculo et religione*. It should be emphasized, however, that Villena's concern for the civic value of poetry in no way constitutes a radical break with the past: he seems, rather, to have adopted the one aspect of Italian humanism which conformed most closely to the central tenet of the Provençal-Catalan Consistories.[40] The same process of assimilation, of grafting Italian humanistic works onto a medieval intellectual framework, may be detected in Santillana's *Proemio*.

Further insights into the benefits to be had from the practice of poetry are given by the list of themes prescribed for the competitions of the Barcelona consistory: 'Algunas vezes loores de Santa María, otras de armas, otras de amores e de buenas

---

[39] Baldwin, *Medieval Rhetoric*, pp. 186–95; McKeon, 'Rhetoric in the Middle Ages', in *Critics and Criticism*, ed. Crane, pp. 260–96, at pp. 288–92.

[40] Di Camillo, *El humanismo*, pp. 101–02; Pedro M. Cátedra, 'Enrique de Villena y algunos humanistas', in *Nebrija*, ed. García de la Concha, pp. 187–203, at p. 202, where he reports the view of Garin and Ullman that *De seculo* was Salutati's most 'medieval' treatise.

costumbres' (p. 167). These themes all derive from the earlier tradition of the Toulouse Academy. With the exception of 'armas', they were given considerable prominence in the treatises of Guilhem Molinier. In the final version of *Las Leys*, he cuts out a whole section devoted to rhetorical tropes, and replaces it with a long prefatory discourse on God, love and philosophy.[41] True poetic eloquence presupposes virtue, in a way that recalls the ideal orator of classical antiquity: the 'vir *bonus* dicendi peritus'. If the science of poetry was discovered in order to enable men to 'miels dir sa voluntat', this 'voluntat', or will, must first be given a spiritual, courtly, and ethical education.

The question of human will is interesting. There is evidence from a quite different quarter that Villena's list of themes was not compiled at random, but that it was influenced by certain aspects of scholastic philosophy. The point may be explained by Dante's *De vulgari eloquentia*. Here, we are told that there are three topics suitable for the finest verse form, the *canzone*: *salus, venus* and *virtus*. Basing his argument on Aristotelian concepts, Dante then shows how these correspond to the three levels of human life: vegetable, animal and rational. Each of these attracts man's will in different ways: thus, man seeks safety through arms, pleasure through love and what is right (*honestum*) through virtue.[42] In *El arte*, a higher element is added: spirituality, in 'los loores de Santa María'. Given his fondness for scholastic philosophy, it is possible that Villena argued along similar lines, and that he considered poetry to be a form of eloquence which enabled man to satisfy a fourfold impulse of the will.

b) The *Aeneid* commentary

When Villena takes on the role of literary exegete, he naturally enough classifies poetry from a different point of view. The main effect of this shift in perspective is to alter its relationship with rhetoric.

In the *arbor scientiarum*, which Villena inserts as a gloss on his life of Virgil, knowledge is divided into two classes: 'las [sciencias]

---

[41] See Marshall, 'Observations': 'it is difficult to believe that he was wholly convinced of the usefulness of an encyclopedic survey of rhetoric, for version C of the *Leys* [i.e. no. 3] omits completely the substance of the fourth Book of the original version. It is likely that in the years between the two versions, the practical utility of this part of the work had shown itself to be negligible' (p. 52).

[42] *De vulgari eloquentia*, II, ii, 1-9, in *Opere*, p. 765.

lícitas e licenciadas de usar, que son sesenta, e las quarenta [que] son
vedadas e supersticiosas ho que enderesçan a provechos particulares
e non ha bien común'.[43] It should be emphasized that this
classification does not represent a consistent methodological
outlook on Villena's part, but corresponds to the local demands of
this particular text. For although in the prologue to his *Arte cisoria*
he also divides wisdom into one hundred component parts, licit
knowledge is there subdivided into three rather than four, and
poetry does not figure in the system at all. Moreover, even within
the *Aeneid* commentary itself, substantial differences in approach
may be found. At the end of the prologue, 'methafísica', 'física' and
'éthyca' constitute the three main branches and, in accordance with
exegetical tradition, Virgil's poem is subordinated to the latter (f.
13ᵛ). I have been unable to trace any close parallel between the *arbor
scientiarum* of the *Aeneid* translation and other intellectual systems of
the Middle Ages, and am unconvinced that Hugh of St Victor was
a major influence here, as Carla de Nigris has recently claimed.[44]
Whether or not I am right in thinking that this classification is
Villena's own invention, as the chart on page 75 shows, poetry falls
within the category of licit knowledge, and, with philosophy,
theology and the mechanical arts, occupies an autonomous position
within it. What this implies will become clear later; but first, some
hypotheses about the three subdivisions of poetry, and the dual
placement of rhetoric under *poesía* and *física*.

There are two possible ways of interpreting the terms *retórica,
oratoria* and *causídica*. One is to suppose that the last two terms
possess no literary connotations, and are simply kinds of rhetoric
(*causídica* being judicial, or forensic oratory: 'lo que pertenece a
seguir y defender las causas y pleitos', *Diccionario de autoridades, s.v.*).

[43] BN Madrid, MS 17.975, f. 46ᵛ. All quotations are from this MS (emended
where necessary by BN Madrid, MS 10.111); references will also be given to the
ed. of the prologue and first three Books (without glosses) by Ramón Santiago
Lacuesta, *La primera versión castellana de 'La Eneida' de Virgilio*, Anejos del *BRAE*,
38 (Madrid: Real Academia Española, 1979).

[44] For the *Arte cisoria*, see ed. Díaz Retge, p. 77; Carla de Nigris, 'La
classificazione delle arti magiche di Enrique de Villena', *Quaderni Ibero-Americani*,
53–54 (1979–80), 289–98. I have not seen her article in *Annali della Facoltà di
Lettere e Filosofia dell'Università di Napoli*, 21 (1978–79). For a general survey of
intellectual systems in the Middle Ages, see James A. Weisheipl, 'Classification of
the Sciences in Medieval Thought', *MS*, 27 (1965), 54–90; Baldwin, *Medieval
Rhetoric*, pp. 154–69, 179–81 (on Hugh of St Victor, John of Salisbury and
Brunetto Latini).

Las sesenta sciencias lícitas y licenciadas de usar (BN Madrid 17.975, ff. 4v-5r, emended by BN Madrid 10.111)

PHILOSOPHIA

methafísica
- ynventiva
- abstratyva

éthica
- iconómica
- política
  - derecho municipal
  - derecho natural
  - derecho civil
  - derecho de las gentes
- monástica

alquímica

física
- phisionomía
- metheora
- gramátyca
- lógica
- dialéctica
- rectórica
- geometría
- arismética

- música
- prespectiva
- astronomía
- astrología
- pensaria
- muratoria
- dispusitoria
- estragemata

POESIA
- oratoria
- istórica ——— ystryónica
- causídica

THEOLOGIA
- scriptoria
- predicatoria
- contemplatoria
- los derechos sacerdotales

MECANICA
- agricultura
- medecina
- cirugía
- theátrica
- cisoria
- navigatoria
- architectónica
- statuaria
- lapicidio
- aurificio
- ferreficio

- agyogrofía
- vitraria
- coraria
- peliparia
- sardónica
- vestimentaria
- armatura
- lanificio

Retórica is classed separately on the grounds that it denoted the theory of rhetoric, and the other two its practice: the distinction between orator and rhetorician had been made before (e.g. by Cicero, and again, in mid-fifteenth-century Castile, by Lucena).[45] In other words, the classification was made purely on the basis of discourse, and the justification for classing poetry as a primary branch of knowledge was that, historically, it was considered to be the most authoritative form. That poetry preceded prose in the evolution of literary language was one of the commonplaces of medieval thought (the theory had been widely disseminated by Isidore and hence became a central argument in Santillana's defence of poetry; see below, pp. 204–05).

However, a case could be made for interpreting *oratoria, causídica* and *istórica* as genres of *poesía*. If we took the first of these to mean demonstrative, or epideictic, oratory, there would be no difficulty in giving it a poetic value. As Curtius has observed, epideictics, which was concerned with 'laude ac vituperatione' (Quintilian, *Institutio*, VIII, pref., 8), exerted the most powerful influence of all oratorical genres upon medieval poetry: it gave rise to the varied eulogies of countries, towns and people which provided popular subject matter for both narrative and lyric verse (*European Literature*, pp. 155–66). Curtius does not, however, mention that this genre also provided the basis for the pseudo-Aristotelian approach to poetry, favoured, to cite a relevant example, by the Italian scholar Benvenuto da Imola. His Dante commentary was well known in early fifteenth-century Castile, and helped to disseminate the idea that praise and blame were the two components of satire.[46] But what of the enigmatic *causídica*? It could be that Villena had in mind the school rhetorical exercise known as *controversiae*, fictitious matters of dispute, which were often written in verse.[47]

Villena also establishes a close literary link between poetry and

---

[45] Cicero, *De oratore*, I, xx, 19; Juan de Lucena, *Libro de vita beata*, in *Opúsculos literarios de los siglos XIV a XVI*, ed. Antonio Paz y Melia, Sociedad de Bibliófilos Españoles, 9 (Madrid, 1892), pp. 105–205, at pp. 109, 114 (Cartagena labelled as 'rethórico', Santillana as 'orador' and Mena as 'poeta').

[46] Hardison, *The Enduring Monument*, pp. 32–36; see also my article 'Juan de Mena's *Coronación*: Satire or *Sátira?*', *JHP*, 6 (1981–82), 113–38. On the presence of Benvenuto in Spain, see Louis M. La Favia, 'Il primo commento alla *Divina commedia* in Spagna', *Hispano-Italic Studies*, 1 (1976), 1–8.

[47] *European Literature*, pp. 154–55.

istórica, with its subdivision *istriónica*. To deal with the problem in inverse order, *istriónica* probably does not denote the more despised aspects of the *histriones*' profession, but rather the performance of tragedies and comedies. According to medieval convention, it was thought that these classical genres were recited, accompanied by appropriate gestures, on stage by *juglares*. Villena's glosses on classical theatre, which have been annotated in such detail by Pedro Cátedra, indicate a keen antiquarian interest in the subject as well as a desire on his part to dignify contemporary *entremeses*, or *representaciones*, such as those he prepared for the coronation of Fernando de Antequera.[48]

More controversial is the relation of poetry to history. In theory, the two were quite separate, indeed the allegorical form of poetry meant that they were considered to be in total opposition. This distinction endured well into the Romantic era when poetry was contrasted to rational scientific discourse.[49] Isidore's *Etymologiae* handed down a particularly influential formulation of the dichotomy. His authority, for example, was invoked by Juan de Mena when, in an important gloss on *La coronación*, he referred to:

> la licencia atribuýda a la poesía, la qual es poder hablar por más hermosas palabras y fictiones, trayendo fondón de aquéll[a]s el seso verdadero de aquello en que hablan. Porende sepan aquellos que no tienen esta manera en el metrificar o versificar que no puede poesía ser dicha su obra, ca según dize Ysidoro en el octavo libro de las *Ethimologías*, en el título 'de poetis': por hablar historialmente, poniendo la verdad en lo que ver[s]ificó, no es contado Lucano entre los poetas.[50]

This trenchant definition is included here for rhetorical reasons—to lend weight to his own status as allegorizing poet—

---

[48] 'Escolios teatrales de Enrique de Villena', in *Serta philologica F. Lázaro Carreter natalem diem sexagesimum celebranti dicata* (Madrid: Cátedra, 1983), II, 127–36. Valuable references also in Edwin J. Webber, 'Further Observations on Santillana's "Dezir cantares"', *HR*, 30 (1963), 87–93.

[49] See M. H. Abrams, *The Mirror and the Lamp: Romantic Theory and the Critical Tradition* (Oxford: University Press, 1953), p. 101.

[50] *Todas las obras del famosíssimo poeta Juan de Mena con la glosa del comendador Fernán Núñez sobre 'Las trezientas', agora nuevamente corregidas y enmendadas* (Antwerp: Martín Nucio, 1552), gloss to st. 17, l. 8, f. 289ᵛ. It was commonplace to discount Lucan as a true poet on the grounds that he eschewed allegory, and that his narrative followed the natural, rather than the artificial, order of events. Boccaccio, e.g., classed him as a 'metrical historian' (*De genealogia*, XIV, 13); for further references, see Osgood, *Boccaccio on Poetry*, pp. 173–74; Berthe M. Marti, 'Literary Criticism in the Medieval Commentaries on Lucan', *Transactions of the American Philological Association*, 72 (1941), 245–54.

rather than as an objective precept. There can be no doubt that Mena was aware of the difficulties involved in its practical application. In the case of Homer, whom he eulogizes so enthusiastically in the prologue to his translation of the *Ilias latina*, he shows that the distinction between poet and historian was utterly invalid. He was both poet and historian, a writer who created the truth of history. Characters and events are recorded not as they actually existed, but in the form given to them by the power of the poet's imagination:

> Ca no fue más desastrada la postrimería de Priamo de quanto Homero quiso, ni Hetor más llorado, ni más enamorado París, ni Achiles más famoso ... de quanto la rica pluma de Homero, por sabia mano ministrada, quiso moderar y perpetuar.[51]

Whether the fall of Troy took place exactly as Homer portrayed it is, Mena suggests, an issue of secondary importance:

> E pongamos que estos hechos fueron assí, o más allende de quanto assí, ¿pudieron más durar de quanto naturaleza [los] sostuvo? Cierto no, si el claro ingenio de Homero no los desnudara de las ciegas tinieblas de olvidança ... dando a todos éstos ... la biva y perpetua immortalidad. (p. 40)

This enthusiasm for the poet's power to control and transform fact returns us to Villena. His classification of 'istórica' as a subdivision of poetry is supported by his emphatic demand that contemporary chroniclers should learn all the rhetorical and poetic techniques exemplified so brilliantly by Virgil's epic:

> en mano del coronista está de fazer durar la fama gloriosamente de quien le ploguiere ho de afear los malos fechos quanto quisiere, e de escurescer la fama ... de qual quisiere, mayormente sy fuere enseñado en la retórica e en la poesía, que l[a] sabrá fazer tan coloradamente que non podrá alguno conoscer si fue parcial en su dezir. (f. 9ʳ)

It is true that there were precedents for the view that historians should employ an ornate literary style: it was this use of rhetoric that differentiated them from mere chroniclers.[52] But Villena's

---

[51] *La Ylíada en romance, según la impresión de Arnao Guillén de Brocar (Valladolid, 1519)*, ed. Martín de Riquer, Selecciones Bibliófilas, 3 (Barcelona, 1949), pp. 39–40. See also María Rosa Lida de Malkiel, *La idea de la fama en la Edad Media castellana* (Mexico City: Fondo de Cultura Económica, 1952), pp. 278–90.

[52] See Gervaise of Canterbury: 'Historicus diffuse et eleganter incedit, cronicus vero simpliciter graditur et breviter. Projicit historicus ampullas et sesquipedia verba; cronicus vero, silvestrem musam tenui meditatur avena', quoted from Chaytor, *From Script to Print*, p. 56.

assertion that Castilian historians should emulate Virgil's use of 'aposturas poéthicas' and 'el orden artificial' (glosses on f. 12^{r-v}) seems to me an extreme position—certainly far more extravagant than Fernán Pérez de Guzmán's sober recommendation that the chronicler should possess 'buena retórica para poner la estoria en fermoso e alto estilo'. According to Derek Carr, the contrasting approaches of these two writers could well be evidence of a polemic in which Pérez de Guzmán advocated a rhetorical style 'that was more in keeping with the Renaissance ideal of elegant simplicity' in face of Villena's defence of the florid *dictamen* esthetic.[53] Whatever the case, when Villena censures recent chroniclers for their 'manifiestas adulaciones e parcialidades' (f. 12^v; ed. Santiago Lacuesta, p. 41), it is not because they lack impartiality, but because they lack the literary skill to conceal their bias.

The glosses on the ignorance of contemporary chroniclers are important not just because of what they tell us about Villena's attitude to history; they also explain why he makes poetry one of the four primary branches of knowledge. In one of his more vituperative attacks on the inadequacies of their literary style, he comes to the conclusion that 'los fazedores dellas [las corónicas] non fueron criados con leche retorical, ne mantenidos de la vianda poéthyca, nutritiva de los generosos entendimientos' (f. 12^v; ed. Santiago Lacuesta, p. 41). This food image is explained in the following manner:

> leche lamó ha la doctrina de la retórica porque es dulce como la leche, e más se deleyta en ella el entendimiento que el gusto en lo dulce, e aun porque se deve aprender en la tierna hedat porque es más fácil que la poesía ha cuyo respecto ésta leche puede ser dicha. (f. 12^v)

Two points should be noted: firstly this passage conforms to a widespread view of rhetoric which reduced its classical tripartite function (*docere, delectare, movere*) to that of giving pleasure. Rhetoric becomes the art of adornment, which engages and pleases the intellect, rather than the art of instructive persuasion. There seems therefore to be a distinct shift in emphasis away from ideas implicit in *El arte*, which suggested a less narrow approach to rhetorical

[53] Derek C. Carr, 'Pérez de Guzmán and Villena: A Polemic on Historiography?', in *Hispanic Studies in Honor of Alan D. Deyermond: A North American Tribute*, ed. John S. Miletich (Madison: HSMS, 1986), pp. 57–70, at p. 67. See also Fernán Pérez de Guzmán, *Generaciones y semblanzas*, ed. R. B. Tate (London: Tamesis, 1965), p. 2.

eloquence. As we shall see in the following chapter, however, the *colores rhetorici* are not to be despised as mere surface glitter: they play a vital part in the meditative process of interpreting allegorical poetry, by attracting the subtler minds to probe the text's deeper layers of meaning.

Secondly, we are reminded of the conventional pedagogic theory that there was a definite order in which one should learn the various branches of wisdom. That the study of rhetoric is thought suitable for 'la tierna hedat' confirms that it is considered here to be a somewhat mechanical affair, involving little more, perhaps, than instruction in figures of thought and speech. (We should not forget that while working on the *Aeneid*, Villena translated *Ad Herennium*, one of the most popular rhetorical manuals of the Middle Ages, which was primarily concerned with practical matters of style.) But rhetoric could occupy a more exalted position in educational schemes; its most famous apologists, Cicero and Quintilian, argued that when combined with philosophy it provided the ideal training for the man whose life was to be devoted to affairs of state (*De oratore*, iii, 15; *Institutio*, I, pref. 12–13). And the attempt to revive this ideal was one of the peculiar characteristics of Italian humanism.[54] In Villena's programme of studies, the ultimate goal is knowledge of poetry:

> Ha la doctrina de la poesía llama vianda porque es [de] mayor substancia que la retorical leche, e pertenesce ha los que son ya en complida hedat; que es cosa que mascando, es [a] saber con grand trabajo, se ha de rescebir, e non se puede sorver como la leche de retórica, ha cuyo respecto la poesía es vianda. (f. 12ᵛ)

The conviction that poetry stands at the pinnacle of intellectual achievement is reiterated even more forcefully in the third gloss on his critique of contemporary chroniclers: 'non ha de ser la primera dotrina la poesía', asserts Villena, 'mas postrimera, después que en los otros saberes fuere informado' (f. 12ᵛ).

Support for this view could be found in two related areas of literary thought. It is part of the belief, which had been in existence since classical antiquity, that allegorical poetry possessed immense

---

[54] Hanna H. Gray, 'Renaissance Humanism: The Pursuit of Eloquence', *JHI*, 24 (1963), 497–514; Jerrold E. Seigel, *Rhetoric and Philosophy in Renaissance Humanism: The Union of Eloquence and Wisdom, Petrarch to Valla* (Princeton: Univ. Press, 1968). As we shall see in the final chapter, some scholars believe that the same phenomenon is at work in XVc Castile, and parade Santillana as a leading figure in the revival of classical rhetorical ideals.

philosophical value. For the Middle Ages as for the Renaissance the epitome of the poet-philosopher was Virgil. Villena's assertion that the *Aeneid* was a veritable ocean of wisdom, containing 'todas las diversidades de buena doctrina' (f. 15^r), simply conforms to a thousand-year tradition stretching from the early commentators, Servius and Macrobius, to such exegetes as the Italian humanist Cristoforo Landino, writing in the late fifteenth century.[55] The corollary of the belief in the encyclopedic scope of allegorical verse was that a corresponding degree of erudition was necessary to interpret it. This was one of the basic assumptions of the grammar curriculum; it evolved a method of literary study, the *enarratio poetarum*, which, when it reached its peak of sophistication in the twelfth century, was thought to offer the finest form of intellectual training.

Allegory, therefore, and the exegetical techniques of the schools, conferred upon poetry the status of philosophy; indeed, there was often scarcely any significant difference between them, given the imprecision with which the two terms were used. But this was not invariably the case. Whenever a serious attempt was made to define the terms *poesia* and *philosophia* and to discuss the relationship between them, even the most ardent apologists of poetic study were careful to distinguish between their respective aims and methods.

This fact is of supreme importance. It is worth giving two examples which will set Villena's ideas into sharper focus. Bernard Sylvester was one of the most influential of all commentators on the *Aeneid*. Like Villena, he makes poetry an autonomous branch of knowledge, alongside the mechanical arts, eloquence and philosophy. Unlike him, however, he does not consider it to be the ultimate target of man's intellectual ambition. In spite of the claims made for the rhetorical and philosophical genius of Virgil, poetry is subordinated to both eloquence and philosophy. It is a propedeutic science: the study of it is a means of paving the way for greater things, rather than being *la postrimera dotrina*, as the Castilian writer later argues.[56]

The same phenomenon occurs in the *Metalogicus* of John of Salisbury. On the one hand, there is the conviction that the study of the finest poets, such as Virgil and Lucan, was of enormous

---

[55] See McKeon, 'Poetry and Philosophy'; Curtius, *European Literature*, pp. 203–13, 443–45; Domenico Comparetti, *Vergil in the Middle Ages*, trans. E. F. M. Benecke (London: Swan Sonnenschein, 1895), pp. 63–69.

[56] McKeon, 'Poetry and Philosophy', pp. 303–05.

educational value (all intellectual disciplines were interrelated, and all were put to use in the *enarratio poetarum*). But on the other, there is the paradoxical distrust of poets themselves—a paradox which, as McKeon has pointed out, goes back to Plato ('Poetry and Philosophy', pp. 307–09). Consequently, poetry is not given an autonomous identity, but firmly classed as part of grammar, which in its turn is subordinated to philosophy and theology.

Villena has much in common with both of these twelfth-century humanists (we shall see more parallels in chapter IV, when we examine his concept of meditative study). The crucial difference is that he bestows much greater status upon poetry, thus anticipating the literary theorists of the sixteenth century, for whom it was an architectonic science, serving the highest good of man.[57] But it is important to remember that Villena was not discussing poetry in an academic context, as were Bernard Silvester or John of Salisbury, but advocating a programme of studies for the educated layman. His radical position stems from this, rather than from a desire to compare the relative merits of poetry, philosophy and theology as an object of study. Poetry embodies the intellectual aspirations of 'los romancistas leedores' and constitutes the soundest training for those engaged in 'la vida civil'. This proposition is argued from two different, but related, angles. *El arte de trovar* demonstrates the value of verse composition as a means of polishing man's powers of verbal expression; the *Aeneid* commentary demonstrates that poetry is fundamental for the acquisition of wisdom. And both texts attempt (with varying degrees of clarity) to lend authority to the composition and study of verse by setting these activities within the intellectual and philosophical framework of *las ciencias*.

To end this chapter, and to highlight the polemical implications of Villena's programme, it is worth quoting the views of Alonso de Cartagena, who reacted strongly to the spread of lay literacy and whose attempts to influence contemporary aristocratic literary taste were clearly articulated in three works. Shortly after the *Aeneid* translation was completed, the Bishop of Burgos outlined a quite distinct pattern of intellectual and spiritual development for the nobility. In his commentary on Seneca's Epistle 88 (which circulated as a separate treatise under the title *De las siete artes liberales*), he adapts a scheme borrowed from St Thomas Aquinas: grammar, logic, then the other liberal arts, followed by natural

---

[57] Weinberg, *A History of Literary Criticism*, see index, *s.v.* 'architectonic'.

philosophy and, in 'la hedat perfecta', by moral philosophy (which requires 'mucha esperiencia' and 'el coraçón libre de las pasiones'); last of all comes the study of theology.[58] These views were later modified in the Latin Epistle sent to the conde de Haro, where he deems this Thomistic sequence to be more appropriate for the professional scholar: drawing on the authority of Aegidius Romanus, he suggests that the nobility have no need of arts of the quadrivium (*Tratado*, ed. Lawrance, p. 57). Cartagena's position narrowed itself even further in a work written only a year or so before his death in 1456. Dedicated to Fernán Pérez de Guzmán, *El oracional* is a philosophic compendium set, significantly, within the framework of a treatise on prayer. It combines a distaste for the empty rhetoric of pagan literature with a eulogy of 'la suave e sana eloqüencia de los santos doctores'.[59] Whereas Villena had claimed that the pursuit of rhetoric and wisdom could legitimately be carried out within the realm of secular letters, for Cartagena this was impossible. For him the noble layman had, like Pérez de Guzmán, to pass beyond, into the world of 'la Santa Escriptura' and its 'canon muy sacro ... guiador de nuestras fablas e aun pensamientos'.

---

[58] *Cinco libros de Séneca* (Alcalá: Miguel de Eguía, 1530), f. xxiii[v].

[59] *El 'Oracional' de Alonso de Cartagena, edición crítica (comparación del manuscrito 160 de Santander y el incunable de Murcia)*, ed. Silvia González-Quevedo Alonso (Valencia: Albatros; Chapel Hill: Hispanófila, 1983), p. 49. See also Francisco López Estrada, 'La retórica en las *Generaciones y semblanzas* de Fernán Pérez de Guzmán', *RFE*, 30 (1946), 310–56, at pp. 339–49.

CHAPTER III

Aspects of Allegory: Enrique de Villena's *Aeneid* Commentary

The two most fertile sources for ideas about the nature of allegory in the first half of the fifteenth century are Villena's huge exposition of the *Aeneid*, Bks I–III, and the even more daunting commentaries by Alfonso de Madrigal on the Bible and the *Chronici canones* of Eusebius and Jerome. Karl Kohut's useful survey gives a clear view of the complex range of attitudes displayed by the theologian toward classical poets and their eloquent fables.[1] He scorned the *mendacia poetarum* and the stupidity of pagans 'que a los hombres llamaron dioses e les dieron honra de verdadero dios' ('Der Beitrag', p. 206, n. 66). The diversity of these gentile gods and other mythological characters, each with a multitude of distinct interpretations, annoyed and frustrated him: the ancient poets' inconsistent treatment of myth, the very substance of their art, was a source of 'grande confusión'. Their incompetence as mythographers is often underlined by his habit of contrasting the terms *poeta* with *sabio* or *auctor*.[2]

Yet despite the distrust and misgivings, Madrigal was orthodox enough to teach that poetic fables could conceal valuable truths and he went to great lengths to extract them. More striking is his

---

[1] 'Der Beitrag', pp. 202–26. See also Ronald G. Keightley, 'Hercules in Alfonso de Madrigal's *In Eusebium*', in *Renaissance and Golden Age Essays in Honor of D. W. McPheeters*, ed. Bruno M. Damiani (Potomac: Scripta Humanistica, 1986), pp. 134–47.

[2] According to Cicero in *De natura deorum* there were four Apollos; but, complains Madrigal, the poets 'assí fablan de Apolo como que fuesse uno solo e todas las cosas que a todos los llamados Apolo convenieron, a éste solo atribuyen, como que otro no oviesse; de lo qual fizieron grande confusión en tanto que aun los sabios que con diligencia las cosas buscaron no pudieron enteramente distinguir entre las cosas que a uno conviene e a otro'. See *El libro de las diez questiones vulgares propuestas al Tostado* (a collection of expositions of classical myth), included in vol. I of *Comento sobre Eusebio*, 5 parts (separately foliated) in 3 vols (Salamanca: Hans Gysser, 1506–07), f. ii^r.

admiration for Ovid and the poet's power to confer immortality. And, to cap it all, he betrays an unparalleled interest in metrics and a keen appreciation for the seductive power of poetry with its 'dulces palabras que aun los muy entendidos gozan en las oýr'.[3] His literary sensibility emerges too in his theoretical utterances on the nature of allegory. He writes, for example, that poetic fiction was not inevitably allegorical since 'algunas vezes por lo que dezían no significavan cosa, mas sólo era para fermosura de la fabla o para continuación de las cosas que dezían' (*Diez questiones*, f. xxxi[r]). With this attitude he was able, like Juan de Mena and other lay writers of the time, to exploit his commentaries for literary ends and to use his vernacular adaptations of Ovidian tales for experiments in the sublime style (see below, p. 125).

Clearly then, the biblical and mythological commentaries of Madrigal offer a rich fund of ideas about poetic fables and their interpretation. In spite of the work of Kohut and Keightley much remains to be done in order to situate his approach within the exegetical traditions of the Middle Ages, and in particular to clarify his position within the intellectual currents of fifteenth-century Castile. A major contribution to this end has been made by Pedro Cátedra, who in several recent studies has detected a polemic amongst Madrigal's contemporaries concerning the application of allegory. In some quarters there was a hostile reaction to the allegorical interpretation of profane authors. A trace of it may be found in the preaching of Vicente Ferrer who, in the face of the growing popularity of the allegorization of such classics as Virgil and Dante, revived the Thomistic argument that the fourfold interpretation should be limited to the exposition of Holy Scripture.[4]

Another topic with a long pedigree in European academic and theological circles was the polemic over what some considered to be an excessive emphasis on the spiritual levels of exegesis, at the expense of the literal meaning. Of those who defended the *sensus litteralis* the most influential was Nicholas of Lyre, whose biblical commentaries figured in many an aristocratic library of fifteenth-century Castile.[5] His approach clearly suited the tastes and abilities

[3] Kohut, 'Der Beitrag', p. 206.

[4] See Cátedra, 'La predicación castellana de San Vicente Ferrer', esp. p. 278; the relevant sermon is listed on p. 248 (BNM 9.433, ff. 33[r]-43[r]).

[5] Santillana owned a copy of Fray Alfonso de Algezira's translation of Nicholas's *Postillae* on Genesis-Psalms (commissioned originally by the Counts of

of the lay reader and corresponds to the style of most vernacular commentaries and glosses, which were devoted, in the main, to the elucidation of historical or linguistic difficulties. Moreover, as Cátedra has shown, Nicholas's position was implicitly endorsed in Villena's exegesis of 'Quoniam videbo'. As we shall see in this and the next chapter, the importance Villena attached to a rational analysis of the surface meaning also characterizes his *Aeneid* commentary. However, in what follows I do not propose to give an account of contemporary intellectual polemics, nor explain Villena's debt to the previous exegetical tradition (Cátedra's forthcoming edition and study of the *Eneida* will doubtless do that). My aims here are more limited: to give a basic description of Villena's theories of allegory as expressed in the Virgilian commentary, and to show how they are related to ideas expressed elsewhere in his *oeuvre*. As so often in this book, we shall see how literary theorizing plays a part in the broader strategies of the text in which it is incorporated.

The first reference to the nature and function of allegory in Villena's commentary on the *Aeneid* occurs in a gloss on the underlying aims of the poem. In the eyes of the simple reader, we are told, the poem appears to relate the epic deeds of Aeneas. In fact, the narrative was merely a pretext: it enabled Virgil to lend historical authority to the newly-established House of Augustus, and, more important still, to convey moral and spiritual lessons relevant to all levels of society (ff. 10ᵛ–11ʳ; ed. Santiago Lacuesta, pp. 39–40). 'So el velo poéthico e colores rectoricales', Villena concludes, 'discretamente e palliada fiere aquel señal adó non parescía tyrar' (f. 10ᵛ; p. 39). An explanation of the poetic *pallium* follows in the accompanying gloss:

> *Velo* llama ha la cubierta ho palliación con que los poethas suelen fablar. Que ansí como el velo cubre la cosa sobre que está, pero non tancto que por su delgadez non se conosca que algo está deyuso e se muestra, aunque non tan claramente como syn velo, ansí los dezires poéthicos fablan por tales encubiertas que ha los non entendidos paresce escuro e velado, e ha los entendidos claro e manifiesto. (f. 10ᵛ)

Three elements make this passage an important theoretical statement. First, it embodies the notion that veiled obscurity is the

---

Niebla: Schiff, *La Bibliothèque*, pp. 215–25); for other copies, see Lawrance, 'La biblioteca del conde de Haro', entries 8, 13, 15. For Villena and early XVc exegetical trends, see Cátedra, *Exégesis—Ciencia—Literatura*, pp. 29–43.

very essence of true poetry. Poets appear to say one thing, but in reality say another. Such was the basic rhetorical definition of allegory: 'Allegoria, id est alieniloquium', wrote Isidore; 'Aliud enim sonat et aliud intellegitur'.[6] His view that without this mode of discourse poetry could not be distinguished from history was repeated by generations of literary critics and poets, including Boccaccio and Juan de Mena (see above p. 77).

Secondly, these lines provide yet another example of the concept of intellectual elitism which, as *El arte de trovar* amply demonstrated, played such an important part in Villena's work. More than any other form, allegorical poetry preserved the vital distinction between the ignorant and the wise.

But what gives this quotation its special interest and importance is the way the metaphor of the veil indicates how form possesses a definite function in conveying the message of the text. It establishes a relationship between reader and book; it suggests the content without entirely revealing it, and thus attracts readers, drawing them into the deeper levels of the text. 'Los dezires poéthicos fablan': the truly significant relationship is between the poem and the individual, rather than between the author and the public at large. Poets plant their messages, as it were, under a layer of fiction, and the extent to which their creations then 'speak' is determined solely by the ability of the reader. As we shall see, the implications of this are far-reaching.

Not until the end of the prologue does Villena tell us more about the poetic veil. The glosses to the list of prefatory *avisamientos* fall into two groups: one concerns poetic genres, the other deals with the use of allegory. To match the four kinds of poetry (tragedy, comedy, satire and lyric) Villena gives four reasons why 'los poethas escrivieron sus obras figuratyvamente' (f. 20ʳ).[7] For the sake of convenience I alter the order in which they are listed; discussion of the first two need not detain us long.

---

[6] *Etymologiarum sive originum libri XX*, ed. William M. Lindsay, Oxford Classical Texts, 2 vols (1911; Oxford: Clarendon, 1971), quotation from I, xxxvii, 22 and 26.
[7] This number seems to have appealed to him: there were four main categories of licit knowledge: poetry, philosophy (with four sub-categories), mechanical arts and theology; and also four of magic: 'mathemática', 'prestigio', 'encantación' and 'maleficio'.

1 Ethics

Figurative language is used on the grounds of moral propriety: 'por encubrir ha los malos la materia de los vicios de que avían de tractar, reprehendiéndolos por que non aprendiesen nuevas maneras de culpas' (f. 20ʳ). It was a commonplace that allegory, indeed any kind of obscurity, was legitimate in order not to cheapen knowledge by exposing it to the eyes of the vulgar herd or, as here, to protect potentially dangerous material from being acquired by ill-intentioned readers.[8] However, Villena is not just paying lip-service to a literary convention: his conviction that the *Aeneid* contained forty branches of 'ciencias vedadas' as well sixty licit kinds of wisdom gives a real sense of relevance to this otherwise lifeless topos. Unfortunately, we are allowed only rare glimpses of his views on which passages of the *Aeneid* might conceal 'materia de los vicios' (his commentary stops short of the sixth book, which was traditionally thought to contain the most esoteric aspects of Virgil's encyclopedic wisdom). But one such moment is his gloss on Bk I, ch. 16, where he refers to 'la sciencia de los señales, a que dizen auspicium' (one of the ten branches of *mathemática*). 'Maguer tenga alguna raýz de verdat', he explains, 'pues que la yglesia lo defiende, los cathólicos non deven en ello parar mientes' (f. 38ᵛ). He does not share his knowledge further, with the tantalizing implication that he knows exactly how reliable this prophetic method is.

Tradition furnished Villena with a second moral motive for employing allegory and related figures of speech. Tropes such as periphrasis and metaphor were permitted, indeed encouraged, by such authorities as Cicero, Quintilian and Isidore if they enabled the writer to avoid improper or obscene expressions.[9] As an indication of Villena's concern to emphasize the ethical character of the poet, it is worth noting how he integrates both this and the previous justification of allegory into his cameo of the virtuous man, whose eloquence should be restrained by 'quatro taciturnidades'. Of the four precepts laid down by Villena, two are relevant here: 'quo no diga malas palabras, porque las malas palabras corrompen las

---

[8] e.g. Boccaccio, *De genealogia*, XIV, 12; see Osgood, *Boccaccio*, p. 170, for bibliography. The notion was also common in biblical exegesis, e.g. St Augustine, *De doctrina Christiana*, IV, viii, 22.

[9] See Jacques Fontaine, *Isidore de Séville et la culture classique dans l'Espagne wisigothique* (Paris: Études Augustiniennes, 1959), I, 145, 289–90.

buenas costumbres', and 'que non descubra los secretos de los saberes que le Dios revelare ... ha los malos e indignos, por donde se acrescentaría su poderío de mal fazer' (f. 28ᵛ).

2 *Brevitas*

The second reason for poets to employ allegory, observes Villena, is 'por fablar breve, e que pudiesen dezir en pocas palabras mucha sustancia' (f. 20ʳ). This concept is not to be confused with the rhetorical ideal of *abbreviatio*, which, together with its stylistic opposite *amplificatio*, was thought by the authors of the *artes poeticae* to offer the writer a useful tool in his attempts to rework hackneyed themes in a novel manner.[10] Nor is it mainly concerned with the ideal of concise narrative treatment: the brevity that governed the overall length of a given work—'la gracia de brevedat de que se pagan oy los modernos', as Villena once referred to it.[11] What is in question here is the concept of sententious, compendious verse: 'sermo brevis magnam in se continens sententiam'.

We may not readily associate this kind of *brevitas* with allegorical discourse. But in fact it accords with the broad rhetorical definition of allegory, *alieniloquium*. It does not mean simply 'to say one thing, and signify another' (i.e. by irony, enigma and so on), so much as 'to say one thing, and signify many more'. Thus, it is related to the famous 'texto/ glosa' dichotomy:

Fiz vos pequeño libro de testo, mas la glosa
non creo que es chica, antes es bien grand prosa,
que sobre cada fabla se entiende otra cosa
sin la que se alega en la razón fermosa.[12]

This was an intellectual as much as a stylistic concision. Its

[10] Ernest Gallo, 'The *Poetria nova* of Geoffrey of Vinsauf', in *Medieval Eloquence: Studies on the Theory and Practice of Medieval Rhetoric*, ed. J. J. Murphy (Berkeley: Univ. of California Press, 1978), pp. 68–84.

[11] *Arte cisoria*, p. 73; see also his contempt for contemporary laymen who 'non quieren estar en el leer de las estorias quanto cumple al entender dellas, e si luenga es la razón déxanla començada'; for their benefit he divides the *Aeneid* into short chapters, 'por que la brevedat dellos combide e afalague al leedor' (BNM MS 17.975, f. 16ᵛ). See also the excursus 'Brevity as an Ideal of Style', in Curtius, *European Literature*, pp. 487–94.

[12] Juan Ruiz, Arcipreste de Hita, *Libro de buen amor*, ed. G. B. Gybbon-Monypenny, Clásicos Castalia, 161 (Madrid: Castalia, 1988), st. 1631.

potential drawback was obscurity. This is a major preoccupation of Juan Manuel, whose many utterances on problems of literary form centre on the contrast between a discourse that is 'alongada e declarada' and one that is 'abreviada e escura'.[13] The relevance of this compression for exegetical theory is obvious. As Germán Orduna has put it, writing about Juan Manuel:

> La palabra condensada aparece rodeada de una corteza que es necesario penetrar con esfuerzo para luego desplegar su contenido, de modo que el signo lingüístico se torna lenguaje vivo por operación del receptor.[14]

Orduna's 'lenguaje vivo' is a most apt way to describe the function of brevity. It allows for interpretative freedom in the exploration of 'mucha sustancia'. As we shall see, the concept of multiple meaning exerted a great attraction over Villena.

Brevity could cause problems when used as a criterion of practical criticism, especially when applied to the classical epic. As Curtius has pointed out, Homer and Virgil, as model authors, were supposed to exhibit all the rhetorical excellences, and critics sometimes found it difficult to reconcile the ideal of brevity with the length of their poems (*European Literature*, p. 489). It is a dilemma shared by Villena: he records the anecdote in which Augustus praised an epigram by Virgil because of 'la brevedat de los versos tancta substancia comprehendientes' (f. 7ᵛ), yet enthusiastically labels his finest work as a 'grand tratado prolixo e difuso, siquiere estendido, cubierto de velo poético' (f. 3ᵛ). Certain passages are paraded as models of *amplificatio*: the description of the isle of Tenedon exemplifies 'una de las maneras con que los retóricos pueden alongar fermosamente sus palabras por [que] los dezires sean copiosos plaziblemente' (f. 57ʳ).

---

[13] For the most comprehensive exposition of this aspect of Juan Manuel's work, see Barry Paul Taylor, 'Juan Manuel, *El conde Lucanor*, Parts II–IV: Edition—Stylistic Analysis—Literary Context', unpublished Ph.D. thesis (King's College, Univ. of London, 1983), especially pp. 43–64; also Macpherson, 'Don Juan Manuel', pp. 8–10; Paolo Cherchi, '*Brevedad, oscuridad*, synchysis in *El Conde Lucanor* (Parts II–IV)', *Medioevo Romanzo*, 9 (1984), 361–74.

[14] See Germán Orduna, '"Fablar complido" y "fablar breve et escuro": procedencia oriental de esta disyuntiva en la obra literaria de don Juan Manuel', in *Homenaje a Fernando Antonio Martínez*, Publicaciones del Instituto Caro y Cuervo, 48 (Bogotá, 1979), pp. 135–46. His view that Juan Manuel was influenced by Islamic concepts has rightly been challenged by Taylor, who shows that the ideas on brevity and obscurity fall within the well-defined traditions of classical and medieval rhetoric.

3 Social considerations

These account for the third reason why poets cloaked their work under a veil of allegory:

> por que fuese común ha todos; ansí que los moços lo oviesen por pastraña, e los de mayor hedat e non letrados por ystoria, los letrados por allegoria e allende desto secretos de natura e moralidades en ello especular podiesen.
> (f. 20ʳ)

There is nothing unusual in the view that readers of quite distinct intellectual abilities perceived different levels of meaning in an allegorical text: the conviction was reiterated in both theological and secular contexts, from Augustine to Petrarch.[15] But Villena was not, I think, merely acknowledging a theoretical tradition. It seems to me to be relevant to his preoccupation with the social commitment of the wise man to disseminate his knowledge; the poet-sage and the philosopher share this same obligation, but they fulfil it in different ways. I shall return to this subject later, but first it is necessary to explain what was meant by *pastraña, ystoria* and *allegoria* and to say something about the corresponding levels of reader.

It was traditional to classify fiction according to its relation to truth. Isidore, influenced by the classifications of *De inventione*, I, xix, 27 and *Ad Herennium*, I, viii, 13, handed down the following scheme:

> historiae sunt res verae quae factae sunt; argumenta sunt quae etsi facta non sunt, fieri tamen possunt; fabulae vero sunt quae nec factae sunt nec fieri possunt, quia contra naturam sunt. (*Etymologiae*, I, xliv, 5)

Villena's first category, the *pastraña*, corresponds to Isidore's *fabula* and he does not concern himself with it. His silence is hardly surprising given his admiration for the moral mysteries of the poem, and it indicates the same contempt for this class of fiction as one encounters in the remarks made in a similar context by Boccaccio. For him, there are four kinds, the lowest of which was

---

[15] See Augustine's *Confessions*, Bk XII, especially chs 27–28 and 31. According to Alan of Lille in his *Anticlaudianus*, 'the sweetness of the literal sense will soothe the childish hearer; moral instruction will infuse the developing sensibility; and the sharper subtlety of allegory will excite the advancing intellect': quoted from Judson Boyce Allen, *The Friar as Critic: Literary Attitudes in the Later Middle Ages* (Nashville: Vanderbilt Univ. Press, 1971) p. 24; for Petrarch, see 'La *Collatio laureationis* del Petrarca', ed. C. Godi, *Italia Medioevale e Umanistica*, 13 (1970), 1–27, at p. 21 ('eadem sit claritas in subiecto, sed, pro captu spectantium, diversa').

the 'delirantium vetularum inventio', or 'old wives' tale'. This contains no truth at all, neither at a literal nor deeper level and as Boccaccio scornfully concludes, it has nothing whatever to do with real poetry.[16]

Villena's second class of fable, the *ystoria*, was the domain of the mature yet unlearned reader. The precise meaning of this term is hard to pin down: like other words relating to fiction and allegory, he employs it with disconcerting flexibility.[17] However, it is safe to assume that it denotes not the *historia* of Isidore, the factually true narrative, but the term as defined by Boccaccio. It is, in other words, the verisimilitudinous tale. The Italian distinguishes two kinds of such fiction. The first is favoured by the great epic poets, Homer and Virgil, who seem to write true stories, 'yet their hidden meaning is far other than appears on the surface'.[18] This is manifestly not what Villena had in mind for the unlearned reader. His *historia* approximates Boccaccio's second category, the sort written by the better comic poets Plautus and Terence. Their work operates purely on the literal level: 'if the events they describe have not actually taken place, yet since they are common, they could have occurred, or might at some time'.[19] The value of this sort resides in the incidental moral teaching that emerges from the portrayal of human foibles. It is similar to the Christian parable.

Villena lavishes great praise on Virgil's skill in weaving his tale with such subtlety thaf it utterly convinces the unlearned reader. He concludes the glosses on the second book with the exclamation:

[16] *De genealogia*, XIV, 9; quoted from *Genealogie deorum gentilium libri*, ed. Vicenzo Romano, Scrittori d'Italia, 200–01 (Bari: Laterza, 1951), at II, 707. His fourfold classification of *fabula* derives largely from Macrobius (Osgood, *Boccaccio*, p. 164).

[17] In *Los doze trabajos*, *historia* could denote: a) a tale that was historically true: 'la verdat de aqueste trabajo fue así como la istoria lo cuenta ... sin ficción poética o semejança metafórica alguna' (ch. II: the Nemean lion; p. 25); b) a tale based on the principles of verisimilitude: the 'istoria nuda' is 'metafórica, e paresce verdat e es posible de ser' (ch. VI: Diomedes; p. 59); c) the euhemeristic interpretation of the allegory: 'E ya sea esta metáfora fuese figurativamente puesta, non es sin real e verdadera istoria' (ch. VI, p. 60; see also ch. XI, p. 117); d) a fabulous tale: 'aquesta istoria es fabulosamente contada por non semejable de verdat manera' (ch. VIII: Antaeus the giant; p. 74). According to Morreale, Villena was more precise in his use of *parabólico, metafórico* and *fabuloso*, p. xiii, n. 3.

[18] Osgood, *Boccaccio*, p. 49; 'longe tamen aliud sub velamine sentiunt quam monstretur' (ed. Romano, II, 707).

[19] Osgood, *Boccaccio*, p. 49; 'Et hec si de facto non fuerint, cum comunia sint esse potuere vel possent' (ed. Romano, II, 707; i.e. Isidore's *argumentum*).

con quanto artificio engeñosamente compuso Virgilio la texedura deste segundo libro, que paresce ha la gente común tan veresímile que todos afirmarían contesciese de la manera por él contada, antes que por la vía que los otros actores lo cuentan. (f. 118ʳ)

He is not content merely to eulogize this aspect of Virgil's narrative brilliance. His commentary contains numerous passages in which he puzzles over details of the text according to the criterion of verisimilitude. Here is a typical example taken from the glosses to Bk II. These start with an inquiry into the length of time taken by Aeneas to recount the many adventures that befell him prior to his arrival at Dido's court. 'Duró aquel razonamiento bien tres horas', remarks Villena, adding a comment that clearly demonstrates how his methods are based on solidly empirical principles: 'segund paresce en la tardança que un buen leedor puede fazer en estos dos libros' (f. 55ʳ). The same procedure is followed in order to prove how late everybody retired to bed (which in turn reveals how infatuated Dido must have been with the hero). He decides that the banquet must have lasted four hours, the blessing of the wine half an hour, the minstrel's song one hour, Aeneas's story three, and therefore, 'todo junctado son ocho horas e media, onde paresce que era pasada media noche grand rato, aunque era en tienpo de las noches grandes (f. 55ʳ). These calculations are a common feature of Villena's exegetical method, both in this work and in *Los doze trabajos*. Quite apart from the obvious delight he took in speculating on such matters, they are included to illustrate the approach that was expected from a reader whose lack of literary training limited his understanding of the allegory to the superficial realities of Virgil's tale.[20]

However extravagant it might appear to us, the attention devoted to the narrative details had a fundamental theoretical justification. The underlying truth of allegory is revealed by a scrutiny of the literal level.[21] This is illustrated by the approach

[20] See also the final gloss on Bk II: 'Plazible será ha los leedores saber en qué tiempo del año e quántos del mes e qué noche fue esta presa de Troya de que faze mención en este libro, pues que non se falla en los ystoriales que fasta agora desta materia han escripto. E por ende ha solaz de aquéllos quise añader esta nota inbestigando por congecturas' (f. 117ᵛ); see also his comment on the existence of the Calidonian boar in *Los doze trabajos*, p. 117; on what Morreale calls Villena's 'ingenuo sentido de la verosimilitud histórica', see pp. xix–xx.

[21] See Morreale, *Los doze trabajos*, pp. x–xiv; it was also a basic precept of biblical exegesis, see Henri de Lubac, *Exégèse médiévale: les quatre sens de l'Écriture* (Paris: Aubier, 1959), I, 425–87.

adopted by the third category of reader—'los letrados'—who realize that the verisimilitude of the poem is deceptive. They understand that Virgil's most impressive achievement was that throughout this apparently real-life tale he planted:

> ciertos pasos en diversos capítulos para que los que ovieren elevados engenios conoscan aya mesclada fycción en la mayor parte, si ha ello pararen mientes, advertiendo e convivando unos dichos con otros. (f. 118ʳ)

Exactly what this operation involves is made clear when Villena himself speculates on the feasibility of Aeneas's various adventures. His summary of the epic hero's travels shows that although the individual episodes may be acceptable enough, when considered as a whole they most definitely fall outside the bounds of possibility:

> todo junctado fue andamio de más de veynte e cinco leguas, syn los rodeos e detenciones e destorvos e ocupaciones e fablas que tomaron grand parte de tiempo. E aunque andoviera una legua por hora, que fuera mucho ha pie e armado, mayormente cuando llevava el padre a cuestas, non pudiera complirse desde el primer sueño fasta en la mañana, segund él lo pone. (f. 118ʳ)

By this rational method of analysis Villena is able to conclude that 'en la ymposibilidat desto paresce la ficción, así que fallará fructo saciatyvo ha su appetytu cada uno de los leedores; los vulgares la literal corteza, e los de mayor yngenio coligiendo las dispersas congecturas' (f. 118ʳ).

It is not always necessary to employ the comparative method to discover whether allegorical secrets have been embedded in the text. At times, the fabulous nature of the *historia* is more obvious, a clear hint that it is just a pretext to trigger the erudite's quest for deeper meaning. Such is the case with the whole of Bk III. Impugning the 'árida declaración e de poco fructo' of 'Servius' (i.e. not the original commentary by that author but the scholia that accumulated under his name), Villena declares that Virgil would not have imagined 'tan estranios acaescimientos ... sy mayor provecho en ello non thesaurizava' (f. 118ᵛ). The notion that the absurdity of the text could indicate allegorical intent has precedents in patristic commentaries, such as those by Augustine and Jerome, and it is also to be encountered in the exegetical work of Alfonso de Madrigal.[22] Rhetorical extravagance was also a clue that the tale had

---

[22] See Beryl Smalley, *The Study of the Bible in the Middle Ages*, 3rd ed. (Oxford: Blackwell, 1983), p. xiv. For Madrigal, see his exposition of the Narcissus myth in *Libro de las diez questiones*, f. 10ʳ.

a deeper significance. For example, the use of *amplificatio* in the description of the island of Tenedon was dictated not just by esthetic reasons, to 'alongar fermosamente sus palabras': it was also employed 'por que oviesen materia los exponedores de pensar que [algund] misterio estava secretizado en la narración desta ysla' (f. 57ʳ).

The importance attached to the outer *cortex*—its rhetorical devices, narrative structure—as a pointer to the *medulla* is emphasized by the way it influences the arrangement of Villena's commentary. Comprehension of the poem as *historia* must precede analysis of it as *allegoria*. Thus, he often postpones his moral exposition of individual passages until the reader has had the chance to acquire a synoptic vision of a whole episode. In a chapter of Bk II, for example, he writes:

> non puse ha cada una particular glosa la declaración moral siquiere aplicación que le pertenescía, reservándol[a] para este lugar e fyn del capítulo. Onde vista toda la textual texedura será formada e mejor entendida.²³ (f. 83ᵛ)

That poets were not merely the apes of the philosophers was an important argument in the defences of poetry written during the Renaissance. According to Boccaccio, for example, they share the goal of portraying truth, yet they arrive at it by quite separate routes. The philosopher proves his theories by use of syllogism, disputing in the lecture-room, and employing 'an unadorned prose style, with something of a scorn for literary embellishment'. By contrast, the poet strives for truth through contemplation, and works in solitude, writing 'in metre, with an artist's most scrupulous care'.²⁴ Although he does not distinguish between the two in the formal context of a theoretical discussion, Villena also sets the poet apart from the philosopher. The framework of his comparison differs from that of Boccaccio in that his overriding concern is with the wise man's position within society. This means that above all else he focusses attention on the way they communicate their knowledge to others. This is to say that the central issue is one of literary form.

---

²³ He alters this procedure in Bk III, which contains 'doctrina muy útil e salutífera, de pocos sabida e de menos practicada'; it thus requires a more detailed exposition: 'en cada una glosa porné la moralidat que le convenga non reservándola ha la fyn del capítulo, segund fize en algunos de los capítulos del segundo libro' (f. 118ᵛ).

²⁴ *De genealogia*, XIV, 17, quoted from Osgood, *Boccaccio*, p. 79.

The point may be illustrated by the dilemma which faced Hercules, the archetypal sage, in the final chapter of *Los doze trabajos*. He was summoned on the death of Atlas, King of Libya, to complete the latter's unfinished treatise on astrology, upon which the good of the state so much depended (astrology being the 'senda que lieva los omnes a Dios', ed. Morreale, p. 130). He did this with such skill that he was able to combine stylistic sublimity with intellectual complexity, yet at the same time preserve lucidity of expression.[25] However, this ideal blend of wisdom and eloquence simply provoked the envy of other philosophers, who, criticizing the work's 'mucha sotileza e entricadura de palabras' compelled Hercules to write a second, stylistically inferior, version (p. 131). Villena then intervenes in the narrative with the following observation on the ideal relationship between form and content:

> en toda obra a dos partes principales que la sostienen. La una la materia ser aprovada, veriguada e fundada, e la segunda el estilo alto e guarnido de rectoricales colores, que es la forma. E quando es tal dura por sienpre e ámanlo todos saber por lo aver desta guisa fecho ... Tanto es nescesaria la pierna del estilo estar firme sin doblegar a la duración de las obras que sin aquélla non avrían tanta actoridat. (pp. 131–32)

The subject-matter, therefore, should be founded on authenticated, unrefuted truth, and clothed in a suitably elevated rhetorical style; works that achieve this balance acquire great authority and perpetual fame (exactly why and how will be explained below). But it is important to note that this digression describes what ought to happen in the perfect state; the circumstances in which Villena chose to place Hercules were quite different. His public resented the complex style of the astrological treatise and even though they were 'enbueltos en inorancia' he had to take their views into account: 'pero en este caso fue forçado a Ercules que la doblegase [la pierna del estilo], por que del todo su obra non fuese desechada e menos entendida o por pocos rescebida' (p. 132). The phrase 'en este caso' needs to be heavily underlined. It illustrates the essentially pragmatic attitude required of the philosopher toward his eloquence. He must follow the basic rhetorical principle of decorum and adapt the style according to the character and intellectual capacity of his particular public.

---

[25] 'Dio conplimiento a las dichas cosas mucho más subtil, alta e declaradamente, suficiente e entendida que por Atalante fueron començadas, aprovándolas con bivas razones e notificando por claras pruevas de manera que algunt tienpo después non son venidas nin vernán a menos' (pp. 129–30).

In *Los doze trabajos*, therefore, Villena envisages form as the extensive use of rhetorical colour to adorn and lend authority to a work; when appropriate, it can be adjusted without affecting in any substantial way the nature of the contents. Form, in short, is regarded as the main obstacle in the dissemination of the philosopher's knowledge. A quite different set of relationships between form, content, author and public is presented in the introductory comments on the *Aeneid*. Here, form does more than embellish and confer authority upon the content: it is not an obstacle, but the very means by which the poet-sage communicates with the widest possible range of public. The poetic veil shifts the burden of communication from the writer to the reader. In other words, instead of having to write according to the lowest common denominator, allegory allows the poet to pack as much substance into his text as he wishes, without alienating the unlearned.

Villena makes much of the notion that Virgil's intention was to speak to all classes of men: the 'doctrina virgiliana', he declares, applies to all ages and social estates (f. 11^r; ed. Santiago Lacuesta, p. 40). The philosophy of this text, unlike that of Hercules's treatise, is truly 'común ha todos', because each reader will find 'fructo saciatyvo ha su appetytu'.

4   The exegete and multiple meaning

According to the prefatory *avisamientos*, the fourth reason why poets employed the veil of allegory was 'por que los exponedores oviesen materia general en que diversas fiziesen exposiciones' (f. 20^r). To say that allegorical verse supplies 'materia general' for a variety of interpretations raises the question of the scope of allegorical exegesis. What is a legitimate interpretation, and were any bounds placed on the imagination of the exegete or did he have total freedom, regardless of the possible intentions of the original author?

The conclusion to the glosses on Bk I offers useful insights into these problems. Here, Villena compares his own interpretation of the poem with that of 'Servius' and notes that there are substantial differences between them. For the earlier commentator, the events of this book concern 'la primèra hedat de la ynfancia', whereas Villena believes it is 'más convenible' (an important phrase) to expound them according to 'la moral vida', and to show how man struggles with sin and Fortune. And although he leaves us in no doubt that he considers his own reading to be superior, the question of a single correct interpretation of the original never arises:

> bien deve ser presumido que todos estos entendimientos fueron en la concebción virgiliana quando fabricó estos yntegumentos, pues que llegó ha la rudidat de nuestros engenios. E por eso fablaron los poethas en esta velada manera, por que pudiesen los exponedores *varias e útiles* declaraciones fazer. (f. 54ᵛ; my italics)

The belief that all interpretations of the *Aeneid* had somehow been anticipated by the poet was one of the traditional legends of Virgilian exegesis. But to argue that Virgil himself saw in the poem all that future generations were to see in it is also a neat way round the question whether the commentator transgresses the poet's intentions. Moreover, since the *Aeneid* was encyclopedic in scope (it contained 'todas las diversidades de buena doctrina', f. 15ʳ), the reader could, in theory, speculate upon an infinite number of 'secretos de natura e moralidades'. These references to 'buena doctrina' and 'moralidades' are vital: they alert us to the fact that the expositions of the poem could be 'varias', but they should also be 'útiles'.

The emphasis on utility, on exploring multiple meaning within the confines of 'buena doctrina', explains why Villena believes his interpretation of Bk I to be 'más convenible' than that of 'Servius'. Even more severe is his criticism in the glosses to the third book of the epic. Once again, the comparison is based not on authorial intention, nor on correctness of interpretation, but on ethical criteria. For 'Servius', Bk III signified the loquacity of youth: this, Villena declares, is an:

> árida declaración e de poco fructo ... e por eso la adapté al estado del ombre que sale de la vida bestial que los vicios le procuraron para recuperar las virtudes e la práctica que en ellas ha de tener. (f. 118ᵛ)

This deprecation of 'Servius' is also, by implication, a criticism of other medieval commentators whose work he no doubt knew. The view that each book of the poem represented a period in man's life from earliest infancy to old age was also the basic premise of Fulgentius and Bernard Silvester, perhaps the greatest and most subtle of all Virgilian exegetes. It remains to be seen exactly where Villena stood in relation to his predecessors, but it could well be that he has most in common with the Italian humanist Cristoforo

Landino who, in the late fifteenth century, also considered the poem to represent man's attempt to reconcile the active and contemplative life.[26]

Returning now to the conflict between interpretative freedom and the concept of appropriateness, the views expressed in the *Aeneid* commentary are put into sharper focus by one of Villena's other exercises in exegesis, *Los doze trabajos*. Here, we are dealing not with the creation of a single writer, but with a compilation of myths culled from a variety of sources: they are the common property of a multitude of 'poetas e istoriales'. For this reason, Villena displays a noticeably free attitude toward what one might call literary ownership. At the start of the treatise, he stresses that his own interpretation of this collection of stories is by no means exhaustive (a claim dutifully reiterated at the end of each chapter), since it is designed, in part, to illustrate the exegetical method, 'el arteficio de la aplicación' (p. 10; see below, pp. 143–51 for further discussion). It is clear, therefore, that he does not wish to shackle the imagination of his readers. In the closing pages, he explains that he has kept his exposition brief:

> por non atar o limitar el entendimiento de los especulativos que leerán este tractado ... a fin que por diversas aplicaciones segunt la diversidat de los ingenios e prespicacidades puedan las moralidades de aquestos trabajos ser variadas e multiplicadas. (p. 140)

The tropological exegesis of the twelve myths and its application to the twelve social estates is—or seems to be—unrestricted. However, as in the commentary on the *Aeneid*, Villena offsets his repeated references to exegetical licence by asserting the aptness of a particular interpretation. The desire to control meaning is instinctive, but it also stems from a confidence in the superiority of his own exegetical skills, a pride which is most strikingly illustrated at the end of the *declaración* of the tenth labour, where he declares that:

> Esta moralidat o alegoria sale de la istoria ante puesta más cercanamente non enbargante que otros entendimientos asaz buenos se podrían a ello dar. Este quiso aquí poner por ser más convenible al estado del disciplo de que en este capítulo fablaré. (p. 103)

---

[26] On these commentators, see the prefatory study to Bernardus Silvestris, *Commentary on the First Six Books of Virgil's 'Aeneid'*, trans. Earl G. Schreiber and Thomas E. Maresca (Lincoln: Univ. of Nebraska Press, 1979); also Comparetti, *Vergil*, pp. 57–60 (on Servius), and 104–12 (Fulgentius).

The assertion that one specific allegorical message emerges from the tale 'más cercanamente' than any other indicates that the criteria that control exegesis are not simply ethical. There is an implicit awareness of the dangers of forcing an interpretation upon the story: the finest commentator, he appears to be saying, is sensitive to the restrictions imposed by the structure of the tale. It is as if each myth is an empty vessel, into which may be placed any content the reader wishes, so long as it fits the contours and patterns of the narrative.[27]

The ideas that have been discussed in the preceding pages were not unique to Villena. The interest he displayed in multiple interpretation, authorial intention and subjective reading was shared by poets and scholars in both the Scriptural and secular exegetical tradition. The emphasis he places, for example, on exploring the text for 'buena doctrina' recalls the influential criterion laid down by St Augustine: for him, as for generations of later theologians who attempted to combat heretical interpretations of Holy Writ, the principle that guided all exegesis was the Catholic concept of *caritas*.[28]

But more relevant to this study is the influence exerted on the vernacular lyric by the concepts that one usually associates with the exegesis of the Bible or classical myth. Just how pervasive this influence was can be judged by the flexible attitude towards authorial intention in the Provençal tradition. One early anonymous poet, aware of the possibilities of multiple interpretation, seems prepared to relinquish all ties with his own creation—though as the final (ironic?) line reveals, he was also conscious of its moral and esthetic limitations:

> Qui aquetz digs estriers enten
> Si mielhs hi dis, no lo.n repren,

---

[27] For further examples, see chs VII and IX (pp. 71–72 and 94); also ch. XI, where the tale of the Calidonian boar is said to have been invented by poets as the vehicle for a particular message: 'por que della que es en parte fabulosa pudiesen mostrar e sacar los especulativos material enxenplo por el qual entendiesen qu'el nuestro cuerpo quando se da a deleites sin enbargo del espíritu se falla así como en región e tierra desierta' (pp. 113–14); also the end of ch. XII, where he submits the treatise to the correction of those who 'moralizan más propiamente' (p. 137). For parallels, see Boccaccio's occasional criticism of Fulgentius (see Osgood, *Boccaccio*, p. xvii, n. 8); and Madrigal, *Comento*, III, part 4, ch. 383: 'No es conveniente el seso de Macrobio en la fábula de Phitón, mas el de Servio' (f. cxxx^v).

[28] See Lubac, *Exégèse*, II, 99–197, especially pp. 99–113.

Quar s'a trop sens una razos,
mout m'es meiller quan quecz es bos.[29]

Parallels may be found too in fifteenth-century Castile. One of Villasandino's rare essays in allegorical verse—his elegy on the death of Enrique III—was contemptuously reinterpreted by Fray Diego de Valencia and given a more forceful political and social dimension in the process. The theoretical justification for appropriating another poet's vision is familiar enough: 'non son los ssesos de una natura/ nin fablan poetas por una entención.[30]

As Allen has shown in his study of the fourteenth-century classicizing friars in England, the artistic and didactic possibilities of exegesis had by that time been exploited to such an extent that, at times, the conventions were subject to the subtlest of parodies (*The Friar as Critic*, pp. 58–63 and 130–2). For Spain—and possibly for Europe as a whole—the *locus classicus* is Juan Ruiz's ironic subversion of the exegetical method in *El libro de buen amor*. Other great poets, notably Jean de Meun and Chaucer, explore the humorous, and very serious, implications of the ideas under discussion here; but to my knowledge, only Juan Ruiz gives such thematic prominence to the concepts of multiple meaning and authorial intention. Clearly, interest in the 'open text' and 'active reader' is not exclusive to the twentieth century, but forms part of a medieval theoretical heritage of whose richness modern scholarship is becoming increasingly aware.[31]

[29] Paterson, *Troubadours and Eloquence*, p. 24. At the other end of the scale of interpretative freedom stood Marcabru, continuously asserting that his verse possessed a unique, incontrovertible meaning (p. 10). For further references to the troubadours' 'cult of ambiguity', see Seidenspinner-Núñez, *Parodic Perspectivism*, pp. 17–21.

[30] *Cancionero de Baena*, ed. Azáceta, no. 35, ll. 7–8 (I, 82); Villasandino's poem is no. 34.

[31] On Juan Ruiz, see, in addition to the book by Seidenspinner-Núñez: Zahareas, *The Art*, pp. 175–76; Priscilla Meléndez, 'Una teoría de la escritura en el *Libro de Buen Amor* de Juan Ruiz, Arcipreste de Hita', *Hispanic Journal*, 4, no. 1 (1982), 87–95; Marina Scordilis Brownlee, *The Status of the Reading Subject in the 'Libro de buen amor'*, NCSRLL, 224 (Chapel Hill: Univ. of North Carolina Press, 1985); E. Michael Gerli, '*Recta voluntas est bonus amor*: St Augustine and the Didactic Structure of the *Libro de buen amor*', RPh, 35 (1981–82), 500–08. See also Eugène Vinaver, *The Rise of Romance* (Oxford: Clarendon, 1971), ch. 2; Lee W. Patterson, 'Ambiguity and Interpretation: A Fifteenth-Century Reading of *Troilus and Criseyde*', Sp, 54 (1979), 297–330; Sylvia Huot, 'Poetic Ambiguity and Reader Response in Boccaccio's *Amorosa visione*', MP, 83 (1985–86), 109–22; Minnis, *Medieval Theory of Authorship*, pp. 201–04

There remains to be discussed one final aspect of Villena's theory of allegory. It will be remembered that the fourth reason why poets wrote obscurely was 'por que los exponedores oviesen materia general en que diversas fiziesen exposiciones' (f. 20ʳ). It is important to note the way in which Villena emphasizes the role of the *exponedor*: the idea that poets write in order that exegetes interpret their creations occurs with such regularity in both the *Aeneid* commentary and *Los doze trabajos* that it is hard to resist the conclusion that, in Villena's opinion, the main justification for allegory lies in the unequalled opportunity it offers the learned to flex their intellectual muscles. The poet and commentator work in tandem across the centuries: the true value of the original poem is a product of both writers. The process is analogous to musical composition and performance. A musical score possesses only latent meaning; its significance is realized only in performance, and whether the full scope of its meaning is explored depends entirely on the skills of the performer.

Though not unprecedented (see the opening lines of the prologue to Marie de France's *Lais*), the emphasis on the role of the interpreter is, I think, unusual in theoretical discussions of allegory.[32] It is particularly significant in this respect that Villena makes no mention of one of the commonest justifications of the poetic veil—namely, that knowledge is valued more highly if it is acquired through great intellectual effort.[33] To include this topical principle in his prefatory *avisamientos* would obviously detract from the value of a commentary whose excellence—according to Villena—resides in the way it clarifies Virgil's moral doctrine and makes it accessible to the layman.

Since his fundamental aim was to make the *Aeneid* 'más tractable ... con menos estudio', he explains that he has not rendered the Latin word for word, but according to the sense: 'de tal guysa que alguna cosa non es dexada ... de lo contenido en su original, antes aquí es mejor declarada e será mejor entendida' (f. 16ʳ; ed. Santiago

---

[32] See Marie's statement that the ancients wrote obscurely so that later scholars could interpret their works ('gloser la lettre') and add their own meaning ('de lor sen le sorplus mettre'); these lines have been the subject of considerable controversy, see, e.g., Leo Spitzer, 'The Prologue to the *Lais* of Marie de France and Medieval Poetics', *MP*, 41 (1943–44), 96–102; Vinaver, *The Rise of Romance*, pp. 15–22; Tony Hunt, 'Glossing Marie de France', *RF*, 86 (1974), 396–418.

[33] See Augustine, *De doctrina Christiana*, II, vi, 8; Boccaccio, *De genealogia*, XIV, 12.

Lacuesta, p. 45). The quality of his work, he adds in a gloss, will be clear to whoever is capable of comparing 'anbos los originales' (f. 16ʳ). That there are two originals demonstrates how he raises the act of translation and exposition to the same status as the act of creation. Virgil is the ideal poet and Villena, we are allowed to infer, is the ideal commentator. This parity between the two literary tasks should not surprise us; as Peter Russell has put it, in spite of their modest claims to the contrary, 'los traductores medievales no parecen compartir en modo alguno la suposición moderna de que preparar una traducción es, por definición, dedicarse a un tipo de trabajo forzosamente inferior al de escribir una obra original'.[34] At times, however, one has the impression that the balance established between the two is tipped in favour of the Castilian. In the gloss on the above passage, for example, he writes: 'non fue solamente tan bien romançado como está en el latýn, *mas aun mejor*' (f. 16ʳ): in the Latin the meanings of mythological characters are 'subintellectas', whereas in his version, they are 'expresadas'. His motive is to emphasize that his audience has access to the *Aeneid* only through his text. Virgil now speaks through him.

A similar desire to exalt the role of the exegete is evident when Villena discusses literary fame. He compares Virgil's *Aeneid* with a chronicle of the same title written by Isidore. The reason why the latter work is little known, he explains, is that:

> las corónicas que non son en alto stillo e guarnescidas de las aposturas poéthicas son poco ementadas porque los entendidos las tienen en poco por cuyo alabamiento avýan de durar. (f. 12ʳ)

In other words, if a writer wishes his work to last he needs to resort to all the resources of rhetoric and allegory: this ensures the approving attention of the learned, without whose scholarly incrustation all literary endeavour is doomed to oblivion. To a certain extent, what Villena says about the relationship between commentators and creative writers has a philosophical justification in the epistemological theories of Boethius (*De musica*, I) and, ultimately Aristotle (*Metaphysics*, 981 b). According to their hierarchical concept of wisdom, knowledge of the abstract and general is superior to knowledge of the concrete and particular. Thus, those who theorize about a science or craft are superior to those who practise or perform it. This faith in the preeminence of

---

[34] *Traducciones y traductores*, pp. 8 and 10; Villena's translation evaluated on pp. 45–50.

the speculative over the practical enabled Juan del Encina, invoking the authority of Boethius, to separate the *poeta* '[que] contempla en los géneros de los versos', from the mere *trobador*.[35]

This theory, however, can provide only a partial explanation of Villena's position. His commentary opens with a passage that leaves us in no doubt about his conviction that his own status, as well as that of his translation, is inextricably linked with the fortunes of his mammoth exegesis. He calls upon future scribes to copy out the work 'con glosas segund aquí está, complidamente ... e non presuman nin atienten el texto solo trasladar' (f. 1ʳ). The overt reason for this command is that the *Aeneid* would be too obscure for lay readers and that, without his accompanying exposition, the benefit of its hidden meaning would be lost. But the extravagance with which he brings home this point suggests that his motives were not wholly altruistic: 'sé ciertos que si les verná voluntad ho deseo de lo trasladar syn las glosas que les viene por temptación e subgeción diabólica' (f. 1ʳ). The divine blessing he then invokes for those who faithfully transcribe his interpretation of the poem is surely prompted by his anxiety to associate himself with Virgil's lasting fame, and thus secure a position as contemporary sage.

The emphasis on his skill and importance as an exegete is undoubtedly the result of the pride taken in the immensity of his achievement: the commentary on the first three books alone equals in length that of other commentators on the whole poem. He also makes much of the fact that he was the first to translate the *Aeneid* complete, with all its 'poéthicas aposturas'.[36] But there are ulterior motives. To underline his own role in the transmission of the poem is merely one tactic within a larger plan to make the *Aeneid* a vehicle for his personal ambitions. It was a means of vindicating his right to indulge in intellectual pursuits, of challenging:

> los del presente tiempo, por detestable que las grandes e generosas personas en esto se ocupen cuidando, e cegados de su ygnorancia, que los dedicados

---

[35] *Arte de poesía castellana*, ed. Francisco López Estrada, *Las poéticas castellanas*, p. 84.

[36] 'En Ytalia algunos vulgarizaron esta *Eneyda*, pero diminutamente ... dexando muchas de la ficciones poéthicas en ella contenidas, sólo curando de la symple ystoria en la mayor parte, especialmente en la materia del quinto libro sobre los juegos que Eneas fizo en Scicilia. E otros del ytaliano en francés e en catalán le tornaron ansí menguada commo estava en el ytaliano, pero nunca alguno fasta agora la sacó del mesmo latýn syn menguar ende alguna cosa salvo el dicho don Enrique' (gloss on f. 15ᵛ).

> ha la sciencial cultura non entiendan de las mundiales cosas e agibles tancto commo ellos e por eso los menosprecian desviando de les encomendar administraciones activas. (f. 2ʳ; ed. Santiago Lacuesta, p. 33)

To counter this contemporary prejudice, Villena draws constant parallels with the practice of ancient Rome, where 'non despresciavan la sciencia ... antes avían por bien que los grandes señores fuesen scientes e letrados' (gloss on f. 7ᵛ).

Juan of Navarre need not have been the most perceptive of monarchs in order to understand what Villena was trying to achieve. In 1425, a few years before the translation was begun, Villena's grandfather died, and his estates were appropriated by the Aragonese crown. Virgil too had had his property confiscated after the civil war, but Augustus wisely returned them when he realized the political value of having such a poet in his service:

> diole bivienda onrada en su imperial casa, e aun segund la oppinión de algunos le dio las rentas de la cibdat de Nápol por que non toviese cuydado de las nescesidades cotydianas, nin fuese ocupado en otra cosa synón en las scientíficas obras. En esto mostró gran discreción el Emperador, dando sus dones a tan sciente persona que con su lengua e dezires le podría fazer tancto servicio. (f. 9ʳ)

The *Aeneid* exposition is a promise of the glorious possibilities offered by his literary and intellectual talents, and perhaps even hints at the composition of the chronicle of Fernando de Antequera, Juan's father—to be written, no doubt, to the same eulogistic ends as Virgil's history of the epic origins of the House of Augustus.[37] Nowhere is this more forcefully put than in the exordial *carta*, where, echoing his threat of eternal damnation to incompetent scribes, Villena links the restitution of his land not just to an earthly but also to a divine reward: 'quanto alcançó de eloquencia despendería loando en sus dichos e scripturas al dicho Rey de Navarra, faziendo durar su fama recordable'. The King should thus be moved by two considerations, 'lo uno por alcançar el eternal premio que non se puede aver syn restitución, lo otro por alcançar fama e nombrad[í]a, seyendo loado por enseñada lengua' (f. 2ᵛ)

We can only speculate on the effect of these lines: civil war broke out between Juan of Navarre and his cousin, Juan II of Castile, and the *Aeneid* never found its way to its original patron.

---

[37] Villena expresses a desire to see such a work published on several occasions, e.g. f. 13ʳ, ed. Santiago Lacuesta, p. 41, and glosses.

All Villena's ambitions came to nothing. Yet his manipulation of history and literary theory suffered one final ironic twist. For after his death, a legend swiftly grew that he dabbled in the black arts. Perhaps he would have appreciated this similarity with Virgil, but he would surely have been less amused by its consequences: when Virgil died, Augustus saved the *Aeneid* from the flames; when Villena died, Juan II put almost the entire contents of his considerable library on the bonfire.

CHAPTER IV

Castilian *Auctores* and Intellectual Nobility

1 The Presentation of the Text

a) The Prologue

No study has yet been devoted specifically to the ways in which
Castilian writers of the fifteenth century introduced their works to
the new aristocratic reading public. But it is during this period that,
as Alberto Porqueras Mayo has observed, the vernacular prologue
'se afianza plenamente como indiscutible y necesaria modalidad
literaria'.[1] The spread of literacy brought authors into closer, more
sophisticated contact with their public; a reader had the opportunity
to reflect upon introductory comments in a way that a listener did
not, and this fact was exploited by poets and prose writers alike.
Thus, in addition to using a wide range of exordial topoi, belonging
to well-established rhetorical traditions, fifteenth-century writers
began to use the prologue in order to explain and justify their work
to a degree that was not previously possible. They were aided in
their endeavours to do this by the fact that they possessed a
ready-made critical system in the *accessus ad auctores*.

The *accessus*, a formal set of introductory comments on a
prescribed text, was a fundamental part of the education system
throughout the Middle Ages. Although better known, perhaps, in
connection with the study of grammar, it was applied to all subjects
of the school and university curriculum. And, although St Jerome
did not use it in his influential prefaces to the Bible, it was
considered appropriate by much later theologians, who felt that it

---

[1] *El prólogo como género literario: su estudio en el Siglo de Oro español*, Anejos de
RLit, 14 (Madrid: CSIC, 1957), pp. 87–88. Porqueras Mayo's brief remarks on the
medieval prologue need to be read very critically: see Martín de Riquer, *RFE*, 42
(1958–59), 298–300. See also Margo Y. C. De Ley, 'The Prologue in Castilian
Literature between 1200 and 1400', unpub. Ph.D. thesis (Univ. of Illinois, Urbana,
1976), which effectively supersedes Porqueras Mayo's study of the earlier medieval
period.

offered a convenient structure for the introductions to their works of biblical exegesis.[2]

In constant use since late antiquity, the *accessus* was subjected to a considerable number of modifications. The full details of these are complex, and need not concern us here. Yet at the height of its popularity in the twelfth century, when collections of *accessus* circulated independently of their texts, a variety of systems had evolved whereby a work could be analysed from both a grammatical and a philosophical point of view. According to one of these, which was in widespread use, a commentator would discuss his text under seven headings: *titulus libri, nomen auctoris, intentio, materia, modus tractandi, utilitas,* and *cui parti philosophiae supponitur.* In order to answer the questions posed by these headings, the scholar would have to draw on all aspects of his academic training: he would need to use etymology so as to explain the implications of the title and to decide whether the work was authentic; he would need also to supply a certain amount of biographical and historical information; allegorical exegesis also came into play in the discussion of the author's true intention (which could then perhaps be contrasted with the work's apparent subject matter); knowledge of literary genres was necessary to explain the *modus tractandi* (the didactic procedure, and the way in which a subject was arranged within the work), and its subdivision *forma tractatus* (the literary forms employed, e.g. comedy, hexameter); then, in his analysis of the last two topics, the commentator would be called on to demonstrate the text's relationship to Christian ethics and to fit it into the general scheme of human knowledge.

In the thirteenth century, with the advent of Aristotelianism, a new system emerged. It entailed a discussion of the work according to Aristotle's four causes: the *causa efficiens* (author), the *causa materialis* (subject), the *causa formalis* (form; subdivided, as before, into *forma tractatus* and *tractandi*), and the *causa finalis* (equivalent to *utilitas* or the *pars philosophiae*). This scheme, and the pre-existing forms of the *accessus*, continued to be used throughout the later Middle Ages, with commentators free to construct new paradigms by combining elements from both the Aristotelian and earlier traditions.

[2] Edwin A. Quain, 'The Medieval *Accessus ad Auctores*', *T*, 3 (1945), 215–64; Hunt, 'The Introductions to the *Artes*'; Curtius, *European Literature*, pp. 221–22; A. J. Minnis, 'The Influence of Academic Prologues on the Prologues and Literary Attitudes of Late-Medieval English Writers', *MS*, 43 (1981), 342–83; *Medieval Theory of Authorship*, pp. 9–72.

As far as Castile is concerned, it was in the fifteenth century that these procedures began to be applied regularly to works written in the vernacular for a non-professional audience. This is not to say that before that date they were confined exclusively to academic or theological circles. Non-latinate readers, faced with texts that bridged a scholastic and lay milieu, could easily have been acquainted with the technical vocabulary and intellectual aims of the *accessus*. The most notable example, as Francisco Rico has shown, is the *General estoria*. Embedded in the historical narrative itself are a whole range of exegetical methods borrowed from the grammatical *enarratio*, including those of the academic prologue. More recently, John Dagenais has suggested that an important strand of parody in the prologue to the *Libro de buen amor* relates to the Ovidian *accessus* that were so popular at the time.[3] There may be other isolated cases, but it seems to me that the earliest, certainly most elaborate, example of an academic *accessus* in Castilian literature designed for a court public is Enrique de Villena's prologue to his translation of the *Aeneid*, completed in 1428.

Villena's prologue is aimed specifically at 'los que se pagan de la vulgar lengua' (f. 3ᵛ; ed. Santiago Lacuesta, p. 35), whose ignorance of Latin prevents them from understanding the traditional methods of exegesis employed to study Virgil's poem. He has in mind, therefore, a distinctly non-academic set of readers—'los que non han visto sus exposiciones'. This moves him to describe the procedure followed by 'el entendido leedor' who:

> ante de començar la ystoria, cobdicia saber quál actor la fizo e de qué nombre titulada e qué es lo que tracta e a qué fyn es fecha e a cúya parte de philosophía pertenesce. (f. 3ᵛ; ed. Santiago Lacuesta, p. 35)

These headings correspond to *auctor, titulus, materia, intentio,* and *pars philosophiae*. But Villena does not adhere rigidly to this scheme, nor draw the reader's attention to the strict formal divisions between the separate topics of his *accessus*. As a result, his prologue is highly discursive in form, especially toward the end, where he expatiates on a number of subjects not usually associated with an academic introduction. And, as one might expect, the many glosses add to the difficulty of following the main lines of his argument;

---

[3] On the *General estoria*, see Rico, *Alfonso el Sabio*, pp. 166–88; on Juan Ruiz, see John Dagenais, '"Avrás dueña garrida": Language of the Margins in the *Libro de buen amor*', *C*, 15 (1986–87), 38–45; 'A Further Source for the Literary Ideas in Juan Ruiz's Prologue', *JHP*, 11 (1986–87), 23–52.

nevertheless, the basic academic patterns can be observed.

He starts with a biography of Virgil; this takes up most of the prologue (ff. 4ʳ–10ʳ; pp. 35–39). Then without pausing to give a separate analysis of the work's title, he moves almost inperceptibly into his explanation of its *intentio*. He observes that Virgil related the deeds of Aeneas in order to praise the house of Augustus. But this was only the poet's secondary intention; his primary goal was to 'reprehender los vicios e favorizar las virtudes por que buenas costumbres en el mundo por esta obra sembradas fuesen' (f. 10ᵛ).

The assertion that the poem has an underlying moral purpose leads Villena on to a brief survey of its *materia*. '¿Qué es lo que tracta?' was the question posed at the outset of the prologue; but this question cannot be answered in isolation, without reference back to Virgil's subtle intentions. 'En esta obra', we are told, 'Virgilio introduze virtuosas costumbres inclinando los oyentes a bien fazer' (f. 10ᵛ; p. 39). Examples are then given to demonstrate how various episodes of the *Aeneid* contain matter useful to all levels of contemporary society.[4] However, Villena emphasizes yet again that the doctrinal value of the work depends on the reader's ability to 'prescrutar el poethal intento' (ff. 10ᵛ–11ʳ; p. 40). Finally, with a passing reference to Servius's view that each book represents a stage in man's life, he brings his discussion of *intentio* and *materia* to a close by declaring that the *Aeneid* is 'un espejo, doctrina en do cada uno puede contemplar su vida, las faltas e reparaciones de aquélla' (f. 11ʳ; p. 40).

At this point, Villena seems to depart from the structure outlined at the start of his introduction. Explaining that Virgil died before he was able to complete the *Aeneid*, he describes how Augustus ordered two scholars to emend the extant twelve books and put them into a form suitable for publication. This was done in such a way that:

> non añadieron de suyo alguna cosa mas quitaron lo que les paresció superfluo, siquier de sentencia ayuno, de manera que lo contenido fincable todo fuese virgiliano. (f. 11ᵛ; p. 40)

---

[4] 'En las respuestas que Eneas avía de los dioses ... inclina non poco ha la religión aprovando las piadosas obras; en las afruentas en que se vido Eneas e commo las pasó syn temor ho flaqueza, inclina los oydores ha esfuerço, siquiera de osar cometer grandes fechos; en los pactos que fueron entre Eneas e el rey Latino ... muestra las práticas commo libran ho han de librar en las cortes ...; en las batallas que ovo ... muestra la instabilidat de la fortuna' (f. 10ᵛ; pp. 39–40).

Although not accounted for in his original scheme, these considerations are not out of place in an *accessus*. They correspond to those sections in which a commentator would list the number of books in a given work, and then guarantee its authenticity. More unexpected, at least from the point of view of a traditional academic prologue, is Villena's bitter attack on the literary incompetence of contemporary chroniclers, who are, he exclaims, totally ignorant of the rhetorical and poetic techniques essential to the art of writing history (see above, p. 79). But this passage is not such a digression as it might at first seem. The comparison between his rendering of Virgil's sublime style and 'la susurración balbuziente de las corónicas' (f. 13^v; p. 41) may be classified as yet another topic of the *accessus*: the *modus tractandi* (or 'manera del proceder', as he later terms it) is in this case rhetorical and poetic.

He now answers the last of his original five questions: '¿a cúya parte de philosophía pertenesce?'. This topic is swiftly disposed of. With the assertion that philosophy is subdivided into three, physics, metaphysics and ethics, he concludes that 'aquesta obra de la *Eneyda* so la parte moral ... es collocada' (f. 13^v; p. 42): a view which had of course been anticipated by much of the earlier discussion, in which the *Aeneid* was put forward as a vast *speculum morale*.

This brief reference to the poem's philosophical category does not, however, end the prologue. Instead, pausing only to exalt the authority and excellence of the work (with the support of quotations from Ovid, Dante and Statius), Villena again reverts to one of the topics of the *accessus*: *utilitas*. Not only will the reader discover all that is necessary 'ha ylluminación de la cavalleril doctrina e conservación de políthyca vida' (f. 15^r; p. 42), but much else besides. However, apart from mentioning in a gloss the innumerable 'provechos singulares en la poesía e otras sciencias' (f. 15^r), which are hidden away in the *Aeneid*, Villena does not attempt to give a detailed exposition of its utility. He contents himself instead with a convenient inexpressibility topos:

> Ciertamente por mí non podrién ser expresados los bienes que nascen e las utilidades que se alcançan de su lectura. Sólo ha aquel pertenesce que los suyos pudiere fasta los más abscondidos penetrar secretos. (f. 15^r; p. 43)

With this encomium, the prologue comes to an end. But the possibilities offered by the vocabulary and methods of the academic *accessus* are still not exhausted. For between the prologue and the translation itself Villena inserts a series of *avisaciones* designed to instruct the inexperienced reader in the rudiments of orthography (ff. 15ᵛ–18ᵛ; pp. 43–45).

These conclude with a dedication of the whole work to its original patron, Juan of Navarre, in which the King is described as 'causa potísima ynscitatyva de tan útil vulgarización ha la vida cevil' (f. 19ᵛ; p. 46). This is intended as flattery; exactly how and why is made clearer in the accompanying glosses. God, affirms Villena, inspired the King to commission his translation: 'todo vino por misterios divinos' (f. 19ʳ). And it is Juan of Navarre, therefore, who deserves the public's gratitude. This is why, he continues, it is appropriate to address him as the:

> causa potýsima siquiere principal deste efecto. Ca maguer se podrié dezir el dicho don Enrique causa eficiente desto, acatando lo que dize el philósopho en el libro *De causis*, que la causa de la causa es causa del causado, por eso el dicho Rey, que fue causa qu'el dicho don Enrique fuese causa heficiente, es causa del causado. (f. 19ʳ)

We are faced here with ideas which clearly owe much to the conventions of the Aristotelian academic prologue to which I referred earlier in this discussion. The distinction between principle and efficient (or instrumental) cause was frequently made in such prologues. However, it seems to have been more usual, particularly amongst religious writers, to claim God as one's direct principal cause. Villena, on the other hand, gives the King a remarkably prominent place in the chain of causality—as an intermediary between God and the translator—and he thus combines conventional dedicatory adulation with the learned formulae of the academic *accessus*.

Villena's prologue is part of his attempt (analysed later in this chapter) to educate his readership. I have examined it at some length here because it shows the ease with which academic methods were transferred from the schoolroom to the court and the flexibility with which they could be employed. But in Villena's case, of course, this transfer was facilitated by the fact that he wrote with centuries of introductory studies on Virgil's masterpiece behind him. His prologue exists within clearly recognizable academic traditions, even though the final product appears very much to be his own creation. However, Villena was not the only one to employ the topics of the *accessus*, as a glance at many prologues to translations and original works will show. Like Villena's prologue, these demonstrate how this system of literary analysis was open to free adaptation, and that writers certainly did not feel bound to explore all its possibilities. Thus Cartagena's discursive prefaces to some of this Senecan translations mention only the author's *entención*; the academic prologue is here moulded to suit the translator's dominant concern that the layman should appreciate the true function of the text. Alfonso de Madrigal is equally independent in the prologue to his translation of the *Chronici canones*: 'la entención e provecho de la obra por ella misma se parece, mas saber quién fue el autor es conveniente'.[5] Some writers, though clearly influenced by the themes of the *accessus*, chose to avoid explicit use of its technical vocabulary. Juan de Mena, for example, prefaced his *Coronación* with four *preámbulos*, the first three of which explain the poem's title (characteristically using etymology), genre and subject matter, but not in the conventional academic terms described above.[6] However, to gauge just how pervasive during this period was the influence of these methods, it is not necessary to undertake an exhaustive survey of their presence in the work of vernacular writers. The influence is best appreciated,

[5] For examples of Cartagena's approach, see his translations of *De la vida bienaventurada* and *De las siete artes liberales*; for Madrigal, see BN Madrid, MS 10.811, f. 1ᵛ; another elaborate example is the preface to the anonymous XVc Castilian commentary on Dante's *Inferno*, I, based almost entirely on the work of Benvenuto da Imola (Escorial MS S-II-13, ff. 36bisʳ–36terᵛ); for extracts, see Edwin J. Webber, 'A Spanish Linguistic Treatise of the Fifteenth Century', *RPh*, 16 (1962–63), 32–40; see also Pulgar's preface to his commentary on *Mingo Revulgo* (he describes its relation to literary 'maneras' [= *modus tractandi* or *qualitas*], its 'fin', 'intención', and concludes with an analysis, by stanza, of its content [= *materia* and *ordo librorum* or *modus tractatus*]). The habit persisted into the XVIc with, e.g., Juan de Padilla's preface to his *Doze triumphos* (the 'argumento' outlines its 'materia', 'intención' and its structural division according to the twelve signs of the zodiac, i.e. *modus tractatus*).

[6] Mena employs the technical vocabulary later, in the main body of his commentary (see below, p. 155). See also the prologue to the *Corbacho*, structured around the following unspecified topics: author, intention, formal division, content and utility; see Colbert I. Nepaulsingh, 'Talavera's Prologue', *RomN*, 16 (1975), 516–19. See also the preface to Rodríguez del Padrón's *Siervo libre de amor*, which opens in an obviously academic style ('El siguiente tratado es departido en tres partes principales', i.e. *modus tractandi*), but which continues in a much more informal manner. Nonetheless, the topics of the *accessus*, though unobtrusive, are still present: *auctor* ('Johán Rodríguez del Padrón'), *modus tractatus* (seguiré el estilo ... de los antigos ... trayendo ficiones'), and *intentio* ('al poético fin de aprovechar e venir a ti en plazer'); in *Obras completas*, ed. César Hernández Alonso (Madrid: Editora Nacional, 1982), pp. 153–56. As we shall see, the academic procedure is more prominent in his introduction to *El bursario*.

I think, by considering the kind of text to which the methods of the *accessus* were deemed appropriate. After all, one might expect men such as Villena, Cartagena, Madrigal or the anonymous Dante commentator to bring these methods before a lay readership, either because of the learned nature of the work being introduced, or because of their own intellectual background. It is much more instructive to note the presence of the *accessus* in contexts which one does not readily associate with the academic world.

The three examples I wish to examine are all prose works, written during the second quarter of the fifteenth century: Diego de Valera's *Tratado en defensa de las virtuosas mujeres*, Juan Rodríguez del Padrón's *Bursario*, and *El Victorial*, by Gutierre Díez de Games. These works exhibit certain obvious formal and thematic differences. The first is an imaginary dialogue, and, as its title clearly indicates, is a reply to the anti-feminist literature which was so popular at the time. *El bursario* is a translation of Ovid's *Heroides*, a collection of epistles by women on the subject of love. And the last work is a biography of the adventurer Pero Niño, the Count of Buelna, and at the same time a treatise on knighthood. However, in spite of their differences they share much common ground; at the core of each lie the standards and ideals of chivalry and courtliness, and each of them is introduced by an *accessus*. But we should note that the topics of the *accessus* are not embedded discreetly within the overall structure of the prologue, as they so often were during this period. On the contrary, all three authors try to bring home to their readers the necessity of approaching their work with a particular set of questions firmly in mind.

Diego de Valera emphasizes the point with the assertion that 'en comienço de toda obra, para ser bien entendida, son quatro cosas necesarias de saber'.[7] But the scheme he then offers the reader is somewhat unusual:

> La primera es el motivo del que faze la obra; segunda, quién es aquel con quien habla; tercera, qué es la materia de que trata; quarta, quál es el fin a que la obra es fecha. (p. 61)

The second of these topics can hardly be said to apply to all literary works; what Valera probably has in mind is some such heading as *qualitas carminis* or *modus tractandi*, equivalent to style or genre. As he subsequently explains: 'escrevía yo como si fablasse con un

---

[7] *Tratado en defensa de las virtuosas mujeres*, ed. María Angeles Suz Ruiz (Madrid: El Archipiélago, 1983), p. 61.

amigo mío a quien mucho pluguiese saber las conclusiones de aquestos maldizientes, no solamente aquellas discriviendo, mas a cada una dellas respondiendo e anulando' (p. 61). The fact that he does not have to hand a traditional academic term to describe his dialogue form indicates a certain degree of vagueness about the nature of the *accessus*: a hypothesis which could be supported by reference to other puzzling aspects of his prologue (e.g. the lack of a firm distinction between *motivo* and *fin*, or his idiosyncratic definition of *lírica*, which, together with his other genre definitions, is set out in the section devoted to *materia*). But these are relatively minor points; what should concern us here is not the looseness with which he applies these academic methods, but the fact that he deems it appropriate to adopt them at all.

This feminist *tratado* belongs to a highly artificial genre—a literary game which was taken seriously in as much as it allowed writers to exercise their rhetorical skills while reeling off a commonplace list of female virtues and vices. But most attractive of all, it seems, was the fact that it enabled them to adopt the conventional courtly postures. However, none of this discouraged Valera from casting a learned veneer over his work; quite the contrary: much of the courtliness derives from the very display of literary erudition. In this respect, his use of the *accessus* is part of those same pretensions which led him to equip this and other treatises with a series of notes and glosses and become what Juan Marichal, in a fundamental essay, has described as 'un pastor mundano' for 'los que no tanto leyeron'.[8]

In one respect, it should not surprise us that Rodríguez del Padrón introduces *El bursario* with an overtly academic prologue. Throughout the Middle Ages, the works of Ovid, including the *Heroides*, formed part of the grammar curriculum, and were thus subjected to all the academic techniques of *accessus* and allegorization. Indeed, a large part of Rodríguez del Padrón's prologue, explaining the work's *titulus, intentio, materia, utilitas*, and *auctor*, is in fact a direct rendering of the *Bursarii*, one of the principal sources of medieval Ovidian scholarship, composed in the early thirteenth century, possibly by William of Orleans.[9] Yet the point to

---

[8] *La voluntad de estilo*, p. 38.

[9] See the thorough study by John Dagenais, 'Juan Rodríguez del Padrón's Translation of the Latin *Bursarii*: New Light on the Meaning of "Tra(c)tado"', *JHP*, 10 (1985–86), 117–39; see also Fausto Ghisalberti, 'Medieval Biographies of Ovid', *Journal of the Warburg and Courtauld Institutes*, 9 (1946), 10–59.

remember is that Rodríguez del Padrón is not noted for his learned aspirations. In his treatise on nobility, *La cadira de onor*, he roundly condemned the practice, favoured by some of his more eminent contemporaries, of conferring upon each other the title of poet laureate. This sneer at the pretensions of men like Santillana and Mena originates in his belief that an aristocratic lineage is sufficient for true nobility; the concept of intellectual nobility, advanced by Villena and others, seems to have been alien to him (see below, pp. 161–62). It is therefore interesting that a writer whom Lida de Malkiel (with some exaggeration in the light of the present evidence) charged with 'arrogante tradicionalismo y resistencia a las nuevas ideas' should feel it appropriate to preserve the scholarly apparatus, in the belief that the *accessus* did not detract from the atmosphere of refined courtliness which pervades his work.[10]

Similar points could be made about *El Victorial*, which is prefaced by a typically scholastic prologue:

> En comienço de cualquier obra quatro cosas son: ynquerir la causa material, e la hefetiva, e la formal, e la final; porque el oydor sienpre deve buscar e querer quién es el autor, e de qué obra trata, e cómo en ella trata, e a qué fin e a qué provecho. La causa material en aquesta obra es oficio e arte de caballería. La causa suficiente [sic; read 'eficiente'?] es quien la hizo. La causa formal es loar los fechos de un buen cavallero. La causa final es provecho.[11]

The hero of this chivalric biography, Pero Niño, is paraded as the ideal noble, the upholder of the rigid concept of the knight as *defensor*. 'El que a de aprender e usar arte de cavallería', asserts the author, 'non conbiene despender luengo tiempo en esqüela de letras' (p. 64). This statement requires careful interpretation. It would be impossible to argue that Díez de Games suscribed to precisely the same blend of active and contemplative life which, as I shall show, characterized the intellectual and social ideals of some of the more prominent fifteenth-century writers. Even so, it seems that bookish learning was not wholly out of place in his scheme of aristocratic education. The emphasis of his objection is on the attendance at the 'esqüela', rather than on the 'letras', a modicum of which would be acquired in a much less formal context. He does

---

[10] María Rosa Lida de Malkiel, 'Juan Rodríguez del Padrón: vida y obras', *NRFH*, 6 (1952), 315–51, at p. 318.

[11] *El Victorial: crónica de don Pero Niño, conde de Buelna*, ed. Juan de Mata Carriazo, Colección de Crónicas Españolas, 1 (Madrid: Espasa-Calpe, 1940), pp. 1–2.

not seem to think it incongruous to expect his noble readers and listeners ('oydor' indicates group reading) to be familiar with procedures that originate in the intellectual habits of a rival class.

To sum up, the *accessus* offered all kinds of vernacular writers an authoritative set of topics with which to present their works to the class of non-professional readers which was gradually evolving during the early fifteenth century. The ease with which academic methods were borrowed is amply illustrated by their presence in the three prologues discussed above. They seem to have rapidly become an accepted, perhaps even expected, procedure for even the most courtly writer. This does not mean that the latter was consciously attempting to ape the academics. In all cases, the scholastic prologue was freely adapted to suit the needs of the individual writer.[12] Its use in the vernacular was the product of the new relationship between the writer and his public, evidence of his desire to communicate more directly, to exercise stricter authorial control and, in the process, to confer greater dignity on his literary status. These ambitions are pictured even more sharply by the phenomenon now to be discussed.

b) Commentaries and glosses

Like the *accessus*, the commentary formed an essential part of the medieval education system. As the major curriculum texts passed through the hands of successive generations of scholars, they accumulated layer upon layer of academic incrustation, in the form of inter-linear or marginal notes, glosses or elaborate commentaries. In some cases, particularly in the fields of theology and law, the longer commentaries took on independent existence and became set texts in their own right, themselves subjected to the critical attentions of later scholars. And also like the *accessus*, the commentary passed beyond the confines of the classroom and the theologian's study. From as early as the thirteenth century, vernacular authors, writing for court circles, began to annotate and comment upon the works of their contemporaries, or upon translations of major classical and patristic authors, or indeed upon their own creations in prose and verse. In doing this, these writers (and their scribes, to whose intervention we owe the existence of

---

[12] James A. Schultz, 'Classical Rhetoric, Medieval Poetics, and the Medieval Vernacular Prologue', *Sp*, 59 (1984), 1–15, offers a salutary warning against too forceful an application of academic and rhetorical patterns to the vernacular prologue. He overstates his case, however, in totally denying their relevance.

many anonymous commentaries and glosses) were responding to the increased demand expressed by the new non-professional reading public for works of greater literary sophistication. To paraphrase Dante, they supplied *cibo* for the *volgari e non litterati* (*Convivio*, I, ix), who were prevented by the pressures of daily life from the formal pursuit of learning.

Dante stood at the head of the vernacular exegetical tradition, for both historical and literary reasons. He wrote at the very start of the rise in lay literacy, and, in his *Vita nuova* and *Convivio* has left us with the most sophisticated examples of vernacular commentaries. His methods were, by and large, wholly conventional. They are based on the techniques and terminology of the Latin commentaries on the Bible and the *Aeneid*, which in turn were borrowed from classical rhetoric.[13] Moreover, the immense literary and intellectual aspirations embodied by the *Divina commedia* spurred later scholars to apply to it the whole range of exegetical methods that had for centuries been reserved for the classics. But Dante was by no means the only poet to explain his own work or to have it annotated and studied by others. Marginal glosses and allegorical commentaries were also added to the poetry of the major European writers of the fourteenth and fifteenth centuries: Petrarch and Boccaccio in Italy, Gower and Chaucer in England, and Christine de Pizan in France.[14]

[13] See Luis Jenaro-MacLennan, 'Autocomentario en Dante y comentarismo latino', *VR*, 19 (1960), 82–123.

[14] For example, Petrarch's *Familiares*, X, 4 (a detailed exposition of his own first *Eclogue*), and the numerous commentaries on his *Trionfi* in the XVc. Boccaccio added three kinds of annotation to his *Teseida*: interlinear glosses on points of grammar and syntax, brief marginal notes, and an extended commentary on the content of the poem; there are also anonymous commentaries and glosses on his *Ameto, Amorosa visione* and *Elegia de Madonna Fiammetta*. John Gower's *Confessio amantis* has a series of Latin glosses on the main points in the verse narrative (absent from the XVc Spanish translation). MSS of certain books of the *Canterbury Tales* contain also Latin glosses. Their authorship has been disputed, but some (e.g. those to *The Man of Law's Tale, The Clerk's Tale* and *The Knight's Tale*) have been confirmed as being by Chaucer himself. Their function is to add authority to the text by quoting extensively from Latin sources or analogues, such as Petrarch, Statius or Jerome: see Robert E. Lewis, 'The Glosses to the *Man of Law's Tale* from Pope Innocent III's *De miseria humane conditionis*', *SP*, 64 (1967), 1–16. In France, the first vernacular commentary was the *Échecs amoureux, c.* 1400, named after the *Échecs d'amour*, the courtly poem which it expounds: see Badel, *Le Roman de la Rose*, pp. 290–315; Christine de Pizan's *Épistre d'Othéa* (*c.* 1400) is followed by her own moral and anagogical exposition; see P. G. C. Campbell, *L'Épistre d'Othéa: Étude sur les sources de Christine de Pisan* (Paris: Édouard Champion, 1924), pp. 36–44. One of the three extant MSS of *L'Avision Christine* (1405) contains a

Examples of this phenomenon may be found in fourteenth-century Castile, such as Juan García de Castrojeriz's commentary on *De regimine principum* by Giles of Rome, the two versions of which acquired enormous popularity in the next century. Certain Bible translations (especially of the Psalms) also included excerpts from scholastic glosses, or even original ones. Before that, as I have already mentioned, Alfonso el Sabio employed all the conventional techniques of literary commentary in his *General estoria*, and, as in so many other fields, his methods must have set an inspirational precedent for the fifteenth century, when the practice of writing commentaries and glosses for the benefit of the aristocratic lay reader finally took root. It is an essential feature of the literature of this period, crucial for our understanding of the literary ambitions of the major authors. Yet for a number of reasons (among them the reluctance of modern editors to publish them, in the belief that they detract from the esthetic merits of the work, and the fact that manuscripts containing glosses are still coming to light) the importance of this subject has yet to be fully recognized.

The field is too heterogeneous to be analysed in detail here.[15] But it is worth making some general descriptive remarks about it as a prelude to the next section, in which I examine some commentaries written specifically on verse, and explain the more significant literary assumptions that underlie their composition.

Considerable impetus was given to the writing of vernacular commentaries by the patronage of royalty and the upper ranks of the nobility—yet another indication of the growth of private reading amongst this class. Annotated texts were dedicated to members of the aristocracy not simply for reasons of courtesy, but as a result of the increased demand for critical and explanatory apparatus to aid private study. The active interest taken by the nobility in the composition of commentaries and glosses is well illustrated by Juan II of Castile. As the most frequent patron of such works, he gives the impression of having consciously sought to emulate the example of Alfonso X. For instance, at the end of

commentary, recently identified as having been written by Christine herself. There are also marginal notes in the hand of a later owner: see J. C. Laidlaw, 'Christine de Pizan—An Author's Progress', *MLR*, 78 (1983), 532–50.

[15] I am currently preparing a bibliography for Research Checklists and Bibliographies (London: Grant and Cutler). For biblical and theological commentaries, see Klaus Reinhardt and Horacio Santiago-Otero, *Biblioteca bíblica ibérica medieval* (Madrid: CSIC, 1986).

the Castilian version of a compilation of Senecan aphorisms (known as *El segundo libro de la providencia de Dios*), Cartagena, who cast the work in its final form, explained that the group of translators worked under the King's supervision and 'añadiéronle las glosas y algunas adiciones en los lugares donde el dicho señor Rey mandó'.[16]

The work of this team offers perfect evidence for the way that most literary glosses were brought into being as a direct result of the increased demand for translations during this period: the two were inextricably interlinked. Alfonso de Madrigal, an important authority on the subject, summarized the orthodox approaches to translation in the preface to his Castilian version of Eusebius/Jerome's *Chronici canones*. There are two basic methods, he explains. This first 'es de palabra a palabra, e llámase interpretación'.[17] This style is the most learned and reliable ('es de más autoridad'), but its very literalness often results in obscurity. Consequently, he continues, it is necessary to add 'algunas breves declarationes, las quales fuessen en manera de postilas sobre algunas partes del testo' (f. 1ʳ). As is well known, the technique of adding brief glosses to a literal translation had earlier been strenuously defended by Cartagena in his famous dispute with Leonardo Bruni over the latter's new and allegedly free translation of Aristotle's *Nicomachean Ethics*.[18] Cartagena himself employed this procedure in his own translations of Seneca, although his glosses are transformed at times into full-scale commentaries.

The second method of translating described by Madrigal consists of rendering 'la sentencia sin seguir las palabras' (f. 1ʳ). It avoids obscurity (and consequently loses authority) because it is employed for the benefit of 'los menores ingenios'; it is called 'exposición o comento o glosa'. However, as the terms used to describe it suggest, this procedure is in reality not so different from the *interpretación*, since the translator also adds explanatory glosses: not in the margin, however, but within the text itself. 'En la

---

[16] *Cinco libros*, f. lxxixʳ. For the Senecan treatises translated and glossed by Cartagena, see Karl Blüher, *Séneca en España: investigaciones sobre la recepción de Séneca en España desde el siglo XIII hasta el siglo XVII*, trans. Juan Conde (Madrid: Gredos, 1983), pp. 133–48; he dates them between 1430 and 1434, the year Cartagena went to Basle (pp. 141–42 and notes).

[17] BN Madrid MS 10.811, f. 1ʳ. For extracts from this prologue (but not the passages quoted here), see Schiff, *La Bibliothèque*, pp. 41–42. Also Russell, *Traducciones y traductores*, pp. 30–33.

[18] See Di Camillo, *El humanismo*, pp. 203–26, especially p. 210.

segunda [manera]', explains Madrigal, 'se fazen muchas *adiciones* et mudamientos por lo qual non es la obra del autor mas del glosador' (f. 1^r; my italics). Madrigal's reference to 'adiciones' and his later emphasis on the way he separates his commentary from the original text indicate how, in practice, the two styles of translation were set apart mainly by attitudes toward literary ownership, authority, and clarity of presentation. The need for interpretative or explanatory notes, whether added parenthetically within the text or placed in the margins, was seldom questioned.[19]

As I have suggested, the first wave of commentaries was inspired by translations; some, in fact, were translations themselves. Thus, side by side with original expositions and glosses, Castilian versions of pre-existing theological and secular commentaries began to be commissioned. They catered for all areas of literary taste, including the Bible (Nicholas of Lyre) and patristic authors (Sts Augustine and Gregory), moral philosophers (Boethius and Seneca), classical historians (Livy and Vegetius), and secular poets, both ancient and modern (Virgil and Dante).[20] But very quickly— from the 1430s on—the practice of textual annotation spread to contemporary Castilian literature. During the next eighty or so years commentaries and, to a greater extent, marginal glosses continued to be written on original works in both prose and verse.

---

[19] Examples of parenthetical glosses are in the Castilian version of *De consolatione Philosophiae* (possibly by Pedro de Valladolid, though he may just be the scribe): a section of the original is first paraphrased, then expounded; thus the first line, 'Carmina qui quondam studio florente peregi', becomes: 'Ay mesquino yo que solía seyer en gran estudio e que he fecho muchos e diversos dictados e que [h]e trasladados muchos libros de filosofía e de griego en latín ansí como la methafísica de Aristótil e la arismética de Nicomanchi [*sic*], padre del dicho Aristótil ....' (BN Madrid, MS 10.193, f. 8^r). For other examples, see Ayala's version of Bersuire's Livy, and the anonymous Castilian versions of Vilagarut's Catalan translation of Seneca's *Tragedies*; on these texts, see *Las décadas de Tito Livio*, ed. Curt J. Wittlin (Barcelona: Puvill Libros, [1983]), I, 107–19; Nicholas Round, 'Las traducciones medievales, catalanas y castellanas, de las tragedias de Séneca', *AEM*, 9 (1974–79), 187–227.

[20] Apart from those already mentioned, see Augustine's *De civitate Dei*, translated for Queen María (1434) by Gómez García del Castillo (via Catalan and French), who includes excerpts of commentaries by Thomas Waleys and Nicholas Trevet. Pero López de Ayala translated Gregory's *Moralium libri* (a commentary on Job) and added his own glosses. He also incorporated Bersuire's glosses on Livy in the text of his version of the Frenchman's translation. Vegetius's *De re militari*, translated *c.* 1400 by Fray Alonso de Cristóbal, contains both a spiritual and literal gloss. As is well known, Santillana commissioned Castilian commentaries on Dante, adapted from those by Pietro Alighieri and Benvenuto da Imola.

They number approximately thirty in all, which, judging by a preliminary comparison, is more than were written in either France or England. And they were attached to all kinds of literary work, ranging from moral didacticism (e.g. Santillana's *Proverbios*) to courtly love (e.g. Pedro de Portugal's *Sátira*) and treatises on the education and manners of the nobility, like Valera's *Espejo de verdadera nobleza*. Worthy of special note as far as poetry is concerned, is the vast *Cancionero de Barrantes* (1479–82), which amongst other things contains the major works of three of the great poets of the fifteenth century (Mena, Santillana and Pérez de Guzmán) accompanied by an almost unbroken series of commentaries and glosses in Castilian and, to a lesser degree, in Latin.[21]

I shall return to some of these commentaries later; but with regard to scope and procedure, the corpus as a whole (including glosses on translations) may be loosely grouped into three categories. The first consists of a series of short notes either interpolated within the text, as I have explained above, or, which is more usual, written separately in the margins. They aim to provide the minimum of information necessary to understand the text and grasp at least a small part of its intellectual or literary background. Thus, they offer concise explanations of historical or mythological references, of etymologies and sources. Their function, in the words of the anonymous translator of Boethius's *De consolatione*, was to expound the text 'sólo tocante a la letra' (Schiff, *La Bibliothèque*, p. 179).

As I have already explained, this style of gloss was closely associated with one of the popular methods of translation. And it is probably from here that Castilian writers drew much of their inspiration to annotate the original works of their contemporaries, exactly as if they had before them translations of the classics. By far the most striking example of this is offered by the brief, but very numerous, glosses attached at an early stage in the manuscript tradition to Mena's *Laberinto*, partially under the supervision of the poet himself.[22] The scope and intention of these are much the same

---

[21] See Brian Dutton and Charles Faulhaber, 'The "Lost" Barrantes *Cancionero* of Fifteenth-Century Spanish Poetry', in John S. Geary (ed.), *Florilegium Hispanicum: Medieval and Golden Age Essays Presented to Dorothy Clotelle Clarke* (Madison: HSMS, 1983), pp. 179–202; Angel Gómez Moreno and Carlos Alvar, 'Más noticias sobre el *Cancionero de Barrantes*', *RFE*, 66 (1986), 111–13.

[22] These notes are contained in five MSS: BN Paris, fonds espagnol, MS 229, Colombina 83–6–10, Lázaro Galdiano MS 208, Bartolomé March (Madrid) MS

as the marginal notes in manuscripts of *De consolatione Philosophiae*, and though they seem insubstantial, the scribes who added them clearly believed that, along with the rubrics, they offered vital assistance in guiding the reader through the text. Leaving aside the difficult question of authorship, their importance resides less in the information they convey (though this is by no means always insignificant), than in what they reveal about the way Mena's poem was presented to contemporary readers. It would be impossible even without the glosses to ignore entirely the ambitiously learned nature of *El laberinto*, with its wealth of classical allusion and linguistic innovation. But the poem without the glosses is not the same work. By the constant spotlighting and laying bare of Mena's erudition, the reader's responses are conditioned: by being in constant receipt of nuggets of fact, of succinct explanations of the poem's many obscurities, the reader becomes a pupil of Mena, the poet-sage. This is one of the most important implications of commentaries and glosses of even such apparently narrow scope as these, and I return to it below.

The glosses I have just been describing are essentially factual; but there is another kind which, although similar in terms of its brevity, serves a quite different purpose. It is represented by the marginal annotation found in manuscripts of Ayala's translation of St Gregory's *Moralia*, and in those of the anonymous translation of Seneca's *Epistles*, both of which were popular items in aristocratic libraries. The function of these glosses is not to explain by providing a small quantity of concrete information about the text and its sources, but to paraphrase and summarize the author's main arguments. This procedure was strongly advocated by pedagogical theorists as an aid to memorization. But it is also related, of course, to the contemporary fondness for aphoristic literature: the readers of these manuscripts had before them, written out in the margins, a ready-made collection of *sententiae*. Indeed, as José Luis Coy has demonstrated in an important article, Ayala later gathered together his glosses and published them separately under the title *Flores de los 'Morales sobre Job'*.[23]

20–5–6 and Barcelona, Central MS 1967 (I am grateful to Professor Maxim Kerkhof, who is currently preparing an edition of *El laberinto*, for this last reference).

[23] José Luis Coy, 'Las *Flores de los "Morales sobre Job"*, de Pero López de Ayala, y las notas de los MSS 10.136–38 de la Biblioteca Nacional de Madrid', *REH*, 9 (1975), 403–23. Coy notes about 600 correspondences between *Las flores* and the

Although these two kinds of annotation guide the readers' perceptions in different ways (one highlights the learned substratum of the work, the other directs them to what is thought most worthy of memorization), they remain nonetheless closely related. They are both entirely subordinated to the work which they accompany: they lead the reader, so to speak, back to the main text. But the forms of gloss and commentary which are to be considered now are different. The same motives may underlie their composition, in that a commentator, like Cartagena for example, would make the usual claim that the work's historical or mythological references were a source of obscurity, and that his main purpose is to elucidate them, 'contando brevemente quanto bastava a la declaración de la letra'.[24] In practice, however, the approach is far more discursive. The result is that the reader is drawn out into the wider realms of historical and literary discussion or philosophical speculation: the text becomes a point of departure, rather like the text of a sermon. Indeed this resemblance is often made more immediate by the way the work is arranged in the manuscript. A poem like Mena's *Coronación*, for example, could be divided up into separate stanzas, or even fragments of a stanza, and the commentary then written out underneath the text, rather than around it in the margins of the whole page.[25]

This broad and diverse group constitutes the largest of the three categories, and within it one finds a variety of exegetical styles. Some, like Cartagena in his Senecan treatises, ranged over a wide number of subjects. In others, one notices more or less systematic attempts to focus attention upon a particular aspect of the work,

---

marginal glosses; some of the latter have undergone revision, others are copied verbatim. He also points out that the notes provide the source for some passages of *El rimado*.

[24] *Tratado de la providencia*, f. xxxvii\u1d5b; see also: the anonymous translator of Boethius (Schiff, *La Bibliothèque*, p. 179); Diego de Valera, *Tratado en defensa de las virtuosas mujeres*, p. 61; Pedro de Portugal, *Sátira de infelice e felice vida*, ed. Luís Adão da Fonseca, in *Obras completas do Condestável Dom Pedro de Portugal* (Lisbon: Fundação Calouste Gulbenkian, 1975), pp. 9–10; Gómez Manrique, 'La péñola', *Can. cas.*, II, 57.

[25] This layout is adopted by the scribes of the *Cancionero de San Román* (Biblioteca de la Real Academia de la Historia, 2–7–2, MS 2, ff. 190\u1d5b–251\u02b3). The distinction between a commentary and a sermon is not always clear. The work by Cartagena generally known as the *Glosa a San Crisóstomo* probably has more in common with the latter. It is a philosophical discussion of cause and effect based on the proposition that harm is always self-inflicted.

whether historical references (e.g. Santillana on his *Proverbios*), moral philosophy and politics (e.g. Díaz de Toledo on Santillana's *Proverbios* and Gómez Manrique's *Exclamación*), or sources (e.g. the two anonymous commentators on Mena's *Laberinto*). What is striking about all these commentaries which purport to expound the literal level of the text, is the apparent lack of interest in matters of rhetoric. It is true that many glosses examine isolated lexical questions, such as etymology, neologisms and difficulties of translation; this is a noticeable feature of Cartagena's glosses on Seneca. But even so, observations on rhetorical usage are a rarity during the fifteenth century, and seem, on the basis of a rapid comparison, to be rarer than in Alfonso el Sabio's *General estoria*.[26] The extent to which content, not form, is the dominant concern is reflected by the occasional, yet fascinating, use of the commentary as a medium for artistic expression. Poets like Mena, Santillana and Pedro de Portugal sometimes turned their explanations of classical myth and history into carefully wrought anecdotes, notable for the quality of their literary style. In other words, glosses could possess a purely ornamental function, enabling a writer to indulge in the simple pleasure of telling a tale.[27]

Finally, there is a small group of works which, like Virgil's *Aeneid*, Mena's *Coronación* or the *Coplas de Mingo Revulgo*, have been subjected to detailed allegorical exegesis. This is not the place to dwell on the subject of exegetical method, but one observation does need to be made by way of conclusion to this rapid survey of form and content. Recent critics have often pointed out that the allegorical verse of Mena's *Coronación* should not, indeed cannot, be read separately from its prose commentary: the two are fused together to form a unified whole. But the full implications of this unity have not been properly recognized. It is clear that Mena wished his work to be considered as a sort of *prosimetrum* (like Christine de Pizan's *Epistre d'Othéa*), with a few lines of verse

---

[26] For Cartagena's glosses, see Olga Tudorică Impey, 'Alfonso de Cartagena, traductor de Séneca y precursor del humanismo español', *Prohemio*, 3 (1972), 473–94, at pp. 478–79, 488–89. For *General estoria*, see Rico, *Alfonso el Sabio*, pp. 184–87. The outstanding XVc exception is Hernán Núñez's commentary on *El laberinto*, in which rhetorical analysis plays a significant part.

[27] See Lida de Malkiel, *Juan de Mena*, pp. 130–38; Julian Weiss, 'Las *fermosas e pelegrinas estorias*: sobre la glosa ornamental del siglo quince', *Revista de Literatura Medieval*, in press.

alternating with a section of prose, rather than the whole poem followed by its commentary.

The comparison with the *prosimetrum* is also relevant to other poems equipped with commentaries, in that they combine to make a new text. But the principle applies by extension to all substantial allegorical and literal expositions, whether of prose or verse. This is to say that a commentary radically alters the character of a text: it becomes, in the process of annotation and expansion, a different book. The commentator has the power to influence the reader's perceptions about a work, by highlighting those aspects which are of particular interest to him. *El laberinto* as presented by the anonymous Paris commentator (fonds espagnol, MS 229) is an imitation of a classical epic; as presented by the commentator of the *Cancionero de Barrantes* it is a compendium of learning, especially of geographical knowledge. The exegete, like Díaz de Toledo in his analysis of the poems of Santillana and Gómez Manrique, can also use the text as the basis of a creation of his own, by bringing together the contents of the poem and his assessment of its implications and sources, and placing them all on the same plane of perspective. The procedure is the same as that employed in the poetic genre known as *glosa*: both poets and commentators construct something new by elaborating a variation on a given theme.

As I have said, commentators on vernacular texts were at liberty to explain and develop their author's ideas in any way they wished. Nevertheless, they worked within obvious restrictions created by the fact that they were writing for a lay public. That certain issues and exegetical techniques were deemed inappropriate is made clear by Alfonso de Madrigal when, in 1449, he dedicated to Santillana the Castilian version of his Latin commentary on the Eusebius/Jerome *Chronici canones*. He emphasizes that the two versions are complementary, and that the Latin text contains erudition beyond the ken of the average lay reader.[28] One important difference between a professional and non-professional commentary is the way in which sources and authorities are cited. When Latin writers are quoted in vernacular commentaries and glosses, the commentator usually makes a point of translating them. 'Irán algunas auctoridades latinas en el siguiente comento', explains Mena in the prologue

---

[28] See Ronald G. Keightley, 'Alfonso de Madrigal and the *Chronici canones* of Eusebius', *JMRS*, 7 (1977), 225–48.

to his *Coronación*, 'assí métricas como prosaycas'. And then, in an apologetic tone which one normally does not associate with this poet, he continues:

> Y de aquesto los no latinos ruégoles no se enojen, ca házese porque vulgarizando el latín, no parece el arte del latino metro y destrúyese la prosa. Pero hallarán luego lo que quiere cada una dellas dezir, siguiente auctoridad.
> (f. 267ʳ)

But there were exceptions; not all critics and scribes expected a lack of classical erudition on the part of their readers. The most interesting example of this is the anonymous commentary on Mena's *Laberinto* (Paris, MS 229) which consists by and large of classical sources and analogues, quoted in the original Latin, for the salient passages of that epic. Certain evidence suggests that the commentator may have been an Italian writing for the Aragonese court at Naples, sometime toward the end of the century.[29] Whatever the case, he obviously had in mind a select group of readers who were familiar with the works of Virgil, Lucan and others in the original Latin. This manuscript commentary points to one of the reasons why marginal annotation, however slight it may seem, deserves closer attention than it has hitherto received. It helps to place a work in its proper historical context, and to clarify the sorts of readership for which particular manuscripts were destined.

The old association between poetry and philosophy constituted the most important, though often unspoken, premise on which literary commentators based their work. Their point of departure was the fundamental assumption that something—whether factual information, moral or spiritual teaching—could be gleaned from

---

[29] The text of the commentary, though not that of the poem itself, contains a striking number of Italianisms, considerably more than one usually finds even during this period of Italian linguistic influence (I am grateful to Professor Ralph Penny and Mr. Fred Hodcroft for their comments on this matter). The hypothesis is strengthened by other internal evidence (e.g., references to mid-XVc Italian works like Flavio Biondo's *Roma restaurata*), and by the probable Italian provenance of the Paris MS. I discuss these points at greater depth in a forthcoming study of the glosses and commentaries on Mena's epic written during the XV and XVIc. See Florence Street, 'The Text of Mena's *Laberinto* in the *Cancionero de Ixar* and its Relationship to Some Other Fifteenth-Century MSS', *BHS*, 35 (1958), 63–71. This study is inaccurate in several important respects: see Maxim Kerkhof, 'Hacia una nueva edición crítica del *Laberinto de Fortuna* de Juan de Mena', *JHP*, 7 (1982–83), 179–89. A few extracts are published by John G. Cummins, *Laberinto de Fortuna* (Madrid: Cátedra, 1979).

the study of verse. This approach is most closely connected with the exegesis of classical poets, and is epitomized by attitudes toward Virgil's *Aeneid*. But in time, the concept also came to be applied to the moderns. Early commentators on Dante, paralleling the Virgilian exegetes, portrayed his greatest poem as an all-encompassing compendium of the arts and sciences: a view which found ready acceptance in fifteenth-century Castile. Petrarch too, though at first best known as the moral philosopher of *De remediis* and *De vita solitaria*, acquired the status of the poet-sage. According to the commentator of sonnet 116, the poem was intended, in part, to be an erudite display of geographical knowledge, showing that Petrarch 'avía leýdo muchos e diversos cosmógraphos e avía en prompto la recordación dellos'.[30]

One encounters the notion of poetic erudition in many guises during the reign of Juan II. It was a subject of debate amongst the first generation of poets, and Baena, in response to contemporary currents of thought, gave it considerable prominence in his description of the ideal courtier. The concept of the wise and well-read poet acquired a more emphatically classical veneer with the poets of Santillana's generation. They constructed for themselves a poetic world with a distinctly literary frame of reference; and the pass-key to this world was real, or feigned, familiarity with the canon of *auctores*.

According to Keith Whinnom, the use of the term *autor* by a Castilian writer of the fifteenth century does not necessarily mean that he is 'either laying claim to *auctoritas* or pretending to a place in the canon of the classics'. There are occasions when such is the case (for instance when Mena calls Villena 'un autor muy sciente', or when Fernando de la Torre refers to Santillana as 'esta actoridad'), but even so, Whinnom was right to emphasize that we should concentrate not on broad literary terms but on the contents of the text itself. These views are endorsed and developed in Dagenais's reappraisal of the term *tratado* as it appears in the sentimental romance.[31] Following this lead, therefore, I propose to examine

[30] Ed. Carr, 'A Fifteenth-Century Castilian Translation and Commentary of a Petrarchan Sonnet', p. 139.

[31] '*Autor* and *Tratado* in the Fifteenth Century: Semantic Latinism or Etymological Trap?', *BHS*, 59 (1982), 211–18, at p. 214; Dagenais, 'New Light on the Meaning of "Tra(c)tado"', pp. 135–38. For Juan de Mena, see *Laberinto*, st. 125 (quoted from Whinnom, '*Autor*', p. 212); see also *La obra literaria de Fernando de la Torre*, ed. María Jesús Díez Garretas (Valladolid: Universidad, 1983), p. 188.

some of the ways in which the commentary could confer *auctoritas* upon the writer by demonstrating the intellectual and esthetic qualities of his work.

2 The poet as sage

a) Scribes and scholars

The first poet to receive the kind of learned treatment which had traditionally been reserved for the ancient and modern classics was Santillana. When dedicated in 1439 to Juan II and his son Prince Enrique, his *Proverbios* were already equipped with the poet's own historical glosses. In the following decade, however, Pero Díaz de Toledo, who was to become an important propagandist for the literary talents of the Mendoza family, considerably augmented these glosses; in doing so, he both transformed the aphoristic simplicity of the text and elevated the status of the poet. As glossed by Díaz de Toledo, *Los proverbios* became a theological and philosophical tract. The *sententiae* of each stanza are methodically expanded, their meaning and implications explored with continuous reference to biblical and, to a lesser extent, classical authorities (mainly Aristotle and Seneca).[32] This commentary, which exists in a large number of fifteenth-century manuscripts and early printed books, did much to strengthen Santillana's position as the epitome of the union of arms and letters.

In the 1460s, Díaz de Toledo attempted to do the same for a poem by Santillana's nephew, Gómez Manrique. The latter's *Exclamación e querella de la gobernación* is a morally didactic critique of contemporary politics and a demand for firm government. In response to the controversy which it seems to have aroused when it was first circulated amongst the members of Archbishop Carrillo's court, Díaz de Toledo set about proving two things: that Gómez Manrique deserved to inherit the literary mantle of his two most famous relatives, Santillana and Fernán Pérez de Guzmán, and that 'su escrevir non discrepa de los sanctos e profetas que semejante querella quisieron fazer a Dios' (*Can. cas.*, II, 131). To these ends he

---

[32] *Los proverbios con su glosa (Sevilla, 1494)*, ed. Antonio Pérez Gómez, Incunables Poéticos Castellanos, 11 (Cieza: 'La fonte que mana y corre', 1965); for an analysis of the commentary, see Nicholas Round, 'Pero Díaz de Toledo: A Study of the Fifteenth-Century *Converso* Translator in his Background', unpublished D. Phil. thesis (Univ. of Oxford, 1966), pp. 632–40.

drew on all the vast resources of erudition which he had previously brought to bear in his commentary on *Los proverbios*. The arguments which underlie the series of *mundus inversus* images of which the poem is composed are authenticated by citations from writers ranging from St Augustine to Alfonso el Sabio. The result is, as before, twofold: the emergence of a new and scholarly treatise, this time centered on a unified political theme, and the elevation of a poet to the rank of contemporary *auctor* who continues the traditions of the saints and prophets of old.[33]

Whether or not Díaz de Toledo would have pretended to argue that these two aristocratic poets were themselves in possession of the wealth of erudition which he deploys on their behalf is open to question. What he does demonstrate, however, is that these two poems attain one of the most highly valued literary ideals of the Middle Ages, that of brevity: 'sermo brevis magnam in se sententiam continens'. By situating their verse in its literary and philosophical context, by exploring the *sententia* through the *verba*, he proves that the poet could, in Aristotelian terms, be a sage in potentiality, if not in act. With *letrados* like Díaz de Toledo in their service, the nobility could acquire an effortless veneer of intellectual profundity.[34]

But the poet most clearly cast in the mould of polymath, following in the footsteps of Virgil, Dante and Jean de Meun, was Juan de Mena. Epic poets in particular had always been thought to possess universal wisdom, and Mena's ambitions to continue this tradition were plain right from the start of his poetic career, when he transformed his youthful eulogy of Santillana, *La coronación*, into a vast compendium of learning. This aspect obviously appealed to one Italian reader of the poem, who preceded the text with a detailed index, which lists the contents of the stanzas and summarizes the moral lessons to be learnt from each.[35] This work,

---

[33] For Round's assessment of the political unity of this commentary, see 'Pero Díaz de Toledo', pp. 669–70. See also the anonymous commentator on Manrique's *Loores e suplicaciones a Nuestra Señora*, who concludes that the poet wrote 'como discreto e letrado' (*Can. cas.*, II, 149).

[34] This was not an exclusively XVc phenomenon: the XIIIc King of Aragon, Jacme II, used Arnaut de Vilanova for similar purposes. His brief Provençal prayer to the Virgin on ecclesiastical corruption is given a more forcefully erudite dimension by his secretary's detailed Latin exposition. See the 'Ballata alla vergine di Giacomo II d'Aragona', ed. Cesare de Lollis, *RLR*, 31 (1887), 289–95.

[35] See Paris, BN, fonds espagnol, MS 224: e.g. in st. 8, 'fa una moralità et additione singulare come li figlioli non sono tenuti ad obedire li patri in cosa che

which I examine below, was a stepping-stone: it was *El laberinto* that earned him the praise of later generations, particularly in the Golden Age, with the help of the efforts of commentators such as Hernán Núñez and El Brocense. Yet it is not generally recognized that the move to build upon Mena's reputation as a poetic sage, and to establish him as a serious Spanish counterpart to Dante, was first made just twenty years after his death, well before Hernán Núñez began his famous editorial work at the end of the fifteenth century.

The commentator of the Paris manuscript does not, unfortunately, leave any explicit prefatory views on the quality of the Castilian poem. But there is no doubt from the continuous parallels he draws with classical authors that he considers Mena should be taken seriously as a successor to the epic poets Lucan and Virgil. His extensive glosses, which are concerned primarily with clarifying the poem's sources, seem designed to prove that *El laberinto* was a successful *imitatio* of classical verse. This commentary bolstered Mena's standing from an esthetic point of view; it is complemented by the approach of the cleric and *littérateur* who compiled and annotated the *Cancionero de Barrantes*. He adopts a broader perspective and places the work squarely within the tradition of encyclopedic poetry. That it represents a true marriage of Mercury and Philology is clear from his opening analysis of the poem's title. For him it stands not so much for the twists and turns of Fortune as for the labyrinthine intricacies of wisdom. Borrowing Isidore's definition of Daedalus's construction, he asserts that:

> Semejante es este tratado a este laberinto ... porque ay dentro en él mucho trabajo .... Es comento o escriptura de materias grandes e difíciles, en el qual tratado o scriptura el que entrare o leyere le conviene que lieve para lo entender ovillo de cuerda asaz luenga, que es ayuntamiento de saber muchas e diversas facultades así istorial como de poesía e otras ciencias que continuamente toca. (Bartolomé March, MS 20–5–6, f. 39ʳ)

This author epitomizes the attitude of most vernacular commentators. They were not predominantly concerned with assessing the esthetic merit of a text, or with analysing its form and structure, or the local use of rhetorical colour (although interest in these is not entirely absent). Their main task, as they saw it, was to exploit the possibilities of the content: to show that the text could be fitted into the orthodox scheme of learning, to prove, in short,

---

sia contra li divini precepti' (f. Bʳ). See **also** Lida de Malkiel, *Juan de Mena*, pp. 323–98.

that a poet or prose writer spoke with the force of authority. This, as Pero Díaz de Toledo put it, was 'un digno trabajo' (*Can. cas.*, II, 131).

This approach has much in common with the concept of *exponere reverenter*, so favoured by medieval grammarians and theologians. In the words of the nineteenth-century French scholar, Charles Thurot:

> En explicant leur texte, les glossateurs ... ne cherchent pas à entendre la pensée de leur auteur, mais à enseigner la science elle-même que l'on supposait y être contenue. Un auteur *authentique*, comme on disait alors, ne peut ni se tromper, ni se contredire, ni suivre un plan defectueux, ni être en désaccord avec un autre auteur authentique. On avait recours aux artifices de l'exégèse la plus forcée pour accomoder la lettre du texte à ce que l'on considérait comme la vérité.[36]

This attitude gives the commentaries of Villena and Díaz de Toledo their characteristic flavour. But there were dissenting voices. Not all commentators invariably followed the guidelines of reverent exposition; some occasionally adopted a more openly critical stance, and illustrate how attitudes toward authority gradually evolved in the course of the later Middle Ages and early Renaissance. Taking their cue from late medieval biblical exegetes, secular comment-ators began to approach their pagan authors with an awareness of their weaknesses as well as their genius. As Alistair Minnis has put it, 'at the end of the Middle Ages, *auctores* became more like men', and were treated as 'familiar authors'.[37] In the Castilian commentary tradition, the most interesting case of this critical deference is Hernán Núñez's exposition of *El laberinto*, in which Mena's knowledge of classical antiquity is both praised and judiciously corrected by the later scholar. This kind of criticism was foreshadowed by the anonymous commentator of Paris MS 229; according to him, Mena's skill in imitating classical models, though impressive, is not an unqualified success. To give just one example, he takes issue with the allusion to Queen Artemisa in stanza 64: 'su ystoria es vulgar e la descrive Valerio más a propósito de las palabras aquí scriptas'.[38]

Much more severe is Cartagena in his Senecan commentaries. As

---

[36] Quoted from Gérard Paré *et al.*, *La Renaissance du XII siècle: les écoles et l'enseignement*, Publications de l'Institut d'Études Médiévales d'Ottawa, 3 (Paris: J. Vrin, 1933), pp. 147–50, at p. 149, note 1.

[37] *Medieval Theory of Authorship*, pp. 211–17, at p. 216.

[38] f. 17ᵛ; see also Street, 'The Text of Mena's *Laberinto*', p. 71.

the national philosopher, Seneca represented the summit of pagan wisdom, and Cartagena occasionally addresses him with a familiarity reminiscent of Petrarch's letters to Cicero. But even so, not every word he wrote was to be accepted without question. Cartagena's horror at the admiration expressed by Seneca for suicide, in his treatise *De providencia*, I, exemplifies how the Stoic's philosophy was uncompromisingly subjected to the standards of Catholicism (*Cinco libros*, f. xxxix[r]–[v]). But more relevant here, particularly for its implications with regard to private study, is what Cartagena has to say about Seneca the poet. Commenting on the collection of aphorisms which makes up the second book of *De la providencia*, he offers the novice reader the following general advice:

> quien en esta copilación leyere mucho deve mirar de qué lugares son las doctrinas aquí puestas, que todos los dichos de Séneca no son de ygual auctoridad. (*Cinco libros*, f. lii[v])

Maxims taken from the *Tragedies* are not necessarily to be trusted, he argues, since they come not from Seneca, but from the mouths of his fictional characters. One finds the same concern that the reader should identify the truly 'authoritative voice' of the text a few decades earlier in an anonymous Castilian commentary on Boethius. The commentator warns the reader not to be misled by the opening scene, since the first poem conveys not the despair of Boethius the philosopher, but that of his poetic persona.[39] These exhortations to consider the context of a particular passage and not to accept passively all that one finds in the work of the ancients, links up with the attempts of other writers to inspire readers to cultivate their critical faculties. As we shall see in the third section of this chapter, they were urged to approach the authoritative text in a frame of mind that was both analytical and meditative.

b) Self-exegesis

Five major authors of the period equipped their original works with commentaries and glosses: Santillana (*Los proverbios*), Mena (*La coronación* and, possibly, *El laberinto*), Pedro de Portugal (*Coplas*

---

[39] For Cartagena, see Blüher, *Séneca en España*, p. 146. The compilation of aphorisms, included in *Cinco libros*, and known as *El segundo libro de la providencia de Dios*, is not to be confused with XVc translation of Seneca's *De providentia*, II, which circulated separately. The Boethius commentary is in BN Madrid MS 174; see f. 5[v].

de contemptu mundi and *La sátira de infelice e felice vida*), Diego de Valera (*Tratado en defensa de las virtuosas mujeres* and other treatises) and Gómez Manrique (the consolatory poem to his sister, Juana de Mendoza).[40]

There were a number of motives behind the adoption of these scholarly procedures. As I have already mentioned, an interesting, though relatively minor, factor was the urge to retell *estorias* for their own sake. But what concerns us here is the way that vernacular poets and prose writers did not rely solely on the efforts of *letrados* such as Pero Díaz de Toledo to bolster their status as men of learning in the eyes of their courtly public. They were so keen to lay bare the intellectual framework of some of their most important compositions precisely in order to prove that they themselves were in possession of the knowledge that could be extracted from their work. Plain though it is, this attitude toward self-exegesis was never explicitly stated; for this, we must turn, once again, to Dante. Intensely conscious, as ever, of his authorial dignity, Dante asserts that if modern vernacular poets claim for themselves the same poetic licence as their classical forebears, they should not do so unless they are capable of explaining their work's allegorical structure or rhetorical devices:

> grande vergogna sarebbe a colui che rimasse cose sotto vesta di figura o di colore rettorico, e poscia, domandato, non sapesse denudare le sue parole da cotale vesta, in guisa che avessero verace intendimento.
>
> (*La vita nuova*, XXV, 10; *Opere*, p. 636)

These words apply specifically to the use of rhetoric and allegory, but I believe that they are also appropriate in a much broader context. For it was to avoid this 'grande vergogna', and to display their poetic erudition, that Santillana and his contemporaries took pains to clarify their mythological and historical allusions, to elucidate obscure vocabulary, to give source references and, occasionally, to discuss theological or philosophical questions arising from the text.

One catches a glimpse of this intellectual pride in being in control of the *texto* and *glosa* in Santillana's preface to his *Proverbios*.

---

[40] See also Pedro de Escavias's commentary on his eulogistic *Coplas dirigidas al condestable don Miguel Lucas de Iranzo* (*c.* 1460), whose extant fragment is contained at the end of the *Cancionero de Oñate-Casteñeda*. It is also possible that Rodríguez del Padrón himself added the notes in the Colombina MS of the *Bursario* (5–5–16). I have not yet seen the recent ed. by Pilar Saquero Suárez-Somonte and Tomás González Rolán (Madrid: Universidad Complutense, 1984).

Here he adopts the role of an intermediary between the novice reader and a vast world of biblical and classical wisdom. The Prince, he observes, is probably too young to be familiar with all the exemplary figures alluded to in his verse, particularly since they are drawn from a notably diverse range of sources. He will take it upon himself, therefore, to explain and summarize the stories behind these historical characters, adding the significant rider, with all the self-satisfaction of an amateur scholar, that he will specify 'los dichos libros e aun capítulos'.[41] The detail with which he pretends to list his sources could expose him to the accusation that his proverbs are wholly unoriginal, plagiarized from Plato, Socrates, Ovid and other 'philósophos e poetas'. This criticism is treated with studied indifference: 'lo qual yo no contradiría, antes me plaze que assí se crea e sea entendido' (p. 220). It is easy to understand why: for by revealing the origins of his wisdom he demonstrates that he is in possession of received truth, part of that great chain of knowledge which stretches back to 'aquellos que por luenga vida e sotil inquisición alcançaron las esperiencias e causas de las cosas' (p. 220).

Two points need to be made about the meaning and tone of these prefatory statements. Firstly, to use the terminology of the schools, Santillana presents himself not as an *auctor* but as a *compilator*. The distinction is important. It grew into being with the development of concordances, tables of contents and all the other devices used to facilitate the private study and the dissemination of authoritative texts. The compiler did not claim personal responsibility for the content of the text, only its presentation. Even so, because his methods of organizing excerpted material could attain high degrees of sophistication, and because he was thought to fulfil an important intellectual and social function, the compiler earned for himself considerable prestige, especially from the fourteenth

---

[41] *Obras completas*, ed. Gómez Moreno and Kerkhof, p. 217. Santillana is not always exact, however: see *ed. cit.*, p. 245 note 66 and p. 249 note 75. For other examples of his dubious source references, see my art. cited in note 27, above; also, see below, pp. 224–25. It is interesting that Mena and Valera also take pains to give sources for their arguments, and do so with a good deal more precision. Gómez Manrique and Pedro de Portugal, on the other hand, appear more interested in recounting *estorias* and do no more than give very general references (see Pedro's remark to his sister, in the introduction to *La sátira*: 'la fize no autorizada de los grandes e scientíficos varones ... porque la vuestra muy llena industria saberá de quáles jardines salieron estas flores mías', *Obras*, ed. Fonseca, p. 8).

century onwards. Like other late medieval vernacular writers, Santillana exploited the status associated with this literary role; his poem is presented as a compilation of accepted wisdom, cast in a form that has the authority of Solomon's Proverbs and Provençal poetics. Maybe even the fact that he attached an exegetical apparatus to it implies that, like John Gower, he wished to claim for himself a limited *auctoritas*. If so, the hint was certainly not lost on later writers.[42]

We can flesh out the authorial image projected by the prologue, text and commentary by placing the work as a whole in its historical context. *Los proverbios* was dedicated to the *infante* don Enrique only a year or so after he had been placed under the tutelage of Alvaro de Luna, who, naturally enough, appointed members of his own household as guardians.[43] The antagonism between his political faction and Santillana's household may account for the learned presentation of this poem, as well as for the self-conscious and acerbic tone of its prologue. The uncompromising refutation of the faceless *reprehensores*, who are crass enough to doubt the compatibility of arms and letters, and who quibble over the poem's versification, could well be a sneer directed at the intellectual and literary skills of the Prince's newly appointed *ayos*. A far better choice, the work seems to tell us, would have been the compiler of *Los proverbios*, who has the modesty to disclaim philosophical originality, yet who is wise enough to produce a text of sufficient authority to merit its own commentary.

It hardly needs to be emphasized that the urge to elucidate one's text was not constant in the literature of this period. The commentary was just one option open to the writer who wished to parade his learning before the public. As anyone familiar with early *cancionero* verse will know, it was more usual for poets to endeavour to impress their readers with extravagant lists of pagan and patristic *auctores*, and accumulated references to characters from history and myth. Baena's *Dezir a Juan II* is an extreme yet wholly traditional example of this fashionable practice. This allusive, and at times consciously hermetic, approach also underpins many of Santillana's

---

[42] Minnis, *Medieval Theory of Authorship*, pp. 190–210; 'Late-Medieval Discussions of *Compilatio* and the Role of the *Compilator*', *Beiträge zur Geschichte der deutschen Sprache und Literatur*, 101 (1979), 385–421. Apart from Díaz de Toledo's commentary, see the references to *Los proverbios* by Fernando de la Torre, *Obra literaria*, ed. Díez Garretas, pp. 149 and 188.

[43] *Crónica de don Alvaro de Luna*, p. 147.

own compositions. His elegy on the death of Villena, *La defunsión* (1434), opens with an extended series of mythological references, couched in the highly Latinate style which characterizes his most ambitious work. Then, after a seventy-five line introduction, he declares, with heavy irony:

> Si mi baxo estillo aun non es tan plano
> Bien commo querrían los que non leyeron,
> Culpen sus ingenios que jamás se dieron
> A ver las ystorias, que non les explano.
> (st. 10; *Obras completas*, p. 159)

In homage to Villena, Santillana portrays himself as a member of that literary elite, glorying in the exclusive knowledge of *las estorias*. Here, his refusal to expound the text and his disdainful isolation from the unread stand in striking contrast to the image of a generous lay exegete he later attempted to project in *Los proverbios*.

Both the arrogance of *La defunsión* and the charitable didacticism of *Los proverbios* are present in another major work of the 1430s: Juan de Mena's *Coronación*. This is the most elaborate poetic commentary of the period, but it is also by far and away the most personal. Mena enters upon a dialogue with his public, employing techniques of apostrophe and invocation which recall Dante's addresses to the reader in the *Divina commedia*. Like Dante, Mena establishes a relationship with the reader which varies in character and intensity, but which is created with one fundamental end in view: to encourage an active participation in the poem, both on a literary and moral level. This pedagogic dimension of the poem and commentary is of utmost importance and I shall return to it later. But one aspect of Mena's direct addresses to the reader is relevant here, since Mena frequently (indeed more than any other vernacular commentator) takes advantage of the possibilities of self-exegesis to defend the complex literary style he chose to employ in his verse.

As Lida de Malkiel has shown, Mena was a prominent figure in the movement to construct a sublime poetic style based on a Latinate vocabulary and syntax. And *La coronación* contains the earliest and some of the most extreme examples of his attempts to do this. In fact, Mena seems to have experimented deliberately in the knowledge that he could fall back on his commentary, and there explain the meaning of a particular phrase and justify his use of it.

He defends his Latinate vocabulary on many occasions. Early in the poem, for example, he refers to 'el copioso thesoro' of sun in

Spring (st. 2, l. 3; f. 269^r). In explaining this word in a gloss, Mena is not satisfied just by supplying its etymology. More important is the emphasis he places on its appropriate usage: 'Por este nombre "copioso", podemos entender abundoso, y aquesto *bien* se puede atribuyr al abundoso thesoro del sol, pues alumbra sobre todos los luminosos cuerpos' (my italics; f. 270^v). Later, at a crucial stage in the poem's argument, Mena describes how the protagonist crosses to the other side of the hellish river; the verb he employs to depict this escape is 'convolar' (st. 24, l. 1). To understand this, however, the reader is obliged to turn to the commentary where he discovers that it means 'traspassar assí como el ave que vuela, esto es con mucha ligereza' (f. 294^v). But yet again, Mena offers more than a simple definition. He stresses the inherent rightness of his vocabulary, and invites the reader to savour the apt expression given to his ideas:

> assí como aquel que sale del pecado mortal que se entiende por este río, luego este tal con mucha ligereza puede convolar al estado de gracia, y porende está aquí propiamente esta palabra.[44]   (f. 294^v)

Mena does not restrict this vindicatory approach to the more obscure terms, but extends it to words which, though in everyday use, take on a specific metaphoric meaning within the allegory of the poem. Thus, to cite just one example, in his gloss on the description of the sages and poets who have gathered on Parnassus to honour Santillana, he asserts: 'Bien dixo la copla en dezir "rica gente", ca no ay mayor riqueza que la sabiduría, como dize Boecio' (gloss to st. 34, l. 4; ff. 302^v–303^r).

In addition to discussing isolated lexical matters and metaphors, Mena exploits the commentary to justify the broader issues of his literary procedure. The overriding theme of the poem, as I have shown elsewhere ('Juan de Mena's *Coronación*'), is not contemporary satire or the eulogy of Santillana, but the moral and spiritual development of man. A taut structure was of immense importance to Mena in marking out the separate stages in this development and in demonstrating that there was a close causal relationship between fame, wisdom and virtue. And his anxiety to illustrate his theme by means of a well-ordered, logical sequence of events is vividly

---

[44] For other examples of his defence of Latinisms, see the glosses to st. 24, l. 7, 'perdurable' (f. 294^v); st. 34, l. 8, 'caucasea' (ff. 299^v–300^r); similarly, the detailed analysis of the lines 'Y las cunas clareciera/ donde Jupiter naciera' (st. 1, ll. 6–7), is to prove that this obscure periphrasis 'no fue superfluo' (f. 268^v).

expressed by the two statements which act as a frame to the entire work. 'Porque de los enormes e desordenados hechos', writes Mena in his *exordium*, 'no se pueden concluyr devidos fines, pensé de poner en orden de escriptura quatro preámbulos' (f. 266ʳ). Fully aware of the dangers inherent in the obscurity of the verse and the sheer size of the commentary, he hopes that the four-part prologue will enable the reader to steer a clear course through the world of learning represented by *La coronación*. At the very end of the work, his concern to avoid literary chaos is reiterated with even greater urgency. In his closing prayer for earthly fame, he declares:

> Si la mi escritura defectuosa o ignorante procede, [el] deleznable tiempo destruyrá la su denostada recordación. E si *ordenadamente* prosigue, la cuenta de los largos años será a ella vida con gloriosa recordación. (My italics; f. 315ʳ)

Neither of these passages should be dismissed as empty formulae; they mask the confidence of a man who knows where the true strength of his poem lies. *La coronación* has been constructed with the same eye for narrative patterns and the same craftmanship that were later to go into *El laberinto*. But what interests us here is the way that, at key stages in the commentary, the poet's pride surfaces to draw attention to the logic behind his representation of man's spiritual and moral progress. In stanzas 6 to 13, the protagonist witnesses the tortures of the damned, and comes to rest in a stage of fearful incomprehension. In the section that follows he is given moral instruction by the Fury Tisiphone. But morality should not be formed passively; the individual himself should attempt to seek answers. Thus, in stanza 13, the protagonist questions the three Furies about the underlying causes of damnation. Glossing this question (which he later labels with the logical term 'proposición'), Mena writes:

> En este lugar se prosigue el propósito del dezir por esta manera: hasta aquí era dicho de las penas de aquéstos. E por haver adelante determinada la causa por que las padecían, muéstrase aquí la pregunta que se hizo a Tesíphone, Furia infernal. Aquesto por proceder por orden en el dezir.[45] (f. 285ᵛ)

One encounters this concern to show that the narrative follows a

---

[45] The Antwerp edition reads 'y por ver determinadamente la causa, porque las padecían, muéstrase aquí' etc. I have emended this second sentence on the basis of *La coronación (?Toulouse, 1489)*, ed. Antonio Pérez Gómez, Incunables Poéticos Castellanos, 10 (Cieza: 'la fonte que mana y corre', 1964), f. 34ʳ.

coherent pattern on other occasions, but nowhere more plainly than in the commentary to those stanzas leading up to the climax of the poem. The protagonist has at last reached the end of his journey and, in a fit of exultation, invokes the inspiration of Apollo. Then, in stanza 32, there is the following apostrophe, which once again displays the poet's passion for order:

> Ved sesos interiores,
> por dónde començaremos
> las hazañas e loores
> de nuestros antecessores,
> o qué orden les daremos.
> (f. 330ʳ)

At this point, he begins the description of Mount Parnassus, with its symbolic trees and host of pagan poets and philosophers. The commentary which corresponds to this section opens with a passage which affords an interesting insight into Mena's attitude towards his powers of organization:

> En esta parte, la copla comiença de recontar de aquellos apartamientos de la selva, y aquesto por tanto porque hasta aquí exclamó demandando socorro a la sabiduría para lo expressar, después hizo mención a los sentidos para la retener y representar, *porende con razón se pudo poner aquí la presente copla*, començando a expressar de los árboles de la montaña. (My italics; f. 301ᵛ)

The sequence adopted in the verse (invocation—apostrophe — description) is straightforward enough; yet Mena hammers home its logic with an insistence that borders on insecurity.

His intense preoccupation with this aspect of the poem can be explained by reference to one of the major esthetic concerns of the *artes poeticae*. Under the influence of Horace (whose contribution to poetics was thought to reside principally in his emphasis on the methodical disposition of *materia*), Geoffrey of Vinsauf and John of Garland promoted the ideals of conceptual clarity and the organic development of one's theme. They stress that, before being committed to paper, the poem should be perfectly planned in the mind's eye: an archetype, or mental image, of the poem must be conceived before actual composition is begun. Only in this way will it be possible to achieve a lucid and logical structure.[46]

---

[46] Geoffrey of Vinsauf states that the poet, like the architect, first conceives a complete mental image of his project before committing it to paper: 'totamque figurat/ Ante manus cordis quam corporis; et status ejus/ Est prius archetypus quam sensilis ... sitque prius in pectore quam sit in ore./ Mentis in arcano cum rem digesserit ordo,/ Materiam verbis vestire poesis', *Poetria nova*, ll. 46–48, 59–61,

Apart from resorting to the commentary to prove his ability to *proseguir ordenadamente*, Mena also employs it to justify the poem's basic allegorical conceit: the crowning of a real-life Santillana in the presence of a fictional protagonist. At the very outset of the work, the reader learns that the action is set 'en una selva muy brava/ de bosques Thessalianos' (st. 2, ll. 7–8; f. 269^r). Then, prompted perhaps by the contempary fashion for beginning narrative *dezires* with this hackneyed motif, he assures the reader that his allegorical wood is relevant to his purpose: 'Sufre la ficción de aqueste hablar el propósito del dezir, según adelante más claro parescerá' (f. 270^v). More interesting is the meticulousness with which the reader is asked to distinguish between Mena the poet and Mena the protagonist. The latter is merely a narrative device to enable the poet to impress the fiction upon the reader's mind 'más palpablemente' (f. 270^v). As he emphasizes on two further occasions (at the end of the introduction and in the conclusion, glosses to sts 3 and 51 respectively), his fictional presence does not imply that he himself is worthy to be counted amongst the sages of Parnassus. The final stanza, which describes his sudden and inexplicable disappearance from the scene, is added:

> por evitar una callada question que de aquí podría resurgir de alguno que dixera que esta coronación tanto redundava a honor de mí como del señor Yñigo López, a cuya advocación se hizo.... Si yo escreví de la mi subida fue por que subido pudiesse mejor fingir algo de lo que dixe que arriba vi. (f. 314^v)

Whether or not one takes these protestations of modesty seriously, there can be no doubt about the intensity of Mena's self-consciousness at this stage of his poetic career.

But there was another 'callada question' to dispose of. Santillana, a contemporary figure who was very much alive at the time of writing, is incorporated into the abstract timelessness of the narrative. So to undercut the possible incredulity of his readers, Mena has the protagonist himself question the verisimilitude of the situation (st. 42). As he explains in the accompanying gloss, he used this rhetorical ploy 'por satisfazer a los tales con el replicato de la donzella que adelante parecerá' (f. 309^v). And the *donzella*'s reply,

---

ed. Faral, *Les Arts poétiques*, pp. 198–199. See also Douglas Kelly, 'The Scope of the Treatment of Composition in the Twelfth- and Thirteenth-Century Arts of Poetry', *Sp*, 41 (1966), 261–78, especially pp. 272–76; *Medieval Imagination: Rhetoric and the Poetry of Courtly Love* (Madison: Univ. of Wisconsin Press, 1978), pp. 26–56.

given in the following stanza and further developed in its corresponding gloss, is that Santillana leads a double life consisting of immortal fame and virtue, coupled with temporal power here on earth. Moreover, Mena later adds, Santillana himself is a symbol of 'qualquier hombre virtuoso' (gloss to st. 48, l. 9; f. 313ʳ).

The *Coronación* commentary is valuable for many reasons. But in my view its overriding interest is as a display of artistic self-consciousness unparallelled in fifteenth-century Castilian poetry. Mena is never content simply to explain what individual passages mean at an allegorical level, or to support his ideas by invoking traditional *auctores*. Throughout, there is an emphasis on the reasons why he chose to write in the way he did: an anxiety to highlight the aptness of his vocabulary and metaphors, the soundness of his structure, and the correspondence between his allegorical motifs and his overall thematic purpose. There is also an obvious desire to exert authorial control over the interpretation of the work. He explicitly rejects the possibility that certain mythological references possess a relevant allegorical function: their purpose is purely decorative.[47] No doubt he would have endorsed Dante's argument that the true meaning of allegorical verse is that which is given to it by the creator: 'Intendo anche mostrare la vera sentenza di quelle [canzone]', he wrote in the *Convivio*, 'che per alcuno vedere non si può *s'io non la conto*, perché è nascosa sotto figura d'allegoria' (I, ii, 17; *Opere*, p. 681).

But the commentary is more that just the vehicle for the literary ambitions of a young *letrado* hoping to impress his fellow poets. It expresses the author's defensiveness as much as his pride, and constitutes a form of protection against adverse criticism; it thus foreshadows Díaz de Toledo's attempts to safeguard Gómez Manrique's budding reputation against those who interpreted his *Exclamación* 'a no sana parte'. Mena's self-exegesis is both a personal manifesto of his intellectual and literary prowess and a defensive wall constructed around his newly-established position as a contempory poetic *sabio*.

---

[47] See the glosses to the myths of Clytia and Salmacis, in sts 25 and 34 respectively; also Mena's comment on the philosophers' thrones, mentioned in st. 35, which are 'de fieras esculpidas'—these wild beasts have no deep significance and are mentioned merely in order to 'afermosear la fábula' (f. 304ᵛ).

3   Literary education

When, in the first decade of the fourteenth century, Dante addressed the secular, non-professional readers of his *Convivio*—the 'volgari e non litterati'—he spoke to them of two kinds of education: the philosophical and the literary. On the one hand, he summoned them to take part in his banquet of wisdom, and on the other, he invited them to adopt his commentary as a model of literary interpretation. Its exegetical procedures, he declared, would guide them in their future attempts to understand the workings of allegory:

> non solamente darà diletto buono a udire, ma sottile ammaestramento e a così parlare e a così intendere l'altrui scritture.   (I, ii, 17; *Opere*, p. 681)

About one hundred years later, Castilian writers responded to the spread of lay literacy in similar fashion. Their academic prologues, commentaries and glosses, together with reference manuals such as Boccaccio's *De montibus* and Madrigal's *Comento sobre Eusebio*, offered the layman an array of practical wisdom and concrete information about specific texts and the literary-historical problems arising from them.[48] But these forms of critical apparatus also reflect an implicit desire to provide the inexperienced with 'sottile ammaestramento' in the art of reading. This pedagogic tendency is most apparent in the work of Villena and Juan de Mena. Their efforts to educate their readers reveal a hitherto unexamined aspect of their literary personalities, and help us to see more clearly why they felt the study of poetry could contribute so substantially to the creation of an aristocratic intellectual elite.

a)   Villena's 'contynua lectura e reposado estudio'
Echoing Dante's appraisal of his *Convivio*, Villena maintained that *Los doze trabajos de Hércules* could serve as a practical treatise on the exegetical method. The bare bones of his commentary on the Hercules myths supplied, as he put it, the 'manera e arteficio' which would enable Pero Pardo to work out his own interpretation of the text (ed. Morreale, p. 14). In short, the latter would learn by

---

[48] Boccaccio wrote *De montibus* as a practical guide for those who 'se rebuelven en saber las istorias de los antigos', but whose ignorance of the texts' geographical allusions endangers 'el seso istorial' (anon. trans. owned by Santillana, BN Paris, fonds espagnol 458, f. 1ʳ). Madrigal defined Eusebius's *Chronici* as a 'llave et glosa ... de todas las ystorias' (Schiff, *La Bibliothèque*, p. 42).

example how to manipulate the various levels of allegorical meaning and, from being a novice reader, he would develop into one of the *leedores especulativos* whom Villena mentions with so much admiration throughout his work. But what was meant by the term 'speculative reader'? And what exactly was involved in literary study that it should be given pride of place in his scheme of knowledge? To answer these questions we must return to his commentary on the *Aeneid*.

Glossing the opening lines of the prologue, he explains that he compiled this 'información prohemial' so as to encourage the lay reader to devote serious attention to the work as a whole. Without his *accessus*, he claims, 'ne se moviera tancto su voluntad a la contynua lectura e reposado estudio de la obra' (f. 4ʳ). This statement is crucial; it summarizes ideas which recur throughout the *Aeneid* commentary and which are also to be encountered in his two other exegetical works, *Los doze trabajos* and the gloss on 'Quoniam videbo coelos'. These ideas about the methods and circumstances of literary study originate in the fundamental tenets of medieval pedagogical theory, and hence offer yet another example of the way that the aristocracy began to construct an intellectual ideal using materials borrowed from the academic world.

Firstly, the implications of 'contynua lectura'. At its most basic, this phrase suggests the ability to read fluently. At the end of the prologue, Villena includes a series of 'avisaciones al nuevo leedor', which are in the main designed to teach the rudiments of punctuation and orthography. Their importance is underlined in a gloss which shows that he clearly entertains a low opinion of his contemporaries' ability to read their mother tongue:

> Queriendo aun dar mayor cumplimiento ha su doctrina, informa ha los romancistas cómo lean, puncten e pausen, por que mejor entiendan el fructo de la obra. Ca para los letrados non era menester, que ya saben e han visto quan pocos buenos leedores de romance se fallavan, e porque [por] mal leer se podrié mal entende[r] e non alcançar el fructo que devrién e podrién alcançar bien leyendo. (f. 16ᵛ)

This is straightforward enough: the first step towards under-standing a text is to know how to punctuate, where to pause and take breath. Controlled reading is especially necessary because it enables one not just to perceive the grammatical structure of the sentence, but also (and the full significance of this will become clearer in due course) to reflect on the deeper meaning hidden from immediate view: 'por que aya mayor espacio de pensar lo que lee, e pensando lo entienda' (f. 17ᵛ). Villena's emphasis on skilful reading is entirely conventional. Compare it, for example, with the observation of one of the most important teachers of Salamanca University, the jurist and rhetorician Juan Alfonso de Benavente:

> ad hoc quod aliquis bonus litteratus fiat, has scientias per ordinem debet scire. Primo debet scire bene legere, quia sicut baptismus est ianua omnium sacramentorum ... sic bene legere totius discipline et omnium scientiarum ianua et fundamentum existit.[49]

'Contynua lectura' also consists of daily reading and memorization. For the benefit of 'el perezoso leedor', Villena divided his translation into 366 chapters, one specifically for each day of the year (f. 16ᵛ). Classical texts were frequently split up into chapters by their fifteenth-century translators in order to facilitate their study by vernacular readers. In the case of Virgil's epic, however, this practice is not employed simply as a concession to those idle aristocrats who, as Villena puts it, 'non quieren tancto estar en el leer de las estorias quanto cumple al entender dellas, e si luenga es la razón déxanla començada' (f. 16ᵛ). This is no doubt one motive, but it is by no means the whole story. One of the most important precepts laid down by pedagogical authorities was that the student should keep beside him a text-book complete with glosses from which he should select a daily passage for study and meditation. It was a practice designed primarily to train the memory, the source and foundation of all sound wisdom. How widespread a notion this had become could be illustrated by reference to many medieval authorities from both academic and theological circles.[50] But it is particularly relevant to fifteenth-century Castile that the importance attached to selecting a 'thought for the day' should have the added authority of Seneca. Attacking, in his second epistle, those who

---

[49] *Ars et doctrina studendi et docendi*, ed. Bernardo Alonso Rodríguez, Bibliotheca Salmanticensis, II, Textus, 1 (Salamanca: Universidad Pontificia, 1972), p. 52; also pp. 100–03. The treatise (1453), was primarily intended as a guide to teaching and studying law, but Benavente claimed that the pedagogical principles (drawn from a wide range of classical and medieval sources) held good for any subject whatever. I am grateful to Emilio de la Cruz Aguilar of the Universidad Complutense de Madrid for bringing this work to my attention, and discussing its contents with me. He has published a translation, *Arte y teoría de estudiar y enseñar*, RFDUCM, 67 (1982), 227–55; 68 (1983), 211–18.

[50] Benavente, *Ars*, pp. 88–91; in a different context, Ramon Llull divided his *Libre de contemplació en Deu* into 366 chapters to provide material for daily prayer and medition.

stray thoughtlessly from book to book, he argues that every day one should return to a small but choice group of works offering the finest *exempla* and most reliable *consolatio*. Then, he tells Lucillus:

> quando muchas cosas abrás leýdo escoge una, la qual aquel día te quede en la memoria. Ca yo mesmo tengo esta forma e regla, que de muchas cosas que yo cada día leo e aprendo, retengo en mí una.[51]

These ideas must have influenced Villena's distribution of the *Aeneid* over 366 chapters—particularly since he reassures the reader that each will contain 'sentencia complida' (f. 16^v). Viewed in this way, the poem and commentary may be seen as a kind of vade-mecum, offering the laity a year-long source of edification and delight.

The emphasis placed on daily selection and disciplined memorization leads naturally on to the concept of meditative reading, or 'reposado estudio'. However, before this goal could be reached, there were certain other steps to follow.

It was traditionally advocated that before embarking upon detailed textual analysis, the student should first acquire a general overview (Benavente, *Ars*, p. 71). With an initial impression of the work's scope and purpose in mind, one is then equipped to proceed to an examination of its constituent parts. This is done according to the well-known scholastic method of the *divisio*, which, as Benavente puts it, 'illustrem et perspicuam totam efficit orationem'.[52] In other words, the process is one of a gradual narrowing of focus. It is a procedure which Villena clearly encourages his readers to follow in their approach to the *Aeneid*. Firstly, in his

---

[51] BN Madrid, MS 9.215, f. 2^r. See also *Epistle* 94, cited by Benavente as an authority for his advice on daily memorization (p. 91); and Santillana's recommendation to his nephew, Pedro de Mendoza, that the *Epistles* should be 'vuestro compañero e comensal continuo' in *Obras completas*, ed. Gómez Moreno and Kerkhof, p. 458.

[52] Benavente, *Ars*, p. 72, quoting the *Novella commentaria* of Juan de Andrés, an authority on canon law, and citing Cicero, *De inventione*, I, xxii, 31. The *divisio* was an essential part of the rational process, hence fundamental in the acquisition of wisdom; see Hugh of St Victor: 'Modus legendi in dividendo constat ... Doctrina autem ab his quae magis nota sunt incipit, et per eorum notitiam ad scientiam eorum quae latent pertingit. Praeterea ratione investigamus; ad quam proprie pertinit dividere, quando ab universalibus ad particularia descendimus dividendo, et singulorum naturas investigando', *Eruditionis didascalicae libri septem*, ed. J.-P. Migne, PL, 176 (Paris, 1854), cols 739–838, at col. 772 (Bk III, x). For the influence of these methods on Dante, see Jenaro-MacLennan, 'Autocomentario', pp. 83–90, 120–22; for Mena, see *Coronación*, e.g., glosses to stanzas 1–4.

prologue, he sets before them a broad view of the poem as a whole, and urges them to consider 'la yntención collectiva de la eneydal compusición' (f. 3ᵛ; ed. Santiago Lacuesta, p. 34). The *argumentos* (defined as 'aquello mediante lo qual la verdat de la cosa saber se puede', f. 18ʳ) fulfil the same function, but on a smaller scale: they help to acquire an appreciation of the full significance of a passage before descending to particular details. Continuing in this way, distinctions are then made, by a variety of scribal devices, between paragraphs, sentences and clauses, until, as Villena exlaims:

> todo syn confusión venga ha noticia del leedor, que alguna dubda notable non quede por solver e paresca claramente lo que la textual texedura contiene, e se vea el artificio del ordenador reluzir con cierta regla scientífica e plazible.⁵³ (f. 17ᵛ)

Even when examined in this fashion, however, the text does not necessarily reveal all its secrets. For this, readers should then appeal to their imaginative and critical faculties and subject individual passages to the methods of the *quaestio*. This entails putting questions to the text, searching for contradictions or inconsistencies, and finding solutions to the problems posed.⁵⁴ It is, to a great extent, a comparative approach, requiring the ability to perceive relationships both between component passages and between those passages and the whole. How Villena puts this technique to work in his exegesis of the *Aeneid* has already been discussed in the chapter on allegory. The deeper levels of the poem are laid bare 'ynbestigando por congecturas', 'convivando unos dichos con otros', or 'coligendo las dispersas congecturas' (ff. 117ᵛ–18ʳ). According to Villena's meticulous calculations, the account of Aeneas's wanderings in Bk II is unacceptable in terms both of fact and of verisimilitude. But, as he points out, 'en la ymposibilidat desto paresce la ficción' (f. 118ʳ). The incredible nature of the narrative was, in other words, a deliberate tactic on the part of Virgil; he consciously placed 'ciertos pasos en diversos capítulos' to act as hidden signals for the inquisitive reader to

---

⁵³ BN MS 17.975: 'todos ... vengan' emended on basis of BN MS 10.111, f. xviiiᵛ.

⁵⁴ Benavente, *Ars*, pp. 73, 77–78; see also Villena's commentary on 'Quoniam videbo coelos tuos', which consists of. his solutions to the 'fermosa serie de qüistiones' that arise from Psalm 8.3 (ed. Cátedra, p. 90); also, *La coronación* (references to 'calladas questiones' at ff. 309ᵛ and 314ᵛ), and the anonymous Dante commentary (Escorial, MS S-II-13, ff. 48ᵛ and 52ᵛ).

question the reality of the literal level and thus arrive at a more profound understanding of the author's intentions.

Villena's advice to place each passage within its broad context extends beyond the individual work and applies with equal force to literature as a whole. As he declares in one section of the prologue, whoever wishes to learn the secrets of myths ('las ystorias') and to grasp the intentions of the *auctores* 'cumple que vea muchos ystoriales e abeze su entendimiento ha la universal aprehensiva' (f. 12^r; ed. Santiago Lacuesta, p. 41). What this recommendation of wide reading involves is explained more precisely in the accompanying gloss:

> el diligente leedor sabrá los secretos de las ystorias, que son los yntegumentos ho pasos obscuros, abezando su entendimiento por contynuo leer; e non solamente una ystoria mas muchas, e muchos actores de una mesma ystoria, por que falle en algunos dellos lo que otros non avrán dicho. Ansí que ha la universidat de las ystorias e[s]tienda su entendimiento. (f. 12^r)

In this context, 'contynuo leer' does not imply the concepts of literary dissection and critical comparison which we have discussed above. One reads widely not to get a different perspective on the same story, but simply to accumulate more facts about it. (Villena's own handling of the Hercules myth is a practical example of this.) All wisdom, all history and myth form a unified whole, and, in accordance with this view, readers should strive to fill the gaps in their perception of that unity and seek to acquire 'la universal aprehensiva'.

So far, we have concentrated on the analytic modes of literary study, which were based on the methods of the *quaestio* and *divisio*. We turn now to the association between reading and meditation which, evoked by the phrase 'reposado estudio', Villena established as one of the principal goals of the aspiring reader.

First of all, it should be emphasized that it would be inaccurate to interpret this reference to calm or restful study as merely yet another instance of the theory of literature as recreation: a flight from the sin of idleness, a temporary escape from care and toil before returning refreshed to the daily business of living. It is true that these ideas were so pervasive in medieval literary thought that they may well be encompassed by the term 'reposado estudio'; but, in this particular context, they could offer only a partial explanation of it.

Judging by its very frequency, *reposo* was without doubt a basic element in Villena's stock of philosophical terms. It corresponded to the Latin *quies* and, like that word, it spanned a wide semantic range. Besides denoting physical rest, it also had important moral and intellectual implications, which can be illustrated by examples drawn from the two earlier essays in exegesis, *Los doze trabajos de Hércules* and the gloss on 'Quoniam videbo'.[55] In the introduction to the former work, Villena informs his patron, Pero Pardo, that the twelve myths have almost unlimited allegorical potential. They are best examined, he continues, 'catando con reposado ojo de la investigativa' (ed. Morreale, p. 11). Later, towards the very end of the treatise, the advice is repeated, as Pardo is encouraged to multiply the meanings of the tales 'en el reposo de vuestro entendimiento' (p. 121). What Villena has in mind here when he talks of intellectual repose, is the concept of *lectio*, one of the fundamental principles of both monastic writers and the academics of the grammar curriculum.

In brief, *lectio* entailed a meditation on the written word. It was often described in gustatory terms: theological authors in particular spoke of 'tasting' a text with the 'palatum cordis', or 'in ore cordis'.[56] In monastic circles, it suggested a prayerful reading; for the schoolmen, whose authorities stretched back to Cassiodorus, the meditation was, on the other hand, more intellectual in emphasis: its objective was not rest in God, but the acquisition of knowledge. According to Hugh of St Victor, the analytical mode of reading led naturally on to that state of inward reflection which represented the culmination of all wisdom: 'Meditatio principium sumit a lectione; nullis tamen regulis stringitur aut praeceptis lectionis. . . . Principium ergo doctrinae est in lectione, consummatio in meditatione'.[57] This movement away from the mechanical

---

[55] For the philosophical and theological background of the term *quies*, see Jean Leclercq, O.S.B., *Otia monastica: Études sur le vocabulaire de la contemplation au Moyen Age*, Studia Anselmiana, 51 (Rome: Herder, 1963), pp. 13–26, 84–113.

[56] Jean Leclercq, O.S.B. *The Love of Learning and the Desire for God: A Study of Monastic Culture*, trans. Catharine Misrahi, 2nd ed. (London: SPCK, 1978), pp. 18–22, 26, 88–93.

[57] *Didascalicae*, III, xi (PL, col 772); see also Cassiodorus, *Institutiones*, I, preface, 3–7 (meditative reading recommended as a school exercise); John of Salisbury, *Metalogicus*, I, xxiv; Benavente, *Ars*, p. 47; both Hugh and John state that their pedagogical methods could also be used by the private reader: *Didascalicae*, III, viii; *Metalogicus*, I, xxiv, where Salisbury distinguishes *lectio* (which concerns the 'occupationem per se scrutantis scripturas' and the 'scrutinium meditantis'), from *praelectio*, a term borrowed from Quintilian, signifying the act of teaching and

application of the methods of *divisio* and *quaestio* enables us to put into sharper focus Villena's thoughts on the multiple interpretation of allegory. The most advanced readers of the *Aeneid* or *Los doze trabajos* were able to explore the potential meanings of these texts precisely because they were no longer bound by the need to investigate the written word by means of the rules and precepts of grammatical technique. The text becomes a point of departure for intellectual speculation—a concept which, as we shall see, exerted a strong influence on the basic structure of Mena's *Coronación*.

Lectio supplies the most important philosophical background for such phrases as 'reposado estudio' or '[el] reposado ojo de la investigativa'. But we can fill in more details of Villena's picture of literary study by examining some other academic associations of the word *reposo*.

Firstly, in certain contexts, *reposo* brings to mind widely held theories regarding the physical circumstances of study. Prominent amongst these was the notion that for the intellect to function properly it had to be free from the demands of the flesh: the body had to be at complete rest. Benavente, for example, suggests late evening, after the siesta, and early morning as the two most profitable times for the student to meditate on his lessons: food should have been properly digested, and the mind refreshed by adequate sleep (*Ars*, pp. 50–51). Villena, by contrast, thinking perhaps of the circumstances of his non-clerical readership, advocates night as the most appropriate occasion for study. 'En aquella sazón', he explains in his gloss on 'Quoniam videbo':

> es más dispuesto el humano entendimiento a sobir por la escalera de contenplación, cesados ya los trabajos del día e callados los tumultos, cuando los mienbros corporales piden reposo e las virtudes intellectuales se despiertan. (ed. Cátedra, p. 104)

Here, *reposo* is employed in its more usual sense, in order to draw the sharp contrast between bodily rest and intellectual vitality: the latter is wholly dependent upon the former.

Moral integrity constituted another important precondition for scholarly pursuits. The notion—which was entirely common-place—influenced much of Villena's writing, and occupies a central

---

studying texts according to grammatical principles (ed. J.-P. Migne, PL, 199 (Paris, 1855), col. 853).

position in his exegesis of the *Aeneid*.[58] Glossing the allegorical significance of Carthage, he asserts that the city stands for 'la tranquilidat en que la conciencia se siente librada de la fortuna de los vicios'. Then, in an interesting variation on exegetical tradition, he interprets the nymphs who inhabit this port as the truths that disclose themselves 'al entendimiento, quando está en lugar apartado' (they were more usually interpreted as the temptations of the flesh). What Virgil was trying to prove is that:

> la puridat de la conciencia e reposo de aquélla dispone el entendimiento a entender fázilmente las intelegibles e scientíficas cosas.   (f. 28ᵛ)

Therefore, the act of reading, more especially the interpretation of allegorical texts, has serious intellectual and ethical implications. 'Reposado estudio' presupposes a tranquil, yet alert, state of mind, freed from the allurements of worldly pleasure. It exercises both the active and contemplative mental faculties: reason and memory. It engages men on the daily task of discovering and retaining wisdom, and leads them gradually along the path to becoming members of Villena's intellectual and social elite of 'generosos entendimientos'.

b) *La coronación* as literary manifesto

At the core of Mena's poem lies the image of the journey, depicting the various stages in man's progress toward true knowledge of God and of the relation between wisdom and virtue. But the narrative does more than just portray and analyse; it also encourages the reader to share in the action of the poem, to emulate the moral and spiritual aspirations of the protagonists. The work thus becomes a manifesto of social conduct, embodying the ideals of 'la política vida'. Yet were this the sole aim, we might reasonably object that Mena had selected an unnecessarily cumbersome vehicle to express his views. However, the difficulties imposed by the poem and commentary exist, in a very real sense, for their own sake. The work is designed as an exercise, in which the reader travels not just toward a goal of ethical understanding but also toward one of intellectual improvement.

That the reader undertakes two kinds of journey is clear from

---

[58] *Tratado de la consolación*, ed. Carr, pp. 125–27, 130–31 (the topos of the philosopher's solitude), *Los doze trabajos*, ed. Morreale, pp. 92 and 107 (the virtuous master and student, citing pseudo-Boethius, *De disciplina scholarium*). See also Hugh of St Victor, *Didascalicae*, III, xiii (quoting the topos 'mores ornant scientiam'); Benavente, *Ars*, pp. 233–37.

the very start of *La coronación*. 'Porque de los enormes y desordenados hechos no se pueden concluyr devidos fines', writes Mena in his *exordium*:

> pensé de poner en orden de escritura quatro preámbulos en este exordio comentual, por que el fin de mí convocado sea casa de descanso del peregrinante principio. (f. 266ʳ)

The image employed here—that of the journey through the text—is not in itself unusual (graphic examples of it may be found in other prologues of the period).[59] But what makes it worth closer attention is the way that the concept of the reader as a pilgrim travelling toward his 'casa de descanso' takes on a thematic status within the poem and commentary. It is in fact woven so tightly into the fabric of the work that the broader moral issues cannot adequately be understood without reference to it.

Throughout both the prose and verse sections of *La coronación*, Mena casts himself in the role of a literary and intellectual mentor, guiding the unlearned through the complexities of the narrative and teaching and entertaining them along the way. To strengthen the bond linking master and pupil, Mena has employed a variety of rhetorical and poetic devices (verisimilitude, *admiratio*, apostrophe and so on), which are commonly found in contemporary allegorical narratives; one of these, the apostrophe, though not in itself unusual, takes on a special importance within the action of the poem.

Mena's direct addresses to the reader are designed to encourage participation in the action of the poem. Readers are expected to identify with the poetic 'yo', to experience the same fears and learn the same lessons as the protagonist. However, this participation in the fictional narrative is not absolute. For just as Mena has two identities—that of commentator and protagonist—so do the readers. On the one hand, they are supposed to empathize with the

---

[59] Cartagena divided his *Memorial de virtudes* into chapters because 'los caminantes una jornada con la yantar acostunbran partir, porque menor trabajo siente aquel a quien la tenprada folgança interrunpe. Pues que asý es, sy algund trabajo concibieres de su letura dél, por la distinción de los libros asý como a un término acostando te lo amengua' (Escorial MS h-III-11, f. 2ʳ). The identical image is repeated in the prologue to his translation of *De senectute*: see López Estrada, 'La retórica en las *Generaciones y semblanzas*', p. 348. The concept is given an interesting twist by the Barrantes commentator on Mena's *Laberinto*: his exposition is the 'ovillo de cuerda' which guides the reader round the labyrinth of the poem: Bartolomé March MS 20-5-6, f. 39ʳ.

protagonist and, so to speak, view the action from the inside; but on the other, they must remain detached and contemplate it from without, as a fictional artifice. The force of this dichotomy is illustrated by the series of apostrophes in stanzas 5 to 11.

At the start of the protagonist's journey down the river of Hell, he exlaims that he will relate the torments of the damned 'por que tú, lector, te asombres' (st. 5; f. 272ʳ). In the stanzas that follow, the rapid enumeration of the mythological figures is accompanied by a sequence of direct and indirect addresses to the readers, urging them to share the narrator's horror and fear (sts 6–10). Then, interrupting the review of evil *exempla*, comes the crucial invocation of stanza 11:

> De otras muchas personas
> del linage feminino
> por no espantar a las donas,
> ni robarles sus coronas,
> sus martyrios no assigno.
> Aunque la tal excepción
> te saluda en discreción,
> exortando que no hagas
> del tal linage de plagas
> ligera contemplación.
> (f. 284ᵛ)

We can ignore the assertion that the description of damned women has been cut short so as not to frighten the good ladies of the court (or, as Mena ironically adds, 'por no ponerles en gran espanto en los tiernos coraçones suyos, ca hartas pudiera hallar de quien dezir', f. 284ᵛ). The demands of brevity and the desire to avoid the distraction of the contemporary anti-feminist debate are undoubtedly stronger motives for his silence. Of much greater importance are the exhortation of the second half of the stanza and the explanatory remarks made in the accompanying gloss. Here, Mena declares that even though he does not mention the damned by name, 'por eso no es de dexar de considerar la tanta pena y dolor que está aparejada a todos aquellos que en el mal les plaze perseverar siempre' (f. 284ᵛ). In other words, the reader is required to pass beyond the concrete and specific, and grasp the underlying moral and theological principle. Contemplation of the eternal truths must not be hindered by emotional involvement with the external show of things. Thus, the bond of empathy which had been forged between the reader and protagonist over the preceding stanzas is momentarily broken, as Mena demands a fundamentally different response to the text: one which taxes the reader's mental powers of perception and abstraction.

The notion that one should see through the form in which an idea is cast and, in a state of emotional detachment, consider the truth that lies behind it, has a close and interesting parallel in a passage in Dante's *Divina commedia*. When, at one notably dramatic stage in his journey through Purgatory (X, 106–11), Dante begins to describe the agonized suffering of the proud, he breaks off his account with the exclamation:

> Non vo' però, lettor, che tu ti smaghi
> di buon proponimento per udire
> come Dio vuol che'l debito si paghi.
> Non attender la forma del martire:
> pensa la succession; pensa ch'al peggio,
> oltre la gran sentenza non può ire.

Like Mena, Dante exhorts readers not to concentrate on the individual act of punishment, which, by arousing terror and despair, might deter them from persevering in their quest, but to consider its purpose, and its place in the overall divine scheme. This apostrophe, and many others like it, have been examined in great depth by Erich Auerbach.[60] They belong, broadly speaking, to a well-defined medieval rhetorical tradition though, as Auerbach has shown, they are unsurpassed in their range of tone and poetic power (being those of a man who claims for himself the inspiration of divine grace for his vision of the other world). The lines from *Purgatorio* have not been introduced here in order to compare the respective literary merits of the two poets, nor even as a possible source for stanza 11 of Mena's poem. Their relevance consists in their being an analogous response to similar social and literary conditions. For both poets, writing at a time when a new, more intimate relationship was being created between author and public, used the apostrophe as, in Auerbach's words, 'an act of teaching . . . a mobilization of the reader's forces' ('Dante's Addresses', p. 273).

We gain deeper insights into the nature of this intellectual mobilization by examining what Mena has to say in the commentary about this particular passage of the poem. His gloss not only

---

[60] 'Dante's Addresses to the Reader', *RPh*, 7 (1953–54), 268–78, and, in the context of the growth in lay literacy, *Literary Language*, pp. 297–303.

strikes home the message of the stanza, but also stands as a general statement of literary policy:

> Quiere dezir esta copla que deve [el] hombre las cosas que son encargadas de tener al juyzio del leedor que se deven ver y catar con estudio sotil y memoria reposada y ojo atento y contemplación prolongada por que sepa el estilo de la escriptura y la intención y propósito del que la ordenó quál fue y a qué fin se endereça, assí lo malo commo lo bueno: lo bueno para en ello perseverar, y lo malo para apartarse dello. (ff. 284ᵛ–85ʳ)

We immediately recognize the presence here of traditional academic attitudes towards the task of reading. Firstly, there is the *lectio*, with its emphasis on penetrating, meditative study and reminiscence (or 'memoria reposada', which evokes the *reposo* or *quies* so dear to Villena). Secondly, this state of mind is supposed to lead toward a better understanding of the work's 'estilo', 'intención' and 'fin', terms which owe an obvious debt to the conventional topics of the *accessus*: the *forma tractatus* (and, perhaps, *tractandi*), *intentio* and *finis*.

But more interesting than all this is the way that these lines relate to medieval theories of composition, whereby a work in its totality was planned in the mind of the writer before taking shape on paper. Mena's comments lead us back to the pride he took in the conceptual clarity of his poem: for what he demands from readers at this point in the commentary is the ability to step back from the narrative and sharpen their powers of perception in order to see through the material form in which the poet has clothed his Idea, and reflect on it as he himself conceived it at the time of composition. One might say that the reader's task is to retrace the steps in the creative process and work back to the poet's archetypal vision of good and evil. This is the 'casa de descanso' mentioned at the outset of the work: via a complete understanding of the poem's rhetoric, one arrives at the conceptual principles that determined its form. The act of reading involves a movement from concrete to abstract, from external to inner realities, and from the active pursuit of meaning to the contemplative knowledge of truth.

However, it must be stressed that this intellectual and literary process is subordinated to a moral, and not an esthetic, purpose. There can be no doubt that Mena wishes the reader to dwell appreciatively on the formal merits of his work, but not for too long. The object is to acquire the ability to discriminate between good and evil, and ultimately to apply one's knowledge to real life: 'lo bueno para en ello perseverar, y lo malo para apartarse dello'. Reading the poem, therefore, teaches *prudentia*, the intellectual quality which, amongst other things, comprises good judgement and estimative power. Set apart from knowledge of facts ('sabiduría'), it demands:

> elevación de juyzio, y órgano de capacidad, y memoria a quien la recomendar, y especulativa para discernir, y expressiva para representar.   (f. 298ʳ)

Its aims are primarily ethical and practical, concerning 'el lícito uso de la buena sabiduría'. As one of the four cardinal virtues, it governs 'la política vida, que es puerta de buenas costumbres'.

Mena's treatment of prudence owes much to Aristotle's *Nicomachean Ethics*, a work whose presence looms large in fifteenth-century Castilian thought.[61] But what is particularly interesting is the way the very act of reading *La coronación* is supposed to bring into play the intellectual virtue which is the main theme of the poem itself. Literary study is therefore the nucleus of Mena's moral manifesto, since it trains the individual in those habits of thought which enable one to attain the ideals of social conduct epitomized in the poem by Santillana. This dynamic connection between theme (the ability to discriminate good from evil in human affairs) and function (to teach and exercise this ability) is a characteristic feature of *La coronación*. It sets the work apart from Villena's commentary on the *Aeneid*, which also has prudence as its thematic backbone, and also devotes much space to the problems of literary interpretation.

A second factor that differentiates the two writers' approach to the ethical and intellectual implications of the reading act is the greater interest shown by the younger poet in the psychological aspects of literary response: what one might call the dynamics of perception. This is manifested by Mena's repeated references to the internal senses and the way they receive, analyse and store data from the physical world. We have already seen how prudence is said to consist of various mental faculties (*juicio, memoria, especulativa* and *expresiva*) controlling human action (*la política vida*). Santillana's coronation by the nine Muses is the allegorical expression of this concept. Leaving aside certain enigmatic aspects of this scene (such as the presence of the 'muse' Comedia in place of Thalia), there can be no doubt about Mena's preoccupation with the workings of the mind. Judgement, imagination, memory: Santillana is shown to

---

[61] A detailed history of the influence of the *Ethics* on XVc vernacular writers has yet to be written; see, however, A. R. D. Pagden, 'The Diffusion of Aristotle's Moral Philosophy in Spain, ca. 1400–ca. 1600', *T*, 31 (1975), 287–313.

possess all these.[62] They are the foundation of his understanding of virtue, which in turn enable him to determine the correct course of action. However, Mena's most coherent and lengthy digression on the internal senses occurs before this, in his commentary on stanza 32 when he invokes the five 'potencias interiores' ('seso común', 'imaginativa', 'fantasía', 'estimativa' and 'memoria') to aid him in his attempts to describe Mount Parnassus. To summarize the functions of these senses as set forth by Mena would take up too much space; as his citations of Aristotle's *De anima*, III, and Aquinas's commentary on it indicate, his ideas are in any case part of conventional scholastic philosophy.[63] More relevant to our purpose at this point are the literary and ethical implications of Mena's fascination with the faculties of the mind.

The disquisitions of psychology are far from being gratuitous digressions. They illustrate the belief that literary response is simply another form of human perception and, as such, plays a vital part in man's search for the highest good. Put in Aristotelian terms, it can be described as a motion towards and rest in the desired object: Mena's journey towards the 'casa de descanso'. Literature was the product of prudence, which worked 'ad bonum operantis', and it could activate the mind in exactly the same way as any other phenomenon from the physical world. Thus, understanding a written text could follow the same general pattern as any other learning process; because of this, a perceptive reading of *La coronación*, like the very act of creating it, actualized the five 'potencias interiores', and trained one to make proper value judgements in the outside world.[64]

---

[62] See glosses to st. 40 (ff. 308^r–9^r), particularly the interpretations of Urania ('capacidad de ingenio'), Erato ('hablar alguna cosa semejable a las que avemos aprendido ... y ser inventivo de otra tal o más sotil'), and Polymnia ('dadora de muchas cosas, assí como es la memoria'), which bear a close resemblance to Benvenuto da Imola's commentary on Dante's *Purgatorio*, I, 8–9 (*Comentum super Dantis Aldigherij Comoediam*, ed. J. P. Lacaita (Florence, Barbèra, 1887), III, 6–8).

[63] Harry A. Wolfson, 'The Internal Senses in Latin, Arabic, and Hebrew Philosophic Texts', *Harvard Theological Review*, 28 (1935), 69–133.

[64] For the influence of faculty psychology on literary thought, see Phillips Salman, 'Instruction and Delight in Medieval and Renaissance Literary Criticism', *Renaissance Quarterly*, 32 (1979), 303–32; other examples in Mario Maurin, 'La Poétique de Chastellain et la "Grand Rhétorique"', *PMLA*, 74 (1959), 482–84; Dom Duarte, ed. Joseph M. Piel, *Leal conselheiro* (Lisbon: Bertrand, 1942), pp. 4–5; general background in Judson Boyce Allen, *The Ethical Poetic of the Later Middle Ages: A Decorum of Convenient Distinction* (Toronto: University of Toronto Press, 1982), *passim*, but esp. pp. 32–33, 93–95, 179–82.

4 The noble mind

The ideas outlined in the preceding pages make it possible to piece together a portrait of an intellectual and social ideal. Certain features of this portrait, as in that of Baena's courtier, will remain ill-defined: not until Boscán introduced *Il cortegiano* to Spain did Castilians have a comprehensively formulated theory of social manners and lay learning. But the picture that does emerge allows us to characterize more sharply some of the major aspirations of the nobility during the first half of the century.

The academic methods of textual analysis described above tell us much about the literary trends of the time, but, if we are to understand the wider implications of their use, one point needs to be made with special emphasis right at the start. Namely, that although Villena and Mena attempted to educate their contemporaries in the techniques of *divisio, quaestio* and *lectio*, this does not mean that they wished to turn their aristocratic readers into caricatures of professional scholars, nor that they wished to break down the traditional barriers separating the clerical and military estates. Nor, indeed, do their efforts to promote disciplined literary criticism support a thesis such as that advanced by Helen Nader (*The Mendoza Family*), who sees in Castilian court circles the same kind of scholarly learning as in Renaissance Florence. The goal was not to become a trained scholar—whether Florentine humanist or professional *grammaticus*—but an amateur of letters.

That an important section of the Castilian aristocracy deliberately set their sights on becoming, in the words of Auerbach, 'cultured, but not learned', has already been amply documented by the work of Russell and Lawrance. However, one more contemporary witness is worth quoting for the particularly interesting way in which he places the concept of gentleman scholar within a classical tradition.

In an attempt to distinguish learned from vulgar Latin, the anonymous Castilian commentator of the *Divina commedia*, cites (incorrectly and out of context) the following passage from Cicero's *De oratore*:

> Muchos de los nuestros menos se dan a las letras que al latín, pero destos quantos conoscistes ceviles que muy poco tienen de letras; pero non ay ninguno que no sea literatísimo.[65]

---

[65] Webber, 'A Spanish Linguistic Treatise', p. 38. The commentator's ultimate source, as Webber suggests, is Bk III, xi, 43, where Cicero asserts (via his mouthpiece Crassus) that the diction of the unlearned citizens of Rome surpasses

The contrast between formal erudition and unschooled, yet cultivated, intelligence of the 'ceviles' (Cicero's *urbani*) provides him with an exact framework for a brief appraisal of the pretensions of contemporary aristocrats. 'Como se diría en Castilla', he continues:

> el señor don Fernando de Gusmán, comendador mayor de Calatrava, non se da mucho a las letras latinas, mas por eso non dexa de ser literatísimo. (p. 39)

The choice of Fernando de Guzmán as the epitome of lay learning may surprise the modern reader, who is perhaps best acquainted with him as the savage villain of *Fuenteovejuna*. But evidence supplied by no less a figure than Alonso de Palencia corroborates the picture of him sketched by the anonymous commentator.[66] Whatever the real latinity of this character, however, two points must be noted. That the fifteenth century looked to the heroes of ancient Rome for their models of social and military conduct is well known. This passage, despite its brevity, takes the idea a stage further, by finding in classical antiquity parallels for the intellectual or literary status of the nobility of the author's own day. The Castilian knights, it is implied, were the natural descendants of a much older, and wholly admirable, social group of literate laymen: the refined inhabitants of Rome.

Secondly, though of undoubted interest for shedding more light on the classicizing trend of the period, the commentator's words must be taken in the context of his general approach to Dante's poem, the point of departure for this whole digression on language and learning. In brief, his attitude is dismissive. Soon tiring of his prescribed task of elucidating the first two cantos, he moves on with undisguised enthusiasm to an exposition of 'otra cosa que sea

---

in elegance that of the most erudite orators of other regions: 'Nostri minus student litteris quam Latini; tamen ex istis quos nostis urbanis, in quibus minimum est litterarum, nemo est quin litteratissimum togatorum omnium Q. Valerium Soranum lenitate vocis atque ipso oris pressu et sono facile vincat', *De oratore*, with an English translation by E. W. Sutton and H. Rackham, Loeb Classical Library, 348 and 349 (Cambridge, Mass: Harvard University Press; London: Heinemann, 1942), II, 34. However, the anonymous Castilian's discussion of this and other linguistic issues is not original, but closely based on a letter by the Italian humanist Guarini, as a forthcoming study by Lucia Binotti (University of Pisa) will show.

66 Palencia dedicated to him the Castilian version of his *De perfectione militaris triumphi*, and invited him (as a compliment that should not be taken too seriously) to judge 'si en algo se desviava la traslación vulgar del enxemplar latino'. Quoted from Russell, *Traducciones*, p. 52.

mejor e más provechosa' (p. 33): two prayers of Sts Augustine and Anselm. For him, in other words, the real value of being 'literatísimo' is the ability to study the writings of the Church Fathers, rather than the imaginative fictions of the vernacular poets. Using the same tactics as Cartagena in his attempts to control the reading habits of the Count of Haro, this cleric praises an ideal and at the same time manipulates it to suit the outlook of his own particular estate.

Leaving the clerical view behind, however, two currents of thought help us to define more clearly what it meant, in court circles, to be 'cultured, but not learned'. As I have explained above, one consequence of literary study, as outlined by Villena and Mena, was that it both presupposed and fostered an individual's moral awareness: it could lead to *prudentia*, or wisdom in action. This belief is based on two intellectual and philosophical traditions. Firstly, from the twelfth-century humanists of the grammar curriculum germinated the idea that thorough, meditative textual analysis had an ethical function. The wisdom acquired from *grammatica* was a necessary, and direct, stepping-stone to the practice of virtue: 'operationem cultumque virtutis scientia naturaliter praecedit'.[67] Onto this basic premise were grafted the moral philosophies of Aristotle and Cicero.

These two authorities were largely responsible for shaping fifteenth-century opinions about the relation of the active to the contemplative life. The influence of the *Nichomachean Ethics*, which stresses wisdom as a political virtue, has already been mentioned. The other major classical authority for this philosophical outlook was Cicero's *De officiis*, in which it is also argued that intellectual pursuits should pave the way for the active life. However praiseworthy it may be to study 'las cosas honestas e dignas de cognición', in the final analysis, observes Cicero, 'dexar las cosas que se deven fazer, es cosa contra oficio'.[68] Both *La eneyda* and *La coronación* bear the unmistakable stamp of these views. The dangers of misguided or exaggerated involvement in worldly affairs are forcefully depicted, but neither Villena nor Mena advocates total withdrawal into a cloistered world of books. Their sights are set firmly on man's conduct within contemporary society: although a

[67] John of Salisbury, *Metalogicus*, I, xxiii (PL, 199, col. 853); cf. Mena's aphoristic summary of *La coronación*, st. 46: 'de la sciencia sale e nasce la virtud' (f. 312ʳ).

[68] Cartagena's literal rendering of I, vi, 19 (Madrid, BN MS 7.815, f. 43ʳ).

contemplative existence is 'la propria mano derecha de ombre', as Villena puts it in *La eneyda*, 'non se puede continuar syn ayuda de la actyva' (f. 49ᵛ).[69]

A sense of having actually fused together these two modes of existence was made possible for Castilian aristocrats by the conventional academic theories of literary study. The inward reflection, the meditation on meaning and form that was demanded by Villena and Mena opened a door into the contemplative life. It enabled lay readers to feel they were conforming to the ideals of social virtue prescribed by Aristotle and Cicero, and portrayed allegorically in the very poems they had before them.

Besides being able to project the image of men whose actions were guided by wisdom acquired in 'reposado estudio', it was possible for the wealthy *militares viri* to bolster their inherited (and in most cases newly won) rank, by drawing on the concept of intellectual gentility. The idea that nobility could depend on factors that had nothing to do with accidents of birth was frequently voiced during the Middle Ages (by Dante and Jean de Meun, for example). It was especially influential in fifteenth-century Castile, when writers like Diego de Valera, in his *Espejo de verdadera nobleza*, propagated the ideal of a nobility based on the fusion of lineage, virtue and courtly manners.[70] Occasionally, in works written either by or for the aristocracy, the notion of a noble spirit took on a more philosophical and learned dimension.

The outstanding example of this is Villena's account of 'los generosos entendimientos', which occurs in a key passage of his decription of poetry as an architectonic science:

> ansí commo los que descienden de nobles e grandes parientes antiguados son dichos generosos, ansí los entendimientos que son habituados ha la solicitud e cura de las otras sciencias antiguadas e apartadas son dichos generosos e nobles. E lo que los primeros han por natura, éstos lo alcançan por doctrina, e ha tales entendimientos commo éstos ansí dispuestos, nudre e cría la poesía. (f. 12ᵛ)

---

[69] See also *Los doze trabajos*: 'Los que quieren a la vida contemplativa seguramente venir, primeramente en la activa deven ser ciertos e aprovados' (ed. Morreale, p. 128).

[70] Valera spent much time in Burgundy from where he may have derived his ideas. His treatise was translated into French in the mid-XVc: see Charity C. Willard, 'The Concept of True Nobility at the Burgundian Court', *Studies in the Renaissance*, 14 (1967), 33–48, especially, pp. 40–41; Maurice Keen, *Chivalry* (New Haven: Yale University Press, 1984), esp. pp. 15–16, 132–33, and 151–52.

This is something quite different from the courtly wisdom of Baena, which seems, to me at least, to have been much more ludic in character. Moreover, some members of the aristocracy would probably have rejected outright the suggestion that their social position had much to do with their interest in letters. Rodríguez del Padrón, for example, in spite of the classical allusions and learned tone of much of his poetry and prose, argues forcefully in his treatise *La cadira de onor* that true nobility rests primarily on inherited or legally acquired rank: the concept of poet laureate, with its connotations of an autonomous intellectual aristocracy, is wholly spurious. 'La nobleza', he declares, 'es honorable beneficio por méritos o graciosamente, de antiguos tiempos avido del príncipe o por subcesión, que faze a su poseedor del pueblo ser diferente'. For this view, he has the authority of the highly influential Italian jurist, Bartolus de Saxoferrato, whom he cites on numerous occasions.[71] Had he wished, he could have drawn further support from Alfonso el Sabio. His *Siete partidas*, which figured in many aristocratic libraries, acknowledges that wisdom contributes to *gentileza*, but then states that it is essentially a matter of noble birth and manners.[72]

The clarity with which Villena sets the nobility of letters apart from that of birth brings him close to the position adopted by Seneca (to pick an example of relevance to contemporary Castile). This author's *Epistulae morales* have the concept of the *anima generosa* as a recurring theme, though it is often submerged in the discursiveness of the argument. However, it could not have passed unnoticed by the reader of the Castilian version. For in this anthology, the notion is brought clearly into view by the rubrics that accompany each of the seventy-five letters. Number 21, for example, is headed by the assertion that 'sólo el ingenio estudioso faze al ombre noble e le da grand nombre'.[73] Though not

---

[71] In *Obras completas*, ed. Hernández Alonso, p. 282; of particular interest is his reference to Bartolus's repudiation of Dante's concept of virtue as the basis of civil nobility (p. 276). See also Keen, *Chivalry*, pp. 148–51.

[72] 'E comoquier que estos que lo ganan por sabiduría e por su bondat son por derecho llamados nobles e gentiles, mayormente lo son aquellos que lo han por linaje antiguamente, e fazen buena vida, porque les viene de lueñe como heredad', *Las siete partidas del sabio rey don Alonso el nono [sic], nuevamente glosadas por el licenciado Gregorio López* (Madrid: Juan Hasrey, 1610–11), II, xxi, 12, f. 71ʳ.

[73] Quoted from the translation commissioned by Fernán Pérez de Guzmán, Madrid, BN MS 9.215, f. 16ᵛ (= Seneca's *Ep.* 21); see also chs. 32 and 38 (= *Ep.* 44 and 37). This does not mean that Villena would have identified totally with

necessarily a direct source (given his distrust of liberal studies), Seneca's sharp distinction between social and philosophical nobility would undoubtedly have proved immensely attractive to an aristocrat in Villena's position. It would have armed him with an authoritative riposte to the criticism of those who maintained that serious literary interests were inappropriate, even dishonourable, for a man of his caste.

Anti-intellectual prejudice (of the kind catalogued by Nicholas Round over twenty years ago) prompted another writer to resort to the same argument as employed by Villena. For several reasons his words deserve close attention. In the preface to his Castilian version of St Basil's famous homily *De legendis libris gentilium*, the anonymous translator reviles those who 'quieren obtrectar los estudios de la humanidat, por que nosotros nos damos a los poetas e oradores e otros que los han tractado'. This is one of the earliest occurences of the phrase 'los estudios de la humanidat' in Castilian literature, and Jeremy Lawrance, who attributes this prologue to Nuño de Guzmán, interprets it as the equivalent of the *studia humanitatis* of the Italian Renaissance.[74] This was a revival of the classical ideal of the *paideia*, a plan of liberal studies (law, literature, history, philosophy), which aimed at the creation of the 'all-around man'. For our purposes, what is interesting is the way this writer, by a series of puns on the word *humanidat*, evokes the idea that the dignity of man rested on the nobility of letters. The fact that the translation was dedicated to Santillana is of first importance. It was undertaken to support the literary and intellectual ideals that he himself aspired to. And prominent amongst these, as we shall see in the following chapter, was the conviction that one's inherited position in the social hierarchy could be enhanced by the study of great poetry.

Santillana provides a fitting conclusion to this survey of the new attitudes towards poetry and literary study that accompanied the spread of literacy through the ranks of the rich and powerful landed aristocracy. He epitomized all the aspirations that we have been examining here: he was a poet-sage, the model 'generoso entendimiento'; he demonstrated to his contempories what could be achieved

---

Seneca's approach; see the latter's reservations concerning both eclectic reading (e.g. ch. 33 = *Ep.* 45), and the inherent ethical value of liberal studies (the famous *Ep.* 88, translated by Cartagena as a separate treatise, *De las siete artes liberales*).

[74] Quoted from Schiff, *La Bibliothèque*, p. 343; see Lawrance, 'Nuño de Guzmán: Life and Works', pp. 195–99.

in the realm of lay wisdom (in contrast to scholarship and Latin erudition), thus proving that, according to his own famous dictum, 'la sciencia non enbota el fierro de la lança, ni faze floxa la espada en la mano del cavallero'.[75] If he was thought to embody all these things, it was due in no small measure to his own relentless efforts to cultivate the image of an aristocrat whose life was guided and improved by the meditative literary study that had been advocated so powerfully by Villena and Mena. As he himself once proudly declared, alluding to the exemplary heroes of Greece and Troy, 'ya passaron por mis manos/ sus ystorias con reposo' (*El sueño*, ll. 411–12; *Obras completas*, p. 130).

Santillana is an appropriate conclusion for a quite different reason. Inevitably, the ideas and aspirations that have been examined in this and the previous chapter span a much wider field than is encompassed by the kind of verse that makes up the bulk of *cancionero* poetry. It is easy to see how poems like *La coronación* or *Bías contra Fortuna* were supposed to contribute to the education of an aristocratic elite, but what about the lesser genres, the amorous *canciones* and narrative *decires*? They could scarcely be approached on the same ethical and philosophical terms as the more ambitious sorts of work; indeed for some, there could be no serious justification for them at all. Santillana was fully aware of the problems involved in reconciling the two kinds of poetic activity; the *Proemio e carta* is his attempt to answer them.

---

[75] *Proverbios*, in *Obras completas*, ed. Gómez Moreno and Kerkhof, p. 218. For Santillana's status in contemporary eyes, see Rafael Lapesa, *La obra literaria del Marqués de Santillana* (Madrid: Insula, 1957), pp. 265–80; Russell, 'Las armas contra las letras', pp. 212, 214–16, 225, 230–31; Joaquín Arce, 'El *Triunfo del Marqués* de Diego de Burgos y la irradiación dantesca en torno a Santillana', *Revista de la Universidad de Madrid*, 19 (1971), 25–39. For the frequency with which Santillana's lyric verse was quoted by contemporary and later poets, see Jane Whetnall, 'Manuscript Love Poetry of the Spanish Fifteenth Century: Developing Standards and Continuing Traditions', Unpublished Ph.D. thesis (Univ. of Cambridge, 1986).

CHAPTER V

Literary Theory and Self-Justification: Santillana's *Proemio e carta*

Santillana prefixed his treatise to an anthology of verse compiled at the request of Don Pedro de Portugal. It is generally supposed that the two noblemen first met after the battle of Olmedo (1445), and, on the grounds that the work would have been carried out soon after this encounter, 1446 has been suggested as a possible date of composition. This is not an unreasonable assumption, but in the final analysis, *El proemio* can only be dated with absolute certainty between the years 1445 and 1449.[1] Don Pedro, therefore, was still under twenty years old, while Santillana, on the other hand, was approaching fifty. This age-gap is important: it prompts Santillana to reflect on the fact that he and his fellow poet are also separated (at least in theory) by a fundamental difference in literary outlook.

[1] See Kerkhof, 'Acerca da data do *Proemio e carta*'. The original copy, and the *cancionero* to which it was attached, are now both lost. For a survey of extant MSS, see Angel Gómez Moreno, 'Tradición manuscrita y ediciones del *Proemio* de Santillana', *Dicenda*, 2 (1983), 77–110. *El proemio* exists in only one XVc MS: the *cancionero* which Santillana gave to his nephew, Gómez Manrique (University of Salamanca, MS 2.655), on which all modern eds are based. For its textual authority, see Maximiliaan P. A. M. Kerkhof, 'Algunas notas acerca de los manuscritos 2.655 y 1.865 de la Biblioteca Universitaria de Salamanca', *N*, 57 (1973), 135–43. The main analyses of the text are by Di Camillo, *El humanismo*, pp. 69–108; Lapesa, *La obra literaria*, pp. 247–55; Francis Ferrie, 'Aspiraciones del humanismo castellano del siglo XV: revalorización del *Prohemio e carta* de Santillana', *RFE*, 57 (1974–75), 195–209; Miguel Garci-Gómez, 'Paráfrasis de Cicerón en la definición de poesía de Santillana', *Hispania* [U. S. A.], 56 (1973), 209–12; 'Otras huellas de Horacio en el Marqués de Santillana', *BHS*, 50 (1973), 127–41; ed., Marqués de Santillana, *Prohemios y cartas literarias* (Madrid: Editora Nacional, 1984), pp. 42–76; David W. Foster, *The Marqués de Santillana*, Twayne's World Author Series, 154 (New York: Twayne, 1971), pp. 141–45; López Estrada's prologue and notes to the ed. (by Angel Gómez Moreno) in *Las poéticas castellanas*, pp. 51–63; the annotation to the ed. in *Obras completas*, ed. Gómez Moreno and Kerkhof, pp. 437–54.

1 Poetry in youth and maturity

At the start of the work, Santillana recalls how a messenger informed him of the Constable's request for a collection of 'dezires e canciones' (p. 438). He carried out this commission but not, he tells us, without some initial reservations:

> estas obras—o a lo menos las más dellas—no son de tales materias, ni asý bien formadas e artizadas, que de memorable registro dignas parescan. Porque, señor, asý commo el Apóstol dize: 'Cum essem paruulus cogitabam ut paruulus, loquebar ut paruulus'. Ca estas tales cosas alegres e jocosas andan e concurren con el tienpo de la nueva hedad de juventud, es a saber, con el vestir, con el justar, con el dançar e con otros tales cortesanos exercicios. E asý, señor, muchas cosas plazen agora a vos que ya no plazen o no deven plazer a mí. (p. 438)

This seems clear enough: Santillana not only claims to be dissatisfied with the quality of his work but also betrays a certain uneasiness about associating himself with what he regards as an essentially youthful pastime. However, an undercurrent of ambiguity runs through the whole passage; an ambiguity created by the tension between his theoretical outlook and his literary practice.

In theory, these introductory comments suggest that the poems being equated with dancing and jousting are examples of Santillana's early amatory verse, such as the narrative *dezires* collected in *El cancionero de Palacio*. But for two reasons this passage is unreliable evidence for the contents of the *cancionero* actually sent to Don Pedro. In the first place, given the notorious flexibility of genre terminology, we should not take at face value the description of the anthology as a collection of 'dezires e canciones': this very phrase is used at the end of *El proemio* to cover the whole range of literature discussed in the historical survey (p. 453). Secondly, we must take into account the demands of the modesty topos, a rhetorical convention that obviously influenced the way he presents his work as light-hearted juvenilia (I can think of very few poems ever written by Santillana that can accurately be described as 'cosas alegres e jocosas').

We can, therefore, only guess at the contents of the *cancionero*, and this in turn makes it all the more difficult to assess the real force of the criticism directed at the poems' form and subject-matter. In addition to making allowances for the modesty topos, we should also notice the way Santillana drops several hints designed to moderate his apparently severe criticism of the esthetic merits of his verse. Firstly, he casually leaves room for manoeuvre by suggesting that his criticism applies only to 'las más dellas', and, shortly after the passage quoted above, he slyly indicates that not everyone need share his low opinion of them: 'Mas commo quiera que de tanta insuficiencia estas obretas mías ... sean, o por ventura más de quanto las yo estimo e reputo ... '. (p. 439). Furthermore, there is also the revealing statement that, having gone to the trouble of gathering together these allegedly minor works, he had them written out 'por orden segund que las yo fize' (p. 438). This remark may be interpreted in two ways. It may mean that the poems were arranged chronologically within the *cancionero*, as seems to have been the case with the later anthology presented to Gómez Manrique. Indeed, the latter may well have imitated this practice in the magnificent *Cancionero* he dedicated to the Count of Benavente.[2] The other possibility is that Santillana wished to assure Don Pedro that his anthology contained faithful copies of the originals, in the same way as other European writers in the fourteenth and fifteenth centuries showed a concern for the authenticity of their texts.[3] But whatever the interpretation, this statement testifies to a heightened degree of literary pride which hardly accords with his earlier show of self-criticism.

Equally hard to define is his general attitude towards his work on a more personal level. Having decided to classify it as yet another *cortesano exercicio*, he is bound by the laws of decorum to dissociate himself from it, as he would from any behaviour that could be considered inappropriate or undignified in an aristocrat no longer in the first flush of youth. Nevertheless, Santillana's words once again strike an ambivalent note: 'muchas cosas plazen agora a vos que ya no plazen *o no deven plazer a mí*' (p. 438; my italics). The qualification contained in the last clause might have been added

---

[2] It is not possible to date all the poems in either *Cancionero*, but those that can be dated have been arranged chronologically within generic distinctions. For precedents, see Riquer, *Los trovadores*, I, 17, and III, 1610–11, and Huot, *From Song to Book*.

[3] According to Miguel Angel Pérez Priego, MSS known to have been prepared under Santillana's supervision reveal a poet who is 'insólitamente preocupado por la fijación definitiva de sus textos', *Poesías completas*, I, Clásicos Alhambra, 25 (Madrid: Alhambra, 1983), pp. 3–14, at p. 3; further examples in Macpherson, 'Don Juan Manuel'; Robert K. Root, 'Publication before Printing', *PMLA*, 28 (1913), 417–31; Sarah Jane Williams, 'An Author's Role in Fourteenth-Century Book Production: Guillaume de Machaut's "livre ou je met toutes mes choses"', *R*, 90 (1969), 433–54; Laidlaw, 'Christine de Pizan'.

merely to round out the phrase, but, on the other hand, it also allows the reader to infer that he did in fact continue to enjoy, or even write, frivolous and amatory verse (and as I show below, the chronology of his poems bears out this inference).

Despite its ambivalence, the implicit theoretical assumption of this opening passage is quite clear: poetry must evolve and mature in accordance with the poet's own intellectual and spiritual development. This was a well-established belief, and often put poets in an awkward position with regard to their youthful verse; Dante provides a clear and extremely interesting example. The love poems of his early *Vita nuova* (1292–93) earned him a reputation which seems to have caused him considerable embarrassment in later years. He begins his *Convivio* (1304–07), a learned commentary on three of these youthful poems, with the very same arguments Santillana was to employ in *El proemio*: 'altro si conviene e dire e operare ad una etade che ad altra; perche certi costumi sono idonei e laudabili ad una etade che sono sconci e biasimevoli ad altra' (I, i, 17; *Opere*, p. 680; also, IV, xxiv). But Dante is able to resolve his predicament in a much more radical way than Santillana: he does not reject—or pretend to reject—his earlier poetry ('non intendo però a quella in parte alcuna derogare', I, i, 16), he simply reinterprets it. His allegorical exegesis shows that his passionate amatory verse really contained profound philosophical truths.

Returning to Santillana, immediately following his definition of poetry, in which, among other things, he emphasizes its utility, he deals with the accusation that it consists merely of 'cosas vanas e lascivas' (p. 440). This hackneyed objection is dismissed with the statement that:

> bien commo los fructíferos huertos habundan e dan convenientes fructos para todos los tienpos del año, assý los onbres bien nascidos e doctos, a quien estas sciencias de arriba son infusas, usan de aquéllas e del tal exercicio segund las hedades. (p. 440)

Each stage in man's life, therefore, is marked out by an appropriate conduct, a characteristic form of behaviour that produces 'convenientes fructos'. This had already been hinted at in the opening lines of *El proemio*, but here, from the point of view of literary theory, the concept of decorum has important and far-reaching implications. According to Santillana, the detractors of poetry had attacked it on the grounds that it was inherently immoral. But he is able to counter this charge by resorting to the argument that it should be considered, above all, as a medium of expression; his choice of vocabulary (*usar, exercicio*) draws attention to the fact that poetry is a practical instrument, used for good or evil according to the will of the individual (and of course, as he later explains, the best poets are by definition 'bien nascidos e doctos'). For this reason, if a poem is truly immoral, the blame lies not with poetry itself, but with the poet.

A similar approach (though in an entirely different context) was adopted by St Augustine in the first book of his *Confessions*. Here, he looks back with remorse upon his youthful infatuation with the works of pagan poets, and regrets the many hours wasted attending lectures on the vain and fruitless subject of literature. But the actual words of the poems he criticizes are exempt from all blame. 'Non accuso verba', he explains, 'quasi vasa lecta et pretiosa, sed vinum erroris, quod in eis nobis propinabatur ab ebriis doctoribus'.[4] Although St Augustine's attitude towards pagan culture was uncompromisingly severe in later life, this passage nevertheless set an invaluable precedent for future defenders of poetry. It allowed them to deflect criticism away from the art (the 'vasa lecta et pretiosa') and focus it upon the personality of the poet.[5] And although it is not possible to determine whether he actually had St Augustine in mind, this is precisely the tactic employed by Santillana. He implicitly concedes that some poetry consists of 'cosas vanas e lascivas', while at the same time suggesting that such faults are more a reflection of the moral and intellectual maturity of the poet than of the inherent nature of his art.

Santillana could also have drawn support from the fact that similar arguments were used in defence of rhetoric. Cicero, for example, begins his influential treatise *De inventione* by asking why rhetoric has so often been the cause of evil, rather than of good. He

[4] St Augustine, *Confessions*, with an English translation by William Watts (1631), Loeb Classical Library, 26–27 (1912; Cambridge, Mass: Harvard Univ. Press; London: Heinemann, 1968–70); see Bk I, ch. 16. Though Santillana owned an Italian translation of the *Confessions*, he could well have been familiar with this passage secondhand, via John of Wales, *Florilegium*, VIII, 3, 'de arte poetica'.

[5] For the influence of St Augustine's image of the *vasa pretiosa* on Petrarch, see *Familiares*, X, 4; the view that the art is wholly innocent of the abuses of individual poets is also expressed in his third invective; see also Boccaccio, *De genealogia*, XIV, 6; Albertino Mussato (1261–1329), Epistles VII and XVIII; for Mussato and Petrarch, see Ronconi, *Le origini*, pp. 24–25, 42, 94, 110–11. The argument re-emerges in Encina's *Arte de poesía castellana*, ed. López Estrada, in *Las poéticas castellanas*, p. 81.

observes that eloquence has been grossly misused, but it is not itself at fault. Eloquence, he concludes, is a powerful weapon, and whoever arms himself with it must be prepared to fight for the benefit of the state rather than against it (I, i, l). The image of the weapon was taken up and developed by Alonso de Cartagena in the prologue to his translation of this work. The moral effect of rhetorical precepts depends entirely upon the speaker; and, while accepting the possibility that they may be put to evil use, he asserts that:

> nin por esto son de dexar; ca el fierro non es de dexar, aunque con él se cometen a las veces injustos omecidos e muertos a mala verdat, porque las armas fechas dél aprovechan a esforçar la justicia e a justa defensión de la república e opresión de los injustos e malos.   (ed. Mascagna, p. 34)

Language, according to this approach, is wholly neutral.

The use made of poetry 'segund las hedades' is again discussed in the penultimate section of *El proemio*. Here Santillana forestalls the possible objection that idleness ('una manera de occiosidat') has enabled him to write at such length about the history of verse. Such an accusation, he claims, would be quite unwarranted, considering his age and 'la turbación de los tienpos' (p. 454). This statement owes something to the demands of rhetoric (writers often claimed that outside forces prevented them from giving the necessary polish to their work; it was also a commonplace that old age should not be wasted in idle pursuits). Yet this self-justification is by no means an empty topos. At the time of writing these lines, Santillana was approaching fifty, and still actively involved in the civil strife that marked the period 1445–49.[6] And it is against this background of political turmoil that we should judge his conclusions about the value of the many poets listed in his historical survey. Concerning these 'auctores' he writes:

> Pero es asý que, commo en la nueva edad me pluguiesen, fallélos agora, quando me paresció ser necessarios. Ca asý commo Oracio poeta dize: 'Quem noua concepit olla seruabit odorem'.   (p. 454)

It is significant that he talks here in terms of 'los auctores' rather than of 'la gaya sciencia'. It seems to suggest that he has in mind the study of literature, as opposed to the act of writing it. Interest in

---

[6] Up-to-date documentation offered by Rogelio Pérez Bustamante and José Manuel Calderón Ortega, *El marqués de Santillana: biografía y documentación*, Fuentes Documentales para la Historia de Santillana, 1 (Santillana del Mar: Fundación Santillana and Taurus, 1983), pp. 73–82.

the emotional relief—a kind of catharsis—afforded by literary creativity is far from common in fifteenth-century Castile, though there was, by contrast, a well-established tradition that to read (or to be read to) was an effective means of calming a troubled mind: anxiety, insomnia, or serious personal loss are all remedied by the power of literature to entertain or edify.[7]

The idea that books provided a necessary source of consolation makes a frequent appearance in Santillana's work. In the early 1450s, for instance, he commissioned his son, Pedro González de Mendoza, to translate Decembrio's Latin version of Homer 'por consolación e utilidad mía' (*Obras completas*, pp. 455–57, at p. 456). Towards the end of his letter, he recalls with evident pride that many classical works had been translated at his request, such as Virgil's *Aeneid*, Ovid's *Metamorphoses*, Seneca's *Tragedies*:

> e muchas otras cosas en que yo me he deleytado fasta este tiempo e me deleyto, y son assí como un singular reposo a las vexaciones y travajos que el mundo continuamente trae, mayormente en estos nuestros reynos.   (p. 457)

These lines are an exact restatement of the idea expressed toward the end of *El proemio*. In both, Santillana confesses, with an emphasis not commonly found amongst his contemporaries, that throughout his life literature has been a constant source not only of edification but also, and this is no less important, of sheer enjoyment.

But I do not think we have fully understood the way in which this belief in the consolatory power of literature actually affected his own poetic practice. Only a few years after the composition of *El proemio*, he wrote the lengthy dialogue *Bías contra Fortuna* with the express purpose of consoling his cousin, the Count of Alba, imprisoned in 1448 by Alvaro de Luna. Early on in the prologue,

---

[7] For one of the rare examples of the cathartic view of poetry, see Gómez Manrique in the *Consolatoria* dedicated to his wife on the death of two of their children: 'pensé de hazer este tractado para consolación de tu merced y para mi descanso, por que descansando en este papel como si contigo hablara, afloxase el hervor de mi congoxa, como haze el de la olla quando se sale, que por poca agua que salga, avada mucho y ella no rebienta' (*Can. cas.*, II, 16). For a contrasting view, see Teresa de Cartagena, who begins her *Arboleda de los enfermos* by stating that she had derived immense consolation for her deafness from reading the Psalms (described as spiritual *canciones*). On the other hand, she later asserts that eloquence itself cannot calm one's spiritual afflictions, and it **can even exacerbate** physical pain.

he tells the Count that he decided to 'investigar alguna nueva manera, assý commo remedios o meditación contra Fortuna' (*Obras completas*, pp. 270–335, at p. 271). These words provide the key both to the text and to the self-image its author wished to project. *Investigar* announces the work as a product of that speculative wisdom which, according to the precepts of both Villena and Encina, is the hallmark of the true poet. It is a 'nueva manera' for reasons of form and content: it is the first poem to give full literary expression to a synthesis of Christianity and Senecan stoicism, and it is cast in the mould of a meditative sermon. The poet's 'thema' (a synonym for *materia* which I have not encountered elsewhere), is the question '¿Qué es lo que piensas, Fortuna?'. Stated at the outset and close of the poem, it sets a mood of defiant resignation on which the Count is supposed to meditate as he works his way through the debate between Bías and Fortuna. Implicit throughout is the assumption that the poem is born of Santillana's own contemplative experience, or *reposado estudio*, of Seneca's philosophy.[8]

To return to *El proemio*, Santillana's life-long enthusiasm for poetry is summed up by Horace's axiom (quoted incorrectly) that 'Quem noua concepit olla seruabit odorem'—'the pot will preserve the smell which it acquired when new'.[9] As far as the source of this image is concerned, it is not necessary to argue, as Garci-Gómez has, that Santillana had direct knowledge of Horace's Epistles. (These do not seem to have been particularly well known at the time, although Villena refers to them in his *Tratado de la consolación*; even if Santillana had heard of them, he could not have read them unaided.) He probably learnt of Horace's image at second hand, possibly from Bk I of Augustine's *City of God* (a work that he seems to have known quite well, in spite of some enigmatic references to it in the glosses to his *Proverbios*), or, which I think more likely, from some medieval *florilegium*. In one of his more scathing attacks on pagan culture, St Augustine scorns the Romans for being proud

---

[8] For discussion, with full bibliography, of the poem's form and content, see the introd. to the ed. by Maxim. P. A. M. Kerkhof, Anejos del *BRAE*, 39 (Madrid: Real Academia Española, 1982 [1983]); see also James F. Burke, 'The *Libro de buen amor* and the Medieval Meditative Sermon Tradition', *C*, 9 (1980–81), 122–27.

[9] The correct text is 'Quo semel est imbuta recens, seruabit odorem/ testa diu' (*Epistles*, Bk I, 2, ll. 69–70), an image used to support Horace's views about the durability of moral lessons learnt in impressionable youth.

of teaching their young to read poets who honour heathen gods. As an example of these poets, he refers to Virgil:

> quem propterea parvuli legunt ut videlicet poeta magnus omniumque praeclarissimus atque optimus teneris ebibitus animis non facile oblivione possit aboleri, secundum illud Horatii: 'Quo semel est inbuta recens servabit odorem/ testa diu'.[10]

That Augustine uses the image here for wholly negative reasons is immaterial; as we shall see, this did not deter Petrarch from borrowing it to describe his own innate love of poetry in his third invective. However, it is impossible to say whether this passage provided Santillana's immediate inspiration, since Horace's image soon acquired the status of an aphorism for writers on rhetoric and poetry. It was cited by Quintilian, Matthew of Vendôme and, in the late fifteenth century, by Juan del Encina as an illustration of how the rules of eloquence must be mastered in one's youth.[11]

To sum up, Santillana frames his treatise with two comments on his life-long relationship with poetry. When set side by side, these remarks give rise to a certain degree of ambiguity. For judging by the broad range of authors discussed in his historical sketch, the final affirmation that poetry has been a continuous source of delight clearly includes the kind of verse from which he tried to dissociate himself in the opening lines of *El proemio*. In spite of his claim that courtly poems 'ya no plazen o no deven plazer a mí', he later displays considerable fondness and admiration for the works of poets like Macías and Villasandino, summarizing his feelings with the observation that 'commo en la nueva edad me pluguiesen, fallélos agora'. The posture he adopts at the start is, at least in appearance, strictly orthodox: each age possesses its own distinctive quality, its own legitimate forms of behaviour. Yet by the time he has defined poetry, defended it against the charge of immorality, eulogized its dignity and versatility and, finally, reeled off an impressive list of famous and not so famous poets, his initial concern for the laws of decorum seems to have disappeared.

The weight of tradition regarding decorum was enormous: it would have been difficult for Santillana not to have drawn Don

---

[10] St Augustine, *The City of God Against the Pagans*, with an English translation by George E. McCracken *et al.*, Loeb Classical Library, 411–17 (Cambridge, Mass: Harvard Univ. Press; London: Heinemann, 1957–72), in Bk I, ch 3. See also Garci-Gómez, 'Otras huellas de Horacio', p. 132.

[11] Quintilian, *Institutio*, I, i; Matthew of Vendôme, *Ars versificatoria*, l. 26; Encina, *Arte*, ed. López Estrada, p. 85.

Pedro's attention to the fact that different literary tastes were expected for them. As the quotation from II Corinthians 13. 11, shows ('Cum essem paruulus, loquebar ut paruulus'), the Bible was an authoritative influence on ideas about the inherent appropriateness of each stage in life. Ecclesiastes might also have played a part in setting the tone of the opening lines of *El proemio*; according to Pedro Díaz de Toledo, this book was one source for Santillana's proverb, 'Al tienpo e a la sazón/ Sey conforme,/ Ca lo contrario/ Es ynorme/ Perdición'.[12] One might also detect the influence of St Augustine: the fourth book of *De doctrina Christiana*, which established the ideals of Christian rhetoric, has as a basic principle the notion that each age demands a different form of eloquence.[13] Yet the tradition was not exclusively Christian: Cicero's *De senectute*, for example, was an influential work (Dante cites it in his discussion of decorum in *Convivio*, IV, xxiv and xxvii). This treatise, which was twice translated in early fifteenth-century Castile, once by Cartagena, teaches that:

> El curso es cierto de la hedad, e cierta la carrera de la natura ... e su manera de tiempo es dada a cada parte. ... Así la madureza de la vegez tiene algo que en su tiempo se deve coger.[14]

Santillana's comments on decorum are certainly very brief; nonetheless, it is noticeable that he does not attempt to give much emphasis to the concept of 'la madureza de la vegez'. That this is so is particularly apparent when one contrasts *El proemio* with the discussion of poetry and maturity in Petrarch's third invective, one of this author's most elaborate and forceful literary defences. In many respects the two works are very different, but they have one basic point in common. Both writers confess their permanent love for poetry, and, to convey the full force of their conviction, they both resort to Horace's image of the wine-flask. However, unlike

---

[12] *Los proverbios con su glosa (Sevilla, 1494)*, Incunables Poéticos Castellanos, 11 (Cieza: 'la fonte que mana y corre', 1965), f. d vii^r; for Díaz de Toledo's gloss, see f. d viii^v.

[13] 'Sicut est enim quaedam eloquentia quae magis aetatem juvenilem decet, est quae senilem', ed. J.-P. Migne, PL, 34 (Paris, 1861) cols 15–122, at col. 93; see also Baldwin, *Medieval Rhetoric*, p. 59.

[14] X, 33; Cartagena's translation, BN Madrid, MS 7.815, f. 15^r. The second rendering is anonymous, included in BN Madrid, MS 2.617. Santillana also owned an Italian version (Schiff, *La Bibliothèque*, pp. 59–60). See also Cartagena: 'Nam sicut et alia, sic et scolastica delectabilia etatis cursus transmutat' (*Un tratado*, ed. Lawrance, p. 30).

Santillana, Petrarch claims that he no longer reads the works of poets:

> non que me pese haberlos leído, mas porque ya leerlos me parece superfluo. Leílos mientra la edad lo sufrió, y en tal manera en los meollos me son fincados, que non se pueden arrancar aunque yo quiera.[15]

Then, after illustrating this with the lines from Horace (which, again unlike Santillana, he explicitly borrows from St Augustine), he goes on to stress that although he has retained his innate love of poetry and his respect for the title *poeta* which he sought so earnestly in his youth, his quest for *maturitas* has led him away from secular interests towards the study of theology:

> Como de las manzanas y mieses, de los estudios y entenderes debe ser madureza .... Y porque conosco mi impotencia, demando ayuda del cielo y deléictome en las Letras Sacras .... Madurar a lo menos deseo, si por ventura aún no maduré. (pp. 394–95)

Petrarch's concern for spiritual development is much more clearly articulated than that of Santillana: nothing can detract from the esteem in which he holds poetry, yet nevertheless he relegates it to a specific period of his life. As we have seen, Santillana acknowledges the demands of *maturitas*, but he has no qualms about confessing his dependence upon secular poetry for instruction and entertainment even in his later years.

The third inventive does not seem to have been particularly well known in Castile.[16] This is unfortunate, because in addition to being a strikingly positive defence of poetry, it also offered a compromise between two extremes: Santillana's permanent and undaunted enthusiasm for poetry and the often guilty outlook implicit in the tradition of literary retractions. The only poet, to my knowledge, who comes close to achieving this Petrarchan compromise was Pero López de Ayala, who, as Michel García put it in his discussion of the thematic and metrical variety of the *Rimado de Palacio*, accepted:

> la necesidad de asumir su obra en totalidad y la incapacidad de disociar la experiencia vivida de la escritura .... En la hora del balance, el autor no

---

[15] Trans. Hernando de Talavera (*c.* 1450), *Invectivas contra el médico rudo e parlero* [nos I and III only], ed. Pedro Cátedra, in *Petrarca: Obras*, I: *Prosa*, ed. Francisco Rico *et al.* (Madrid: Alfaguara, 1978), pp. 369–410, at p. 394.

[16] Alan Deyermond, *The Petrarchan Sources of 'La Celestina'*, 2nd ed. (Westport, Conn: Greenwood Press, 1975), lists no references to the *Invectivas* and Hernando de Talavera's translation seems the only sign of interest.

> puede elegir entre sus obras las que mejor le convengan. Lo único que le
> queda es asignar a cada una el marco vital que la rodeó, aunque sólo sea para
> no atribuir al anciano las obras y las locuras del mancebo.
>
> (*Obra y personalidad*, pp. 301–02)

By contrast, the careers of some of the most notable
fifteenth-century poets, such as Juan de Mena, Montoro, Juan
Alvarez Gato and, later, Diego de San Pedro, are distinguished by
their severe, apparently abrupt, renunciation of their secular verse,
which they had been taught to associate with paganism and, above
all, with the sins and folly of youth. Mena, one of the leading
figures of the classicizing movement, provides the most startling
example of this *volte-face*. His intensely didactic *Coplas de los siete
pecados mortales*, which was left unfinished at his death in 1456,
begins with an invocation to the 'christiana musa' in which the
pagan muses who inspired his early verse are passionately rejected:
'las sus tales niñerías/ vayan con la joventud'.[17]

A similar retreat into a world of Christian didacticism occurs in
the work of Fernán Pérez de Guzmán. Towards the end of his life
(at least after 1454), he appeared to 'pasar a lo divino' as Cartagena
put it, and renounce the secular verse of his youth and middle
age.[18] This change seems to be adumbrated in his didactic poetry,

[17] Ed. Gladys M. Rivera, '*Coplas de los siete pecados mortales*' *and First
Continuation* (Madrid: Porrúa Turanzas, 1982), pp. 60–61. For an analysis of this
passage, its influence on later poets such as Juan de Padilla and Fray Iñigo de
Mendoza, and its relation to the ideas of Patristic writers, see Joaquín Gimeno
Casalduero, 'San Jerónimo y el rechazo y la aceptacíon de la poesía en la Castilla de
finales del siglo XV', in *La creacíon literaria de la Edad Media y del Renacimiento (su
forma y su significado)* (Madrid: Porrúa Turanzas, 1977), pp. 45–65; Otis H. Green,
'"Fingen los poetas"—Notes on the Spanish Attitude toward Pagan Mythology',
in *The Literary Mind of Medieval and Renaissance Spain: Essays by Otis H. Green*, ed.
John E. Keller (Lexington: Univ. Press of Kentucky, 1970), pp. 113–23. Palinodes
became something of a literary topos, and should not always be taken at face value.
Perhaps the best illustration of this is Chaucer's conclusion to the *Canterbury Tales*,
an ironic mixture of commonplace formulae and artistic pride; see Olive Sayce,
'Chaucer's "Retractions": The Conclusion of *The Canterbury Tales* and its Place in
Literary Tradition', *MAe*, 40 (1971), 230–48; John Tatlock, 'Chaucer's *Retractions*',
PMLA, 28 (1913), 521–29, traces the development of the term 'retraction' from
Augustine (to review and revise one's work) to Jean de Meun (to withdraw or
reject it).

[18] See Cartagena's prologue to his *Oracional*, written only a short time after the
death of Juan II: 'agora acordades passar a lo divino ... escriviendo ... hymnos e
oraciones', ed. González-Quevedo, p. 45. The dangers of making simplistic
classifications in this poet's work have been pointed out by Lida de Malkiel (*Juan
de Mena*, p. 393), and by Tate, *Generaciones*, p. xiii. Nevertheless, there is some

written in his late forties and fifties. In the lengthy introduction to one of these works, *Los loores de los claros varones de Castilla*, he casts aside the classical writers (Virgil and Ovid) whom Santillana considered to be an essential source of consolation and delight, and looks to Jerome as the model for authorial standards:

> De los ilustres varones
> San Gerónimo tratando,
> non le veo Cicerones
> nin Ovidio memorando,
> antes se quexa, que quando
> fue puesto ante el tribunal
> del juez celestial
> dixo su culpa llorando.
>
> (st. 50; *Can. cas.*, I, 711–12)

This passage demonstrates how poets could draw support for their distrust of secular verse from a long and authoritative tradition stretching back to the early days of the Christian church. As Gimeno Casalduero has shown, Jerome was particularly influential in forming the attitudes of later generations towards pagan literature. His two most important works in this respect were his epistles to Pammachius and Magnus (AD 397–98), in which he argues that although it is permissible to read the works of pagan poets, the true Christian should do so only with the utmost caution: whatever did not accord with Christian teaching should be rejected outright. And in fifteenth-century Castile, this doctrine was popularized by Juan de Mena:

> Usemos de los poemas
> tomando d'ellos lo bueno,
> mas fuygan de nuestro seno
> las sus fabulosas temas;
> las sus ficiones y poblemas

---

evidence to support the hypothesis that after his political retirement in 1432, he began to take an increasingly moral attitude towards poetry. There are fourteen brief occasional poems extant; these are collected in the *Cancionero de Baena*, and most of them (e.g. the exchanges with Villasandino, died *c.* 1424) can be dated before 1430. The longer didactic poems *Confesión rimada*, *Coplas de vicios e virtudes*, *Los loores de los claros varones*, were written before 1452 when they were collected in *El cancionero de los duques de Gor*. These last two poems contain references to social isolation, suggesting they were written after his retirement. Two other didactic works, *La coronación de las quatro virtudes* and *Los proverbios*, were written only 'bien poco tienpo' before *El proemio* (Santillana's comment on p. 453). *La coronación* is post 1445: Pérez de Guzmán refers to his nephew as 'el marqués'.

desechemos como espinas.
(*Pecados mortales*, st. 14; ed. Rivera, p. 64)

But Jerome was not the only fourth-century ecclesiastical writer
to adopt this approach. Similar views were advanced by St Basil in
his homily, *De legendis libris gentilium*. In this work he accepts that
the pagans had something of value to offer, but, like Jerome, he
stresses that their poetry should be read only to extract what was
morally useful. Basil's homily was well known in the later Middle
Ages and early Renaissance, and, as I have already mentioned,
Santillana himself owned a translation of it, possibly by Nuño de
Guzmán (see above, p. 163). This Castilian version was written
about the same time as *El proemio* (c. 1445), and no doubt Santillana
considered what Basil had to say as authoritative confirmation of
his view that poetry did not consist merely of 'cosas vanas e
lascivas'. But on the other hand, Basil's text could also be
interpreted in a much less positive light. About the same time as
Santillana was recommending poetry as a source of entertainment
and moral instruction, another aristocratic bibliophile, the Count of
Haro, was being given a stern lesson on the kinds of literature
appropriate for the noble caste. The author of this lecture was
Santillana's companion, Alonso de Cartagena.[19] Drawing on the
very precepts laid down by Basil, he warned the Count not to be
captivated by the sweetness of those works:

> qui ad inhonestatem videntur allicere, uti sunt amatoria, bucolica, aliaque
> poetarum figmenta, que, licet eloquenti stillo et acuta inventione composita
> sint, magnámque ingenii elevationem ostentent, cum mirabili compositione
> metrorum exquisitisque verbis coagulata dulcem saporem conficiant, in
> nonnullis tamen eorem materia obscena et provocativa libidinum est. (p. 50)

The severity with which Cartagena classes the *figmenta poetarum*
among those works that stimulate licentiousness provides a stark
contrast to Santillana's attitude to poetry. The former reserves
specific condemnation for amatory verse and the tales of Lancelot
and Amadís (p. 54); but for Santillana such works are legitimate,
indeed wholly appropriate, when composed in 'la nueva hedad de
juventud'. Although he acknowledges the fact that there comes a
time when one should put away such 'childish things', his remarks
on courtly poetry are, as we have seen, somewhat equivocal: this
ambiguity suggests, I think, not only a certain degree of literary

---

[19] On Cartagena's literary attitudes, see Lawrance, *Un tratado*, 12–26; López
Estrada, 'La retórica', pp. 339–49; Kohut, 'Der Beitrag', pp. 189–202.

pride in his own work, but also a fundamentally tolerant attitude towards the genre in general.

Before we leave this topic, one final comparison needs to be made with Boethius, one of the most influential *auctores* of the Middle Ages. The famous opening scene of his *De consolatione* depicts the self-pitying attempts of an old man to find consolation for the trials of fortune by retreating to the favourite pastime of his youth, the composition of verse: 'Gloria felicis olim viridisque iuentae/ Solantur maesti nunc mea fata senis'.[20] But the Muses at his bedside are soon chased away by the imposing figure of Philosophy: contemplation and study supplant poetic creation. This crucial passage became the subject of some dispute: like Plato's expulsion of the poets from the ideal republic, Boethius's rejection of the Muses was particularly irksome to those who defended the claims of poetry. They surmounted the problem posed by this formidable authority by re-interpreting his criticism.[21] Nevertheless, it set a firm precedent for the view that poetry could offer no consolation in adversity and, in particular, that it was of no use to man in his preparation to face death. The influence of Boethius may be clearly detected in the opening stanzas of Mena's *Coplas de los siete pecados mortales*, as Gimeno Casalduero has shown ('San Jerónimo', pp. 58–60). But the notions that underlie Boethius's retraction had already been transformed into aphorisms. The vast collection of *sententiae, La floresta de philósophos*, compiled either by or for Fernán Pérez de Guzmán, summarizes a number of the basic themes of *De consolatione*. Among them is the idea that 'Los cantares que en algund tiempo nos heran alegres, en otro nos fazen ser tristes', or that 'Los cantares non consuelan al mezquino, antes le acrecientan el dolor'.[22]

On the face of it, Santillana's own poetic career does not seem to

[20] *The Consolation of Philosophy*, with an English translation by S. J. Tester, Loeb Classical Library, 74 (London: Heinemann; Cambridge, Mass: Harvard Univ. Press, 1973), I, i, 7–8.

[21] Mussato (Epistles VII and XVIII), Petrarch (Invectives I and III) and Boccaccio (*De genealogia*, XIV, 20) argued that Boethius had restricted his attack to the theatrical Muses. Enrique de Villena adopted a different tactic. Dismissing Trevet's explanation that the 'scénicas meretrículas' refer to poetry, he claims that it is far better to interpret them as 'las pasiones del ánima, mayormente ... yra e temor' (*Tratado de la consolación*, ed. Carr, p. 30; see note 5 for the relevant gloss by Nicholas Trevet).

[22] '*Floresta de philósophos*', ed. Raymond Foulché–Delbosc, *RH*, 11 (1904), 5–154; these aphorisms are nos 467 and 469 in the collection.

have been affected by the attitudes of Jerome and Boethius, nor by
the literary recantations of his contemporaries. It is true that his
later poems betray a greater interest in religious, moral and political
matters; but it is also true that, even at the time of writing *El
proemio*, his taste for love poetry or light-hearted occasional verse
had not deserted him. Indeed, the majority of Castilian poems cited
in his history are, in fact, examples of courtly love lyrics.[23]
Therefore, although one can trace a development in Santillana's
work, it seems to have been much less pronounced than in the case
of, say, Fernán Pérez de Guzmán. So it is especially interesting that
this poet was one of the very few men ever to comment adversely
on Santillana's work. In his *Coronación de las quatro virtudes* (written
only just before *El proemio* and dedicated to Santillana), he includes
the following enigmatic reproach:

> entre aquella fermosura
> de las vuestras clavellinas,
> ya vimos nascer espinas
> entre lyrios e verdura.
> (*Can. cas.*, I, 671; st. 65)

Lapesa considers these lines to be an oblique reference to one of
Santillana's extra-marital affairs (*La obra literaria*, p. 275). However,
if we interpret the imagery as a reference to the flowers of rhetoric
or to poetic adornment in general, then this obscure passage
becomes a comment on the use, or rather misuse, of eloquence. It
recalls the image of the dangerous thorns of poetry, as used, for
example, by St Basil in his homily *De legendis libris gentilium*:

> assí como en el coger de las rosas nos guardamos de las espinas del rosal,
> assí tomando de las escripturas lo que fuere útil, declinaremos lo otro que
> podrá dañar.[24]

And as we have seen, this idea was repeated by Mena in his

---

[23] See Whetnall, 'Manuscript Love Poetry', p. 93; see also the exchanges of
preguntas y respuestas with Juan de Mena (post 1439, Lapesa, *La obra literaria*, pp.
266–67). In 1444, Santillana sent doña Violante de Prades seventeen sonnets,
dealing, in the main, with commonplace themes of courtly love. In the original MS
(now lost) they accompany his *Proverbios* and *La comedieta de Ponza*, indicating that
he did not feel it necessary to keep his serious moral and philosophical works
separate from those that might have been considered frivolous 'cortesanos
exercicios'. Even amongst the late devotional sonnets, there are two love poems
(nos 37 and 40) that draw on religious imagery.

[24] From the translation owned by Santillana (Paris BN, fonds espagnol, MS
458, f. 66ᵛ).

exhortation to cast aside the unhealthy elements of classical verse: 'sus ficiones e poemas/ desechemos como espinas'. Fernán Pérez, therefore, seems to imply that his nephew, in spite of his undoubted literary talents, preserves a wholly inappropriate interest in poetry of a non-didactic nature. His heart and mind are still engrossed in contemplation of the Poetic Muses who, as Boethius put it, 'con infructuosas espinas de deleytes matan la mies de la razón' (I, prose I, 9; BN Madrid, MS 10.220, f. 6^v).

Santillana's remarks on poetry in youth and maturity add an extra dimension to his eulogy: instead of arguing from a purely theoretical position, he also bases his defence on personal experience—a widely-recommended rhetorical ploy. The validity both of his definition of poetry and of his explanation of its historical authority is reinforced by the argument that he has spent the greater part of his life in the fruitful and enjoyable study of verse.

2 The definition

In contrast to the apparent diffidence with which he treats his own youthful attempts at writing poetry, Santillana greets Don Pedro's incipient literary interest with open enthusiasm:

> vos quiero certificar me plaze mucho que todas cosas que entren o anden so esta regla de poetal canto vos plegan ... Commo es cierto este sea un zelo celeste, una affección divina, un insaciable cibo del ánimo. (p. 439)

This last statement poses a delicate problem of interpretation, since it is hard to decide exactly how far its formulation is affected by purely stylistic considerations. Tripartite figures of amplification are characteristic of the style of prose adopted throughout *El proemio*, and on most occasions it is obvious that the separate elements are synonymous and have been added simply to give rhythm and grandeur to the phrase. But whether or not this is the case here is hard to tell, for the simple reason that each term is open to more than one possible interpretation. The problem centres mainly on the difficulty of distinguishing between *zelo* and *affección*; they both bring to mind the same two, quite distinct, literary theories: a) the concept of *furor poeticus*, and b) the poet's love of his art.

a) *Furor poeticus*

The term *zelo* (or its alternative *celo*) could denote a variety of emotions ranging from intense passion to jealousy, emulation or desire.[25] It would be quite feasible, therefore, to interpret Santillana's 'zelo celeste' as an attempt to render the idea of poetic fury: a kind of madness, or inner force which is the poet's chief source of inspiration. This possibility is strengthened by the fact that, even without the adjective *celeste*, the word is charged with certain religious overtones which are closely related to the kind of *furor* in question here.

According to Corominas, its earliest attestation is in Berceo's *Sacrificio de la Misa* (st. 27), where the phrase 'summo celo' is used to evokes such passages in the Bible as John 2.17, or Psalm 69.9: 'zelus domus tuae comedit me'. It is that violent fervour which consumed so many Old Testament priests and prophets, inspired by a jealous God. Latinisms abound in *El proemio*, but the choice of *zelo* instead of *celo* is perhaps determined by the desire to recall the biblical notion of being fired by God's passion, and thus emphasize that the poet is driven on by a force over which he himself has no control. Interpreted in this way, Santillana's 'zelo celeste' possibly derives from Isidore's concept of poetic *vesania*:

> Vates a vi mentis appellatos Varro auctor est ... et proinde poetae Latine vates olim, scripta eorum vaticinia dicebantur, quod vi quadam et quasi vesania in scribendo commoverentur .... Etiam per furorem divini eodem erant nomine.[26] (*Etymologiae*, VIII, vii, 3)

Boccaccio also claims that the poet is inspired by an inner force, although he places less emphasis than Isidore on the irrationality of the creative act. His *furor* is a longing for utterance, rather than a kind of madness, or *vesania*: it is a 'fervor quidam exquisite inveniendi atque dicendi, seu scribendi quod inveneris' (*De genealogia*, XIV, 7; ed. Romano, II, 669). Many critics have assumed that this passage is the direct source for Santillana's definition of poetry as 'un zelo celeste' etc. (indeed, that the whole of his definition is based on Boccaccio). This assumption has never been properly examined. Although, for reasons that will become clearer in the course of this discussion, it would be rash to discount Boccaccio altogether, it would be equally unwise to claim that he is

---

[25] See Corominas and Pascual, *DCECH*, *s.v.* 'celo'.

[26] See also Isidore's definition of the term *carmen*: 'qui illa canerent carere mentem extimabantur' (I, xxxix, 4).

the exclusive source for this section of *El proemio*. As I have already suggested, Santillana's 'zelo' (if it means poetic fury) could be an attempt to render Isidore's *vesania*, and, in addition, it calls to mind the biblical *ʒelus*.

One could also interpret 'affección divina' as this irrational impulse. Like *ʒelo*, it had a wide semantic range, but it was often used to highlight the conflict between man's reason and his emotion, and to describe the unstable element in the human temperament.[27] It is not surprising, therefore, that the anonymous translator of Bruni's *Vite di Dante e di Petrarca* should consider it an appropriate term to convey one of this writer's theories about poetic inspiration. Bruni claims that there are two kinds of poet. One achieves mastery of his art by continuous intellectual toil, 'por lección de estorias, e por tractar e volver muchos e varios libros, velando e sudando en los estudios' (BN MS 10.171, f. 43ʳ). The other, which Bruni prefers, acquires his wisdom like St Francis, through the prompting of a spontaneous inner force: 'por interior affección e movimiento e despertamiento de mente' (f. 43ʳ; 'astrazione ed agitazione di mente').[28]

This use of the word *affección* is one of the very few examples of a close verbal parallel between *El proemio* and another text. It would be tempting to conclude, therefore, that Santillana borrowed it

---

[27] *Afección* seems to have entered Castilian in the late XIV or early XVc as a learned equivalent of the Latin *afectio*. The brief reference in *DCECH* (*s.v.* 'afecto') does not cover the range of contexts in which it could be used. See José A. Pascual, *La traducción de la 'Divina commedia' atribuida a don Enrique de Aragón: estudio y edición del 'Infierno'*, Acta Salmanticensia, Filosofía y Letras, 82 (Salamanca: Universidad, 1974), p. 188, and Santiago Lacuesta, *La primera versión castellana de la 'Eneida'*, p. 160. In addition to meaning 'goodwill', 'love' or 'desire for something', *afección* could denote irrationality, or susceptibility to emotional change, as in Mena's dictum 'lo que guía el afición/ las menos vezes acierta' (*Los siete pecados mortales*, st. 11, ed. Rivera, p. 63). See also Cartagena's translation of *De inventione*, where it renders the rhetorical term *affectio*: 'aquella mudación que acaesce en el coraçón o en el cuerpo en algunt tiempo por alguna cabsa, como alegría, cobdicia, miedo, tristeza, dolencia, flaqueza o otras cosas semejantes' (ed. Mascagna, p. 69; [I, xxv, 36]).

[28] *Le vite di Dante e di Petrarca*, in *Humanistisch-philosophische Schriften, mit einer Chronologie seiner Werke und Briefe*, ed. Hans Baron (1928; Wiesbaden: Martin Sändig, 1969), pp. 50–69, at p. 59. Bruni employs a variety of terms to convey this concept and they are generally translated quite literally: 'vigore interno e nascoso' ('vigor interior e oculto o ascondido'), 'furore ed ocupazione di mente' ('furor o ocupación de mente'), 'interna agitazione ed applicazione di mente' ('interior o intrínseco movimiento e aplicación de mente').

from his copy of Bruni's translation. But this temptation should be resisted. For one thing, in spite of their common use of the word, we still cannot tell exactly what kind of inspirational theory lies behind the phrase 'zelo celeste e affección divina'. So far, we have seen three possibilities: Isidore's frenzy (*vesania*), Boccaccio's longing or urge to create (*fervor inveniendi*), and Bruni's idea that one does not have to resort to bookish learning in order to become a poet. And none of these can be confidently ruled out as a possible meaning for Santillana's statement. But there is a much stronger reason why we should be cautious about suggesting that Santillana depended on Bruni for the use of the word *affección*. And this is that in another work in Santillana's possession, the term is employed with a completely different meaning; indeed, this work casts in doubt the whole idea that this part of *El proemio* concerns literary inspiration.

b) *Amor dulcis*: the poet's love of his art
In the anonymous allegorical exegesis of Petrarch's sonnet 116 (to be found, it will be remembered, at the end of Santillana's manuscript of the *Divina commedia*), the commentator explains that the poem is an expression of Petrarch's overpowering desire to 'optener la poesía e ser en aquélla laureado' (ed. Carr, p. 135). And, at the end of the commentary, he describes the poet's craving to acquire 'plazer e fartura de la plática poetal' as an 'afección poetal virtuosa' (p. 138). This interpretation corresponds to one of Petrarch's basic literary theories. In his coronation speech (1341), he takes as his theme two lines (291–92) from Virgil's third *Georgic*: 'Sed me Parnasi deserta per ardua dulcis/ raptat amor'.[29] Although the poet, explains Petrarch, is a divinely-inspired being, he is faced by three daunting obstacles: the inherent difficulty of his task, ill fortune, and the philistinism of his contemporaries. These are all overcome by his 'dulcis amor':

> he who undertakes to climb the 'ardua deserta Parnasi' must indeed long intensely for that which he seeks to attain; and he who loves to climb is doubtless the better prepared thereby to attain through study that in which his mind delights. For study without longing and without great mental pleasure and delight cannot attain the desired results.
>
> (Wilkins, *Studies*, p. 301)

[29] 'La *Collatio laureationis* del Petrarca', ed. Godi, p. 13. For translation, see Ernest H. Wilkins, *Studies in the Life and Works of Petrarch* (Cambridge, Mass: Harvard Univ. Press, 1955), pp. 300–13.

The Castilian commentator could not have known Petrarch's oration (it did not circulate beyond a very small group of friends). Nevertheless they share the conviction that, in spite of all its difficulties, the activity of studying and writing poetry is an essentially pleasurable one; indeed, without the support of this 'dulcis amor' or 'afección poetal', the poet would be incapable of fulfilling his rigorous literary ambitions. The similarity between the two writers may be explained by the fact that they draw on a common source. The 'sweet longing', Petrarch tells us, is comparable to Cicero's definition of *studium*: 'assidua et vehemens ad aliquam rem applicata magna cum voluptate occupatio, ut philosophie, poetrie' (ed. Godi, p. 14). This particular definition comes from *Tusculans*, IV, xvii, 38, but as Petrarch himself points out, it also corresponds to what Cicero says in his influential rhetorical treatise, *De inventione* (I, xxv, 36 and II, ix, 31).

The idea that intellectual quests were undertaken 'magna cum voluptate' exerted a powerful influence on the way medieval poets described their relationship with their art. When Dante, for example, first meets Virgil at the outset of his epic journey, he greets him with the exclamation:

> O degli altri poeti onore e lume,
> vagliami il lungo studio e il grande amore,
> che m'ha fatto cercar lo tuo volume.
> (*Inferno*, I, 82–84)

Boccaccio takes up the theme in *De genealogia*, XV, 10, when he recalls how nothing could distract him from his youthful ambition to become a poet, 'in tantum illum ad poeticam traebat affectio' (ed. Romano, II, 776; 'so great was my one passion for poetry', Osgood, *Boccaccio*, p. 132). This passion, or 'affectio', he goes on to explain, sustained him throughout his long and arduous period of literary apprenticeship.

The concept *studium* (pleasurable and arduous study) also influences Santillana; he too confesses that he is driven on by a 'dulcis amor'. Replying to a *pregunta* in which Juan de Mena calls him 'Perfecto amador del dulce saber', Santillana declares:

> Tanto me plazen las cirras donzellas
> en quien non consiste un punto d'amargo ...
> que, si algo velo, es por obtenellas,
> commo enamorado quando se enamora.
> (*Obras completas*, pp. 382–85, at p. 384)

Indeed, one wonders whether the idea that Santillana was *un enamorado* in pursuit of the Muses influenced Gómez Manrique's portrayal of poetry in his *Planto*. In this work, his uncle's death is lamented by the figure of Poetry, personified as a courtly lady, dressed in robes of blue and white and with Santillana's motto, 'Dios e vos', embroidered on the hem.

One final example will illustrate just how familiar Santillana's circle was with the concept under discussion here. One of the most interesting aspects of Don Pedro's commentary on his *Sátira de infelice e felice vida* is that it takes on a life of its own and becomes, in a sense, an end in itself. Exactly how this came about is explained in the following manner:

> quanto más discorría por las vidas valerosas de la antigua edat, dándome a conoscimiento de las cosas con viso más propinco que de ante, tanto mi mano con mayor gozo escrevía, e con mayor affección e estudio.
>
> (*Obras*, ed. Fonseca, p. 10)

Don Pedro's 'affección e estudio' clearly belongs to the same tradition as Dante's 'lungo studio e ... grande amore', Petrarch's 'dulcis amor', Boccaccio's 'affectio' and the anonymous commentator's 'affección poetal virtuosa': they all apply to a poetic context the concept of *studium*—the intense delight taken in any intellectual quest.

Although I have not found it used in the same kinds of literary context, *zelo* could also be interpreted as an irresistible longing to master the art of poetry. Like *afección*, it could specify a 'passion for something', and not just an emotional upheaval or change.[30] Therefore, considering the ambiguity of the terms and the fact that the ideas they evoke were both accessible to Santillana, it would, in conclusion, be hazardous to attempt to pin down the precise meaning of the assertion that poetry is 'un zelo celeste, una affección divina'. The only unambiguous aspect of this passion (whether understood as inspiration or as love of poetry) is that it is of divine origin. And the association between poetry and the divine was such a commonplace notion that it would be absurd to look for any specific source. That poetry was 'una gracia infusa del señor Dios' was proclaimed with great regularity by writers of Baena's

---

[30] For instance, Diego de Valera wrote his *Tratado en defensa de las virtuosas mujeres* 'movido con zelo de verdad', ed. Suz Ruiz, p. 49; the translator of Sallust's *Catiline Oration* addresses Pérez de Guzmán as 'zelador de saber los grandes e antiguos fechos', Schiff, *La Bibliothèque*, p. 78.

circle. And Santillana himself draws on this theory when, defending poetry against the accusation of immorality, he talks of 'los onbres bien nascidos e doctos, a quien estas sciencias de arriba son infusas'. But, of course, he could also have acquired support from any number of authorities, ranging from Isidore (*Etymologiae*, VIII, vii, 3), to Benvenuto da Imola, who in the introduction to his commentary on Dante cites Cicero's *Pro Archia* to prove that poetry 'quasi por un spíritu divino ynfla o resolla, finchiendo de sciencia' (BN Madrid, MS 10.208; the translation owned by Santillana, f. 6ᵛ; for original, see *Comentum*, ed. Lacaita, I, 13). It is also worth noting that in the margin of his copy of Pietro Alighieri's commentary on Dante, he has drawn one of his characteristic pointing fingers against the following statement: 'e porque estas cosas [las musas] vienen del cielo, por esto son llamadas divinales'.[31] Despite the hackneyed nature of the idea, he still thinks it worth taking note of. However, as we shall see in the discussion of its origins, poetry qualifies for the label 'divine' not only because it is a gift, but also because it was first used in the sacred rites of Judeo-Christianity.

But what of the phrase 'un insaciable cibo del ánimo'? This too covers a broad range of ideas. The 'food that never sates the soul' is the product of both the form and content of verse. In the first place, poetry offers intellectual nourishment. In his *Aeneid* commentary, Villena tells his readers that 'la doctrina de la poesía llama vianda porque es [de] mayor substancia que la retorical leche' (BN Madrid, MS 17.975, f. 12ᵛ). The food image, so commonly associated with learning in the Middle Ages, illustrates how poetry offers an inexhaustible supply of wisdom with which humans can sustain themselves in every circumstance they are likely to encounter.

Yet 'cibo' also relates to the esthetic power of verse. It recalls Jerome's warning in the epistle to Pope Damasus that 'Daemonum cibus est carmina poetarum'. *Cibus* is used here as a metaphor, meaning 'bait': the attractive, gentle rhythms of verse charm the senses of the listeners, and finally captivate their very souls:

> Haec sua omnes suauitate delectant et, dum aures uersibus dulci modulatione currentibus capiunt, animam quoque penetrant et pectoris interna deuinciunt. (Gimeno, 'San Jerónimo', p. 50, n. 4)

Much later, Jerome's belief in the addictive effect of poetry was taken up by Alonso de Cartagena, who, in his Latin epistle to the

[31] BN Madrid, MS 10.207, f. 64ᵛ.

Count of Haro, also compared the 'figmenta poetarum' to 'cibi ... que ... libidinem provocant' (*Tratado*, ed. Lawrance, p. 50). In view of this, it is highly ironic that the fictional Cartagena of Juan de Lucena's dialogue *De vita beata* (1463) should describe Mena's passion for verse in the following terms of approval:

> La poesía (de que tanta gloria, fama y loor nuestro Juan de Mena consigue) es tan dulce, que muchas vezes me juró por su fe, de tanta delectación componiendo, algunas vegadas detenido, olvidados todos aferes, transcordado el yantar y aun la cena, se piensa estar en la gloria. Créolo yo por cierto: ninguna suavedat se le eguala, sy al apetito la invención, y a la invención responden los versos. (ed. Paz y Melia, p. 158)

According to Lucena, it is not just the mind of the listener that succumbs to the seductive power of verse, as Jerome had suggested, but that of the poet as well. Moreover, its attraction resides in more than just its musicality; its esthetic effect derives from the correspondence between form and content, and from the intense satisfaction poets experience once they have given adequate expression to this original thought or intention ('apetito'). A few years later, the minor poet Pero Guillén de Segovia also remarked on the way that the human spirit is enthralled by the appropriate blend of form and content. Poetry, he declares, is:

> ante tanto dulce et aplacible a los sentidos, que comenzada a gustar non se dexa expedir de la mente, mas siempre accompaña aquel dulzor a los sesos que la communican; mayormente quando de aquélla resultan algunos efectos coadjutorios al bueno, lícito y onesto vivir.[32]

These passages enable us to grasp the full range of ideas implicit in Santillana's rather elliptical assertion that poetry is 'un insaciable cibo del ánimo'. Poets, Santillana appears to be saying, will never tire of the pleasure and intellectual nourishment offered by their art. As Lucena put it, once one submits to the attraction of verse 'se piensa estar en la gloria'.

Quite clearly, this part of the definition, with its allusions to 'amor dulcis' and the seductive power of verse, forms a strong thematic link with the closing stages of *El proemio*. There, as I have already explained, Santillana confesses his life-long fondness for the works of the poets: 'commo en la nueva edad me pluguiesen,

---

[32] Kohut, 'La posición', p. 82; see also Leonardo Bruni's appraisal of the *Divina commedia*: 'aquestas bellas cosas esplicadas con gentileza de rimos prenden la voluntad de aquel que las lee, e mucho más de aquellos que más entienden' (BN Madrid, MS 10.171, f. 46ᵛ).

fallélos agora, quando me paresció ser necessarios'. He has proved himself to be, in Mena's words, the 'perfecto amador del dulce saber'.

So far, Santillana has concentrated on the poet's relationship with his art. His allusive remarks bring to mind notions of God-given energy, of a sustained craving for perfection and of the captivating effect of both the form and matter of verse. It is not surprising then that he should conclude the first part of his definition with a reference to poetic exclusivity:

> asý commo la materia busca la forma e lo inperfecto la perfección, nunca esta sciencia de poesía e gaya sciencia buscaron nin se fallaron synón en los ánimos gentiles, claros ingenios e elevados spíritus.   (p. 439)

This passage and the later statement that poetry is infused into the minds of 'los onbres bien nascidos e doctos' have recently been interpreted as evidence that Santillana wished to make poetry the domain of a purely intellectual elite (Di Camillo, *El humanismo*, pp. 105–06). This is surely a misconception (this scholar's interpretation that '"bien nascidos", en este contexto, obviamente significa lo que hoy llamaríamos genéticamente bien dotados', seems particularly forced). The view that nobility, or the broader concept 'courtliness' (*gentileza*), somehow conferred extra status upon one's poetic achievements was by no means unusual amongst Santillana's contemporaries. There is no concrete reason to suppose that Santillana deviates from this norm when he refers to 'ánimos gentiles' and 'onbres bien nascidos'. Indeed, Gómez Manrique felt that the nobility of his uncle actually enhanced the literary merit of his work. In the prologue to the *Planto* in which he laments Santillana's death, he explains that he possessed 'biva e pronta discrición, gracia *gratis data*, profunda ciencia, grandeza de estado, que lo bueno faze mejor' (*Can. cas.*, II, 67). Both he and Santillana, therefore, establish a balance between the qualities that accrue from adherence to the code of *gentileza* and the more tangible merits of acquired learning. The theme of intellectual and social nobility recurs later in *El proemio*, when, in order to prove the dignity of verse, Santillana describes the poetic talents of Roman emperors and the enthusiastic literary patronage of two recent European kings.

However, these comments on poetic exclusivity need to be taken in their context. Elsewhere, as we shall see, Santillana goes to great lengths to prove that the art of poetry has been cultivated by a much broader intellectual and social class than seems to be the case here. The assertion that it is a divine gift infused into 'los ánimos gentiles, claros ingenios e elevados spíritus' probably reflects his opinions about the best kind of verse, but it is clear that there are many other forms of poetry whose value he is willing to recognize. These lines have an obvious rhetorical function within the eulogy. Not only does he exalt poetry by claiming that it does not admit mediocrity, but in doing so he also, of course, pays a supreme compliment to Don Pedro.

We turn now to the second part of Santillana's definition, which concerns the internal requirements of poetry itself:

> ¿qué cosa es la poesía—que en nuestro vulgar gaya sciencia llamamos—syno un fingimiento de cosas útyles, cubiertas o veladas con muy fermosa cobertura, conpuestas, distinguidas e scandidas por cierto cuento, peso e medida? (p. 439)

Compared with his previous remarks this is a straightforward theoretical statement. Poetry has three elements: it possesses a core of utility, masked by a veil or *cobertura*, and is subject to the fixed form of verse. However, two points need to be made about the terminology employed here. Firstly, it is interesting that Santillana should feel it necessary to draw Don Pedro's attention to the fact that *poesía* and *gaya sciencia* were simply different names for the same thing. By the 1440s, *poesía*, *poema* and *poeta* had become fully integrated into Castilian literary terminology and could be used as alternatives for words drawn from the troubadouresque vocabulary (such as *troba, trobar*, etc.) Yet it seems as if these terms of classical origin still retained some of their original force: the *Aeneid* could not be described as a *dezir* or *troba*, but a Villasandino *pregunta* could be called 'un poema'. As is well known, the difference between the two terminological groups was more pronounced in the case of *poeta* and *trobador*. Santillana, in his eulogy of Imperial (p. 452), drew a strict qualitative distinction between the two: the *poeta* was a man of impressive learning (and probably an allegorical poet), while the *trobador* was a mere versifier.[33]

---

[33] The distinction between *poeta* and *versificator* goes back to antiquity: see Quintilian, *Institutio*, X, i, 89; see also Bruni's life of Dante: 'assí como toda persona que es presidente o tiene officio de mandar inpera o manda, mas sólo aquel se llama enperador que es sobre todos, assí que aquel que conpone obras en versos e es alto e muy excelente en conponer las tales obras se llama poeta' (MS 10.171, f. 45ʳ). Bruni then states that it is irrelevant whether the poet writes in Latin or the vernacular, thus ignoring the distinction made by Dante himself in his *Vita nuova*,

Secondly, the term *fingimiento* does not appear to have been particularly common at this time—at least I have not encountered it in any other text before the late fifteenth century.[34] No doubt Santillana's contemporaries would have been reminded (if they needed reminding) that poets write artful lies: 'los poetas fingen'. But originally, *fingir* meant simply 'to create' and lacked the rather derogatory connotations it later acquired as a result of its association with the *figmenta* or *mendacia poetarum*. One wonders whether Santillana's self-conscious preference for *fingimiento* instead of the more usual term *ficción* was an attempt to recapture some of the original force of *fingir*, in order to translate the Greek *poio*, 'I make'. If so, the emphasis in this part of his definition would be on poetry as a craft; the poem is the product of the poet's technique, rather than of his ability to invent pleasing fictions. Santillana does not ignore the notion that the poet transforms reality: he expresses this idea in the phrase 'cubiertas o veladas con muy fermosa cobertura'. If this interpretation of *fingimiento* is correct, it confirms how, as we shall see later, Santillana places the same emphasis on verbal craft as on allegory.[35]

XXV ('poete' = classical poets; 'dicitori' or 'rimatori' = vernacular). See also Encina's distinction between *trobador* and *poeta* in his *Arte*, ed. López Estrada, pp. 83–84.

[34] Corominas suggests the word was first used by Nebrija (*DCECH*, *s.v.* 'fingir'); Covarrubias, in the late XVIc, makes *fingimiento* synonymous with *ficción*. I have encountered several attestations of *enfengimiento*; e.g., in the early Castilian version of Isidore's *Etymologiae*, where the word translates 'figmenta'. See *Las etimologías de San Isidoro romanceadas*, ed. Joaquín González Cuenca, 2 vols (Salamanca: Universidad, 1983), II, *s.v.* The sole extant MS is a XVc *refundición*.

[35] The concept of poet as artisan, which was so common in Provençal poetics, was not unknown in XVc Castile: Gómez Manrique, for example, describes himself as 'un fazedor', and refers to the act of literary creation as a process of polishing and smoothing with 'limas' and other 'herramientos' (compare with Middle English 'maker'). This parallel might also support the hypothesis that Santillana's 'fingimiento' does not refer to 'simulation' or 'figment', but to something that is created by the poet's art. This distinction was also made in certain etymologies of the term *poeta*. Its Greek origins were perceived by Leonardo Bruni (who was, after all, a Greek scholar): 'Questo nome *Poeta* è nome greco, e tanto viene a dire quanto facitore' (*Vite*, p. 60). It is interesting that in the Castilian version 'facitore' is rendered by 'fingidor' (f. 43ᵛ), which thus provides another possible analogy for Santillana's use of the term 'fingimiento' (i.e. 'something manufactured'). Elsewhere 'facitori' is translated by 'fazedores' (once: f. 44ʳ) and by the phrase 'fingidores e fazedores' (twice: f. 44ʳ). Boccaccio adopts a slightly different etymology of *poeta* in order to avoid the word's connotations of untruthfulness. Following Isidore, *Etymologiae*, VIII, vii, 2, he rejects the notion

According to the well-known allegorical definition, poets cloak truth under a veil of beautiful fiction. As Isidore put it, 'Officium autem poetae in eo est ut ea quae gesta sunt, in alias species obliquis figurationibus cum decore aliquo conversa transducant' (*Etymologiae*, VIII, vii, 10). But in Santillana's version, the poetic veil does not cloak reality ('ea quae gesta sunt'), but 'cosas útyles'. This shift in emphasis is, I think, significant, but it needs to be interpreted with care if the underlying aim of *El proemio* is not to be misunderstood.

One misconception that might arise from this passage is that the reference to 'cosas útyles' indicates an overtly didactic approach to literature on Santillana's part. Such a view seems to be held by Di Camillo, for example, who compares the Spanish poet's definition with that given by Boccaccio in *De genealogia*, XIV, 7. He comes to the conclusion that whereas for the latter fiction is used in order to express eternal truths, for Santillana it is employed simply for ornamental reasons; the poet's aim is moral, and his message is explicit. Santillana's attitude, he asserts, is crudely utilitarian (i.e. medieval) and, hence, directly opposed to the views of the humanist Boccaccio.[36] There is no doubt, however, that it is unwise to base any comparison of their literary theories on such broad concepts as truth and utility. For one thing, the distinction between the two has much more appeal to a post-Romantic critic than it would have had to a medieval or Renaissance reader. Boccaccio himself have been swift to point out that some things, such as certain aspects of law (XIV, 4), might be true, but they are not invariably useful; on the other hand, as one medieval commentator on Horace's *Ars poetica*

---

that poetry derives from the Greek verb 'poio, pois' (equivalent, in his opinion, to the Latin 'fingo, fingis', 'I pretend' or 'imagine'), in favour of the explanation that it comes from the Greek noun 'poetes', meaning 'exquisite discourse' (*De genealogia*, XIV, 7).

[36] *El humanismo*, pp. 79–81. Di Camillo later claims that in spite of his medievalism, Santillana was the most advanced literary theorist of his time in Spain, in that he made poetry the highest form of philosophy and went further than even Boccaccio, who had placed poetry on a par with theology (pp. 99ff). However, Di Camillo adduces very little concrete evidence in support of this hypothesis. He bases his argument upon an interpretation of the statement that eloquence is the most noble branch of knowledge known to man. This, as I later show, was a medieval topos, and does not imply that Santillana was attempting to make a serious evaluation of the relative value of poetry, philosophy and theology (or any other branch of knowledge). Certainly, Santillana makes great claims for poetry, but not in the way Di Camillo supposes.

pointed out, the utility of poetry depended upon the quality of moral and physical truth which it contained.[37] For these reasons, I do not think that the substitution of 'cosas útyles' for an underlying truth means that Santillana's attitude towards allegorical poetry is substantially different from Boccaccio's: utility presupposes truth. The basic similarity of the two writers is apparent when one considers that, despite the references to 'the eternal truths of Nature', Boccaccio devotes the whole of Bk XIV (and specifically chapters 6 and 9) to proving the thesis that poetry is a useful art.

Another misunderstanding that might result from the reference to 'cosas útyles' is that Santillana consciously based this part of his definition on Horace's dictum that 'Aut prodesse volunt aut delectare poetae' (*Ars poetica*, 333). Such a claim has been made by Garci-Gómez in an article whose point of departure is that the entire *Proemio* is modelled on Horace's *Ars* ('Otras huellas de Horacio', p. 134). It would be a waste of space to refute this critic's basic premise that Santillana was an expert on Horace's verse. But the assertion that he knew the Horatian theory mentioned above is worth closer examination.

It is true that the idea that poetry could be both useful and pleasurable found its most eloquent exponent in Horace. It is also true that his *Ars* became a set text in the medieval grammar curriculum and that, consequently, it exerted an influence on many aspects of rhetorical and poetic theory (particularly in the twelfth century, when it influenced Geoffrey of Vinsauf, for example). Nevertheless, the *prodesse/ delectare* theory soon became so commonplace that it would be extremely rash to assert, in the absence of concrete evidence, that a particular poet consciously associated it with Horace. Indeed, he was much more likely to relate it to the *corteza/ meollo* topos of medieval sermons: the outer covering, or form, provided the pleasure, and the nourishing core, or content, provided the utility. As far as fifteenth-century Castile is concerned, there is scarcely any evidence that practising poets (as opposed to theologians and academics, like Alfonso de Madrigal), turned to Horace to endorse their views on poetry.

However, Santillana is one of the few poets who could have known the *delectare/ prodesse* theory as expressed by Horace: not at first hand, I suggest, but via Benvenuto da Imola. This writer quotes the relevant lines in his influential commentary on Dante:

---

[37] Bruyne, *Études*, I, 277.

'segund la sentencia de Oracio en la su poetría, los poetas o quieren aprovechar o quieren delectar o juntamente las cosas alegres e ydóneas dezir de la vida' (translation commissioned by Santillana, BN Madrid, MS 10.208, f. 3^r; for original, see *Comentum*, ed. Lacaita, I, 9). But though Santillana had access to Horace's precept, this in itself does not prove that it inspired his reference to 'cosas útyles'; as I have already pointed out, the idea that poetry should be useful had long been axiomatic. What is more, it is also the logical consequence of the belief that poetry was a legitimate branch of knowledge. All sciences had to serve some useful purpose; this was an accepted fact to which Santillana himself refers in the prologue to his *Proverbios*. Citing Aristotle's *Ethics*, Bk I, he declares: 'toda arte, doctrina e deliberación es a fin de alguna cosa' (*Obras completas*, p. 216): a dictum then proved by his series of moral proverbs. There is therefore more than one authority for the conviction that poetry was useful. Had an inveterate name-dropper like Santillana wished Don Pedro to know that he was following Horace, he would certainly have informed him.

But what exactly is meant by the assertion that poetry is 'un fingimiento de cosas útyles'? It will be plain from the discussion so far that I do not belief the phrase should be interpreted in the narrow sense of ethical utility. Obviously, the moral value of poetry cannot be discounted, particularly in the light of Santillana's annotation of his *Divina commedia* manuscript. But if we consider the definition in the context of *El proemio* as a whole, it will become clear that the concept of utility must be interpreted in the broadest possible manner. We shall see in due course that Santillana's ultimate purpose is to argue that poetry is, or should be, a fundamental part of human life, and it is this conviction, rather than the demands of didacticism, that led him to state that 'cosas útyles', rather than truth, are cloaked by the poetic veil.

The third and final element in the definition is the notion that the content of poetry is arranged according to 'cierto cuento, peso e medida'. Throughout his work, Santillana displays a keen interest in verse form, and this interest is echoed on many occasions in *El proemio*.[38] He compares, for example, the French *ballade* with the

---

[38] See, for example, the prologue to *Los proverbios*, where he indignantly rejects the possible accusation that he is ignorant of the metrical rules established by the Provençal theorists; see also his eulogy of Alfonso de Aragón (*La comedieta*, ll. 209–10), and his reply to Gómez Manrique's request for a *cancionero* ('Sea Calíope adalid e guía', sts 2 and 5). For important new insights into aspects of Santillana's

Italian sonnet, *terza rima* and *canzone*; he explains the meaning of the Catalan *novas rimadas*, and that the Catalan decasyllabic line is of Provençal origin; he also recalls that Castilian verse derives its metrical terminology from the Galician school (pp. 445, 447, 449). But the best known, and most controversial, passage concerning formal aspects of poetry is the discussion of the three levels of style, 'sublime', 'mediocre' and 'ínfimo'. Poets who employ the last style, he explains:

> son aquellos que syn ningund orden, regla nin cuento fazen estos romances e cantares de que las gentes de baxa e servil condición se alegran. (p. 444)

We should not read too much into this comment on popular verse (whether ballad or epic): it is a neutral statement of fact, rather than an expression of contempt.[39] Santillana certainly does not deny it the right to be classified as poetry. Indeed, later on in his eulogy, he adduces popular ballads as evidence to prove that poetry has a social value, and plays an integral part in all human affairs. Nevertheless, there is no doubt that, on a theoretical level at least, he considered poetry *de grado ínfimo* to be of inferior quality. As far as we know, court poets began to take a consistently serious interest in popular ballads only toward the end of the fifteenth century, when they started to copy them down and collect them. Perhaps it is no coincidence that this period was also characterized by a movement away from the stylistic exuberance of the literature written during the reign of Juan II.[40] There are two reasons why

---

metrics, see Martin J. Duffell, 'The Metre of Santillana's Sonnets', *MAe*, 56 (1987), 279–303.

[39] For the frustrated attempts to pin down the meaning of these generic terms, see William C. Atkinson, 'The Interpretation of "romançes e cantares" in Santillana', *HR*, 4 (1936), 1–10; Florence Street, 'Some Reflections on Santillana's *Prohemio e carta*', *MLR*, 52 (1957), 230–33; Dorothy Clotelle Clarke, 'The Marqués de Santillana and the Spanish Ballad Problem', *MP*, 59 (1961–62), 13–24; Garci-Gómez, *Prohemios*, pp. 54–76. López Estrada, *Las poéticas*, pp. 106–08. For the three levels of style, see Faral, *Les Arts poétiques*, pp. 86–89, 312–13; Hans R. Jauss, 'Littérature médiévale et théorie des genres', *Poétique*, 1 (1970), 79–101; Franz Quadlbauer, *Die antike Theorie der 'genera dicendi' im lateinischen Mittelalter* (Vienna: Böhlhaus, 1962).

[40] As Peter Russell has pointed out, the popularity of the ballads at the court of Ferdinand and Isabella coincides with the taste for the religious verse of Franciscan poets such as Iñigo de Mendoza and Montesino, 'quienes ... exaltaban el modo de expresarse y las actitudes de la gente común por considerarlos más puros que los de los "galanes" cortesanos' ('Las armas contra las letras', in *Temas*, p. 235 and n.

Santillana would have found this poetry inadequate. Firstly, just as 'la gente de baxa e servil condición' were inferior to him socially, so their pleasures were inherently inferior to his: their verse lacked the grace of *gentileza*. Moreover, their poetry was imperfect from a purely technical point of view. That it did not possess 'cierto cuento, peso e medida' was crucial: as Villena's remark on the implications of Santillana's 'mengua de sciencia' demonstrated, metrical precision and refinement were considered to be the means by which poets gave clarity and concision to their ideas (see above, pp. 69–70).

Perhaps the most interesting example of Santillana's concern with poetic form is the ambitious comparison between the French and Italian styles of literature:

> Los ytálicos prefiero yo ... a los franceses, solamente ca las sus obras se muestran de más altos ingenios e adórnanlas e conpónenlas de fermosas e peregrinas ystorias; e a los franceses de los ytálicos en el guardar del arte: de lo qual los ytálicos, synon solamente en el peso e consonar, no se fazen mención alguna. (p. 446)

These lines are more non-committal than some critics have supposed. He simply observes that the Italians have greater inventiveness, more narrative flair than the French, and this is illustrated by their skill in creating strange and pleasing stories. On the other hand, for technical precision and formal variety one must turn to the French. Each school has its own merits; Santillana does not state an overall preference for one or the other. To frown on the undoubted pleasure he takes in formal virtuosity is merely tendentious (see, for example, Lapesa's observation that the French school is 'rigurosa y vacua', and that Santillana's fondness for it is proof of literary conservatism; *La obra literaria*, p. 254).

It should be clear from the preceding discussion that Santillana's definition of poetry is flexible: it is not a rigorous precept but a comprehensive, yet concise, summary of the various elements of which any poem can be composed. The core of 'cosas útyles' is, as we shall see, constant. But beyond this, the poet is at liberty to focus on technical aspects of verse form, or on the allegorical artifice, the 'muy fermosa cobertura'. Yet the writer whose art embraces all potential elements of poetry will be worthy of the title *poeta*, like Imperial, rather than a mere *dezidor*.

---

34). See also Keith Whinnom, 'Diego de San Pedro's Stylistic Reform', *BHS*, 37 (1960), 1–15.

Finally, something needs to be said about music. We know that by the mid-fifteenth century, lyric poetry was no longer composed purely to be sung. Indeed, Santillana does not make music a defining characteristic or poetry, as Dante, Deschamps or Machaut had done in the previous century. Nevertheless, there is ample evidence in *El proemio* that he had a special interest in music. He remarks, for example, on the musical abilities of two poets in his survey (Machaut and Jordi de Sant Jordi), but he is particularly impressed by the innate musicianship of the French (see p. 446). His enthusiasm for this aspect of their poetry inspires the following general conclusion:

> ¿E quién dubda que, asý commo las verdes fojas en el tienpo de la primavera guarnescen e aconpañan los desnudos árboles, las dulces bozes e fermosos sones no apuesten e aconpañen todo rimo, todo metro, todo verso, sea de qualquier arte, peso e medida? (p. 447)

Quite obviously, it would be wrong to underestimate the close ties that music still had with poetry, even for those writers, like Santillana, whose main ambition was to create a learned style of poetry, designed to be read and studied.

What were the sources of Santillana's definition of poetry? The most widely-held view is that these sections of *El proemio* owe a special debt to Boccaccio's *De genealogia*, XIV, 7. Before I discuss this hypothesis, two preliminary points need to be made. Firstly, although Santillana's copy of the Castilian translation of this work ends at the beginning of Bk V, it is clear from evidence supplied by another manuscript that all fifteen books were originally translated. Secondly, given that Santillana would have read Boccaccio's defence in Castilian, not Latin, any comparison between the two on the basis of verbal similarity must necessarily be somewhat tentative.[41] Boccaccio comments on the form and nature of poetry

[41] The idea that *El proemio* depended upon *De genealogia* was first suggested by Arturo Farinelli who, in a brief footnote to his discussion of Boccaccio's influence in Spain, compared Santillana's definition to a modern Italian translation of the relevant sections of the treatise (*Italia e Spagna* (Turin: Fratelli Bocca, 1929), I, 189–90 and n. 2). This view was reiterated by, e.g. Lapesa, *La obra literaria*, pp. 250–51, and Green, *Spain and the Western Tradition*, III, 8–9. However, Di Camillo (*El humanismo*, pp. 79–94), suggests that the similarities between the two are the result of a common source (e.g. Isidore) or of sheer coincidence. A reasonable argument, but vitiated by his denial that Santillana could have known *De genealogia*, XIV, 7, on the grounds that the theoretical portions of this work were systematically censored by Spanish scholastics, opposed to the ideals of humanism. There is no evidence whatsoever to support this. All the XVc MSS of the Castilian

on many occasions in the fourteenth book of his encyclopedia, but his views are summarized by the statement that opens chapter 7:

> Poesis ... est fervor quidam exquisite inveniendi atque dicendi, seu scribendi, quod inveneris. Qui, ex sinu dei procedens, paucis mentibus, ut arbitror, in creatione conceditur, ex quo, quoniam mirabilis sit, rarissimi semper fuere poete. Huius enim fervoris sunt sublimes effectus, ut puta mentem in desiderium dicendi compellere, peregrinas et inauditas invent-iones excogitare, meditatas ordine certo componere, ornare compositum inusitato quodam verborum atque sententiarum contextu, velamento fabuloso atque decenti veritatem contegere.[42]   (ed. Romano, II, 669)

This definition does have some points in common with *El proemio*: both writers begin with a reference to a kind of poetic fervour; both then claim that poetry descends from God into the minds of a chosen few; finally, both mention the poetic veil and strict verse form. These parallels are undeniable, and probably outweigh in importance the conceptual, linguistic and syntactical differences between the two texts (i.e. Santillana's *zelo* and *afección* could mean something quite different from the Italian writer's *fervor*; his characterization of the poetic elite is more detailed—Boccaccio does not mention social nobility; his reference to metrical regularity comes after the poetic veil; Boccaccio's sentences depend syntactic-ally, and conceptually, upon *fervor*). But in my view, these similarities are not sufficient to prove that Santillana consciously set out to model his definition on that of Boccaccio. The crucial point

---

translation are incomplete; however, BN Madrid MS 10.062 ends with the rubric to BK XIV. Whatever the reasons for the absence of the last two books in this MS, this rubric indicates that the original translation (owned by Santillana) did contain Boccaccio's defence (see Jules Piccus, 'El traductor español de *De genealogia deorum*', *Homenaje a Rodríguez-Moñino*, II, 59–75). See also Garci-Gómez, 'Paráfrasis de Cicerón', who claims that this part of *El proemio* is a faithful rendering of *De oratore*, I, xxxi, 142. I am entirely unconvinced by the details of the comparison between the two texts, by the extraordinary basic assumption that Santillana was a classical scholar and, as I explain below, by the belief that the definition is based on any one specific text.

[42] 'Poetry ... is a sort of fervid and exquisite invention, with fervid expression, in speech or writing, of that which the mind has invented. It proceeds from the bosom of God, and few, I find, are the souls in whom this gift is born; indeed so wonderful a gift it is that true poets have always been the rarest of men. This fervor of poesy is sublime in its effects: it impels the soul to a longing for utterance; it brings forth strange and unheard-of creations of the mind; it arranges these meditations in a fixed order, adorns the whole composition with unusual interweaving of words and thoughts; and thus it veils truth in a fair and fitting garment of fiction' (Osgood, *Boccaccio*, p. 39).

is that the concepts put forward by both writers belong to a common heritage of literary theory, employed in one form or another from the time of the early Christian Church until well beyond the fifteenth century. It would be extraordinary if Santillana had had no knowledge of the ideas in question here before he had read *De genealogia*, XIV, 7, and that he should feel it necessary to resort to this work, or indeed to any other single text, in order to furnish his treatise with a definition of poetry. The theory of divine infusion was one of the main subjects of debate amongst Baena's circle; the medieval education system, and his own experience of reading such poets as Dante and Virgil, would have informed him that poetry could have something to do with allegory; and as for the importance attached to metrical regularity, it would be absurd to explain this by reference to a specific literary source—as we have seen, it was something that preoccupied him as a practising poet on many occasions.

But none of this means that Boccaccio should be ruled out of the discussion altogether, rather that the relationship between the two writers should be viewed in a different light. In reading the Italian's defence, Santillana would surely have been impressed by its sheer scope and eloquence. Many of the details of the argument contained in the last two books would no doubt have been new to him, but not the basic literary theories set out in XIV, 7. For this reason, Boccaccio should be placed in the same category as the other Italian writers whose literary treatises were translated under Santillana's patronage. This is to say that, along with Pietro Alighieri, Benvenuto da Imola and Leonardo Bruni, he is best thought of as yet another authority, though a particularly forceful one, whom Santillana could have invoked in order to support the validity of his definition.

The importance of Bruni's *Vite di Dante e di Petrarca* has passed unnoticed by most critics of *El proemio*. Yet this work supplies much more than biographical details. It also includes a great deal of theoretical material, and in fact all aspects of Santillana's definition may also be encountered here. We have already seen how his discussion of inspiration might help to elucidate the meaning of the term *affección*; to this analogy we must add his remark that the form and content of Dante's poetry captures the will of the reader, and that the title *poeta* is reserved for only the finest poets (see above, notes 32 and 33). But Bruni also describes the general nature of the poet's art, and in terms that partly coincide with Santillana's definition: 'El nombre de poeta significa excellente e maravilloso estillo en versos, cubierto e velado de linda, sotil e alta ficción' (ff. 44ᵛ–45ʳ). These similarities should deter us from considering Boccaccio, or any other single writer, as an exclusive source for the definition. The influence that the Italian authors and commentators must have exerted upon Santillana was of a different order. Their treatises, particularly the two commentaries on the *Divina commedia*, would have confirmed his belief that the study of literature had something of immense value to offer. In this respect, they would undoubtedly have encouraged him to undertake his enthusiastic defence of poetry. Even so, we should look on them not as sources—in the strictest sense of the word—for such basic concepts as the poetic veil and metrical form, so much as a group of writers who helped Santillana to assimilate, clarify and ultimately give concrete expression to ideas with which he and his contemporaries were already familiar.

It will be clear from what I have said that the main value of Santillana's definition does not consist in the originality of its separate elements. His references to divine infusion, the allegorical veil and metrical form would not have struck his fellow poets as being in any way unusual. These matters were discussed at length by the previous generation of poets, such as Villasandino, Diego de Valencia and Manuel de Lando. And as I mentioned before, they constituted the topics of literary debates until the changes in approach to literary theorizing that took place in the sixteenth century. For this reason, we cannot judge whether Santillana was a reactionary or a radical figure only on the basis of what he has to say about the form and nature of poetry. We should concentrate not so much on the theories themselves, as on the way they are used, and on the ultimate purpose of the argument. In other words, Santillana's originality resides not in his definition of poetry but in the fact that he chose to define and defend it at all.

3 The dignity of poetry

Immediately after he has defined poetry and dismissed the view that it consists merely of 'cosas vanas e lascivas', Santillana pauses to ask the following set of questions:

> E sy por ventura las sciencias son desseables, asý commo Tulio quiere, ¿quál de todas es más prestante, más noble e más digna del honbre? ¿O quál más

extensa a todas especies de humanidad? Ca las escuridades e cerramientos dellas ¿quién las abre, quién las esclaresce, quién las demuestra e faze patentes syno la eloquencia dulce e fermosa fabla, sea metro, sea prosa? (p. 440)

Structurally, this is an important passage; in rhetorical terms, it marks the distinction between *expositio* and *narratio*. Up to this point, Santillana has, so to speak, stated his case: poetry is an honourable and valuable activity, the hallmark of an exclusive elite. From this point on, he embarks upon the proof of this argument. The division is clearly indicated by a change of pace in the prose style, brought about by the accumulation of rhetorical questions. But it is also emphasized by the way in which he draws back from his narrow focus upon the art of poetry itself to consider the value of eloquence in general. This last subject constitutes the first of four proofs that support his claim that poetry is a noble and dignified activity.

a) Eloquence and wisdom

The opening premise that 'las sciencias son desseables, asý commo Tulio quiere' is based on a passage in Cicero's *De officiis*, one of this author's most popular works in fifteenth-century Castile: 'Ca todos somos traýdos e induzidos a cobdiciar la cognición e la sciencia, en la qual sobrepujar pensamos que es cosa fermosa'.[43] But it was also a stock medieval aphorism (included, for example, in *La floresta de philósophos*, no. 1060; under the heading 'De los oficios'). Moreover, without the reference to 'Tulio', Don Pedro might legitimately have believed that Santillana had another famous dictum in mind: Aristotle's assertion that 'the search for wisdom is natural in man'.

Aristotle and Cicero also provide the source for the idea that of all branches of knowledge, eloquence is the one that most ennobles mankind. According to *La floresta*, 'la ciencia del bien fablar es la más noble que ningund arte del mundo' (no. 633; from the *Libro del tesoro*, attributed to Aristotle). This aphorism is based on the theory that man is distinguished from beasts by his use of speech, an idea taken up and developed by Cicero, in his youthful *De inventione*:

---

[43] I, vi, 18; quoted from Cartagena's translation, BN Madrid, MS 7.815, f. 42ᵛ. *De officiis* is one of the texts most frequently cited by Santillana; it supported his claims about the compatibility of arms and letters (I, xxi) and about the importance of spending one's *ocio* in intellectual pursuits (III, i, 1-4). For the Italian and Aragonese versions owned by Santillana, see Schiff, *La Bibliothèque*, p. 63. Don Pedro's father translated it into Portuguese.

E por cierto, a mi juizio, los omnes en muchas cosas son más flacos e más
enfermos que los animales brutos, mas en esto les lieva muy grande ventaja,
que pueden fablar e los animales non. Por ende parésceme que alcança muy
fermosa cosa quien en aquello en que los omnes lievan ventaja a las bestias
lieve el ventaja a los otros omnes.[44]

(I, iv, 5; Cartagena's translation, ed. Mascagna, p. 39).

Having asserted that eloquence is the most noble and at the same
time the most characteristic of all human attributes, Santillana
broaches the subject of its relation to knowledge. There is an
indissoluble bond between the two: eloquence, he explains, clarifies
learning and sheds light on its 'escuridades e cerramientos'. This is
a crucial statement, but it needs to be interpreted with caution. It
has led one recent scholar, Ferrie, to the conclusion that Santillana's
attitudes towards rhetoric were those of an Italian humanist. This
supposition is based upon the following argument: many leading
figures of the Italian Renaissance shared Cicero's lifelong preoccupation with the conflicting demands of rhetoric and philosophy and attempted to combine the two into a coherent system.
And Santillana employs rhetoric and praises eloquence in his
Proemio; thus, concludes Ferrie, 'se había incorporado al espíritu y
las convicciones de conocidos humanistas italianos' ('Aspiraciones',
p. 196). This is a serious over-statement. Italian humanists
discussed the relationship between eloquence and wisdom with
greater subtlety and with a greater sense of urgency than other
writers since Antiquity: the subject was one of the central debates
of their movement. But Ferrie has overlooked the fact that
throughout the Middle Ages writers were aware of the inter-
dependence of rhetoric and philosophy, even though they tended to
treat the issue in a schematic and perfunctory manner.[45] As far as

---

[44] This passage was disseminated to an even wider public by Brunetto Latini's
Livres dou Trésor, III, i, 11, where he discusses the social value of rhetoric. It was
also familiar to the members of the XIVc poetic consistories at Toulouse: see *Las
Leys* [third version, 1356], ed. Anglade, I, 83. See also Pérez de Guzmán: 'La
florida eloqüencia/ quanto vale ver lo has/ quando entre el ombre farás/ e las
bestias diferencia' (*Can. cas.*, I, 576; *Coplas de vicios e virtudes*, st. 13); Encina, *Arte*
(ed. López Estrada, p. 77). An alternative tradition, also deriving ultimately from
Aristotle, was that man and beast were separated by the use of reason: Santillana
himself makes it one of the central themes of *Bías*; for Cartagena's references to the
idea, see Lawrance, *Un tratado*, p. 35 and n. 20.

[45] See Seigel, *Rhetoric and Philosophy*, pp. 174–98. That wisdom and eloquence
were interdependent was a topos in discussions of rhetoric; for a Castilian example,
see Pérez de Guzmán, *Coplas de vicios e virtudes*, st. 47 (*Can. cas.*, I, 580–81).

Santillana is concerned, there is no substantial evidence to prove that he was doing anything more radical than simply reworking ideas that derived from the well-known works of Aristotle and Cicero, and which had been transformed into topoi, to be diffused in aphoristic form by *florilegia* such as *La floresta de philósophos*.

It is not, then, necessary to look to Italy for influences. And as a further illustration of this, it is worth mentioning two other medieval authorities who could well have influenced this section of *El proemio*: Isidore of Seville and Alfonso el Sabio. Isidore's discussion of rhetoric in the second book of his *Etymologiae* closes with a comparison between rhetoric and dialectic. These two arts provide quite separate paths to knowledge. The former explains and clarifies, whereas the latter arrives at truth by means of precise (and obscure) reasoning. To demonstrate this idea more clearly, Isidore introduces the image of the open palm and clenched fist. The lucidity of rhetoric, he explains, is symbolized by the open palm: 'Rhetorica ad illa quae nititur docenda facundio' (II, xxii, 1–3), a view that is closely paralleled by Santillana's assertion that the role of eloquence is to *esclarescer, demostrar* and *fazer patente*.

However, his attitude towards rhetoric and philosophy also owes something to the traditions of the seven liberal arts. The trivium, comprising the arts of discourse (grammar, rhetoric and dialectic), was considered to be propedeutic; it opened the way to knowledge of the number-based sciences (arithmetic, music, geometry and astrology) which made up the quadrivium. As expressed by Alfonso el Sabio, the relationship between the two groups is as follows:

> Et estas quatro artes que dixiemos postrimeras son el quadruvio que ensenna a omne saber toda cuenta, e toda concordança, e toda medida, e todo movimiento que en las cosas sean. Et las primeras tres artes, que avemos dicho que llaman trivio, son en estas quatro que dizen quadruvio como en las cerrajas las llaves que las abren, e abren estas del trivio todos los otros saberes por que los puedan los omnes entender mejor.[46]

It would be an exaggeration to say that Santillana's image of the *cerramiento* is modelled on Alfonso's *cerraja* (the notion of enclosed or locked-up knowledge was commonplace). But when considered in the context of the other analogies described above, the similarity

[46] *General estoria: primera parte*, ed. Antonio G. Solalinde (Madrid: Centro de Estudios Históricos, 1930), p. 196; Rico, *Alfonso el Sabio*, pp. 145–54.

is yet further evidence that Santillana's ideas on rhetoric and wisdom firmly belonged to medieval traditions.

Poetry, therefore, shares the methods and function of eloquence. To paraphrase *El proemio*, its purpose is to 'abrir e demostrar escuridades, e fazerlas patentes'. Yet this notion seems rather incongruous in the context of the earlier definition which indicated that the contents of a poem were hidden beneath a veil of obscurity, and the poets' task was to convey their wisdom indirectly by means of ornate fiction. Santillana has, perhaps without realizing it, significantly altered the course of his theoretical argument. This, however, should not surprise us. The overall aim of *El proemio* is rhetorical—to eulogize poetry—and to this end he gathers together whatever proofs are at his disposal and weaves them into his argument wherever appropriate. At this stage in the discussion he wishes to emphasize that poetry is essential to human dignity, and he therefore resorts to the Aristotelian/ Ciceronian notion that nobility derives from thirst for knowledge and use of speech. Onto this basic concept he grafts the authoritative idea that knowledge is clarified and made accessible by 'la eloquencia dulce e fermosa fabla'. But in his enthusiasm to make verse the highest form of eloquence, he does not reconcile the allegorical and rhetorical approaches to poetic theory.

b) The poetry of the Bible
Henceforth, Santillana's procedure is to assert the preeminence of verse over prose, and to trace its origins back to the Bible:

> E, asý, faziendo la vía de los stoycos—los quales con grand diligencia inquirieron el orígine e causas de las cosas—me esfuerço a dezir el metro ser antes en tienpo e de mayor perfección e más auctoridad que la soluta prosa. (p. 440)

The first part of this quotation is another echo of Cicero's *De officiis* ('Audeamus imitari Stoicos, qui studiose exquirunt unde verba sint ducta', I, vii, 23), but the definition of the Stoics' etymological methods is also probably influenced by the broader Isidorean concept of etymology, which included the origins not just of words, but also of all natural and created objects.

From this point on, Isidore beings to figure prominently as an authority on the history of poetry. He supplies, for example, the theory that verse was cultivated long before prose: 'Praeterea tam apud Graecos quam apud Latinos longe antiquiorum curam fuisse carminum quam prosae. Omnia prius versibus condebantur; prosae autem studium sero viguit' (I, xxxvii, 2). But Santillana's technique of amplification leads him to expand the idea that metre was *antiquior* into the assertion that it was also 'de mayor perfección e más auctoridad'. Clearly, the view that poetry is more authoritative follows logically from the original premise that it was more ancient, but the statement that it is 'de mayor perfección' requires further comment. Verse is 'more perfect', so to speak, because it possesses more form than prose; there is a qualitative difference between the two which derives from the fact that just as matter is inferior to form (according to Aristotelian philosophy), so 'la soluta prosa' is inferior to poetry. It lacks the artifice of form, and consists of language in a comparatively unpolished, unfinished state. In other words, 'perfección' is endowed here with all the etymological force of *perficeo*: 'finished', or 'fully-wrought'.

In order to prove the antiquity of poetry, Santillana adduces the argument that parts of the Old Testament were written in verse. Prompted by Josephus and Origen, the man largely responsible for forming the theory about biblical verse was St Jerome. St Jerome wrote as an apologist for Christianity, aiming to counteract the enormous prestige of classical antiquity. He claimed that his religion was in no way inferior to pagan culture, since it too possessed great poets—and these were earlier than either Greek or Roman authors. Much later on, in the Middle Ages and Renaissance, the theory of biblical verse was appropriated by the defenders of poetry in order to give authority to their arguments that the composition of verse did not run counter to Christian morality.[47] Jerome's ideas (elaborated in his epistles and in the preface to his translation of the Bible) were transmitted to the Middle Ages and Renaissance by generations of exegetes and encyclopedists, such as Isidore, and once again, it is this scholar who is cited by Santillana:

---

[47] See María Rosa Lida de Malkiel, 'La métrica de la Biblia (un motivo de Josefo y San Jerónimo en la literatura española)', in *Estudios hispánicos: homenaje a Archer M. Huntington* (Wellesley, Mass: Wellesley College, 1952), pp. 335–39; Curtius, *European Literature*, pp. 40–41, 214–27; 'Zur Literaturästhetik, III', pp. 459–79; Ronconi, *Le origini*, pp. 35, 43, 86–93. Jerome's account of biblical poetics influenced Pero Díaz de Toledo in his commentary on Gómez Manrique's *Exclamación, Can. cas.*, II, 131, and Alfonso de Madrigal, *Comento sobre Eusebio*, I, ff. xxii^v–xxiii^v.

Ysidoro Cartaginés ... quiere que el primero que fizo rimos o canto en metro aya seýdo Moysén, ca en metro cantó e profetizó la venida del Mexías; e, después dél, Josué en loor del vencimiento de Gabaón. David cantó en metro la victoria de los filisteos e la restitución del archa del Testamento e todos los cinco libros del *Salterio*. E aun por tanto los hebraycos osan afirmar que nosotros no asý bien commo ellos podemos sentyr el gusto de la su dulceza. E Salamón metrificados fizo los sus *Proverbios*, e ciertas cosas de Job son escriptas en rimo; en especial, las palabras de conorte que sus amigos le respondían a sus vexaciones. (p. 441)

I have quoted the passage in full because although it follows the general outline of the alleged source, parts of it deserve detailed examination.

Isidore states that Moses wrote in verse on two occasions in the Pentateuch: the song praising God after the crossing of the Red Sea, Exodus, 15.20, and his final sermon to the Israelites, Deuteronomy, 32.1–43 (*Etymologiae*, VI, ii, 7). Yet neither of these passages coincides with those parts of the Pentateuch traditionally thought to be prophecies. Santillana's statement that Moses used verse to prophesy 'la venida del Mexías' is probably influenced by the belief that Deuteronomy as a whole was a prophetic Book, a prefiguration of the new covenant (*Etymologiae*, VI, ii, 7).

The mention of Joshua's song 'en loor del vencimiento de Gabaón' raises similar difficulties, in that it is not possible to identify with any certainty the episode to which Santillana refers, particularly since neither Jerome nor Isidore describes Joshua as a writer of verse. Although Joshua reduced the Gibeonites to slavery (Joshua, 9), no song in the Bible celebrates the event. Perhaps Santillana had in mind the victory over the five kings who had attacked the city of Gibeon (ch. 10): during the battle, Joshua invoked divine aid, calling upon God to stop the course of the sun and the moon. It is true that according to the Bible this invocation does not appear to be a song of praise or celebration, but it may well be that Santillana was influenced by the interpretation of a Bible commentary.

Bible commentaries and glosses could also have shaped his reading of the Psalms, which were a particularly contentious area of biblical scholarship. For although these were cited as examples of hexameter and pentameter, there was considerable dispute as to their authorship. Interestingly, Santillana departs from the views of his immediate source, Isidore, who followed Jerome and stated that the Psalter should not be attributed in its entirety to David. The

Spaniard adhered to a different tradition, which goes back to St Augustine and Cassiodorus. Their argument that Asaph, Idithun and others were merely the performers of individual Psalms was widely disseminated in the later Middle Ages and early Renaissance by the *Glossa ordinaria*, a corpus of Psalter commentaries which was gathered from a wide range of patristic and medieval exegetical sources and used as a standard teaching text.[48] The *Glossa ordinaria* probably also accounts for the inclusion in Santillana's list of the two other poems which were not part of the original canon of biblical verse established by Jerome. This commentary elaborated upon the brief references in the Bible that a choir celebrated 'la victoria de los filisteos' (II Samuel, 6.5) 'e la restitución del archa del Testamento' (II Samuel, 5.17–25 and ch. 22). Of course, it is also easy to imagine that this particular passage was based on Santillana's own reading of the Bible, rather than on any scholarly source.

Little needs to be said about the reference to Solomon's Proverbs (though Santillana might have added Ecclesiastes and The Song of Songs, both ascribed to Solomon and thought to be in verse); of much greater interest is his description of the Book of Job. It was commonly held that most of this Book was in verse; in fact, it was thought that an uninterrupted series of poems stretched from 3.3 as far as 42.6.[49] Yet Santillana notes that only 'ciertas cosas de Job son escriptas en rimo', which suggests, perhaps, that he had only a hazy recollection of the theory that no more than a few chapters of the book were in prose. There is also a suggestion of vagueness about the clause that qualifies the initial statement: certain parts are in verse, 'en especial, las palabras de conorte que sus amigos le respondían a sus vexaciones' (i.e. chs. 11, 15, 18, 20, 22, 25, 32–37). First of all, one wonders what exactly is meant by 'en especial': is it 'for example', thereby implying that other passages were in verse? Or does the phrase have a narrower

---

[48] For Isidore, see *Etymologiae*, VI, ii, 15–17. Madrigal also follows Jerome in his *Comento sobre Eusebio*; acknowledging the popular view that 'los psalmos suelen ser dichos de David', he identified which psalms were actually written by him, and which by other biblical authors (I, f. xxxi^r). For the contrasting tradition, see Cassiodorus's preface to his commentary on the Psalms (ch. 2), with a reference to St Augustine's *De civitate Dei*, XVII, 14. On the *Glossa ordinaria*, see Smalley, *The Study of the Bible*, pp. 46–52, and Minnis, *Medieval Theory of Authorship*, p. 44.

[49] For Jerome, see Lida de Malkiel, 'La métrica', pp. 336–37 and note 4; also Isidore, *Etymologiae*, VI, ii, 14. Both Díaz de Toledo (*Can. cas.*, II, 131) and Madrigal (*Comento*, I, xxiii^v) give an accurate account of this tradition.

meaning, such as 'specifically', or '*id est*', thus restricting the poetry to those chapters containing 'palabras de conorte'? Whatever the case, one senses that Santillana focusses upon these chapters precisely because they were consolatory. Since they offered the reader an abundance of moral advice ('cosas útyles'), they would be 'un singular reposo a las vexaciones que el mundo continuamente trahe', as Santillana put it in the letter to his son. In other words, unable to recollect the full details of the tradition of biblical verse, he resorts to hypothesis based on his own concept of true poetry.

Santillana now leaves the Bible and describes the beginnings of classical verse: 'De los griegos quieren sean los primeros Achatesio Millesio e, aprés dél, Ferécides Siro e Homero, no obstante que Dante soberano poeta lo llama' (p. 441). The source here is once again Isidore's discussion of metre in *Etymologiae*, I, xxxix, 11–12, but he seems to impose a strict chronology on the events which the original itself does not suggest: 'hunc [the hexameter] apud Graecos Achatesius Milesius fertur primus conposuisse, vel, ut alii putant, Pherecydes Syrus. Quod metrum ante Homerum Pythium dictum est, post Homerum heroicum nominatum'. Isidore's 'Achatesius ... vel ... Pherecydes' is transformed, in Santillana's version, into 'Achatesio ... e aprés dél, Ferécides'. This may just be a slip, but it is also characteristic of his attempts to keep the lines of his historical survey clear and simple.

Dante is again used to offset Isidore in the next stage of the historical account. 'De los latinos Enio fue el primero' (taken from *Etymologiae*, I, xxxix, 6), 'ya sea que Virgilio quieran que de la lengua latina en metro aya tenido e tenga la monarchía; y aun asý plaze a Dante, allí donde dize en nombre de Sordello Mantuano:

> O gloria del latyn solo per chui
> mostro cho que potea la lingua nostra,
> o precio eterno del llocho ove yo fuy'.[50]
>   (p. 441)

Given Santillana's fondness for Seneca, Lucan and Ovid, it is surprising that this section on classical literature is so brief. The reason for this is not, I expect, that he had nothing to say about this period, but rather that this succinctness served a rhetorical purpose.

---

[50] *Purgatorio*, VII, 16. This quotation does not coincide with Santillana's own copy of the *Divina commedia*: 'O gloria di latin, disse, per cui/ mostro cio che potea la lingua nostra,/ o prexio e lume del luocho ov'io fui' (BN Madrid, MS 10.186, f. 73^r).

I shall return to this point shortly, but first it is worth summarizing his endeavours to prove the historical authority and dignity of verse. He does this, as we have seen, first by citing the evidence of biblical poetry, and then by drawing support from the work of the ancients. His procedure shows that he adopts a chronology which subordinates secular to sacred verse: poetry was first cultivated by the Hebrews, then the Greek, followed by the Romans. Although this sequence was favoured both by Christian apologists and by secular defenders of verse, it was by no means the only theory about the origins of poetry that circulated in the Middle Ages. As Boccaccio pointed out in *De genealogia* XIV, 8, there also existed a number of other hypotheses, such as that the art was invented by the Babylonians, the Assyrians or the Greeks. And Pero Díaz de Toledo reports witnessing a discussion of the origins of verse, in which some maintained that the first poet was a Sicilian, other that it was Linus, or Orpheus (commentary on *Exclamación, Can. cas.*, II, 131).

As far as Santillana was concerned, however, there was no possible doubt about the priority of the Bible. He brings this section on the origins of poetry to a close with the following emphatic declaration:

> E así, concluyo ca esta sciencia, por tal, es acepta principalmente a Dios, e después a todo linage e especie de gentes. Afirmalo Casiodoro en el libro *De varias causas*, diziendo: 'Todo resplendor de eloquencia e todo modo o manera de poesía o poetal locución e fabla, toda variedat de honesto fablar hovo e hovieron començamiento de las divinas escripturas. Esta en los deíficos templos se canta, e en las cortes e palacios imperiales e reales graciosa e alegremente es rescebida. La plaças, las lonjas, las fiestas, los conbites opulentos sin ella así commo sordos e en silencio se fallan. (p. 442)

The citing of Cassiodorus is intriguing (and not just because it is hard to tell where it ends). This author discusses eloquence on two occasions in *De variis causis*, the vast collection of official letters written during the reigns of the Ostrogothic kings Theodoric and Athalaric. But these passages concern the political importance of rhetoric and grammar, and bear no relation to the statements cited by Santillana.[51] It is possible that *De variis causis* has been confused with the commentary on the Psalms, for it is here that Cassiodorus describes at greatest length the biblical origin of secular eloquence. In the preface, *caput* xv, under the heading 'De eloquentia totius

---

[51] Curtius, *European Literature*, pp. 74–75.

legis divinae', he argues that the rhetorical tropes that characterize the works of pagan authors had previously been used to great effect in Holy Scripture.[52] This work, then, provides the most likely source for this passage in *El proemio*, even though the lack of close verbal parallels and the mistaken attribution to *De variis causis* indicate no more than a second-or third-hand knowledge of the text.

Santillana's aim in his discussion of biblical and classical poetry is not simply to claim that *la gaya ciencia* is an ancient art, and for this reason worthy of respect. He also works on the assumption that there is a fundamental unity in literary tradition. Poetry was born in the religious rites of Judeo-Christianity, but as time progressed, it was put to use in a variety of profane contexts which encompassed the whole spectrum of social class (from the 'palacios imperiales' down to the popular 'plaças', 'lonjas' and 'fiestas'). But this process of secularization does not constitute a break with the past; on the contrary, it is a proof of continuity. Past and present are linked by the fact that poetry has always been a natural human urge—*un zelo, una affección*. It is an instrument that has been indispensable at all stages of human development, making it possible to breathe life first into religious and then into secular affairs. The vitality that poetry injects into the latter is emphasized by Santillana's deliberate choice of examples. He picks out situations which involve large gatherings and glittering ceremony—temples, palaces, squares, festivals and banquets—and then qualifies them by words which underline the liveliness and joy of the occasion: 'resplendor', 'cantar', 'graciosa e alegremente', 'opulentos'.

The unity of literary tradition is also conveyed by the structure of the argument. As we have seen, Santillana dwells at comparative length upon the kinds of verse found in the Old Testament: songs of prophecy and consolation, celebrations of military victories, moral proverbs. Then, but only very briefly, he refers to Greek and Latin poetry, after which he again takes a broader view of the historical development and, in the section allegedly based on Cassiodorus, he lists a whole range of contemporary circumstances which are brought to life by verse. The economy with which he deals with classical poetry is deliberate: it brings modern poetry into closer juxtaposition with its sacred origins.

---

[52] Curtius, *European Literature*, p. 448.

Following the enigmatic mention of Cassiodorus, there is no clear break with the next passage; but there is an obvious shift in emphasis. The reference to the patristic writer enabled Santillana to introduce the notion that the usefulness of poetry in a variety of contexts was evidence of the vigour and continuity of the literary tradition; hence, in the next section, he examines utility as a separate topic, as yet further proof of the dignity of verse.

c) The utility and diversity of poetry

> ¿E qué son o quáles aquellas cosas adonde—oso dezir—esta arte asý commo necessaria no intervenga e no sirva? (p. 442)

This rhetorical question prefaces a brief yet heterogeneous list of circumstances in which verse is thought to be necessary. But before I discuss the sources and implications of the passage, it is worth stressing that its principal value lies in the light it sheds on the definition of poetry as 'un fingimiento de cosas útyles'. As we have seen, Di Camillo has criticized this definition for being too narrow in scope, in the belief that it refers only to moral utility. However, the three examples that follow clearly indicate that Santillana's concept of utility needs to be interpreted in the broadest possible sense:

> En metro las *epithalamias*—que son cantares que en loor de los novios en las bodas se cantan—son conpuestos; e de unos en otros grados aun a los pastores en cierta manera sirven, e son aquellos dictados a que los poetas *bucólicos* llamaron. En otros tienpos, a las cenizas e defunsiones de los muertos, metros elegíacos se cantavan, e aún agora en algunas partes dura, los quales son llamados *endechas*; en esta forma Jheremías cantó la destruyción de Jherusalem. (p. 442)

This passage is for the most part based on Isidore's discussion of metre in *Etymologiae*, I. The definition of the first genre, the wedding song, is a fairly accurate reproduction of 'Epithalamia sunt carmina nubentium, quae decantantur ab scholasticis in honorem sponsi et sponsae' (I, xxxix, 18). The presence here of bucolics is probably also inspired by Isidore, who defined it, somewhat vaguely, as 'pastorale carmen' (I, xxxix, 16). As regards the final genre, there seems to be a slight confusion between elegiac metre and another form of lament, the *threnos*. According to Isidore, the defining characteristic of the elegy is that 'modulatio eiusdem carminis conveniat miseris' (I, xxxix, 14). It could be argued, of course, that this category of poem would not be entirely out of place 'a las cenizas e defunsiones de los muertos'; but on the other hand, Santillana's account of funeral verse has much more in common with Isidore's definition of the *threnos*, 'quod Latine lamentum vocamus, primus versu Ieremias conposuit super urbem Hierusalem. ... Adhibebantur autem funeribus atque lamentis: similiter et nunc' (I, xxxix, 19).[53]

Apart from its value as yet further evidence of Santillana's reliance on Isidore, this passage is important in two respects. Firstly, these brief remarks are another example of his firm belief in the continuity of poetic conventions. The generic terms employed here are borrowed from a classical tradition, yet they are still considered to be applicable to contemporary verse. One can sense, it is true, a certain vagueness about the term *bucólico* (a form used by shepherds only 'de unos en otros grados ... en cierta manera'), but his rather forced use of the word highlights his keenness to describe the continuity of literary practice. Similarly, although he admits that the elegy is an earlier term for *endecha*, he nonetheless stresses that the actual content and function of this kind of poetry have not undergone any substantial change since the time of Jeremiah. The conviction that, in certain crucial respects, poetry is not susceptible of change recurs later in the prologue, in the discussion of the three levels of literary style:

> no es de dubdar que universalmente en todas de sienpre estas sciencias se ayan acostunbrado e acostunbran, e aún en muchas dellas, en estos tres grados, es a saber: sublime, mediocre e ínfymo. (p. 444)

The second important feature of this section is that these three genres, epithalamia, bucolics and elegies, have more in common with oral verse than with the courtly poetry of the *cancioneros*. It is hard to say how familiar Don Pedro would have been with songs 'que en loor de los novios en las bodas se cantan', since it seems that the epithalamium did not constitute a strictly literary genre until the Renaissance. Yet contemporary allusions to wedding celebrations show that such songs did exist before then on a popular level; they also figure quite prominently in the corpus of Christian and Sephardic traditional poetry.[54] The same applies to

---

[53] Madrigal also refers to 'los trenos de Jheremías' (*Comento*, I, xxiiiᵛ).

[54] See Manual Alvar, *Cantos de boda judeo-españoles* (Madrid: CSIC, 1971), especially pp. 11–17 for contemporary references to songs as an integral part of wedding celebrations. The traditional epithalamia were not always sung 'en loor de los novios', as Santillana suggests; they also include tragic themes, obscenity and

what Santillana has to say about the contemporary bucolics. He clearly does not have in mind such artificial forms as the *pastourelle*, but actual songs sung by the shepherds themselves. And with regard to the funeral lament, although numerous examples of *plantos* and *endechas* may be found in *cancionero* poetry (Santillana himself cultivated the genre with some success), he obviously refers to a form which played an active part in the rites of burial and mourning, or to the traditional lyric, rather than to a set piece of a purely literary nature. Given the popularity of the literary genre, the comment that laments are still sung only in certain areas ('aun agora en algunas partes dura'), must be another reference to oral verse (e.g. the *endecha* for Guillén Peraza, *c.* 1443), and perhaps to Sephardic ritual; *endechas* used to abound in the Jewish communities of North Africa, where the *endechera* was an accepted and important figure.[55]

It should not surprise us that Santillana should focus on genres that are not readily associated with *cancionero* verse. His aim is, after all, to emphasize the integration of poetry into the activities of daily life ('¿quáles son aquellas cosas adonde ... esta arte asý commo necessaria no intervenga e no sirva?'). It is not just another aristocratic diversion, another courtly accomplishment like dancing or jousting. The full extent of this integration is emphasized by demonstrating that poetry is involved in two of the most important rites of life and death. But the three genres discussed here are not the only examples of poetic utility to be found in *El proemio*. One should also take into account the examples supplied by the Bible (with their references to war, consolation and moral didacticism); by the passage based on Cassiodorus (which illustrated how poetry could enliven a broad range of public occasions); and finally, in contrast to this, by the concluding sections of *El proemio* (which evoked the immense personal value to be derived from the private study of verse). Poetry is, then, an eminently practical instrument, one which plays a part in all kinds of human affairs. But one might object that Santillana's attempts to justify the social value of poetry are incompatible with his theory that it is an art cultivated by a

---

insults which correspond, according to Thomas Deveny, to 'the ritualistic need for a safety-value whose function is to ensure the consummate happiness of the bride and groom'; see 'Lewdness and Lament in Spanish Wedding Poetry', *RoN*, 23 (1982–83), 175–80, at p. 180.

[55] See Deyermond, *La Edad Media*, p. 59 and n. 37, pp. 221–22; Manual Alvar, *Endechas judeo-españolas*, revised ed. (Madrid: CSIC, 1969), pp. 17–20.

divinely inspired elite (by 'los onbres bien nascidos e doctos, a quien estas sciencias de arriba son infusas'). This would, however, be an unfair criticism; for if we consider *El proemio* as a whole, Santillana quite clearly recognizes that poetry has a legitimate role at all social and intellectual levels. It is not the exclusive property of a cultured minority, though he no doubt considers that this group composes the best poetry. There has been some dispute about his attitude towards popular verse, produced by those who 'syn ningund orden, regla ni cuento fazen estos romances e cantares de que las gentes de baxa e servil condición se alegran'. Whereas, for reasons I have already discussed (pp. 195–96), this kind of verse was thought to be intellectually and esthetically inferior to that written by 'los onbres bien nascidos e doctos', there is no evidence to suggest that he questioned its social value. Poetry *de grado ínfymo* may not be masked by an ornate allegorical veil, nor possess regular form, but it does, on the other hand, contain a measure of 'cosas útyles': it brings pleasure and solace to the lower classes.

d) Poetry in the courts of emperors and kings

The final element in the defence of the dignity of verse illustrates a comment made earlier in *El proemio*, that poetry 'en las cortes e palacios imperiales e reales graciosa e alegremente es rescebida' (p. 442). Immediately following the reference to wedding songs, bucolics and laments, Santillana declares that 'Gayo César, Octaviano Augusto, Tiberio e Tito, enperadores, maravillosamente metrificaron e les plugo toda manera de metro' (p. 442). This information derives ultimately from Suetonius's *Lives of the Caesars*, which Santillana possessed in an Italian translation (see Schiff, *La Bibliothèque*, pp. 150–51; it may, however, derive from Alfonso X who, in turn, took much of his Suetonius from Vincent of Beauvais). But for obvious reasons, the Marquis's account of these Emperors' poetic talents and tastes greatly simplifies the range of opinions contained in the original. Suetonius reports, without comment, that Caesar wrote a few poems in his youth, including a tragedy, *Oedipus*; he reserves his praise for the simplicity of his prose style (I, lvi, 1–7); this provides a striking contrast with what Santillana had earlier said in the prologue to his *Proverbios*: Caesar wrote his poems 'en tan alto e elevado estilo que después de su vida apenas los muy entendidos las entendían' (*Obras completas*, p. 221). Augustus is also said to have had a restrained prose style; although enthusiastic, he made very few attempts to write poetry (II, lxxiv–lxxv, 1–2). Tiberius wrote one Latin poem and several in Greek; he was also a ridiculous pedant (III, lxx, 1–3). Titus is the only Emperor whose literary talents seem faithfully reported by Santillana. Suetonius praised the facility with which he wrote Latin and Greek verse, adding that he could even improvise (VIII, iii, 2).

Of all these Emperors, Augustus acquired the greatest fame as poet and literary patron. Petrarch, for example, in one of his literary defences, referred to the fact that Augustus wrote poetry, and called him 'Pierian spirit'. Similarly, Boccaccio described with admiration how he composed a verse edict which countered Virgil's dying wish that the *Aeneid* be destroyed.[56] In Spain, Enrique de Villena also drew on Suetonius for information regarding Augustus's literary talents. In chapter IV of *Los doze trabajos*, he condemns the ignorance of contemporary nobility and urges them to follow the example 'del grant Octaviano enperador e non menos virtuoso cavallero, que se dio a la arte del versificar e escrivió métricamente muchas e memorables cosas' (ed. Morreale, p. 44). Yet unlike Santillana, none of these writers makes any substantial attempt to incorporate the other Emperors into their defences of literary studies.

Santillana then leaves behind what he calls 'las estorias antiguas', and brings forth two modern examples of royal literacy:

> El Rey Roberto de Nápol, claro e virtuoso príncipe, tanto esta sciencia le plugo que, commo en esta misma sazón micer Francisco Petrarca, poeta laureado, floresciese, es cierto gran tienpo lo tuvo consigo en el Castil Novo de Nápol, con quien él muy a menudo confería e platicava destas artes, en tal manera que mucho fue avido por acepto a él e grand privado suyo.   (p. 443)

The relationship between Petrarch and King Robert was well known, in one form or another, in fifteenth-century Castile: it had become a symbol of enlightened patronage and of the dignity of poetic study. Accounts of the friendship varied, but for the most part they derive ultimately from Petrarch's own exaggerated reminiscences in *De rebus memorandis* Bks I and III, and from the anecdotes related by Boccaccio in *De genealogia*, XIV, 22, and XV, 6.[57] In Spain, the legend was transmitted most faithfully via Fernán Pérez de Guzmán, whose version of Giovanni della Colonna's *Mare*

---

[56] Petrarch, *Epistula metrica*, II, 10, 159–60 (Ronconi, *Le origini*, p. 72); Boccaccio, *De genealogia*, XIV, 4 and 19.

[57] Ernest H. Wilkins, *The Making of the 'Canzoniere' and Other Petrarchan Studies* (Rome: Edizioni di Storia e Letteratura, 1951), pp. 45–53.

historiarum includes a character sketch of King Robert which is a literal translation of passages from *De genealogia*, XIV, 9 and *De rebus memorandis*, I. According to this account, the King was a torpid and uneducated youth, scarcely capable of mastering the basics of grammar. However, after being introduced to the fables of Aesop, he soon became a marvellous philosopher. Nevertheless, much to his regret, he never learnt the art of poetry.

The version given by Enrique de Villena differs considerably, even though he claims to write on the authority of Petrarch: 'en el libro que fizo de las recordables cosas, onde en loor del rey Ruberto de Nápol ... dize que por enxenplo suyo veyéndolo tanto inclinado al saber se dio a la poesía' (*Los doze trabajos*, p. 44). Curiously, the idea that the King took up poetry on the inspiration of Petrarch has less in common with *De rebus memorandis* than with *De genealogia*, XV, 22. Here, Boccaccio relates how Robert utterly scorned Virgil and other poets until, in his sixty-sixth year, he first met Petrarch and heard him unfold the hidden meaning of the *Aeneid*.

Where Santillana derived his information is hard to say. The claim that Petrarch stayed with King Robert 'grand tienpo', had many literary conversations with him, and wrote many works at his court (such as *De rebus memorandis*, the eclogues and many sonnets) probably constitutes his own personal addition to the legend. On the other hand, this belief could be an elaboration of the apocryphal anecdote passed on by the anonymous Castilian commentator whose gloss on a Petrarchan sonnet was owned by Santillana. According to this writer, the poem was composed at the court of Robert who then ordered it to be copied down 'en el registro de sus obras' (ed. Carr, p. 138). The King is thus presented as an active literary patron. But whatever his exact source, it is clear that Santillana has adapted his material with an eye for rhetorical effectiveness, rather than for historical accuracy.

The same principle is at work in the second example of modern royal patronage:

> Johán Bocacio, poeta excellente e orador insigne, afirma el Rey Johán de Chipre averse dado más a los estudios desta graciosa sciencia que a ningunas otras; e asý paresce que lo muestra en la entrada prohemial del su libro de la *Genealogía o linage de los dioses gentyles*, fablando con el Señor de Parma, mensajero o enbaxador suyo. (p. 443)

Poetic, or rather rhetorical, licence allows Santillana to depart from his source to a significant extent: nowhere does Boccaccio suggest that the King of Cyprus was more fond of poetry than of any other branch of knowledge. In fact, the only explicit reference to his intellectual pursuits concerns not poetry, but theology (see Osgood, *Boccaccio*, p. 3). It is also worth pointing out that the manuscript of Santillana's translation of *De genealogia* does not mention the King's name: this might help to explain why Santillana called him 'Johán', rather than Hugo; after all, the King of Cyprus when Santillana wrote *El proemio* was Jean II (reigned 1432–58).

It is, I think, significant that Santillana should select Robert and Hugo as modern examples of poet-rulers. After all, it might seem strange that in the reign of Juan II anyone should feel it necessary resort to foreign rulers in order to prove what had become an obvious fact: that the composition of verse was a vital and popular ingredient of court life. But, as Fernán Pérez de Guzmán's *semblanza* of Juan II shows, it was sometimes thought that the monarch could take his fondness for poetry too far, at the expense of those qualities which 'verdaderamente son virtudes' (*Generaciones*, ed. Tate, p. 39). The choice of Robert and Hugo is deliberately aimed at countering this disapproval. They find their way into *El proemio* purely on the basis of their association with two of the three most fashionable and authoritative writers of the time—Petrarch and Boccaccio. These writers' association with royalty would, in Santillana's opinion, have helped to silence the criticism of those who believed that the patronage of poets and the composition of verse were not entirely appropriate activities for a member of the ruling class. It is ironic that the most prestigious literary figure of the period, Dante, could not be invoked in support of the argument that great literature could be produced under the sponsorship of royalty. Santillana would have been thoroughly disappointed to learn from Bruni's biography that, unlike Petrarch who conscientiously cultivated the friendship of princes, Dante was never welcomed 'graciosa e alegremente' at the courts of kings and emperors, and died in exile.

4   The historical survey

When Santillana traced poetry back to its supposed origins in the religious verse of the Old Testament, he did so not because he wished to write an objective literary history, but because the rhetoric of *El proemio* demanded it. He needed to prove 'la excelencia e prerrogativa de los rimos e metros': the antiquity of poetry was ample demonstration of its dignity. As the fourteenth-century Italian poet, Albertino Mussato, put it: 'Quo magis hanc primis artem scruteris ab annis/ splendidior tanto nobilitate sua est' (Epistle IV, 71–72; Ronconi, *Le origini*, p. 31). But once Santillana has described the literary patronage of Robert of Sicily and Hugo of Cyprus, his historical survey of vernacular poetry seems to take on a life of its own, and grows in dimension to an extent unprecedented at the time. The sheer scope of his treatment (roughly half *El proemio*), illustrates the obvious pride he takes in his wide-ranging knowledge of literary development. There is not the space here to annotate this section in the detail it deserves (particularly since many of the problems are unanswerable).[58] I wish to concentrate on two aspects only: its rhetorical and pedagogical background, and the view of literary growth which it represents.

In spite of the evident pleasure taken in recounting the recent history of poetry, the underlying purpose of Santillana's survey is rhetorical: it would not have been written had it not supported his argument in a number of important ways.[59] Firstly, the very fact that he discusses the past of European poetry at all is significant; for by showing that it actually possesses its own history, he

---

[58] Such as the identity of certain poets: Pau de Bellviure, Juan de la Cerda, Alfonso González de Castro. If Santillana gives prominence to writers who, for us, are shadowy figures, the converse is also true: he knows of only four poems by Macías, although *El cancionero de Baena* records eight; he suggests that Alfonso el Sabio composed Latin lyrics, and—which is perhaps even more extraordinary—appears to have no personal knowledge of his vernacular poems: 'yo vi quien vio dezires suyos' (p. 450). There are other puzzling features: his ignorance of the death of Alain Chartier in the 1430s, the erroneous attribution to him of certain poems, and the reference to King Louis of France (he did not· succeed to the throne until after Santillana's death; his presence, like that of King Jean of Cyprus, is probably due to a scribe's attempt to update the text: I am grateful to Professor Alan Deyermond for information about the last-named monarch). Also enigmatic is the reference to his grandfather's composition of 'cénicos plautinos e terencianos' (p. 451): see Edwin J. Webber, 'Plautine and Terentian *Cantares* in Fourteenth-Century Spain', *HR*, 18 (1950), 93–107; 'Further Observations on Santillana's "Dezir cantares"', *HR*, 30 (1962), 87–93. For useful notes on the historical section, see López Estrada, *Las poéticas*, pp. 106–21, and Gómez Moreno and Kerkhof, pp. 441–53.

[59] Sir Philip Sidney and George Puttenham also 'only use the historical method, and then fleetingly, for an argumentative purpose, to prove that in most societies "good poets and poesie were highly esteemed and much favoured of the greatest princes"' [Puttenham, *Arte*, I, viii], George Watson, *The Literary Critics*, pp. 33–34.

demonstrates that it is a subject in its own right, and deserves to be classed as a science. As we saw in chapter II, this concept influenced Villena's inclusion of a list of previous poetics in his *Arte de trobar*: poetry as *scientia* concerned 'cosas inmutables e verdaderas'. And although Santillana alludes to changes in literary practice and distinguishes between poetic schools, the main impression his survey conveys is one of continuity. For example, he juxtaposes biblical and contemporary verse in order to emphasize their similarities; the three levels of style are universal; the classical genres, epithalamium, bucolic and elegy, are shown to be unchanged—or at least subject to only vaguely perceived mod-ifications; Castilian derives its terminology from the Galician school. These and other passages were designed to counter the accusation that poetry was an ephemeral and hence trivial pastime.

The rhetorical nature of the historical section is further underlined when it is viewed in the context of formal eulogies of the arts and sciences. As Curtius has pointed out, a significant element in these orations was the 'catalogue of notable persons' who had practised the art or science in question. One of the purposes of this catalogue was to establish a canon of authorities whom the audience or dedicatee should attempt to emulate (*European Literature*, pp. 548–49). In *El proemio*, this catalogue is represented by the extensive list of European poets, from whom Don Pedro, the aspiring poet, is encouraged to select his models. Toward the end of the treatise, the young noble is urged not only to persevere with the composition of verse, but also to continue studying fine poetry: 'la inquisición de los fermosos poemas' (p. 454).

The possibility that the concept of *imitatio* was one of the implications of the history is strengthened, I think, when we compare *El proemio* with an anonymous *Règles de la seconde rhétorique*, written in France sometime between 1411 and 1432. This precept-ive poetic is prefaced by a list of about twenty poets, enumerated in chronological order. The scope of this rudimentary history is much more limited that in *El proemio*, its pedagogical function more obvious. According to the author, these poets embody the art of poetry, whose rules are compiled in the treatise. The novice poet, therefore, is required to study and emulate his canon of *auctores*: 'Et affin que quiconques voulra soy introduire à faire aucuns diz ou balades, il convient que on les face selon ce que donnèrent les premiers réthoriques, dont aucuns s'ensuyvent'.[60]

Turning now to Santillana's attitude toward literary development, one of the key passages is his portrayal of the beginnings of secular verse. Here, it will be remembered, he draws on Isidore and Dante for his information about the earliest Greek and Latin poets (see above, p. 208): Achatesius and Ennius were, according to Isidore, the first in their respective languages, but Homer and Virgil were, according to Dante, the greatest. The collation of evidence supplied by the two authorities is inspired by Santillana's keenness to distinguish between those who first practise the art, and those who later achieve mastery of it. 'E asý commo dize el philósofo, "de los primeros, primera es la especulación"', observed Santillana in his discussion of the early vernacular poets Arnaut Daniel and Guido Guinizelli (p. 444). This aphorism is a crude reformulation of the Aristotelian theory of potentiality and act, a process of 'becoming' which entailed the gradual elimination of an inherent shortage. A beginning is naturally the point of most shortage, the point from which an object strives to reach its fully-developed state. Thus, Santillana appears to be saying, these early essays in sonnet form must have shared the inferiority common to all beginnings; they must have been purely speculative attempts at a style of verse which had not yet acquired a concrete and clearly defined form. The same process of growth underlies Villena's summary account of the development of vernacular poetics: Raimon Vidal 'por ser començador no fabló tan complidamente' (El arte, p. 164). This comment, as we have seen (ch. II, p. 65), conforms to a theory of knowledge whereby, given a sufficient quantity of wise men, learning gradually accumulates and, in time, becomes more refined. And one senses that this general principle is also at work in Santillana's assessment of the state of contemporary Castilian verse. Toward the end of El proemio he declares:

> Desde'l tienpo del Rey don Enrrique, de gloriosa memoria, padre del Rey nuestro señor, e fasta estos nuestros tienpos, se començó a elevar más esta sciencia, e con mayor elegancia, e ha avido onbres muy doctos en esta arte. (pp. 451–52)

Santillana seems conscious of surveying the history of verse from one of the peaks in its development. In Castile, progress has been achieved through the labours of 'onbres muy doctos', who have

---

[60] Recueil d'arts de seconde rhétorique, ed. E. Langlois (Paris: Imprimerie Nationale, 1902), p. 11.

created the circumstances favourable to the innovative talents of a poet like Francisco de Imperial: 'sy alguno en estas partes del occaso meresció premio de aquella triunphal e láurea guirlanda, loando a todos los otros, éste fue' (p. 452). Imperial is as far removed from the beginnings of poetry in the Peninsula as Homer was from the work of Achatesius, or Virgil from that of Ennius.

5 The conclusion

Santillana brings his eulogy to a close with a skillfully constructed *peroratio*, in which he emphatically restates the principal themes of the previous sections. He begins it with a grandiose reference to the poetic consistories of Toulouse:

> Pero de todos éstos ... asý ytálicos commo proençales, lemosís, catalanes, castellanos, portugueses e gallegos e aun de qualesquier otras nasciones, se adelantaron e antepusieron los gállicos cesalpinos e de la provincia de Equitania en solepnizar e dar honor a estas artes. (p. 454)

This list of poetic schools is more than just rhetorical padding (it corresponds to the figure of speech called *enumeratio*): by summarizing the nations who have cultivated the art of poetry he reaffirms his earlier point that eloquence (of which poetry is the finest kind) is 'extensa a todas especies de humanidad' (p. 440). But Santillana refrains from giving more historical information about the ceremonies of the Toulouse Consistory. It is unnecessary to go into detail, he explains, because 'ya en el prólogo de los mis *Proverbios* se ha mencionado' (p. 454). This cross-reference is a stratagem designed to confirm his status as an expert of long standing on matters of literary history, and thus give added authority to his previous arguments. But had Don Pedro actually consulted the work in question he might have been disappointed. None of the promised information whatsoever is supplied in that earlier prologue; one is left wondering exactly how much Santillana could have known about the Toulouse school, and why he chose to ignore the Barcelona Consistories, with which he must have been more familiar.[61]

---

[61] It is doubtful that Santillana had first-hand knowledge of these Provençal-Catalan poetics (though there were MSS in Barcelona, to which he might have had access in his youth). His bold claim to have read them is probably no more than a bluff which, along with the obscurely rhetorical prose, was designed to impress

However, we can have no doubts about the motives behind this puzzling reference to 'los gállicos cesalpinos e de la provincia de Equitania': its purpose is to endorse the theme of those earlier sections in which Santillana brought forth evidence to prove the dignity of verse. But here, in the recapitulation, the theme is taken a stage further. He previously showed why poetry should be honoured; his concluding allusion to the French Consistories is an attempt to show how one school of poets have formalized their respect and paid tribute to their art in a series of solemn rituals. Thus, theory has actually been put into practice.

All this, Santillana continues, is yet further proof that poetry deserves to be held in the greatest esteem:

> Por las quales cosas e aun por otras muchas ... podrá sentyr e conoscer la vuestra magnificencia en quánta reputación, extima e comendación estas sciencias averse deven; e quánto vós ... devedes extymar que aquellas dueñas, que en torno de la fuente de Elicón incessantemente dançan, en tan nueva edad no inméritamente a la su compañía vos ayan rescebido. (p. 454)

Like the previous quotation, this passage demonstrates how Santillana not only repeats an earlier idea but at the same time adds an extra dimension to it. Poetry is a noble art, practised by an elite of 'los onbres bien nascidos e doctos'; consequently, Don Pedro should consider it a great honour to have been chosen as a member of this select group. The notion that being a poet confers honour upon an individual lays the ground for the final exhortation:

> Por tanto, señor, quanto yo puedo exorto e amonesto a la vuestra magnificiencia que, asý en la inquisición de los fermosos poemas commo en la polida horden e regla de aquéllos, en tanto que Cloto filare la estanbre, vuestro muy elevado sentido e pluma no cessen; por tal que, quando Antropos cortare la tela, no menos délficos que marciales honores e glorias obtengades. (p. 454)

Four points need to be made about this passage. Firstly, it follows

---

Prince Enrique and his fellow courtiers. His references coincide almost exactly with the description given by Villena in his *Arte*—dedicated, of course, to Santillana: e.g., the poetic competitions took place 'en el collegio de Tolosa, por abtoridad e permissión del rey de Francia'; compare with Villena's 'se fundó el collegio de Tholosa de trobadores con authoridad e permisión del rey de Francia' (ed. Sánchez Cantón, p. 165). Moreover, in the poem itself, he does not follow the precepts outlined in the preface: see H. R. Lang. 'Observações às rimas do *Cancionero de Baena*', in *Miscelânea de estudos em honra de D. Carolina Michaëlis de Vasconcellos* (Coimbra: Imprensa da Universidade, 1930), pp. 476–92, at pp. 476–80.

the requirements of the formal *laudatio*, or panegyric, of the sciences. As Curtius has suggested, these often ended by encouraging the dedicatee to devote himself to the study of whichever science was being praised (*European Literature*, p. 548). Secondly, Santillana encourages Don Pedro not just to write poetry, but also to study it; in other words, to become *un poeta* (a man of wide learning, with a thorough knowledge of classical myth and a highly polished verse technique), rather than *un dezidor*. Thirdly, this exhortation recalls another theme that underpins *El proemio* as a whole: Don Pedro is urged to preserve his interest in poetry until the very end of his life—it is not just another pastime appropriate for one's youth. And finally, these lines introduce a completely new topic, that of literary fame.

Lida de Malkiel's book on this subject makes it unnecessary for me to go into any detail here, although her conclusions concerning Santillana need to be modified. Neglecting to mention *El proemio*, she observes that he mentions fame only in passing, and that 'no demuestra sincera pasión de fama' (*La idea de la fama*, pp. 276–78). This is to underestimate his attitude towards literary glory. Santillana was by no means indifferent to its appeal, as is clearly shown by the comments and other marginalia scribbled in his manuscripts. He marks out passages concerning fame with noticeable frequency, and indeed, on the basis of this evidence, it seems that his interest in this topic is exceeded only by his preoccupation with the theme of fortune. In *Inferno*, IV, 76–78, Virgil and Dante are met by the shades of Homer, Horace, Ovid and Lucan. Virgil explains that although they were pagan, their literary fame has acquired for them the honour of being given a special place in Limbo, rather that among the souls of the damned:

> L'onrata nominanza
> che di lor suona su nella tua vita
> Grazia acquista nel ciel che si gli avanza.
> (BN Madrid, MS 10.186, f. 7ʳ)

'¡Nota maravillosa opinión!' exclaims Santillana.[62] Whatever the

---

[62] See also *Inferno*, XXIV, 46–51; *Purgatorio*, XI, 100; these passages and Santillana's marginalia are transcribed by Mario Schiff, 'La Première Traduction espagnole de la *Divine comédie*', in *Homenaje a Menéndez y Pelayo en el año vigésimo de su profesorado: estudios de erudición española* (Madrid: Victoriano Suárez, 1899), I, 269–307, at pp. 291, 293 and 298. References to literary fame are also noted in his MS of Benvenuto da Imola's commentary on the *Inferno*: see the glosses on I, 106–07 and II, 7–9 (where Benvenuto mentions the poet's power to confer

precise shade of meaning intended by this remark, he was undoubtedly impressed by Dante's bold conception of the power of literary glory. The quality of one's poetic achievements generates more that just earthly renown: literary fame has a transcendental value. The fruits of 'esta sciencia' which is, Santillana emphasized, 'acepta principalmente a Dios' (p. 442), bring the poet a further, divine, reward. Thus, it is important to realize that the final exhortation, in which Don Pedro is encouraged to devote his life to the quest for both literary and military glory, is not just a passing acknowledgment of a contemporary fashion, tacked on to the end to the eulogy as an afterthought: it is the logical conclusion to all that Santillana has said about the value and dignity of poetry.

6 Final considerations

That *El proemio* holds the key to the intellectual aspirations of the leading member of Spain's literate aristocracy has long been recognized. But these ambitions have not, in my view, been adequately interpreted: partly because scholars have tended to approach the problem with preconceived and ill-defined notions about the work's general cultural background. To compensate for this it seemed important to carry out a thorough analysis of the content, structure and sources of *El proemio* before attempting to discuss its wider implications. However, the detailed approach I have adopted has, almost inevitably, obscured the broad outlines of Santillana's argument; so, by way of a general summary, the following points should be made.

Very seldom does Santillana identify the sources of *El proemio*. Even when he names a specific authority (Cicero, Isidore, Dante, Cassiodorus and Horace) he never gives precise references. This has particularly interesting implications when we consider the textual inaccuracies that are frequently to be found in his eulogy.

Santillana's most important source is Isidore's *Etymologiae* (Bks I, xxxviii–xxxix, 'de prosa', and 'de metris'; VI, ii, 'de scriptoribus et vocabulis sanctorum librorum'; and possibly, VII, vii, 'de poetis'). Judging by the amount of material he has been able to extract from Isidore's chaotic and widely-spread observations on

---

immortality, and the relationship between literary fame and talent: BN Madrid, MS 10.208, ff. 48^r and 58^r).

the nature and origins of poetry, it is clear that at one stage he must have been very familiar with parts of this encyclopedia, either in the original or in a Castilian *refundición*. But although his definition of epithalamium, for example, comes remarkably close to that given by Isidore, at other times he departs from his source to a considerable extent. His treatment of biblical poetry provides a striking example of this. His references to the Books of Joshua and Samuel, and his account of the consolatory verse of Job, indicate that he relied on memory and a series of not unreasonable guesses in order to reconstruct the tradition of biblical verse. However well he once knew Isidore, it seems that at the time of writing *El proemio* he did not feel it necessary to check his sources. The same might also apply to his quotation from Dante's *Purgatorio*, VII, 16 (see above, p. 208 and note 50), which does not coincide either with his own copy of the *Divina commedia* or with any version recorded by modern textual criticism. Finally, the puzzling reference to Cassiodorus's *De variis causis* confirms that he often based his argument on a vague recollection of a source rather than on the actual text itself (see above, p. 209–10).[63]

On some occasions, of course, the mere reference to an authority does not necessarily imply that Santillana had any particular text at all in mind: some of the ideas introduced at key points in his argument had become aphorisms. This could be the case with the statement that 'las sciencias son desseables, asý commo Tulio quiere'; other examples are the misquotation from Horace: 'Quem noua concepit olla seruabit odorem', and the two Aristotelian tags, 'de los primeros, primera es la especulación' and 'la materia busca la forma e lo inperfecto la perfección' (p. 439; on poetry as divine infusion). Both of these are echoes of Aristotle's theory of potentiality and act, outlined in *Physics* I and *Metaphysics* V. But the basic elements of this theory had become so commonplace, almost a habit of mind, that there is no reason to assume that Santillana associated these aphorisms with any particular treatise.

I do not wish to exaggerate the inaccuracies of *El proemio* or Santillana's vagueness with regard to his sources. After all, he

---

[63] Although he read and annotated his MSS, Santillana can be as vague about his sources as another aristocratic writer, don Juan Manuel. Ian Macpherson has put the difficulty of ascribing precise sources to his work down to the fact that he 'acquired the bulk of his material aurally, from conversations with his Dominican friends, rather that from long hours of private study, and that as he wrote he relied more on memory than manuscript for his inspiration', 'Don Juan Manuel', p. 6.

sometimes departs from the original text for an obvious rhetorical purpose (e.g. his treatment of Suetonius on the Roman Emperors, or Petrarch and Boccaccio on Robert of Sicily and Hugh of Cyprus). It is also possible that he did not have any reference books to hand when he wrote *El proemio*, and that he was therefore unable to check all the details of his argument. Indeed, it is also worth bearing in mind that he need not have relied exclusively on written sources in order to compile material for his treatise. We have perhaps underestimated the fact that much information, and possibly even the inspiration for writing an extended treatise about poetry, could have come from literary discussions: discussions that would have taken place over a long period of time, and not only with fellow poets, but also with the numerous *letrados* in his employment as translators (such as Martín de Avila, the much-travelled Latin secretary to Juan II, or Pero Díaz de Toledo, who provides a fictionalized picture of such literary-philosophical discussions in his *Diálogo sobre la muerte del Marqués*).

These three points help to explain some of the vague and perplexing aspects of *El proemio* and its sources. However, given the tendency of some recent critics to associate Santillana with the Italian humanists, it is worth emphasizing the rather obvious fact that this impressive literary defence is the work not of a professional scholar, but of an aristocratic dilettante. He was, of course, an extraordinarily cultured aristocrat by the standards of his time; nevertheless, in spite of his wide and close reading of vernacular literature, his methods, according to his friend Fernando de la Torre, remain those of 'onbres sin letras'.[64]

The passage whose sources are most difficult to trace is Santillana's definition of poetry. The problem is due both to the lack of substantially close verbal parallels and to the traditional character of the theories he put forward. In fact, the raw material of the entire treatise is drawn form a common stock of literary theories employed, in a variety of contexts, throughout the Middle Ages and early Renaissance. Apart from the definition, one might also point to the conventional nature of Santillana's views on eloquence and wisdom and the association between rhetoric and poetry. Although in many respects a synthesis of traditional ideas,

---

[64] *Obra literaria*, ed. Díez Garretas, p. 148; see also Pero Díaz de Toledo's admiring comment on Santillana's proverbs: 'mucho era de maravillar como no seyendo doctrinado en las letras que sentiesse e escriviesse tan bien e tan moral e virtuosamente', *Los proverbios con su glosa*, f. a vi[r].

El proemio is by no means an abstract work, written, so to speak, in a historical vacuum. It is the response of a specific individual to the conditions of a particular period of Castilian history. The treatise is not itself polemical, but it is, nevertheless, a reaction against contemporary scepticism about the value of poetry and the part it should play in the life of the nobility.

The doubts and misgivings of many fifteenth-century writers (some of whom I mentioned in the first section of this chapter) are concisely expressed by Fernán Pérez de Guzmán. This author, whose sententious style captures many contemporary commonplaces, observed on one occasion that the art of poetry was 'más graciosa/ que útil nin honorable'.[65] Clearly, *El proemio* is the perfect antithesis to this view. Santillana devotes most of his energy to proving that, in addition to being pleasurable, poetry is both useful and honourable. Its utility derives from several factors: it possesses immense consolatory power (as a source of both moral doctrine and entertainment); it plays an integral part in all aspects of human life; and as a form of eloquence, it clarifies and transmits wisdom. That poetry is an honourable activity ·follows on from the original premise that it serves some useful purpose; however, Santillana draws on a number of other arguments in order to reinforce this point. Poetry has impressive historical authority stretching back to the Bible (and the implication of its historical continuity is that it may legitimately be classed as a science); it has close, and fruitful, associations with royalty (and not only with such maligned monarchs as Juan II); at its finest, it is both the product and the hallmark of an exclusive intellectual and social elite; and, as a logical consequence to all this, it is a valid means of acquiring eternal fame.

But *El proemio* is far from being just a series of theoretical statements. The most striking aspect of the work (apart from the historical survey) is, in my view, its value as a personal document which enabled Santillana to express the keenness and continuity of his enthusiasm for verse. Whatever the range of meaning implicit in the enigmatic phrase 'un zelo celeste, una affección divina, un insaciable cibo del ánimo', one essential ingredient is the notion of the poet's love for his art. The intellectual and esthetic attraction of

---

[65] *Coplas de vicios e virtudes*, st. 5 (*Can. cas.*, I, 576); see also his comment on Juan II's taste for 'obras más plazibles e deleitables que útiles nin onorables' (*Generaciones*, ed. Tate, p. 39).

poetry captivates the heart and mind of the writer; the study and composition of verse, however arduous, are nonetheless undertaken with intense mental delight. And, Santillana promises, the pleasure that poetry has to offer is not transient: 'Quem nova concepit olla seruabit odorem'; it lasts throughout the life of those who have been welcomed into the company of 'aquellas dueñas que en torno de la fuente de Elicón incessantemente dançan'. Parallels with these ideas may be found, sporadically, in the words of other writers, but no other Castilian poet lays such emphasis on his undiminished appetite for this 'cibo insaciable'.

In one sense, Santillana's enthusiasm possesses its own logic. Speech is man's defining characteristic; and, according to the traditional Ciceronian view, man should strive to cultivate those qualities that set him apart from the beasts. Eloquence becomes an ideal to be pursued. And poetry is the finest form of eloquence. Thus, Santillana's declaration of his undying love for this art, and the eulogistic terms in which his arguments are couched, combine to make *El proemio* a vindication of his own intellectual and spiritual nobility.

CONCLUSION

This study offers a picture of the literary theorizing carried out by a particular group of aristocratic and professional writers: it will, I hope, contribute towards a more comprehensive account of the literary tastes and attitudes of late medieval Spain. To acquire that broader picture, however, one would of course have to expand the geographical and chronological boundaries; no less importantly, the evidence examined here would need to be complemented by studies employing different methods, and pursuing different goals. Urgently needed are more stylistic analyses of courtly verse, especially for the earlier period; for the later decades, considerable progress has already been made by, to cite obvious examples, Rafael Lapesa and Keith Whinnom. Even so, nothing of the scope of the books by Roger Dragonetti or Paul Zumthor has yet been attempted for Castilian poetry. Also valuable would be a broad paleographic survey of the *cancioneros* themselves; in one important respect, Jane Whetnall's recent thesis makes a fascinating contribution, but more could be done along the lines of, say, Julia Boffey's monograph on the English lyric, or the work by Elspeth Kennedy and Barry Windeatt on scribal responses to the literary text.[1]

A broader context for the theoretical issues examined here could be supplied by a study of life, patronage and education in the Castilian courts. But one should not limit the field of literary criticism to court writers. Those writing in an academic or theological milieu, especially at the end of the century, must also be taken into account by future scholars. Nebrija's approach to poetry and the task of literary criticism has received some attention, and so has that of Alfonso de Madrigal. But in spite of the work of Kohut and Keightley, Madrigal's historical and theological commentaries

---

[1] Rafael Lapesa, 'Poesía de cancionero y poesía italianizante', in *De la Edad Media*, pp. 145–71; Keith Whinnom, *La poesía amatoria de la época de los Reyes Católicos* (Durham: University, 1981); Roger Dragonetti, *La Technique poétique des trouvères dans la chanson courtoise: contribution à l'étude de la rhétorique médiévale* (Bruges: De Tempel, 1960); for Zumthor, Boffey, Kennedy and Windeatt, see Introduction, notes 4, 7 and 16.

remain one of the last great uncharted areas of Castilian culture during the late Middle Ages.[2]

As far as the present book is concerned, one of the conclusions that must inevitably be drawn from the preceding pages is the fact that there is no convenient label to tag onto the literary thought of the period. There are two reasons for this. Firstly, there is a notable diversity of sources. A few of these can be identified with certainty: Santillana's use of Isidore and Baena's *refundición* of Alfonso X are obvious examples. By and large, however, we are faced with ideas that cannot safely be ascribed to a single individual, but rather to broad intellectual traditions or literary and scholastic practices. This is to say that although we can detect the guiding hand of patristic writers (Jerome, Basil, Augustine), or scholastic and humanist commentators on Virgil and Dante ('Servius', Benvenuto da Imola, Boccaccio and Bruni), we can seldom point to a single individual as having been solely responsible for the formulation of a particular concept. And none can reasonably be described as authorities for the whole range of ideas present in the work of Baena, Villena, Mena or Santillana.

This point applies with special force to the Latin arts of rhetoric and poetry, both classical and medieval. These had a part to play in the transmission of ideas about the nature and function of poetry: they helped shape, for example, the basic premises of the Provençal and Catalan poetic consistories, which in turn influenced the association between rhetoric and poetry made by Villena in his *Arte de trovar*. The extent to which manuscripts of these works circulated in Castile from the thirteenth to the fifteenth centuries has been amply documented by Charles Faulhaber.[3] Although the impact of these texts on rhetorical theory and practice has still to be properly determined, after 1400 there was a sharp increase in the number of manuscripts of classical treatises, such as Horace's *Ars*, Cicero's *De inventione*, and the more novel *De oratore*; Ciceronian doctrine was

---

[2] For Nebrija, the most recent relevant study is by Luis Gil, 'Nebrija y el menester del gramático', in *Nebrija*, ed. García de la Concha, pp. 53–64.

[3] *Latin Rhetorical Theory in Thirteenth and Fourteenth Century Castile*, UCPMP, 103 (Berkeley: Univ. of California Press, 1972); 'Retóricas clásicas y medievales en bibliotecas castellanas', *Abaco*, 4 (Madrid: Castalia, 1973), 151–300; 'Medieval Spanish Metrical Terminology and MS 9589 of the Biblioteca Nacional, Madrid', *RPh*, 33 (1979–80), 43–61; 'Las retóricas hispanolatinas medievales (siglos XIII–XV)', *Repertorio de Historia de las Ciencias Eclesiásticas en España*, 7 (1979), 11–65; also fundamental will be Spurgeon Baldwin's forthcoming ed. of the Castilian translation of Brunetto Latini's *Trésor*.

also transmitted via the popular Castilian version of Brunetto Latini's *Trésor*. Yet it seems to me that until the end of the century their relevance lies principally in academic rather than lay circles. Contrary to the views of, say, Miguel Garci-Gómez, classical treatises did not play a dominant part in shaping the ideas of the court poets about the nature and function of poetry.

Of all texts available to fifteenth-century readers, Horace's *Ars* had the most to say about these matters: perhaps his most famous contribution was his dictum that poetry should be both *dulce et utile*. But the belief that poetry served these two ends had become so hackneyed by this time that the scarcity of explicit references to Horace as an authority for the theory is surely significant. Occasional references to him may indeed be found in the work of, for example, Juan de Mena, Diego de Valera and Carlos de Viana, but there is nothing to suggest that these vernacular writers had enough interest in, or knowledge of, Horace to qualify even remotely for the label 'Horatian'. The same may be said of Aristotle, whose most relevant text for the purposes of this study is the *Nicomachean Ethics*.[4] If I have laboured this fact it is to emphasize the point that we should not approach the criticism and theory of this period from the narrow perspective of schools, classical and otherwise, and that it is inappropriate to talk in terms of a single theoretical tradition. What stands out is the absence of one dominant figure whose authority is such that we may justifiably classify the reign of Juan II under a particular theoretical category.

But there is another important factor: as far as ideas are concerned, there was little change in the basic premises on which

---

[4] Diego de Valera cites Horace as an authority for the five parts of the *ars dictaminis*; I have not found a source for this in the medieval scholia on the *ars poetica* (*Tratado en defensa de las virtuosas mujeres*, ed. Suz Ruiz, p. 80). Rodríguez del Padrón talks of the 'poético fin de aprovechar e venir a ti en plazer', though significantly without specifying Horace (*Siervo libre de amor*, ed. Hernández Alonso, p. 156). Carlos de Viana alludes to him briefly in the preface to his translation of Aristotle's *Ethics*; for Juan de Mena, see the confused reference in *La coronación*, f. 308r. As for Aristotle, James F. Burke has suggested that the author of *El libro del Cavallero Zifar* knew the *Poetics* in the version of Averroës, since a copy was owned by the Archbishop of Toledo, his possible patron: 'A New Critical Approach to the Interpretation of Medieval Spanish Literature', *C*, 10 (1982–83), 273–79; Nepaulsingh has interpreted the structure of *El corbacho* in the light of Aristotle-Averroës, though he refrains (wisely) from claiming a direct influence: *Towards a History*, ch. 4; the only explicit reference to the *Poetics* that I know of is that by Alfonso de Madrigal, in his Latin commentary on Eusebius: see Kohut, *Las teorías literarias*, p. 20 and n. 85.

literary debate was conducted until well into the sixteenth century, when writers looked afresh at the poetics of Aristotle and Horace. There are, of course, shifts in emphasis and attitude at various times and places, but on a purely theoretical level it is misleading to apply the terms medieval or Renaissance to the kinds of literary theory and criticism discussed here. The appropriateness of these terms is determined not by the ideas themselves, so much as by the way the conventional arguments were manipulated and the various rhetorical ends to which they were put.[5]

As I have said, the Castilians derived their ideas about the composition and study of poetry from an eclectic range of theoretical and literary traditions. Attempts were made—mainly by Villena and Santillana—to synthesize and establish a coherent theoretical tradition relevant to Castilian literature, but it seems to me that such attempts were partial and, for the following reason, ultimately unsuccessful. Although the poetry of Santillana and Mena continued to be read and admired after their deaths, their literary theorizing had no subsequent influence. Indeed, if present manuscript evidence is anything to go by, three of the five major texts (the prologues of Baena and Santillana, and Villena's *Arte*) were not widely disseminated; *La coronación* was probably the best-known work (since it was attached to numerous editions of *El laberinto*), and this is not immediately recognizable as a work of literary theory. So it is easy to understand the sense of isolation that pervades the introduction to Encina's *Arte de poesía castellana*:

> Y bien creo aver otros que primero que yo tomassen este trabajo y más copiosamente, mas es cierto que a mi noticia no ha llegado, salvo aquello que el notable maestro de Lebrixa en su arte de romance acerca desta facultad muy perfectamente puso.   (ed. López Estrada, p. 79)

The theoretical sections of Encina's *Arte* closely resemble Santillana's *Proemio*. The basic arguments they employ to defend poetry are identical (the dignity of human speech, the art is not to be blamed for the abuses of the individual poet, and so on). These similarities have led López Estrada, who has examined them in some detail, to suggest that Encina knew the earlier text.[6] For

---

[5]   A similar point has been made by David Robey, 'Humanist Views on the Study of Poetry in the Early Italian Renaissance', *History of Education*, 13 (1984), 7–27, at p. 9.

[6]   '*El arte de poesía castellana* de Juan del Encina (1496)', in *XIXe Colloque International d'Études Humanistes, Tours, 5–17 juillet 1976: l'Humanisme dans les lettres*

reasons I have already mentioned, this is not necessarily so; but whatever the case, the main interest resides not so much in conceptual similarities as in the differences in sources: Encina's substantial references to Quintilian point to the new developments taking place in Nebrija's time when a new set of classical authorities were being invoked. Similarly, when Hernán Núñez praises the antiquity of poetry, ranking it as a form of philosophy with immense civic importance, he bases his familiar arguments on Strabo.[7] He uses Horace, Aristotle and Quintilian as authorities for historical observations on authors and genres that do not differ substantially from ideas disseminated throughout the Middle Ages by Isidore. In spite of many underlying continuities, the history of literary theory in the fifteenth, as in other centuries, seems a history of fresh starts.

Although it is not easy to find neat labels for the writers whose ideas I have been discussing, a general pattern does emerge, in that they were united by the social bias of their literary thought. The dominant concern was with the dual contribution poetry could make to the creation of an aristocratic ideal. When considered from the point of view of composition, the rhetorical value of poetry was emphasized: it was seen as a medium for the courtly qualities of wit, *graciosidad*, and lucidity. When considered as the subject of *reposado estudio*, its philosophical value was brought to the fore: poetry was prized as a source of consolation and example, and as a means of giving a contemplative dimension to the active life. This duality in the poetic theorizing of the period reminds us how there were, put crudely, two literatures in the Middle Ages: the classical and the vernacular. Each, broadly speaking, had its own set of theories, and each evoked its own separate responses: classical poetry was discussed from the point of view of study, vernacular from that of composition. But for a number of reasons, these two literatures, which had for centuries run parallel to each other, finally began to converge. This development was encouraged by a blend of social and political factors: not just literary fashion, but also by the spread of lay literacy amongst a baronial class anxious to use the written word as a means of enhancing social status and gaining political influence.

---

espagnoles, ed. Augustin Redondo, De Pétrarque à Descartes, 39 (Paris: J. Vrin, 1979), pp. 151–68.

[7] In his commentary on Mena's *Laberinto*, gloss on st. 123 (Antwerp, 1552, ff. 112r-13v).

We see this convergence begin around 1430 with Baena's *Cancionero*, to be followed soon after by Juan de Mena's *Coronación* and Santillana's *Proverbios*. In these works, the critical methods which had traditionally been reserved for the classics began to be applied to contemporary poetry. From then on, the lengthy prose prologues, commentaries and glosses took deep root in fifteenth-century Castile, and indicate how the private study of poetry had become firmly entrenched in the literary life of the time. The results of this development were far-reaching, and may be summarized on two related levels, the personal and the national.

The application of scholastic critical devices to the vernacular text helped bolster the status of lay writers. It added an extra dimension to their literary personae, enabling them to take on the guise of a pedagogue, or *sabio*, expounding their own work. As Marichal put it in relation to Díez de Games's use of the academic prologue, it allowed them to express 'la decidida voluntad del escritor por mantener y afirmar su derecho a la voz literaria' (*La voluntad de estilo*, p. 59). These aspirations may be detected in many other aspects of literary style and production; they are reflected in a particularly interesting way by the composition of *cancioneros* recording the output of a single poet. Personal anthologies were compiled sporadically throughout Europe before the fifteenth century, but only at that time did they become truly fashionable. In some cases—and for Castile there are the possible examples of the luxury *cancioneros* by Santillana and Gómez Manrique—these collections follow a chronological arrangement, which suggests that they too were considered as a form of literary biography, a complement to the new genres of *semblanza* and personal history. As Brian Tate has reminded us in an important review-article on Marichal's book, interest in the individual is not an exclusively Renaissance phenomenon. But this use of the *cancionero* is typical of the vernacular humanism of the late Middle Ages. Poets like Santillana and Gómez Manrique did more than just borrow thematic motifs from the past; they also took the idea that poetry was worthy of serious study and possessed immense educational value. In applying this concept to their own verse they conferred upon themselves and their work the dignity of wisdom and enhanced authorial status.[8] Indeed, the idea that modern poets

---

[8] On individual anthologies, see Huot, *From Song to Book*, pp. 211–327, where the practice is traced back to the XIVc. For Santillana and Gómez Manrique, see

could emulate classical *auctores* had become deeply rooted by the
end of the fifteenth century, when Hernán Núñez wrote his
commentary on Mena's *Laberinto*; perhaps it was even a platitude.
At the start of the sixteenth it was mercilessly and obscenely
satirized by *La carajicomedia*, which parodies not only the style of *El
laberinto*, but also the basic literary outlook which the poem and its
commentaries represent.

As Spain began to create its own modern classics, it also, as a
direct consequence, began to elaborate the concept of a national
literature. This development went hand in hand with the patriotic
antiquarianism which characterized the popularity of such 'Spanish'
writers as Seneca, Lucan and Quintilian, and which gave rise to the
myth of the Cordoban Aristotle. The emerging desire to trace a
national literature was, of course, a European phenomenon:
England looked to Chaucer as the father of its verse, France to
Jeun de Meun and Machaut, Italy to Dante and Petrarch.[9] These
countries were able to find their modern classics in the fourteenth
century; Castile sought hers in the fifteenth. One reason why this
should have been so was, I suspect, the absence of a courtly lyric
tradition in Castilian. The proliferation of *cancioneros* compiled
between 1440 and 1470 suggests a general trend to establish such a
tradition and a keenness to preserve it with a written record. This
was done partly at the expense of the Galician-Portuguese
anthologies. The major reason for the loss of these *cancioneiros* was
because the verse they contained had become linguistically un-
fashionable. But it is striking that they did not arouse the
antiquarian interest that Provençal poetry did in France and Italy: it

Biblioteca Universitaria, Salamanca, MS 2.655 and Biblioteca de Palacio, MS II
1.250. See also R. B. Tate, 'The Literary *Persona* from Díez de Games to Santa
Teresa', *RPh*, 13 (1959–60), 298–304.
   [9] On antiquarianism, see Lawrance, 'Nuño de Guzmán: Life and Works', pp.
148–63; on the concept of a national literature, see López Estrada, 'La teoría de la
poesía nueva en las lenguas vernáculas', in *Introducción*, pp. 155–58; for elsewhere in
Europe, see Badel, *Le 'Roman de la Rose'*, pp. 494–96; Pierre Jodogne, 'Les
"Rhétoriqueurs" et l'humanisme: problème d'histoire littéraire', in *Humanism in
France at the End of the Middle Ages and in the Early Renaissance*, ed. A. H. T. Levi
(Manchester: University Press, 1970), pp. 150–75 (esp. pp. 163–64); Cynthia
Brown, 'The Rise of Literary Consciousness in Late-Medieval France: Jean
Lemaire de Belges and the Rhétoriqueur Tradition', *JMRS*, 13 (1983), 51–74;
Minnis, *Medieval Theory of Authorship*, pp. 177–209; on Chaucer, see also Derek
Brewer (ed.), *Chaucer: The Critical Heritage*, 2 vols (London: Routledge and Kegan
Paul, 1978), vol. I (1385–1837).

is as if Castilian poets and compilers were too preoccupied with the task of establishing the modern lyric to be concerned with its historical antecedent.

The notable exception to this was Santillana, who illustrated the continuities between past and present by explaining that many contemporary technical terms, 'los nonbres del arte', derived from Galician-Portuguese. To us, this statement may seem a glimpse of the obvious; to his fellow poets, it may possibly have come as something of a revelation. Evidence for a lack of interest in and certainly lack of knowledge of the Galician-Portuguese school comes from the manuscript tradition ('tradizione povera, tradizione sterile', in the words of Tavani). This evidence is supported by the comments of Santillana himself. Though he is fully aware of their historical significance, he confesses that he has no personal knowledge of the *cantigas* of Alfonso X, and his acquaintance with the rest of the corpus is confined to memories of an anthology seen in his distant youth. Moreover, roughly ten years before *El proemio*, in the prologue to *Los proverbios*, he offered a different view of the true context of Castilian verse. There, more under the influence of Enrique de Villena than of personal experience, he boasted that the appropriate formal models for this contemporaries to follow were supplied by the Provençal-Catalan treatises of Vidal, Foixà and Molinier. If this shift in perspective illustrates the fragmentary view Castilians had of their lyric traditions, it also highlights Santillana's anxiety to place his own verse within a solid historical framework.

Others besides Santillana reflect this concern to establish a literary tradition for Castilian poetry, and it is especially noticeable in the two preceptive poetics written at opposite ends of the century. Shortly before his death, Villena recalled the heyday of the Barcelona Consistory, and paraded its activities as an example to be followed. His treatise, shown to have the authority of long-established conventions behind it, offered precepts designed to fix the new Castilian lyric within a set of immutable rules. He attempted, in short, to lay a course for Castilian verse by grafting it onto the traditions of his youth. Much later, Encina showed himself to be no less fascinated by the literary progress and present-day authority of his craft. But though he shared the concerns of Villena and Santillana, he wrote from a different perspective and with different motives. His is a much cruder formulation of historical development: Castilian is, he declares, the direct descendent of Latin verse, though her immediate forebears were Italian. To prove his point he explains how the verb *trobar* derives from the Italian 'to find'. Neither the etymological nor the historical explanation makes any reference to other vernacular traditions, Iberian or otherwise. His silence might conceivably have been born out of ignorance; it is rather more likely to have been the inspired by the conviction that Italy provided the more illustrious models.[10] This historical perception is indicative of the mood of the entire treatise. After two generations of Castilian court poets, he writes with supreme confidence about the achievements and current strength of his literary school. Poetry in Spain, he concludes, 'ya florece más que en ninguna otra parte'. Encina's confidence is also reflected in the very form of his theoretical prologue. As a blend of two genres, the eulogy and the preceptive poetic, his *Arte de poesía castellana* reconciles the two theoretical approaches to poetry mentioned above. It justifies the study of verse using the arguments of the ancients and defines rules for its composition by adducing examples culled from the modern classics, Santillana and Mena. It is thus a culmination of the trend to dignify Castilian poetry by exemplifying the *translatio auctoritatis* from the classics to the vernacular.

Yet if the first poetic of the fifteenth century attempted to set rules for the future, the final one attempted to preserve the past. In spite—or, paradoxically, because—of his confidence in the strength of his tradition, Encina, taking his cue from Nebrija, suggests the possibility of decline. Castilian poetry has reached a stage 'de donde más se podía temer el decendimiento que la subida', and consequently he decides to 'encerrarla debaxo de ciertas leyes y reglas, por que ninguna antigüedad de tiempos le pueda traer olvido' (p. 78). The very same paradox motivated the vast enterprise of Hernando del Castillo. His *Cancionero general* and its many reprints attest to the continuity of taste between the late Middle Ages and early Renaissance. His pride in the textual authenticity of its contents also reflects the necessity of preserving accurate records of an established school of writing (was he conscious too of the scarcity of *cancioneros* compiled in the thirty years immediately preceding his?).[11] The solid generic arrangement

[10] Ed. López Estrada, p. 82. I take 'los nuestros' to mean Castilian poets. However scant his knowledge, it is hard to accept that Encina believed both Dante and Petrarch predated Galician-Portuguese and Catalan troubadours.

[11] Anthologies compiled between 1470 and 1511 were devoted, in the main, to the work of earlier poets; as Jane Whetnall has observed, 'no major manuscript

of this collection is reminiscent of the Galician-Portuguese *cancioneiros* copied at roughly the same time for the Italian antiquarian Angelo Colocci. These are based, it is true, upon collections made at the close of a much earlier era, but their methods of organization mirror identical concerns: rather than focussing on the achievements and personalities of individual poets, the aim of all these anthologies is to offer a broad overview of a tradition as a whole. Hernando del Castillo was certainly responding to the continued popularity of *cancionero* verse, but his desire to structure and codify it according to its various genres betrays his awareness that the Castilian tradition was beginning to change its course.

---

collections containing new love lyric have survived from the closing decades of the fifteenth century .... The source manuscripts that fed Castillo's vast compilation seem to have disappeared' ('Manuscript Love Poetry', p. 1). As Deyermond's article on 'The Silent Century of Portuguese Court Poetry' indicates, one could make similar points about Resende and the compilation of the *Cancioneiro geral*.

SELECT BIBLIOGRAPHY

Manuscript sources

Escorial,
  MS h-III-11, Alonso de Cartagena, *Memorial de virtudes*
  MS K-III-31, ff. 69ʳ–89ᵛ, Alvar Gómez de Castro's extracts of *El arte de trovar*
    by Enrique de Villena
Madrid, Biblioteca de Bartolomé March,
  MS 20–5–6, ff. 39ʳ–68ᵛ, Juan de Mena, *El laberinto*, and anonymous late XVc
    commentary (*Cancionero de Barrantes* fragment)
Madrid, Biblioteca Nacional,
  MS 174, Boethius, *De consolatione Philosophiae*, trans. Pero López de Ayala [?]
  MS 10.171, ff. 25ʳ–62ʳ, Leonardo Bruni, *Le vite di Dante e di Petrarca*,
    anonymous XVc Castilian translation
  MS 10.186, Dante, *Divina commedia*, trans. Villena; Petrarch, sonnet 116, with
    anonymous Castilian commentary and translation.
  MS 10.207, Pietro Alighieri, commentary Dante's *Divina commedia*, anonymous
    XVc Castilian translation
  MS 10.208, Benvenuto da Imola, commentary on Dante's *Inferno*, anonymous
    XVc Castilian translation (fragment: cantos I–VII, part of VIII)
  MS 10.811, Eusebius/ Jerome, *Chronici canones*, trans. Alfonso de Madrigal
  MS 17.975, Virgil, *Aeneid*, Bks I–III, trans. and commentary by Enrique de
    Villena
Madrid, Biblioteca de la Real Academia de la Historia,
  Colección Salazar, MS N-73, anon. XVc Castilian glossary
Paris, Bibliothèque Nationale,
  fonds espagnol, MS 224, Juan de Mena, *La coronación*
  fonds espagnol, MS 229, ff. 2ʳ–76ᵛ, Juan de Mena, *El laberinto*
  fonds espagnol, MS 458, Boccaccio, *De montibus*; St Basil, *De legendis libris
    gentilium*, anonymous XVc Castilian translation

Printed sources: primary

Alfonso X, *Las siete partidas del sabio rey don Alonso el nono [sic], nuevamente glosadas
    por el licenciado Gregorio López*, 3 vols (Madrid: Juan Hasrey, 1610–11)
——, *General estoria: primera parte*, ed. Antonio G. Solalinde (Madrid: Centro de
    Estudios Históricos, 1930)
St Augustine, *The City of God Against the Pagans*, with an English translation by

George E. McCracken *et al.*, Loeb Classical Library, 411–17 (Cambridge, Mass: Harvard Univ. Press; London: Heinemann, 1957–72)

——, *Confessions*, with an English translation by William Watts (1631), Loeb Classical Library, 26–27 (1912; Cambridge, Mass: Harvard Univ. Press; London: Heinemann, 1968–70)

——, *De doctrina Christiana*, ed. J. -P. Migne, PL, 34 (Paris, 1861) cols 15–122

Averçó, Luis de, '*Torcimany*' *de Luis de Averçó: tratado retórico gramatical y diccionario de rimas, siglos XIV–XV*, ed. José María Casas Homs, 2 vols (Barcelona: CSIC, 1956)

Benavente, Juan Alfonso de, *Ars et doctrina studendi et docendi*, ed. Bernardo Alonso Rodríguez, Bibliotheca Salmanticensis II, Textus 1 (Salamanca: Universidad Pontificia, 1972)

——, *Arte y teoría de estudiar y enseñar*, trans. Emilio de la Cruz Aguilar, *RFDUCM*, 67 (1982), 227–55, and 68 (1983), 211–18

Benvenuto da Imola, *Comentum super Dantis Aldigherij Comoediam*, ed. J. P. Lacaita, 5 vols (Florence: Barbèra, 1887)

Bernardus Silvestris, *Commentary on the First Six Books of Virgil's 'Aeneid'*, trans. Earl G. Schreiber and Thomas E. Maresca (Lincoln: Univ. of Nebraska Press, 1979)

Bernart Amoros, 'Le Chansonnier de Bernart Amoros', ed. E. Stengel, *RLR*, 41 (1898), 349–80 [prologue and 1st part only]

Biographies des troubadours: textes provençaux des XIIIᵉ et XIVᵉ siècles, ed. Jean Boutière, A. H. Schutz, Irenée-Marcel Cluzel, 2nd ed. (Paris: Nizet, 1973)

Boccaccio, Giovanni, *Genealogie deorum gentilium libri*, ed. Vincenzo Romano, Scrittori d'Italia, 200–01 (Bari: Laterza, 1951)

——, *Boccaccio on Poetry: Being the Preface and the Fourteenth and Fifteenth Books of Boccaccio's 'Genealogia Deorum Gentilium'*, trans. Charles G. Osgood (1930; New York: Bobbs-Merrill, 1956)

Boethius, Anicius Manlius, *The Consolation of Philosophy*, with an English translation by S. J. Tester, Loeb Classical Library, 74 (Cambridge, Mass: Harvard Univ. Press; London: Heinemann, 1973)

Bruni, Leonardo, *Le vite di Dante e di Petrarca*, in *Humanistisch- philosophische Schriften, mit einer Chronologie seiner Werke und Briefe*, ed. Hans Baron (1928; Wiesbaden: Martin Sändig, 1969), pp. 50–69

Cancionero de Juan Alfonso de Baena, ed. José María Azáceta, Clásicos Hispánicos, 3 vols (Madrid: CSIC, 1966)

'*Cancionero de Baena*' *Reproduced in Facsimile from the Unique Manuscript in the Bibliothèque Nationale*, ed. Henry R. Lang (New York: Hispanic Society of America, 1926)

Cancionero castellano del siglo XV, ed. Raymond Foulché–Delbosc, NBAE, 19 and 22 (Madrid: Bailly-Baillière, 1912–15)

Cartagena, Alonso de, *Un tratado de Alonso de Cartagena sobre la educación y los estudios literarios*, ed. Jeremy N. H. Lawrance, Publicaciones del Seminario de Literatura Medieval y Humanística (Bellaterra: Universidad Autónoma de Barcelona, 1979)

——, *El 'Oracional' de Alonso de Cartagena: edición crítica (comparación del manuscrito 160 de Santander y el incunable de Murcia)*, ed. Silvia González-Quevedo Alonso (Valencia: Albatros; Chapel Hill: Hispanófila, 1983)

——, See also under Cicero, Seneca

Cicero, Marcus Tullius, *De oratore*, with an English translation by E. W. Sutton and H. Rackham, Loeb Classical Library, 348–49 (Cambridge, Mass: Harvard Univ. Press; London: Heinemann, 1942)

——, *La rethórica de M. Tullio Cicerón* [i.e. *De inventione*, I], trans. Alonso de Cartagena, ed. Rosalba Mascagna, Romanica Neapolitana, 2 (Naples: Liguori, 1969)

Classical and Medieval Literary Criticism: Translations and Interpretations, ed. Alex Preminger *et al.* (New York: Frederick Ungar, 1974)

Crónica de don Alvaro de Luna, Condestable de Castilla, Maestre de Santiago, ed. Juan de Mata Carriazo, Colección de Crónicas Españolas, 2 (Madrid: Espasa-Calpe, 1940)

Dante Alighieri, *Opere*, various eds, in *Encyclopedia Dantesca* (Rome: Instituto della Enciclopedia Italiana, 1978), VI, 619–1002

Díez de Games, Gutierre, *El Victorial, crónica de Don Pero Niño, Conde de Buelna*, ed. Juan de Mata Carriazo, Colección de Crónicas Españolas, 1 (Madrid: Espasa-Calpe, 1940)

Encina, Juan del, see under *Las poéticas castellanas*

Guiraut Riquier, 'La supplica di Guiraut Riquier e la risposta di Alfonso X di Castiglia', ed. Valeria Bertolucci Pizzorusso, *Studi Mediolatini e Volgari*, 14 (1966), 9–135

Hugh of St Victor, *Eruditionis didascalicae libri septem*, ed. J.-P. Migne, PL, 176 (Paris, 1854), cols 739–838

Imperial, Micer Francisco, '*El dezir a las syete virtudes' y otros poemas*, ed. Colbert I. Nepaulsingh, Clásicos Castellanos, 221 (Madrid: Espasa-Calpe, 1977)

Isidore of Seville, *Etymologiarum sive originum libri XX*, ed. William M. Lindsay, Oxford Classical Texts, 2 vols (1911; Oxford: Clarendon, 1971)

John of Salisbury, *Metalogicus*, ed. J. -P. Migne, PL, 199 (Paris, 1855), cols 823–946

López de Mendoza, Iñigo, Marqués de Santillana, *Obras completas*, ed. Angel Gómez Moreno and Maximilian P. A. M. Kerkhof (Barcelona: Planeta, 1988)

——, *Poesías completas*, I, ed. Miguel Angel Pérez Priego, Clásicos Alhambra, 25 (Madrid: Alhambra, 1983)

——, *Los proverbios con su glosa (Sevilla, 1494)*, ed. Antonio Pérez Gómez, Incunables Poéticos Castellanos, 11 (Cieza: 'la fonte que mana y corre', 1965)

——, *Bías contra Fortuna*, ed. Maxim. P. A. M. Kerkhof, Anejos del *BRAE*, 39 (Madrid: Real Academia Española, 1982 [1983])

——, *Prohemios y cartas literarias*, ed. Miguel Garci-Gómez (Madrid: Editora Nacional, 1984)

——, see also under *Las poéticas castellanas*

Lucena, Juan de, *Libro de vita beata*, in *Opúsculos literarios de los siglos XIV a XVI*, ed. Antonio Paz y Melia, Sociedad de Bibliófilos Españoles, 9 (Madrid, 1892), pp. 105–205

Madrigal, Alfonso de, *Comento sobre Eusebio*, 5 parts [each foliated separately] in 3 vols (Salamanca: Hans Gysser, 1506–07)

Mena, Juan de, *Todas las obras del famosíssimo poeta Juan de Mena con la glosa del comendador Fernán Núñez sobre 'Las trescientas', agora nuevamente corregidas y enmendadas* (Antwerp: Martín Nucio, 1552)

——, *La Ylíada en romance, según la impresión de Arnao Guillén de Brocar (Valladolid, 1519)*, ed. Martín de Riquer, Selecciones Bibliófilas, 3 (Barcelona, 1949)

——, '*Coplas de los siete pecados mortales' and First Continuation*, ed. Gladys M. Rivera (Madrid: Porrúa Turanzas, 1982)

Metge, Bernat, *Lo somni*, ed. Marta Jordà, Les Millors Obres de la Literatura Catalana, 41 (Barcelona: Edicions 62, 1980)

Molinier, Guilhem, *Las Flors del gay saber estier dichas las Leys d'amors*, ed. A. Gatien-Arnoult, 4 vols (Toulouse: J.-B. Paya, 1841–48)

——, *Las Leys d'amors: manuscrit de l'Académie des Jeux Fleuraux*, ed. Joseph Anglade, 4 vols (Toulouse: Édouard Privat; Paris: Auguste Picard, 1919–1920)

Pedro de Portugal, *Obras completas do Condestável Dom Pedro de Portugal*, ed. Luís Adão da Fonseca (Lisbon: Fundação Calouste Gulbenkian, 1975)

Pérez de Guzmán, Fernán, *Generaciones y semblanzas*, ed. R. B. Tate (London: Tamesis, 1965)

——, [?] *Floresta de philósophos*, ed. Raymond Foulché–Delbosc, *RH*, 11 (1904), 5–154

Pero da Ponte, *Poesie*, ed. Saverio Panunzio, Biblioteca di Filologia Romanza, 10 (Bari: Adriatica, 1967)

Petrarch, Francis, 'La *Collatio laureationis* del Petrarca', ed. C. Godi, *Italia Medioevale e Umanistica*, 13 (1970), 1–27

——, *Invectivas contra el médico rudo e parlero* [nos I and III], trans. Hernando de Talavera, ed. Pedro Cátedra, in *Petrarca: Obras*, I: *Prosa*, ed. Francisco Rico *et al.* (Madrid: Alfaguara, 1978), pp. 369–410

Las poéticas castellanas de la Edad Media, ed. Francisco López Estrada (Madrid: Taurus, 1984 [1985]) [treatises by Baena, Santillana and Encina]

Raimon Vidal *et al., The 'Razos de trobar' of Raimon Vidal and Associated Texts*, ed. J. H. Marshall (London: Oxford Univ. Press, 1972)

Receuil d'arts de seconde rhétorique, ed. E. Langlois (Paris: Imprimerie Nationale, 1902)

Rodríguez del Padrón, Juan, *Obras completas*, ed. César Hernández Alonso (Madrid: Editora Nacional, 1982)

——, *Bursario*, ed. Pilar Saquero Suárez-Somonte and Tomás González Rolán (Madrid: Universidad Complutense, 1984)

Ruiz, Juan, Arcipreste de Hita, *Libro de buen amor*, ed. G. B. Gybbon- Monypenny, Clásicos Castalia, 161 (Madrid: Castalia, 1988)

Seneca, Lucius Annaeus, *Cinco libros de Séneca*, trans. Alonso de Cartagena [*De la vida bienaventurada, De las siete artes liberales, De los preceptos y doctrinas, De la providencia de Dios*, I and II] (Alcalá: Miguel de Eguía, 1530)

Torre, Fernando de la, *La obra literaria*, ed. María Jesús Díez Garretas (Valladolid: Universidad, 1983)

Los trovadores: historia literaria y textos, ed. Martín de Riquer, 3 vols (Barcelona: Planeta, 1975)

Valencia, Fray Diego de [?], *Tratados castellanos sobre la predestinación y sobre la Trinidad y la encarnación, del Maestro Fray Diego de Valencia OFM (siglo XV): identificación de su autoría y edición crítica*, ed. Isaac Vázquez Janeiro (Madrid: CSIC, 1984)

Valera, Diego de, *Tratado en defensa de las virtuosas mujeres*, ed. María Angeles Suz Ruiz (Madrid: El Archipiélago, 1983)

Villena, Enrique de, 'El *Arte de trovar* de don Enrique de Villena', ed. F. J. Sánchez Cantón, *RFE*, 6 (1919), 158–80

——, *Los doze trabajos de Hércules*, ed. Margherita Morreale, Biblioteca Selecta de Clásicos Castellanos, n.s., 20 (Madrid: Real Academia Española, 1958)

——, *Tratado de la consolación*, ed. Derek C. Carr, Clásicos Castellanos, 208 (Madrid: Espasa-Calpe, 1976 [1978])

——, *Exégesis—Ciencia—Literatura: la 'Exposición del salmo "Quoniam videbo"' de Enrique de Villena*, ed. Pedro M. Cátedra, Anejos del *AFE*, 1 (Madrid: El Crotalón, 1985)

——, *La primera versión castellana de 'La Eneida' de Virgilio*, ed. Ramón Santiago Lacuesta, Anejos del *BRAE*, 38 (Madrid: Real Academia Española, 1979)

——, [?], 'A Fifteenth-Century Castilian Translation and Commentary of a Petrarchan Sonnet: Biblioteca Nacional MS 10.186 folios 196ʳ–199ʳ', ed. Derek C. Carr, *RCEH*, 5 (1980–81), 123–43

Printed sources: secondary

Aguirre, Elvira de, *Die 'Arte de trovar' von Enrique de Villena* (Cologne, 1968)

Aguirre, José María, 'Reflexiones para la construcción de un modelo de la poesía castellana del amor cortés', *RF*, 93 (1981), 55–81

Allen, Judson Boyce, *The Friar as Critic: Literary Attitudes in the Later Middle Ages* (Nashville: Vanderbilt Univ. Press, 1971)

——, *The Ethical Poetic of the Later Middle Ages: A Decorum of Convenient Distinction* (Toronto: Univ. of Toronto Press, 1982)

Alvar, Carlos, and Angel Gómez Moreno, *La poesía lírica medieval*, Historia Crítica de la Literatura Hispánica, 1 (Madrid: Taurus, 1987)

Aston, Margaret, *The Fifteenth Century: The Prospect of Europe* (London: Thames and Hudson, 1968)

Atkinson, William C., 'The Interpretation of "romançes e cantares" in Santillana', *HR*, 4 (1936), 1–10

Auerbach, Erich, 'Dante's Addresses to the Reader', *RPh*, 7 (1953–54), 268–78

——, *Literary Language and its Public in Late Latin Antiquity and in the Middle Ages*, trans. Ralph Manheim, Bollingen Series, 74 (New York: Bollingen Foundation, 1965)

Badel, Pierre-Yves, *Le 'Roman de la Rose' au XIVᵉ siècle: étude de la réception de l'oeuvre* (Geneva: Droz, 1980)

Bahler, Ingrid, *Alfonso Alvarez de Villasandino: poesía de petición* (Madrid: Ediciones Maisal, 1975)

Baldwin, Charles Sears, *Medieval Rhetoric and Poetic (to 1400), Interpreted from Representative Works* (1928; Gloucester, Mass: Peter Smith, 1959)

Battesti-Pelegrin, Jeanne, *Lope de Stúñiga: Recherches sur la poésie espagnole au XVᵉ siècle*, 4 vols (Aix-en-Provence: Université de Provence, 1982)

Bibliography of Old Spanish Texts, 3rd ed. by Charles Faulhaber *et al.* (Madison: HSMS, 1984)

Blecua, Alberto, '"Perdióse un quaderno": sobre los *Cancioneros de Baena*', *AEM*, 9 (1974–79), 229–66

Blüher, Karl, *Séneca en España: investigaciones sobre la recepción de Séneca en España desde el siglo XIII hasta el siglo XVII*, trans. Juan Conde (Madrid: Gredos, 1983)

Boase, Roger, *The Troubadour Revival: a Study of Social Change and Traditionalism in Late Medieval Spain* (London: Routledge and Kegan Paul, 1978)

Boffey, Julia, *Manuscripts of English Courtly Love Lyrics in the Later Middle Ages*, Manuscript Studies, 1 (Cambridge: D. S. Brewer, 1985)

Brownlee, Marina Scordilis, *The Status of the Reading Subject in the 'Libro de buen amor*', NCSRLL, 224 (Chapel Hill: University of North Carolina Press, 1985)

Bruyne, Edgar de, *Études d'esthétique médiévale*, 3 vols (Bruges: De Tempel, 1946)

Burke, James F., 'The *Libro de buen amor* and the Medieval Meditative Sermon Tradition', *C*, 9 (1980–81), 122–27

Caravaggi, Giovanni, 'Villasandino et les derniers troubadours de Castille', in *Mélanges offerts à Rita Lejeune* (Gembloux: Duculot, 1969), I, 395–421

Carr, Derek C., 'Pérez de Guzmán and Villena: A Polemic on Historiography?', in *Hispanic Studies in Honor of Alan D. Deyermond: A North American Tribute*, ed. John S. Miletich (Madison: HSMS, 1986), pp. 57–70

—— and Pedro M. Cátedra, 'Datos para la biografía de Enrique de Villena, *C*, 11 (1982–83), 293–99

Carreras y Artau, Tomás and Joaquín, *Historia de la filosofía española: filosofía cristiana de los siglos XIII al XV*, 2 vols (Madrid: Asociación Española para el Progreso de las Ciencias, 1939–1943)

Catálogo-índice de la poesía cancioneril del siglo XV, ed. Brian Dutton *et al.* (Madison: HSMS, 1982)

Cátedra, Pedro M., 'Enrique de Villena y algunos humanistas', in *Nebrija y la introducción del Renacimiento*, pp. 187–203 (see under V. García de la Concha, ed.)

——, 'Escolios teatrales de Enrique de Villena', in *Serta philologica F. Lázaro Carreter natalem diem sexagesimum celebranti dicata* (Madrid: Cátedra, 1983), II, 127–36

——, 'La predicación castellana de San Vicente Ferrer', *BRABLB*, 39 (1983–84), 235–309

——, 'Algunas obras perdidas de Enrique de Villena con consideraciones sobre su obra y su biblioteca', *AFE*, 2 (1985), 53–75

Chaytor, H. J., *From Script to Print: An Introduction to Medieval Vernacular Literature* (1945; London: Sidgwick and Jackson, 1966)

Clarke, Dorothy Clotelle, 'On Santillana's "una manera de deçir cantares"', *PQ*, 36 (1957), 72–76

——, 'The Marqués de Santillana and the Spanish Ballad Problem', *MP*, 59 (1961–62), 13–24

Comparetti, Domenico, *Vergil in the Middle Ages*, trans. E. F. M. Benecke (London: Swan Sonnenschein, 1895)

Corominas, Joan, and José A. Pascual, *Diccionaro crítico etimológico castellano e hispánico* (Madrid: Gredos, 1980–)

Cotarelo y Mori, Emilio, *Don Enrique de Villena: su vida y obras* (Madrid: Sucesores de Rivadaneyra, 1896)

Cummins, John G., 'The Survival in the Spanish *Cancioneros* of the Form and Themes of Provençal and Old French Poetic Debates', *BHS*, 42 (1965), 9–17

Curtius, Ernst Robert, 'Zur Literarästhetik des Mittelalters', *ZRPh*, 58 (1938), 1–50, 129–232, 433–79

——, *European Literature and the Latin Middle Ages*, trans. Willard R. Trask (London: Routledge and Kegan Paul, 1953)

Dagenais, John, 'Juan Rodríguez del Padrón's Translation of the Latin *Bursarii*: New Light on the Meaning of "Tra(c)tado"', *JHP*, 10 (1985–86), 117–39

——, '"Avrás dueña garrida": Language of the Margins in the *Libro de buen amor*', *C*, 15 (1986–87), 38–45

——, 'A Further Source for the Literary Ideas in Juan Ruiz's Prologue', *JHP*, 11 (1986–87), 23–52

De Ley, Margo Ynés Corona, 'The Prologue in Castilian Literature between 1200 and 1400', unpublished Ph.D. thesis (University of Illinois, Urbana, 1976)

Deyermond, Alan D., *Historia de la literatura española*, I: *La Edad Media*, Letras e Ideas: Instrumenta, I (Barcelona: Ariel, 1973)

——, 'Juan Ruiz's Attitude to Literature', in *Medieval, Renaissance and Folklore Studies in Honor of John Esten Keller*, ed. Joseph R. Jones (Newark: Juan de la Cuesta, 1980), pp. 113–25

——, 'Baena, Santillana, Resende and the Silent Century of Portuguese Court Poetry', *BHS*, 59 (1982), 198–210

—— and Francisco Rico, *Historia y crítica de la literatura española*, I: *Edad Media* (Barcelona: Editorial Crítica, 1980)

Di Camillo, Ottavio, *El humanismo castellano del siglo XV* (Valencia: Fernando Torres, 1976)

Duffell, Martin J., 'The Metre of Santillana's Sonnets', *MAe*, 56 (1987), 276–303

Dutton, Brian, 'Spanish Fifteenth-Century *Cancioneros*: A General Survey to 1465', *KRQ*, 26 (1979), 445–60

Eddy, Nelson W., 'Dante and Ferrán Manuel de Lando', *HR*, 4 (1936), 124–35

Egan, Margarita, 'Commentary, *vita poetae*, and *vida*: Latin and Old Provençal "Lives of Poets"', *RPh*, 37 (1983–84), 36–48

Faral, Edmond, *Les Arts poétiques du XIIᵉ et du XIIIᵉ siècle: recherches et documents sur la technique littéraire du Moyen Age* (1924; Paris: Champion, 1962)

Faulhaber, Charles, *Latin Rhetorical Theory in Thirteenth and Fourteenth Century Castile*, UCPMP, 103 (Berkeley: Univ. of California Press, 1972)

——, 'Retóricas clásicas y medievales en bibliotecas castellanas', in *Abaco*, 4 (Madrid: Castalia, 1973), 151–300

——, 'Las retóricas hispanolatinas medievales (siglos XIII–XV)', *Repertorio de Historia de las Ciencias Eclesiásticas en España*, 7 (1979), 11–65

——, *Libros y bibliotecas en la España medieval: una bibliografía de fuentes impresas*, Research Bibliographies and Checklists, 47 (London: Grant and Cutler, 1987)

Ferrie, Francis, 'Aspiraciones del humanismo español del siglo XV: revalorización del *Prohemio e carta* de Santillana', *RFE*, 57 (1974–75), 195–209

Foster, David W., *The Marqués de Santillana*, Twayne's World Author Series, 154 (New York: Twayne, 1971)

Fraker, Charles F., *Studies on the 'Cancionero de Baena'*, NCSRLL, 61 (Chapel Hill: Univ. of North Carolina Press, 1966)

——, review of Lange, *El fraile trobador* [see below], *HR*, 42 (1974), 341–43

Garci-Gómez, Miguel, 'Otras huellas de Horacio en el Marqués de Santillana', *BHS*, 50 (1973), 127–41

——, 'Paráfrasis de Cicerón en la definición de poesía de Santillana', *Hispania* [U.S.A.], 56 (1973), 207–212

García, Michel, *Obra y personalidad del Canciller Ayala* (Madrid: Alhambra, 1983)

——, 'Las traducciones del Canciller Ayala', in *Studies in Honour of R. B. Tate*, pp. 13–25 (see under I. Michael, ed.)

García de la Concha, Víctor (ed.), *Nebrija y la introducción del Renacimiento en España: Actas de la III Academia Literaria Renacentista* (Salamanca: ALR, Universidad de Salamanca, 1983)

Ghisalberti, Fausto, 'Medieval Biographies of Ovid', *Journal of the Warburg and Courtauld Institutes*, 9 (1946), 10–59

Gimeno Casalduero, Joaquín, 'Pero López de Ayala y el cambio poético de Castilla a comienzos del XV', *HR*, 33 (1965), 1–14

——, 'San Jerónimo y el rechazo y la aceptación de la poesía en la Castilla de finales del siglo XV', in *La creación literaria de la Edad Media y del Renacimiento (su forma y su significado)* (Madrid: Porrúa Turanzas, 1977), pp. 45–65

Gray, Hanna H., 'Renaissance Humanism: The Pursuit of Eloquence', *JHI*, 24 (1963), 497–514

Green, Otis H., *Spain and the Western Tradition: The Castilian Mind in Literature from 'El Cid' to Calderón*, 4 vols (Madison: Univ. of Wisconsin Press, 1963–66)

——, '"Fingen los poetas"—Notes on the Spanish Attitude toward Pagan Mythology', in *The Literary Mind of Medieval and Renaissance Spain: Essays by Otis H. Green*, ed. John E. Keller (Lexington: Univ. Press of Kentucky, 1970), pp. 113–23

Greenfield, Concetta C., *Humanist and Scholastic Poetics, 1250–1500* (Toronto: Associated Univ. Presses, 1981)

Guiette, Robert, 'D'une poésie formelle en France au Moyen Âge', *Revue des Sciences Humaines*, 54 (1949), 61–68

Hardison, O. B., *The Enduring Monument: A Study of the Idea of Praise in Renaissance Literary Theory and Practice* (Chapel Hill: Univ. of North Carolina Press, 1962)

——, 'Toward a History of Medieval Literary Criticism', *Medievalia et Humanistica*, n.s., 7 (1976), 1–12

Hunt, Richard William, 'The Introductions to the *Artes* in the Twelfth Century', in *Studia medievalia in honorem admodum reverendi patris Raymundi Josephi Martin* (Bruges: De Tempel, 1949), pp. 85–112

Huot, Sylvia, *From Song to Book: The Poetics of Writing in Old French Lyric and Lyrical Narrative Poetry* (Ithaca: Cornell Univ. Press, 1987)

Impey, Olga Tudorică, 'Alfonso de Cartagena, traductor de Séneca y precursor del humanismo español', *Prohemio*, 3 (1972), 473–94

Jaeger, C. Stephen, *The Origins of Courtliness: Civilizing Trends and the Formation of Courtly Ideals 939–1210* (Philadelphia: University of Pennsylvania Press, 1985)

Jauss, Hans R., 'Littérature médiévale et théorie des genres', *Poétique*, 1 (1970), 79–101

Jeanroy, Alfred, *La Poésie lyrique des troubadours*, 2 vols (Paris: Henri Didier; Toulouse: Édouard Privat, 1934)

——, 'Les *Leys d'amors*', in *Histoire littéraire de la France*, 38 (Paris: Imprimerie Nationale, 1949), pp. 139–233

Jenaro-MacLennan, Luis, 'Autocomentario en Dante y comentarismo latino', *VR*, 19 (1960), 82–123

Jodogne, Pierre, 'Les "Rhétoriqueurs" et l'humanisme: problème d'histoire littéraire', in *Humanism in France at the End of the Middle Ages and in the Early Renaissance*, ed. A. H. T. Levi (Manchester: University Press, 1970), pp. 150–75

Joset, Jacques, 'Pero López de Ayala dans le *Cancionero de Baena*', *MA*, 4th series, 30 (1975), 475–97

Keen, Maurice, *Chivalry* (New Haven: Yale University Press, 1984)

Keightley, Ronald G., 'Alfonso de Madrigal and the *Chronici canones* of Eusebius', *JMRS*, 7 (1977), 225–48

——, 'Hercules in Alfonso de Madrigal's *In Eusebium*', in *Renaissance and Golden Age Essays in Honor of D. W. McPheeters*, ed. Bruno M. Damiani (Potomac: Scripta Humanistica, 1986), pp. 134–47

Kelly, Douglas, 'The Scope of the Treatment of Composition in the Twelfth- and Thirteenth-Century Arts of Poetry', *Sp*, 41 (1966), 261–78

——, *Medieval Imagination: Rhetoric and the Poetry of Courtly Love* (Madison: University of Wisconsin Press, 1978)

Kennedy, Elspeth, 'The Scribe as Editor', in *Mélanges de langue et de littérature du Moyen Age et de la Renaissance offerts à Jean Frappier* (Geneva: Droz, 1970), I, 523–31

Kerkhof, Maximiliaan P. A. M., 'Acerca da data do *Proemio e carta* do Marqués de Santilhana', *PFG*, 12 (1972–73), 1–6

——, 'Hacia una nueva edición crítica del *Laberinto de Fortuna* de Juan de Mena', *JHP*, 7 (1982–83), 179–89

Kohut, Karl, *Las teorías literarias en España y Portugal durante los siglos XV y XVI: estado de la investigación y problemática*, Anejos de *RLit*, 36 (Madrid: CSIC, 1973)

——, 'Der Beitrag der Theologie zum Literaturbegriff in der Zeit Juans II von Kastilien: Alonso de Cartagena (1384–1456) und Alonso de Madrigal, genannt el Tostado (1400?-55)', *RF*, 89 (1977), 183–226

——, 'La posición de la literatura en los sistemas científicos del siglo XV', *IR*, n.s., 7 (1978), 67–87

——, 'La teoría de la poesía cortesana en el *Prólogo* de Juan Alfonso de Baena', in *Actas del coloquio hispano-alemán Ramón Menéndez Pidal*, ed. Wido Hempel and Dietrich Briesemeister (Tübingen: Max Niemeyer, 1982), pp. 120–37

Laidlaw, J. C., 'Christine de Pizan—An Author's Progress', *MLR*, 78 (1983), 532–50

Lang, H. R., 'Observações às rimas do *Cancionero de Baena*', in *Miscelânea de estudos em honra de D. Carolina Michaëlis de Vasconcellos* (Coimbra: Imprensa da Universidade, 1930), pp. 476–92

Lange, Wolf-Dieter, *El fraile trobador: Zeit, Leben und Werk des Diego de Valencia de León (1350?-1412?)*, Analecta Romanica, 28 (Frankfurt: Klostermann, 1971)

Lapesa, Rafael, 'La lengua de la poesía lírica desde Macías hasta Villasandino', *RPh*, 7 (1953–54), 51–59

——, *La obra literaria del Marqués de Santillana* (Madrid: Insula, 1957)

——, 'Poesía de cancionero y poesía italianizante', in *De la Edad Media a nuestros días: estudios de historia literaria* (Madrid: Gredos, 1967), pp. 145–71

——, *Historia de la lengua española*, 9th ed. (Madrid: Gredos, 1983)

Lausberg, Heinrich, *Manual de retórica literaria: fundamentos de una ciencia de la literatura*, trans. José Pérez Riesco, 3 vols (Madrid: Gredos, 1966–69)

Lawrance, Jeremy N. H., 'Juan Alfonso de Baena's Versified Reading List: A Note on the Aspirations and the Reality of Fifteenth-Century Castilian Culture', *JHP*, 5 (1980–81), 101–22

——, 'Nuño de Guzmán and Early Spanish Humanism: Some Reconsiderations', *MAe*, 51 (1982), 55–85

——, 'Nuño de Guzmán: Life and Works', unpublished D. Phil. thesis (Univ. of Oxford, 1983)

——, 'Nueva luz sobre la biblioteca del conde de Haro: inventario de 1455', *AFE*, 1 (1984), 1073–111

——, 'The Spread of Lay Literary in Late Medieval Castile', *BHS*, 62 (1985), 79–94

——, 'On Fifteenth-Century Spanish Vernacular Humanism', in *Studies in Honour of R. B. Tate*, pp. 63–79 (see under I. Michael, ed.)

Leclercq, Jean, O.S.B., *Otia monastica: études sur le vocabulaire de la contemplation au Moyen Age*, Studia Anselmiana, 51 (Rome: Herder, 1963)

——, *The Love of Learning and the Desire for God: A Study of Monastic Culture*, trans. Catharine Misrahi, 2nd ed. (London: SPCK, 1978)

Le Gentil, Pierre, *La Poésie lyrique espagnole et portugaise à la fin du Moyen Age*, 2 vols (Rennes: Plihon, 1949–53)

Lida de Malkiel, María Rosa, *La idea de la fama en la Edad Media castellana* (Mexico City: Fondo de Cultura Económica, 1952)

——, 'Juan Rodríguez del Padrón: vida y obras', *NRFH*, 6 (1952), 313–51

——, 'La métrica de la Biblia (un motivo de Josefo y San Jerónimo en la literature española)', in *Estudios hispánicos: homenaje a Archer M. Huntington* (Wellesley, Mass: Wellesley College, 1952), 335–59

——, *Juan de Mena: poeta del prerrenacimiento español*, 2nd ed. (Mexico City: El Colegio de México, 1984)

López Estrada, Francisco, 'La retórica en las *Generaciones y semblanzas* de Fernán Pérez de Guzmán', *RFE*, 30 (1946), 310–52

——, '*El arte de poesía castellana* de Juan del Encina (1496)', in *XIXᵉ Colloque International d'Études Humanistes, Tours 5–17 juillet 1976: l'Humanisme dans les lettres espagnoles*, ed. Augustin Redondo, De Pétrarque à Descartes, 39 (Paris: J. Vrin, 1979), pp. 151–68

——, *Introducción a la literatura medieval española*, 5th ed. (Madrid: Gredos, 1983)

Lubac, Henri de, *Exégèse médiévale: les quatre sens de l'Écriture*, 4 parts [in 3 vols] (Paris: Aubier, 1959–64)

McKeon, Richard, 'Rhetoric in the Middle Ages', in *Critics and Criticism Ancient and Modern*, ed. R. S. Crane (Chicago: Univ. Press, 1952), pp. 260–96

——, 'Poetry and Philosophy in the Twelfth Century: The Renaissance of Rhetoric', in *Critics and Criticism*, pp. 297–318

Macpherson, Ian, 'Don Juan Manuel: The Literary Process', *SP*, 70 (1973), 1–18

Maravall, José Antonio, 'La concepción del saber en una sociedad tradicional', in *Estudios de historia del pensamiento español: serie primera—Edad Media*, 3rd ed. (Madrid: Ediciones Cultura Hispánica, 1983), pp. 203–54

——, 'La "cortesía" como saber en la Edad Media', in *Estudios de historia*, pp. 257–67

——, 'El Pre-Renacimiento del siglo XV', in *Nebrija y la introducción del Renacimiento*, pp. 17–36 (see under V. García de la Concha, ed.)

Marichal, Juan, *La voluntad de estilo: teoría e historia del ensayismo hispánico* (Barcelona: Seix Barral, 1957)

Márquez Villanueva, Francisco, 'Jewish "Fools" of the Spanish Fifteenth Century', *HR*, 50 (1982), 385–409

Marshall, J. H., 'Observations on the Sources of the Treatment of Rhetoric in the *Leys d'amors*', *MLR*, 64 (1969), 39–52

Massó Torrents, Jaume, 'Inventari dels bens mobles del rey Martí d'Aragó', *RH*, 12 (1905), 413–590

——, *Repertori de l'antiga literatura catalana: la poesia*, I [only one vol. published] (Barcelona: Editorial Alpha, 1932)

Meléndez, Priscilla, 'Una teoría de la escritura en el *Libro de buen amor* de Juan Ruiz, Arcipreste de Hita', *Hispanic Journal*, 4, no. 1 (1982), 87–95

Menéndez y Pelayo, Marcelino, *Historia de las ideas estéticas en España*, Edición Nacional, 4 vols (1883–89; Madrid: CSIC, 1962), I [on the Middle Ages]

Menéndez Pidal, Ramón, *Poesía juglaresca y orígenes de las literaturas románicas: problemas de historia literaria y cultural*, revised ed. [of *Poesía juglaresca y juglares*, 1924] (Madrid: Instituto de Estudios Políticos, 1957)

Michael, Ian, and Richard A. Cardwell (eds), *Medieval and Renaissance Studies in Honour of Robert Brian Tate* (Oxford: Dolphin, 1986)

Minnis, Alistair J., 'Late-Medieval Discussions of *Compilatio* and the Rôle of the *Compilator*', *Beiträge zur Geschichte der deutschen Sprache und Literatur*, 101 (1979), 385–421

——, 'The Influence of Academic Prologues on the Prologues and Literary Attitudes of Late-Medieval English Writers', *MS*, 43 (1981), 342–83

——, *Medieval Theory of Authorship: Scholastic Literary Attitudes in the Later Middle Ages*, 2nd ed. (London: Scolar Press, 1988)

Nader, Helen, *The Mendoza Family in the Spanish Renaissance, 1350–1550* (New Brunswick: Rutgers Univ. Press, 1979)

Nepaulsingh, Colbert I., *Towards a History of Literary Composition in Medieval Spain* (Toronto: Univ. of Toronto Press, 1986)

Nieto Cumplido, Manuel, 'Aportación histórica al *Cancionero de Baena*', *Historia, Instituciones, Documentos*, 6 (1979), 197–218

——, 'Juan Alfonso de Baena y su Cancionero: nueva aportación histórica', *Boletín de la Real Academia de Ciencias, Bellas Letras y Nobles Artes de Córdoba*, 52 (1982), 35–57

Olson, Glending, *Literature as Recreation in the Later Middle Ages* (Ithaca: Cornell Univ. Press, 1982)

Orduna, Germán, '"Fablar complido" y "fablar breve et escuro": procedencia oriental de esta disyuntiva en la obra literaria de don Juan Manuel', in *Homenaje a Fernando Antonio Martínez: estudios de lingüística, filología, literatura e historia cultural*, Publicaciones del Instituto Caro y Cuervo, 48 (Bogotá, 1979), pp. 135–46

Pagden, A. R. D., 'The Diffusion of Aristotle's Moral Philosophy in Spain, ca. 1400–ca. 1600', *T*, 31 (1975), 287–313

Paré, Gérard, *et al.*, *La Renaissance du XIIe siècle: les écoles et l'enseignement*, Publications de l'Institut d'Études Médiévales d'Ottawa, 3 (Paris: J. Vrin, 1933)

Parkes, Malcolm B., 'The Literacy of the Laity', in *Literature and Western Civilization: II, The Medieval World*, ed. David Daiches and Anthony Thorlby (London: Aldus Books, 1973), pp. 555–77

——, 'The Influence of the Concepts of *Ordinatio* and *Compilatio* on the Development of the Book', in *Medieval Learning and Literature: Essays Presented to Richard William Hunt*, ed. J. J. G. Alexander and M. T. Gibson (Oxford: Clarendon, 1976), pp. 115–41

Paterson, Linda M., *Troubadours and Eloquence* (Oxford: Clarendon, 1975)

Pearsall, Derek (ed.), *Manuscripts and Readers in Fifteenth-Century England: The Literary Implications of Manuscript Study* (Essays from the 1981 Conference at the University of York) (Cambridge: D. S. Brewer, 1983)

Pérez Bustamante, Rogelio, and José Manuel Calderón Ortega, *El Marqués de Santillana: biografía y documentación*, Fuentes Documentales para la Historia de Santillana, 1 (Santillana del Mar: Fundación Santillana and Taurus, 1983)

Piccus, Jules, 'El traductor español de *De genealogia deorum*', in *Homenaje a Rodríguez-Moñino* (Madrid: Castalia, 1966), II, 59–75

Porqueras Mayo, Alberto, *El prólogo como género literario: su estudio en el Siglo de Oro español*, Anejos de R*Lit*, 14 (Madrid: CSIC, 1957)

Potvin, Claudine, 'Les Rubriques du *Cancionero de Baena*: étude pour une gaie science', *Fifteenth Century Studies*, 2 (1979), 173–85

Quadlbauer, Franz, *Die antike Theorie der 'genera dicendi' im lateinischen Mittelalter* (Vienna: Böhlaus, 1962)

Quain, Edwin A., 'The Medieval *Accessus ad auctores*', *T*, 3 (1945), 215–64

Reinhardt, Klaus, and Horacio Santiago-Otero, *Biblioteca bíblica ibérica medieval* (Madrid: CSIC, 1986)

Rico, Francisco, *Alfonso el Sabio y la 'General estoria': tres lecciones*, 2nd ed. (Barcelona: Ariel, 1984)

Riera i Sans, Jaume, 'Sobre la difusió hispànica de la *Consolació* de Boeci', *AFE*, 1 (1984), 297–327

Ringler, William, '"Poeta Nascitur non Fit": Some Notes on the History of an Aphorism', *JHI*, 2 (1941), 497–504

Riquer, Martín de, review of Porqueras Mayo, *El prólogo*, *RFE*, 42 (1958–59), 298–300

——, 'Don Enrique de Villena en la corte de Martín I', in *Miscelánea en homenaje a Monseñor Higinio Anglés* (Barcelona: CSIC, 1961), II, 717–21

——, *Història de la literatura catalana*, 3 vols [on Middle Ages] (Barcelona: Ariel, 1964)

Ronconi, Giorgio, *Le origini delle dispute umanistiche sulla poesia (Mussato e Petrarca)*, Strumenti di Ricerca, 11 (Rome: Bulzoni, 1976)

Root, Robert K., 'Publication before Printing', *PMLA*, 28 (1913), 417–31

Round, Nicholas G., 'Renaissance Culture and its Opponents in Fifteenth- Century Castile', *MLR*, 57 (1962), 204–15

——, 'Pero Díaz de Toledo: A Study of a Fifteenth-Century *Converso* Translator in his Background', unpublished D. Phil. thesis (Univ. of Oxford, 1966)

——, 'Five Magicians, or the Uses of Literacy', *MLR*, 64 (1969), 793–805

——, 'The Shadow of a Philosopher: Medieval Castilian Images of Plato', *JHP*, 3 (1978–79), 1–36

Russell, Peter E., 'Fifteenth-Century Lay Humanism', in *Spain: A Companion to Spanish Studies*, ed. P. E. Russell (London: Methuen, 1973), pp. 237–42

——, 'Las armas contra las letras: para una definición del humanismo español del siglo XV', in *Temas de 'La Celestina' y otros estudios: del 'Cid' al 'Quijote'* (Barcelona: Ariel, 1978), pp. 207–39

——, *Traducciones y traductores en la Península Ibérica (1400–1550)* (Bellaterra: Universidad Autónoma de Barcelona, 1985)

Saenger, Paul, 'Silent Reading: Its Impact on Late Medieval Script and Society', *Viator*, 13 (1982), 367–414

Saintsbury, George, *A History of Criticism and Literary Taste in Europe from the Earliest Texts to the Present Day* (1900; Edinburgh: William Blackwood, 1949), I [the classical and medieval period]

Salman, Phillips, 'Instruction and Delight in Medieval and Renaissance Literary Criticism', *Renaissance Quarterly*, 32 (1979), 303–32

Santiago Lacuesta, Ramón, 'Sobre "el primer ensayo de una prosodia y una ortografía castellanas": el *Arte de trovar* de Enrique de Villena', *Miscellanea Barcinonensia*, 42 (1975), 35–52

Schiff, Mario, *La Bibliothèque du Marquis de Santillane: Étude historique et bibliographique de la collection de livres manuscrits de don Iñigo López de Mendoza, 1398–1458, marqués de Santillana, conde del Real de Manzanares, humaniste et auteur espagnol célèbre* (1905; Amsterdam: Van Heusen, 1970)

Schultz, James A., 'Classical Rhetoric, Medieval Poetics, and the Medieval Vernacular Prologue', *Sp*, 59 (1984), 1–15

Scudieri Ruggieri, Jole, *Cavalleria e cortesia nella vita e nella cultura di Spagna* (Modena: Mucchi, 1980)

Seidenspinner-Núñez, Dayle, *The Allegory of Good Love: Parodic Perspectivism in the 'Libro de buen amor'*, UCPMP, 112 (Berkeley: Univ. of California Press, 1981)

Seigel, Jerrold E., *Rhetoric and Philosophy in Renaissance Humanism: The Union of Eloquence and Wisdom, Petrarch to Valla* (Princeton: Univ. Press, 1968)

Smalley, Beryl, *The Study of the Bible in the Middle Ages*, 3rd ed. (Oxford: Blackwell, 1983)

Spingarn, Joel E., *A History of Literary Criticism in the Renaissance*, 2nd ed. (1899; New York: Columbia Univ. Press, 1954)

Street, Florence, 'Some Reflections on Santillana's *Prohemio e carta*', *MLR*, 52 (1957), 230–33

——, 'The Text of Mena's *Laberinto* in the *Cancionero de Ixar* and its Relationship to Some Other Fifteenth-Century MSS', *BHS*, 35 (1958), 63–71

Tate, R. B., 'The Literary *Persona* from Díez de Games to Santa Teresa', *RPh*, 13 (1959–60), 298–304

Taylor, Barry Paul, 'Juan Manuel, *El conde Lucanor*, Parts II–IV: Edition— Stylistic Analysis—Literary Context', unpublished Ph. D. Thesis (King's College, Univ. of London, 1983)

Thomas, Antoine, *Jean de Gerson et l'éducation des dauphins de France* (Paris: Droz, 1930)

Tittman, Barclay, 'A Contribution to the Study of the *Cancionero de Baena* Manuscript', *Aquila*, 1 (1968), 190–203

Vàrvaro, Alberto, review of Fraker, *Studies*, *RPh*, 22 (1968–69), 108–11

Vinaver, Eugène, 'A la recherche d'une poétique médiévale', *CCMe*, 2 (1959), 1–16

——, *The Rise of Romance* (Oxford: Clarendon, 1971)

Walsh, John K., and Alan Deyermond, 'Enrique de Villena como poeta y dramaturgo: bosquejo de una polémica frustrada', *NRFH*, 28 (1979), 57–85

Watson, George, *The Literary Critics: A Study of English Descriptive Criticism* (Harmondsworth: Penguin, 1962)

Webber, Edwin J., 'Plautine and Terentian *Cantares* in Fourteenth-Century Spain', *HR*, 18 (1950), 93–107

——, 'Further Observations on Santillana's "Dezir cantares"', *HR*, 30 (1962), 87–93

——, 'A Spanish Linguistic Treatise of the Fifteenth Century', *RPh*, 16 (1962–63), 32–40

Weinberg, Bernard, *A History of Literary Criticism in the Italian Renaissance*, 2 vols (Chicago: Univ. Press, 1961)

Weisheipl, James A., 'Classification of the Sciences in Medieval Thought', *MS*, 27 (1965), 54–90

Weiss, Julian, 'Juan de Mena's *Coronación*: Satire or *Sátira*?', *JHP*, 6 (1981–82), 113–38

Whetnall, Jane, 'Manuscript Love Poetry of the Spanish Fifteenth Century:

Developing Standards and Continuing Traditions', unpublished Ph.D. thesis (Univ. of Cambridge, 1986)

Whinnom, Keith, 'Diego de San Pedro's Stylistic Reform', *BHS*, 37 (1960), 1–15

——, '*Autor* and *Tratado* in the Fifteenth Century: Semantic Latinism or Etymological Trap?', *BHS*, 59 (1982), 211–18

——, *La poesía amatoria de la época de los Reyes Católicos* (Durham: University, 1981)

Willard, Charity C., 'The Concept of True Nobility at the Burgundian Court', *Studies in the Renaissance*, 14 (1967), 33–48

Williams, Sarah Jane, 'An Author's Role in Fourteenth-Century Book Production: Guillaume de Machaut's "livre ou je met toutes mes choses"', *R*, 90 (1969), 433–54

Wilson, Elizabeth R., 'Old Provençal *Vidas* as Literary Commentary', *RPh*, 33 (1979–80), 510–18

Windeatt, Barry A., 'The Scribes as Chaucer's Early Critics', *Studies in the Age of Chaucer*, 1 (1979), 119–41

Wolfson, Harry A., 'The Internal Senses in Latin, Arabic, and Hebrew Philosophic Texts', *Harvard Theological Review*, 28 (1935), 69–133

Zahareas, Anthony N., *The Art of Juan Ruiz, Archpriest of Hita* (Madrid: Estudios de Literatura Española, 1965)

Zumthor, Paul, 'Recherches sur les topiques dans la poésie lyrique des XIIᵉ et XIIIᵉ siècles', *CCMe*, 2 (1959), 409–27

——, *Essai de poétique médiévale* (Paris: Seuil, 1972),

INDEX